SO-AEZ-513

CRIMINAL JUSTICE

A Community Relations Approach

Charles P. McDowell, Ph.D.

PILGRIMAGE
A Division Of Anderson Publishing Co.
Cincinnati, Ohio

CJ Criminal Justice Studies

CRIMINAL JUSTICE
A Community Relations Approach

Copyright © 1984 by Anderson Publishing Co.

ISBN: 0-932930-55-7

Project consultants: Michael Braswell, Ph.D.
Steven Brown, Ph.D.

Cover design by Jonathan Donehoo

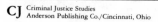 Criminal Justice Studies
Anderson Publishing Co./Cincinnati, Ohio

DEDICATED
TO
CARROL W. TRUMBULL
1918 - 1983

Preface *

Two forces in recent history have come together in a way that no one had anticipated, and the result has been a strong public interest in the criminal justice system. The first force was the civil rights movement, which focused attention on many of the weaknesses and inadequacies of society in general and the criminal justice system in particular. The turbulent decades of the 1960's and 1970's produced what appeared to be a widespread breakdown in law and order along with cries for a more compassionate and equitable social system.

The second force was the effort on behalf of the Federal government (primarily through the now-defunct Law Enforcement Assistance Administration) to modernize criminal justice in America by providing Federal funds to state and local governments. The first force — the civil rights movement — drew attention to a multitude of problems, and the second force — Federal funding — gave local governments the opportunity to do something about them. To be sure, society's problems are far from over, but few would claim that we have not made considerable progress. As a minimum the general public is better informed and more articulate in its expectations; large numbers of people from diverse backgrounds have found careers in the criminal justice system; and, there is a very real public sentiment which demands quality in the administration of justice.

One consequence of these advances is that criminal justice courses have also matured. Indeed, academic programs have gone beyond the earlier, narrow law enforcement or police science programs into curricula which explore the full spectrum of the criminal justice system. The final step is to relate criminal justice to the community of which it is a part. This is an inescapable objective, for criminal justice does not exist nor can it operate apart from the community: it is organic to it. This text recognizes this fact and attempts to look at the entire criminal justice system in the light of its community setting.

This book does not present the system in its "ideal," theoretical perspective: instead it looks at the courts, police, and corrections as they really are — warts and all. It attempts to distinguish between the "private" and "public" control systems and points out the conflicts inherent in both systems. In the process the book stresses two themes. The first is that the criminal justice system is a public enterprise and is subject to the principles which govern all public bureaucracies. The second is that the criminal justice system consists of people who deal with other people and that human considerations are never far from the surface.

The student must bear in mind, however, that each community is at least somewhat different and to understand the criminal justice system one must first understand his own community. Hopefully this text will help serve as a guide or at least give the student an idea of what to look for.

No undertaking of this scope is an individual effort, and this book is no exception. I have many people to thank for their help and support. I would particularly like to acknowledge Dr. Norman G. Kittel, who contributed the information in chapters 10 and 12. I would also like to thank Dr. Stephen Brown for his thoughtful criticism of the manuscript and for his helpful suggestions. I am particularly indebted to Dr. Michael Braswell and his wife Susan for their superb management of this project on behalf of Pilgrimage. Finally — but certainly not least — I owe a debt of gratitude to my wife, Cynthia, for her encouragement and help.

---

*It should be noted that although this book has been written utilizing the masculine gender, no sexism is intended. Women are, in fact, playing an increasingly vital role in all Criminal Justice areas.

Contents

vii

INTRODUCTION 1

The American system of criminal justice is enormously complex and touches the lives of everyone. The type of contact a given individual may have with the criminal justice system can take a variety of forms: serving on a jury, getting a traffic ticket, hiring an ex-offender, being robbed, or getting directions from a police officer. Some of these contacts are unpleasant; few could be described as fun.

Some of our contacts with the criminal justice system are vicarious (for instance, what we see on television or at the movies). Some contacts are second hand and include what we are told by friends. Yet other contacts are not really contacts at all, but anticipations: the elderly citizen who is afraid to go out after dark for fear of being attacked; the rape victim who refuses to report the crime because she fears humiliation at the hands of the authorities; and the young boy who is frightened of the police because an over-zealous parent has told him that if he misbehaves, "the cops will take him away and put him in jail."

There are numerous ways people can have contact with the criminal justice system, and many of these contacts (real or imagined) leave the individual with impressions and feelings. These feelings in turn shape attitudes and provide much of the basis by which he or she views both the criminal justice system and his or her relationships with it. People, both as individuals and as members of groups, can and do have divergent and conflicting attitudes toward the criminal justice system. Adding to the confusion, the system itself is characterized by diversity, internal contradictions, and fragmentation. How can the average person make sense out of what seems to be chaos? How is the criminal justice system itself supposed to respond to the wide range of feelings and expectations held by the people it nominally serves? These are by no means simple questions, and there are no easy answers. Perhaps the best way to understand the system, especially as it functions within the total community, is to look at it from several different perspectives.

The Administration of Justice as a Public Enterprise

The administration of justice is essentially a public entrprise: it is basically carried out by government. Criminal justice agencies are government agencies, and this simple fact has profound significance. Only certain kinds of affairs can or should be carried out by the government. Moreover, the fact that an enterprise is a public function goes a long ways toward enabling us to understand how its processes are organized and administered. Some of the important points to consider in looking at the administration of justice as a public enterprise include the following.

Justice as a Collective Good

Economists sometimes use the term "collective goods" to describe an indivisible benefit: something which benefits all members of society whether or not any given individual chooses to use it or even to pay for it. For example, most homeowners pay school taxes whether or not they have children in the public schools. They do so because public education is a collective good which benefits all citizens and is something from which society as a whole derives a benefit. Criminal justice is another indivisible benefit. The police are as close as the nearest telephone, and in an emergency they can marshal enormous resources for the benefit of an individual. To see this in action, one need only watch what happens at a serious traffic accident .

CITY MAN INJURED IN MOTORCYCLE ACCIDENT

The caption cited above appeared in a local newspaper. The article which followed took up less than two inches and simply stated that a local resident was seriously injured when he struck an automobile which was making an improper turn into a shopping center. The article noted that the man was in stable condition in a local hospital and the driver of the car was charged in the accident. Most people would skim the article without giving it a second thought; few would realize the high drama that was involved. Let's take a look at what happened.

The driver of the car made a sharp left turn without first giving a signal because on an impulse he decided to go into a

2

convenience store in a shopping center. He said he did not see the motorcycle approaching in the traffic lane he crossed. The motorcycle struck the front fender of the car at about 35 miles per hour. The driver was thrown from the motorcycle facefirst into the windshield, which shattered on impact. When the vehicles came to a stop, the driver of the motorcycle was obviously critically injured.

The county Emergency Medical Transportation Service received a number of calls simultaneously, each reporting the accident. The dispatcher gave the call to the nearest mobile intensive care unit, instructing them to respond "emergency traffic to a 10-50PI involving a motorcycle." The dispatcher then notified the fire and police departments by direct line. The Fire Department dispatched an engine (for manpower) and a rescue squad (the fire station from which this equipment responded was only a few blocks away). The police dispatcher gave the call to two patrol units and a supervisor, all of whom likewise responded with lights and sirens.

In less than two minutes all of the original units dispatched were at the scene of the accident. The victim obviously had compound fractures of both legs and both arms; it appeared that his neck and back might have been broken, he was bleeding heavily and was in respiratory distress. Emergency first aid was started by the fire department personnel while the ambulance paramedics set up their equipment. The police assisted with the victim, re-routed traffic, and began the investigation of the accident. Because of the seriousness of the victim's injuries, it took about half an hour to stabilize and prepare him for transportation. The paramedics were in direct radio contact with the emergency room at the hospital and were able to control the bleeding, relieve the respiratory distress and immobilize the broken arms and legs. The victim's neck was likewise immobilized and he was secured to a "backboard" so he could be moved without aggravating his injuries. He was finally placed in the mobile intensive care unit and rushed to the hospital. The police controlled the crowd of bystanders, photographed and measured the accident scene, and took the driver of the car into custody for further questioning after having his car impounded. The fire department personnel cleaned up the accident scene, washing down the gasoline from the motorcycle and sweeping up the glass and other debris from the wreck before departing.

Within an hour from the moment the accident happened,

everything was back to normal at the scene. The victim, although critically injured, was responding well in the Intensive Care Unit of the hospital. The firemen were back in their station. The driver of the car was in the process of making a statement, and all of the bystanders had departed.

What did this utilization of the city and county's resources cost the victim? Nothing. They are collective goods available to all of us.

Although the administration of justice is a collective good, it is somewhat selective in how it is used, paid for, and perceived. The poor, even though they pay fewer taxes, tend to receive a disproportionate share of criminal justice services; yet many of them resent the quality of the service they receive, alleging a dual standard in the administration of justice. Although affluent citizens may pay more taxes, they often seem to derive little benefit from the money spent and are especially annoyed by actions of the courts and prisons which they perceive as foolish, if not actually dangerous.

If the criminal justice system operated in a market economy and users paid for what they got, many who need the police would not be able to afford them. If the district attorney charged for his services, how many victims could afford to pay for the prosecution of those who harmed them? Who would pay for the prisons? The administration of justice, by its very nature, must be a public undertaking. At least in theory this assures all of equality before the law and makes the services of the entire criminal justice system theoretically available to all. Public agencies, however, do not always seem to function in the interest of their clientele — why is this?

Criminal Justice Agencies as Instruments/Institutions

Downs has noted that bureaus come into existence in four ways. First, a bureau can emerge through what Max Weber called the "routinization of charisma."[1]   An organization can emerge from the teachings or philosophy of some charismatic leader; many religions are formed this way. Second, a bureau may be created in order to carry out a specific function which is either not being met at all, or which is being satisfied inadequately by an existing bureaucracy. This happened when municipalities took over firefighting from the insurance companies.

4

Third, a new agency can split off from a parent organization, as the Air Force did from the Army after World War II. Fourth, a new organization can be created through "entrepreneurship." This occurs when a group of advocates promote a particular policy and gain enough support to establish an organization to carry out that policy.[2]   A good example is the recent formation of a number of women's groups dedicated to achieving specific feminist objectives.

When some segment of the public perceives a problem and their concern is brought to the attention of the authorities, action of some type is likely to result. If the appropriate public agency has the authority to act on the problem, it will probably do so. If there is no authority to act, then legislation may be introduced giving some public agency the proper authority. The police, courts, correctional systems, and prosecutors are all authorized to deal with some aspects of what may be considered public problems.

To the extent that a public agency effectively fulfills the purpose for which it was created, it may be regarded as an instrument for achieving some goal or objective. However, Carroll Quigley has rather dryly noted that instruments invariably become institutions. He remarked that an institution is an instrument which has taken on activities and purposes of its own, separate and different from the purposes for which it was formed. As a consequence, an institution achieves its original purpose with decreasing effectiveness.[3] There are three reasons for this. First, "instruments" are composed of people, and over time people tend to substitute their own goals for those of the institutions of which they form a part. Second, the kinds of bureaucratic rules which are essential for the efficient management of the organization tend to become more important than the objectives of the organization. Finally, many organizations are reluctant to change and fall behind the times through simple inertia. For these reasons, many public agencies tend to become vested interest institutions more concerned with advancing their own interests than achieving the purpose for which they were created.

Peter has noted that much of what happens goes wrong. "In time, every post tends to be occupied by an employee who is incompetent to carry out its duties ... work is accomplished by those employees who have not yet reached their level of incompetence."[4] This so-called Peter Principle is certainly not without merit; we can all find examples of people who have been promoted beyond their level of competence.

However, the problem is not simply a matter of public organizations which are filled with people who cannot do what they are supposed to do. It is often more a matter of organizations that no longer do what they were formed to do because they have either been captured by tradition or because they have had their resources redirected in favor of protecting the personal interests of their members. In some cases the organization has simply not kept pace with change. Kharasch has embodied this idea in his "Institutional Imperative" which states, "Every action or decision of an institution must be intended to keep the institutional machinery working."[5] He continues by stating, "To speak of any goal or purpose of an institution other than keeping the institutional machinery running is no more meaningful than to speak of the goal of an automobile exhaust or the purpose of the hum of a sewing machine."[6]

Problems of goal displacement and even incompetence are not unusual, but why do they seem to be so common and so difficult to deal with in public agencies? Look at it this way: if a private company provides a service, and if the quality of that service diminishes over time, consumers who want that service will look to other, better sources. This will eventually cut into the profit picture of the company and give them a clear message: shape up or get ready to go out of business. The private sector economy is very sensitive to this kind of message. The calculus by which private businesses evaluate their performance is very basic: they can measure the value of their outputs by their profits. If people do not buy a given product or service, it is either because it is not wanted in the first place or because it can be obtained better or cheaper elsewhere. This does not generally apply to government and is certainly not the case with the criminal justice system. Police departments do not compete with one another; neither do the courts or prisons. Moreover, public agencies generally do not have to justify either their existence or their actions once they have been created. Unfortunately, agencies like police departments and courts are not directly accountable to the public in any realistic way, and there are no reliable means for measuring the quality of their outputs. This is one reason there tend to be such tremendous differences among agencies which have similar social responsibilities. Understanding criminal justice entails an appreciation of the fact that its processes are carried out for the most part by public agencies, many of which are as responsive to their own "institutional imperatives" as they are to the needs of the community. The general lack of direct accountability on the part of these agencies, combined with their inability to accurately measure the value of their outputs, creates many possible situations for discontent on the part of the citizenry.

It is not unusual for a government agency to engage in public relations efforts to polish a tarnished image. However, if the basic problem lies in the fact that the actions of the agency are not responsive to the needs of the clientele, then public relations alone will not solve the problem. Criminal justice agencies are by no means exempt from the problems that beset all organizations and it is important that the various elements of the system remain mindful of the subtle changes which can transform them from effective instruments into sluggish, unresponsive institutions. This means, among other things, that they must continually remind themselves that they operate within the broader context of society and that they are not separate entities. This calls for a dual awareness. On the one hand, each agency must carefully monitor its external environments: it must know who and what its clients are and how to meet their needs as efficiently and effectively as possible. Agencies must be especially sensitive to change and willing to adapt to new requirements. On the other hand, they must also keep a watchful eye on internal factors as well. Since criminal justice agencies are composed of people, "people problems" within the organization can be a major source of trouble. The management of human resources is one of the most important tasks of management — but a responsibility which is too often overlooked or given insufficient attention. The rapid rise of unions in the public sector (particularly among police) is clear evidence that problems in this area have been ignored or mishandled.

Power and Power Settings In Criminal Justice

Power is the ability to act. More appropriately, power is the ability to make others act. The State is vested with considerable power. It has the authority to compel its citizens to do certain things (such as stop at red lights) and not to do others (such as steal or commit murder). Of course, there are people who disregard laws and do as they wish. In such cases the state may apply its coercive powers in apprehending and punishing them. However, power is far more subtle than the foregoing suggests, for not all power is mandated by legislation and executed without ambiguity. Organizations and individuals attempt to obtain power for a variety of reasons: to carry out the intended purposes of the organization, to increase the amount of control exercised over the immediate environment, and to aggrandize the position of specific individuals. A great deal of what people do involves getting and exercising power, often for its own sake, and sometimes to the detriment of the public.

From the perspective of a public agency, it is again important to remember that organizations, like people, are not isolated from the rest of society. What an organization becomes and how it fulfills its social functions is determined in large measure by its relationships with other people and organizations. The cluster of people and organizations vital to the interests of an agency may be described as its "power setting." This power setting is composed of a number of major elements:

The Executive

An organization's executive is the person who has ultimate authority over the organization, such as the chief of police, district attorney or the warden of a prison. These people are not sovereign in the sense that they wield absolute power; indeed, their powers are limited by law, custom, or the superordinate bodies to which they must report, such as city councils or legislative committees. The executive is the person within the organization who is supposed to shape its policies into operational realities. The power of the executive may show itself in what he is able to accomplish or even in what he cannot get done. It should be apparent that the executive is an individual person and his decisions will be influenced by the kinds of things that influence all other people. Simply because he legally occupies a position of executive authority by no means proves that he ought to be the person in that particular position. Some executives are incompetent. To the extent that a given executive is incapable of discharging his duties, the entire organization and its clientele will suffer to some degree.

Rivals

Any organization that competes with another organization is its rival. Competition may be functional (competition for the same task) or allocational (competition for resources). In general, there is very little functional rivalry among criminal justice agencies — there is usually just one police department in town, whether you like it or not. This lack of functional competition may be a major factor in the relatively low quality of the output of some agencies. On the other hand, criminal justice agencies do have many allocational rivals. The police department must compete with all other municipal departments for its budget, just as the state department of corrections must compete with other state agencies for its funds. There may even be fierce competition for funds within an agency, and this is what produces some of the "politics" within an organization. If there is an ample supply of money for everyone, allocational conflicts tend to be minor and of little importance. However, when the competition for funds becomes acute, the resulting rivalries can get intense and even unpleasant. Recent voter initiatives based on citizen dissatisfaction with government taxation, several years of double-digit inflation, and recent economic depression have created a serious financial crunch for all levels of government. This is important because not all agencies, or bureaus within agencies, will survive during periods of economic hardship. Because of this, one can expect to see shifts in the delivery of public services, including criminal justice services. Money needed for expensive programs will be much harder to get and many agencies will be forced to maintain current levels of service in the face of greater demands and shrinking budgets. This will ultimately produce clientel dissatisfaction in areas where services must be cut or otherwise modified. Indeed, the 1980's look as if they will be years beset with major challenges to the various levels of government, and many changes can be anticipated.

Beneficiaries

Some people clearly benefit from the services of various agencies. The person whose house is on fire is a direct beneficiary of the services of the fire department, just as welfare recipients are direct beneficiaries of the welfare department. Direct beneficiaries are inclined to take an active interest in the affairs of the agencies which provide their benefits and tend to support both the agencies and their policies. The direct beneficiaries of an agency often exert a collective influence in advancing the interests of the agency which takes care of them.

Other people are indirect beneficiaries and tend to give little thought to the agencies which provide them the indirect benefits they receive. For example, although prisons do keep some dangerous offenders out of circulation, those of us who are safe from those prisoners give little thought to the benefit we receive or to the people who provide it. Indirect beneficiaries more or less ignore the agencies which serve them, thus allowing them to pretty well manage themselves as they see fit. This only encourages the lack of accountability previously discussed.

Criminal justice agencies have relatively few direct beneficiaries. Perhaps their most important direct beneficiaries are the people who supply them with resources. This would include those who sell radios, cars, weapons, supplies, equipment, and facilities. As a collective good, justice is not supposed to be directed in favor of any particular group, and for this reason the criminal justice system does not generally seek to benefit any particular segment of the public. Since most people are indirect beneficiaries of the system, most do not devote a great deal of personal effort to understanding how the system works. Many members of the community more or less take it for granted that those who work within the system do pretty much whát they are supposed to. Although many members of the criminal justice system decry this apathy and urge citizens to take a more active interest, in the absence of some means for making people see themselves as direct beneficiaries, this appeal will meet with little success.

Sufferers

Just as some people are beneficiaries, others many suffer from the actions of those same agencies. How a person suffers is a function of what the agency does to him. Very few agencies of government take direct action against the individual; the criminal justice system is an exception. Those believed to have committed crimes are arrested by the police, prosecuted in the courts, and incarcerated in prisons. As direct sufferers these people have a direct interest in what the criminal justice system does.

There are also indirect sufferers. This includes some minorities, young people, the elderly, and businessmen. Some minorities may feel (correctly or otherwise) that they have been singled out for special attention. Young people likewise may believe they are discriminated against, just as some elderly people may believe they are inadequately protected. Some businessmen may believe the system does not give them adequate protection and that it is too easy for criminals to prey upon them. The validity of these feelings is not the main point; what is important is that people see themselves in a particular and subjective relationship to the criminal justice system. If a person believes he or she is a sufferer, then he or she really is a sufferer! As W.I. Thomas has said, "What is real in perception is real in its consequences." It should be noted in passing, however, that some people ought to suffer! That is the price of violating the law or of being disorderly; however, no person should be punished solely because of his age, race, sex or national origin. As we will see later, this is easier said than done.

Regulatees

Ours is a highly complex society, and in order to achieve harmony there must be a variety of regulations which govern the behavior of the individual. People simply cannot be allowed to do as they please. Such regulations exist and many are enforced by the criminal justice system. The same police officer who is expected to protect you from an armed robber is also expected to protect you from yourself. This is done through the regulation of such activities as traffic, alcohol consumption, and the use of drugs. The state imposes many regulations by requiring licenses of different types — for driving, to own or carry guns, and to practice certain occupations. This kind of regulation is a necessary and proper government fucntion. Although most people accept this kind of regulation, some become unhappy when they are personally called to task for infractions. The simple matter of getting a traffic ticket clearly illustrates the point. Nearly all veteran police officers have been confronted with the verbal abuse of the motorist who is unhappy because the officer is "harassing" him instead of "catching crooks." In recent years the police and courts have come under heavy criticism for enforcing laws which regulate morals, particularly those which deal with the use of recreational drugs or sexual behavior among consenting adults. Some people become unhappy when the police refuse to regulate the behavior of other people on demand. In this type of situation, someone insists that the police take action against a troublesome friend, neighbor, or acquaintance and when informed that it is not within the scope of police authority to do so, the complainant may become angry or hostile, because he sees himself as a rejected beneficiary who ends up a sufferer!

Allies

People or groups who are willing to support an agency in the event of conflict are its allies. Alliances can be made for peculiar reasons, and in the criminal justice system one can become an adversary of one element of the system simply by becoming the ally of another. For example, public defenders have a different set of goals than do police officers and prosecutors. Even the police and the prosecutor may find themselves at opposite ends on some issues. Perhaps more important is the issue of how the public emerges as an ally of the system. Some criminal justice agencies, especially the police, want citizen alliances; others, such as the courts, could often care less. The police need allies for a number of reasons. They need the help of citizens who report crimes and who assist them in the identification of offenders. They may also need political support, especially at budget time. The courts do not require the same kind of citizen assistance: those who are needed can be subpoenaed. There is very little citizens can do to assist the prisons, although citizen assistance is vital in the case of community-based corrections. Alliances are not made for their own sake; allies are courted when they are needed and they are recruited for specific purposes. Crass as this may sound, it is one of the realities of life.

Downs has noted that different bureaus may have radically different power settings, either because they do not contain the same elements, or because individual elements are organized very differently.[8] If we are to understand the criminal justice system, we must examine each of its major components in the light of its own power setting. Anything less would reduce the study of the system to the simple restatement of cliches. Finally, if we are concerned with the pattern of relationships between the community and the criminal justice system, it is important that we see just how the community contributes to the power settings of the various parts of the criminal justice system. In doing so, it might be possible to identify sources of conflict and to correct them. This is important because at every point where the system touches the community, some aspect of its power setting is involved.

By understanding the nature of power settings, members of the community can influence the quality of justice. Complex relationships can be clarified and strengthened, and channels of communication can be widened. By the same token, members of criminal justice agencies can use their understanding of power settings to establish a more effective outreach to the community. Community leaders (including those within the criminal justice system) can make use of the multitude of power settings within the community to improve the quality and scope of their respective roles.

Community Ecology & Criminal Justice

Studying the criminal justice system in a college course is a lot like dissecting frogs in a biology class. One takes the frog, cuts it up, and looks at the parts. We do pretty much the same things with the criminal justice system in most courses: we divide it up into its major elements and then look at the parts. But the frog in biology lab is dead and all we can learn from its corpse is its anatomy and morphology; it is not the same creature it was when it was alive. In a way, the same is true of the criminal justice system. The "live" criminal justice system is an organic part of the community and it is deeply entwined in the full range of community structures and processes. You cannot hope to fully understand the criminal justice system without looking at it "alive" in its ecological relationship with the rest of the community.

The word "community" is a term used to describe a broad array of human groupings, some of which have little in common with one another. It is clear that communities vary on the basis of size, location, degree of ubanization, social composition, and economic base. It is less clear that they also vary on the basis of what they provide for, and what they expect from their residents. Some people could survive quite well in one kind of community whereas another would be a disaster for them. Some communities are close-knit and supportive while others are cold and impersonal. Criminal justice, which is a process that takes place within the community, will also vary from place to place. Some communities have higher expectations of the system than others, just as some are more willing to invest resources in the system than are others.

To better understand community ecology, let us take a brief look at some of the major variables that are involved. The combination of variables discussed below — although the list is by no means complete — is what gives a particular community its own unique criminal justice system and also explains why there is so much variation from one place to the next.

The Idea of "City"

When we speak of community, most of us think of the town in which we live; the idea of "community" is closely identified with the concept of "city." A city, in its simplest sense, is an aggregate of people within a common geographic boundary. Unfortunately, nothing is quite that simple. Cities have life cycles and where a city is in terms of its life cycle says a great deal about the place and its inhabitants. Perhaps one of the best-known classifications of cities using this approach was done by Lewis Mumford, who set forth a six-stage cycle of the growth and decline of the city.

THE LIFE CYCLE OF THE CITY*

Stage 1; The Eopolis. This is the village community which, by contemporary standards, we would consider to be both primitive and quaint. The eoplois represents the first permanent (as distinguished from *nomadic*) settlement of an area. People have made the place their home and have begun the domestication of animals. The hallmark of this stage of community development is the generation of surplus. In this primitive kind of community, social associations are based on blood ties; that is, on *kinship*. The villages tend to be composed of clans or tribes of persons related to one another. At least initially, this kind of community has very little contact with "outsiders."

Stage 2: The Polis. The association of villages or kinship groups into a somewhat larger grouping, perhaps in order to provide for mutual defense, leads to the development of the "polis." The bringing together of these various groups soon produces a division of labor which ultimately leads to the development of the trades and crafts. The polis, according to Mumford, remained a collection of families whose way of life remained basically homogenous. Considerable control could still be exercised over the individual by his family and

*Lewis Mumford, *The Culture of Cities*. New York: Harcourt, Brace and Co., 1938.

associates and the roles each person was expected to perform were still largely determined for him.

State 3: The Metropolis. The metropolis is a regional center which is usually strategically located along some major transportation route (the older ones were usually located along water routes). The metropolis is somewhat of a "mother" city, attracting residents from other, smaller communities. They are attracted to the metropolis because of its commercial and mercantile functions. The trade between the metropolis and other cities along its transportation route provides a cultural cross-fertilization, further enhancing the division of labor and the specialization of trades and crafts. Of course, all of this produces a new set of social relationships which include a much broader range of associations than the family or kinship group. It is in the metropolis that we see the first signs of a beginning class struggle, for it is in the metropolis that the "ties that bind" loosen and the inequalities of society become patterned and obvious. The metropolis is characterized (at least in the Western world) by mass literacy, a relatively fluid class system, and the use of inanimate energy (the latter was in fact the basis of the industrial revolution which itself was one of the major factors producing the modern industrial state). It is now possible for a metropolis to form in geographic areas not previously suitable: we are no longer dependent on navigable waterways for transportation. The combined use of air routes, railways, and motor transport has given a new meaning to geography. In the metropolis we find people as individuals rather than as members of families or clans, and this means that the kinds of controls which must be placed on them must come from sources outside the family. Hence, the need for extensive laws and ordinances and for agencies to enforce and adjudicate them.

Stage 4: The Megalopolis. Mumford says that this stage marks the beginning of the decline of the city. The utopian view that the growth in technology can cure social ills begins to be offset by the dystopian view which suggests that technological growth either generates or intensifies more social evils than it reduces or cures. In the megalopolis the city concentrates on bigness and power — on economies of scale, and the owners of the instruments of production and distribution subordinate every other fact of life to the achievement of riches and the display of wealth. Standardization and mechanization prevail; the megalopolis ushers in an age of cultural aggrandizement: scholarship and science by tabulation; sterile research; elaborate fact-finding with no reference to rational intellectual purpose or any ultimate possibility of social use. It would seem that at this point the community no longer supports the needs of its residents but virtually consumes them as a kind of fuel needed to stoke a huge social machine gone wild. Rigidity and ossification take place, and the citizen becomes an appendage to his own institutions.

Stage 5: Tyrannopolis. In this stage Mumford sees parasitism and exploitation as pervading all aspect of social, economic, and political life. Place-hunting, privilege-seeking, bonus-collecting, favor-currying, nepotism, grafting and tribute-exacting become rife in both government and business and is accompanied by widespread moral apathy and a general failure of civic responsibility. Each group and each individual takes what it can get away with; the motto becomes: "Me First!" Wars, disease, and starvation emerge and productive work in the arts and sciences ceases.

Stage 6: The Nekropolis. This is Mumford's final stage, and in it he paints a picture which is harrowing and bleak: war, famine, and disease wrack both the city and the countryside. The cities themselves become mere shells. Nekropolis is the city of the dead, where flesh is turned to ashes and life is turned into a meaningless pillar of salt. Mumford described Nekropolis in his *Culture of Cities*, which was written in 1938. That was less than a decade before the devastation of Hiroshima, Nagasaki, Stalingrad, Berlin, and Leipzig.

Although Mumford's life cycle of cities presents an interesting overview of their historical, social, political, and technological growth, it is also important because it reminds us that cities can serve different functions. Although the basic functions of the police are the same in Dallas and New York City, there are apt to be significant differences in how the two departments discharge their responsibilities. Although the residents of both cities expect similar products from their police departments, the kind of organization and procedures that work in the central business district of Dallas might not be nearly as effective inTimes Square in New York City. One cannot conclude that either department is better than the other, it as would be a subjective value judgement. New York and Dallas are simply different kinds of cities and each has its own pressures, problems, and needs. The administration of justice within a given city can only be fully understood in the light of the needs and makeup of that particular city. As a result, it is unfair to compare criminal justice agencies in one city with those in another, unless the two cities are nearly comparable in all major respects. Some of the factors which play a role in community diversity are its population size and composition, the technological environment, the social structure of the city, and its political economy.

Population The size of a community's population is important. Typically, the more populous the city, the greater its diversity and heterogenity. In smaller communities people tend to be bound together by somewhat closer ties of kinship, occupation, and social convention. In larger communities, they tend to be bound together by interdependent economic needs and political interests.

Other population factors, such as racial composition and population density also play an important role in defining a given community. Members of minority groups who come to cities in search of opportunity often find only further disappointment and a new definition of poverty. Many seek out the comfortable familiarity of ethnic or racial enclaves and in the process contribute to the cleavages already found in most cities.

Density, which refers to the number of persons per square mile of land area, is also a subtle but important factor. Population density is in part a function of the extent to which population increases and area expansion keeps pace. What this means is that some cities have been able to expand their boundaries to accommodate growing populations. On the other hand, some cities have been locked in, their boundaries fixed because they are surrounded by incorporated areas and cannot expand. When this happens, a "central city" may find itself surrounded by other, smaller incorporated cities. The suburban cities may then provide much of the labor force used by the central city but contribute little to its tax base (as most local taxes are based on property taxes). When this happens, the central city does not accurately reflect the total number of people who impact on it, and any actual growth within the central city automatically increases its population density.

The relationship between crime and population density has been widely debated. It has been shown that crime rates tend to be highest in the central city and diminish as one moves out towards the suburbs. It has also been shown that population densities tend to follow the same pattern. However, the relationship is more apparent than casual. High density alone would no doubt provide more opportunity for many kinds of crime, but the key seems to be the quality of the density. As Harries points out, "It would seem that conventional measures of population density (persons per acre or persons per acre of residential land) are quite inadequate as predictors of criminal environments. A crowding index such as persons per room, is apparently a much better measure since it approximates human reactions to space and is more likely to help us predict areas of social pathology."[9] Where large numbers of people are crowded together under conditions which strain the human capacity for effective adjustment, there may indeed be good grounds for anticipating conflict, disorder, and violence.

The Technological Environment Technology has been described as a blessing and a curse; in reality, it is a combination of both. [10] Technology has brought about tremendous social change, solving old problems and creating new ones. Technology is closely related to the nature of the labor force, and plays a major role in determining the economic base of the community. For example, some cities are essentially manufacturing towns whereas others may be mill towns, college towns, service centers, or military towns. Advances in technology or changes in the economy can have a dramatic impact on these kinds of towns. The recession in the automotive industry, for example, created enormous difficulties for Detroit and other "car cities." The development of the microelectronics industry resulted in the emergence of such places as "Silicon Valley" in California and the rapid growth of cities like Richardson, Texas (home of Texas Instruments).

The kind of industries that develop in a given area helps determine the nature of the work force of the area. Technology is also changing cities, and not all of the changes have been good. The older, traditional cities have become plagued with problems. As one writer has noted, "The inner-city has changed. Middle-class whites have abandoned the city for the suburbs, leaving behind growing percentages (often large majorities) of lower-class blacks, the elderly, and the poor. This is the new clientele who are the objects of urban bureaucracies, and it should be no surprise to find these bureaucracies under attack in the inner cities...."[11]

Not only are communities in the process of changing, the criminal justice system is itself undergoing rapid change. Driven by advances in technology, the system is employing more sophisticated equipment and processes. This is bringing about some fundamental changes in the way the police and courts perform their functions. This in turn has produced a call for different kinds of employees than those hired by criminal justice agencies in the past. The technological environment is a constantly changing and often confusing component of the community ecology, and cannot be ignored in any serious attempt to understand the criminal justice system.

Social Structure We live in a stratified society in which people tend to group together according to their levels of income, education, and social values. These groupings reflect social class. One's social class is not always easy to determine, as there are no definite rules for assigning class position (except at the uppermost levels of society). It is determined by a combination of factors, including one's occupation; prestige within the community; possessions, wealth and residence; patterns of social interaction; degree of class consciousness; value orientations; and the amount of power one wields within the community.

Communities can differ considerably in their distributions of social classes. There are very wealthy communities which contain large numbers of very upper class and upper middle class residents, just as there are very poor communities with large numbers of working class people. Since each social class has its own value orientations and outlook (especially with respect to the criminal justice system), the class composition of the community will play a major role in the nature and quality of the criminal justice system within the community.

Political Economy   McKinney and Howard note that, "Ecology produces demands; culture determines the type and quality of responses that government will make; and political economy identifies the strategy — that is, how, when, and in what manner these demands will be satisfied. The political economy perspective allows us to view public organizations in terms of the power government officials exercise."[12] This is a synthesizing perspective; it allows us to tie together a number of the points that have already been touched on.

Government has limited resources, and although (in theory) it may be legally able to do a great many things, as a matter of practical reality, it actually does very few of them. Put another way, government must make some rational decisions about how it will allocate and spend its resources. The limitation is not so much on government's *willingness* to do things in the public interest as on its ability to pay for those things. A given community can only raise so much in the way of revenues and its expenditures must roughly equal those revenues. This means that government must not only decide *what* it will do, but *how much* as well. This is why many government agencies operate at less than desirable levels of effectiveness. It it were possible to hire as many employees as were needed, and to purchase all the equipment required, then providing effective public services would be no problem.

How then does government decide what services it will provide and the exact extent of those services? First, government provides what it considers to be "essential services" which include public safety and education; beyond that, it seeks a utility maximization which basically provides the greatest social benefits for the largest number of people at the lowest possible cost. This calls for an estimation of minimum levels of service consistent with need and ability to pay. Second, the services which are provided are the result of a public policy process, and this process is influenced by a wide range of considerations including (but not limited to) the power setting of the government agencies; citizen expectations and tolerances; pressure group activities; the class structure of the community and political expediency. For example, in one community an intelligent and well-meaning woman decided that a shelter was needed for battered women. This shelter, which was actually a "safe house," was to be a refuge for women with limited financial means who faced physical violence in their own homes. While staying in the home the women could be given counseling and could be provided with information concerning their legal rights. At the time there was no such refuge. Public policy dictated that women who were being abused should either call the police and secure criminal charges against their abusers or should seek civil remedy in the appropriate court. This lady wanted the city to fund the Womens' Shelter; that is, she wanted to alter the public policy concerning the plight of abused women. In order to achieve this objective, she went to a number of politically active sources: the Council on the Status of Women, several women's organizations, and the local media. Contact was made with female members of the city council and the county commission. Pressure was placed on the key political personages, such as the local state representative and state senator, the mayor and city manager, and even the governor's office. After an intensive and well orchestrated campaign, money was appropriated to fund the women's shelter. A site was located and made ready and the shelter was opened for business. Although use of the shelter has been relatively limited, it is still too early to evaluate the undertaking; however, it does illustrate the fact that public policy and the provision of services can be shaped by individuals and special interest groups. Of course, one complaint often articulated by certain citizen's groups (most notably the poor) is that they lack the power to shape public policy. That is, they see themselves as consumers who have little say in the quality of the product they receive and this argument is certainly not without merit. Members of the community who lack power have few realistic avenues of access to either the legislative bodies (city councils) or the administrators of the agencies themselves (police chiefs, district attorneys).

Two facts are quite evident: (1). the decade of the 1980's is going to require considerable imagination and innovation in the delivery of public services, and (2) city governments are going to be faced with major problems in funding public programs. The whole issue of political economy will become an important point in the development of rational public policy, and the entire criminal justice system will feel the consequences.

Summary

We now have three major frames of reference with which we can explore the relationship between the community and the criminal justice system. At this point it is fair to ask, "Exactly how will these broad frames of reference help us to understand community-criminal justice relations?"

In the first place, by looking at the full range of criminal justice services and practices as *public* enterprises we can see the basis for many of the strengths and weaknesses of the system. The concept of collective goods tells us that criminal justice is designed for *everyone's* benefit, yet experience shows us that in reality it is selectively distributed — and not everyone "benefits" from it! We also see how the problem of goal displacement can convert an *instrument* into an *institution*, watering down the overall effectiveness of its operations. That this has happened to the criminal justice system will be made painfully clear in subsequent chapters.

Second, by looking at the criminal justice system from the perspective of power and power settings, we will be able to see some of the subtle (and not so subtle) forces that work on both individuals and groups in the shaping of both policies and operations. The idea of an agency's executive gives us a device for examining how individual responsibility "at the top" influences what an agency does — or fails to do. The idea of the executive is also important because it provides a point where subjective and objective factors cross in the development and implementation of policy. The concepts of functional and allocational rivalry enable us to understand the kinds of competition which force decisions in various ways, and which determine not only what will be done but how it will be accomplished; it also shows why a great deal of an agency's resources are consumed in "playing politics" instead of "delivering the goods." The concept of power is vitally important, as it is based on the premise that give-and-take relationships are part of a *zero-sum game* in which winners can only win at the expense of losers.

The third frame of reference — community ecology — underscores the fact that criminal justice can only be understood in context — specifically, in the context of the community of which it is a part. The elements which make up the ecology of a community are staggering in their complexity. Likewise, the size of a community and its composition in terms of its structure, population density, and level of technology are critical variables in the larger equation.

The criminal justice system draws upon the community and reflects its composition in various ways. Gross inequalities in power relationships almost always result in an inequitable distribution of services. Factors associated with class weave in and out of the full range of criminal justice practices, from hiring police officers to determining which offenders will be given active time for their crimes and who will be placed on a probated sentence. These same class factors also influence the kinds of expectations a community has of its criminal justice system, including the kinds of services it is willing to tolerate and the kinds of services it will demand.

The whole issue of criminal justice and community relations would be simple and problem-free if there were just one set of rules which applied with equal effectiveness in all community settings. Unfortunately, this is not the case. Just as communities vary dramatically, so does the nature of criminal justice within the community. Thus, the study of one is actually the study of the other.

Discussion Questions

1. What are some of the ways you can tell if an "instrument" has become an "institution"?

2. Are most people *direct* or *indirect* beneficiaries of the criminal justice system? What are the consequences of this?

3. Why do you think so many people support the efforts of government to regulate the behavior of citizens — but at the same time resist being regulated themselves?

4. How would you describe the *kind of community* in which you live? How does the kind of community you live in influence the quality of criminal justice?

5. Do you think social class really makes a difference in how people are treated by the criminal justice system? If so, give some specific examples.

6. Is social policy made "fairly"? Do you think that special interest groups demand too much?

7. Describe the "collective goods" provided by government in your community. Do they *really* benefit everyone? Would we be better off without some of them?

8. How can you have "allocational rivals" in a government agency? Give an example.

9. Do you think it is possible for the criminal justice system to convince citizens that they are *direct beneficiaries*? If so, how?

10. How has technology made city life more complex in recent years? Has this hurt the quality of justice?

11. Have recent trends in society limited the impact of class on the freedom of the individual?

12. To what extent is a person's access to "justice" determined by his status, and what particular status-related factors are likely to be the most important?

Glossary

ALLIES — Any person or group willing to support an organization, especially when it becomes involved in a conflict.

BENEFICIARIES — Those who benefit from an organization's functions. Beneficiaries may be *direct* or *indirect* beneficiaries.

COLLECTIVE GOODS — A benefit which exists for everyone regardless of whether they pay for it or how much others also benefit from it. Collective goods are usually provided by public agencies.

INSTITUTION — A formal organization which devotes a significant amount of its efforts and resources towards its own maintenance as opposed to accomplishing the objectives for which it was originally established.

INSTRUMENT — The means for accomplishing an end. Organizations are ideally instruments for meeting some objective. (e.g., solving a social problem or providing a needed service).

ORGANIZATION — A group of individuals formally associated with one another for the purpose of accomplishing a collective objective. An organization may be either an instrument or an institution.

PETER PRINCIPLE — The thesis that an individual will rise within the hierarchy of an organization until he reaches his level of incompetence.

POPULATION DENSITY — The number of people per square mile of land area.

POWER SETTING — The external environment and relationships of an organization, composed of people or other organizations which are affected by (or affect) the organization.

REGULATEES — People whose activities are regulated by an organization's functions.

RIVALS — Any competing organization. Rivals can be *functional* (that is, have a competing function) or *allocational* (that is, compete for funding from the same source).

SOCIAL STRATIFICATION — The distribution of the population on the basis of social class differences.

EXECUTIVE — The person within an organization who has legal authority over the organization (e.g., the police chief; the District Attorney; or a Warden).

SUFFERERS — Those who are adversely affected by an organization's functions. Sufferers may be *direct* or *indirect* sufferers.

Notes

[1] Anthony Downs, *Inside Bureaucracy* (Boston: Little, Brown and Company, 1967), p. 5; see also Max Weber, *The Theory of Social and Economic Organization* translated by A.M. Henderson and Talcott Parsons (New York: The Free Press of Glencoe, 1947), p. 363.

[2] Downs, *Inside Bureaucracy*, p. 5.

[3] Carroll Quigley, *The Evolution of Civilization* (Indianapolis: Liberty Press, 1979), pp. 101-102.

[4] Lawrence J. Peter and Raymond Hall, *The Peter Principle* (New York: William Morrow & Co., Inc., 1969), p. 27.

[5] Robert N. Kharasch, *The Institutional Imperative* (New York: Charterhouse Books, 1973), p. 24.

[6] Kharasch, *Institutional Imperative*, p. 24.

[7] Downs, *Inside Bureaucracy*, pp. 44-47.

[8] Downs, *Inside Bureaucracy*, pp. 44-47.

[9] Keith D. Harries, *The Geography of Crime and Justice* (New York: McGraw-Hill Book Company, 1974), p. 83.

[10] Emmanuel G. Mesthene, "The Role of Technology in Society," in *Technology and Man's Future*, edited by Albert H. Leich (New York: St. Martin's Press, 1977), pp. 159-160.

[11] Jerome B. McKinney and Lawrence C. Howard, *Public Administration: Power and Accountability* (Oak Parks, Illinois: Moore Publishing Co., Inc., 1979), pp. 104-105.

[12] McKinney and Howard, *Public Administration*, pp. 106-107.

SOCIAL CONTROL AND CRIMINAL JUSTICE 2

All communities are aggregations of people who are involved in various kinds of interaction with one another. Due to differences in status, ethnicity, religion, education and so on, conflicts cannot be avoided. It is certain that some people will behave in ways which are unacceptable to others. In fact, the majority of people would probably *like* to behave unacceptably from time to time, but avoid doing so because they fear the consequences. It is obvious that an orderly society must have ways to control the behavior of its citizens.

Some of the most effective forms of control come from *within* the individual and are a product of his socialization process. These controls represent the internalization of the values of his group and focus attention on the powerful influence of primary associations. These socializing agents will be discussed under the heading of the *private control system* later in the chapter. The focus of this text is on the controlling role of the criminal justice system, and we will turn our attention first to more formal means of social control — laws.

The concept of law is at the same time complex and simple. Laws direct our behavior in many ways. Yet laws are themselves the product of many factors and are constantly changing. It is impossible in the scope of a single chapter — or even a single book — to describe in detail the origins and structure of law and the legal system; however, without at least some overview of the relationship between law and the individual, it would be virtually impossible to explore the relationship between the criminal justice system and the community. The discussion which follows is offered as a simplified "springboard" which will enable us to examine both the criminal justice system and its relationship to the community.

Law and Social Control

Without law there would be no criminal justice system; in fact, there would probably be no cities as we know them. Business, industry, science, the arts — if they existed at all — would be radically different from what we associate with those terms. Indeed, the situation was crisply summarized by Thomas Hobbes when he said that in a land without laws there would be "no arts, no letters, no society, and which is worst of all, continual fear and danger of violent death, and the life of man solitary, poor, nasty, brutish, and short."[1]

Therefore, before we examine the relationship between the criminal justice system and the community, we must first consider the role played by law. We should attempt to clarify the relationship between the criminal justice system and law as well as the relationship between the community and law. This should ultimately provide a better understanding of the relationship between the criminal justice system and the community. This is an important undertaking because the concept of law is probably the most significant element within a complex series of interrelated issues.

The Functions of Law

Laws, like most social institutions, serve a purpose. Before we try to discover how well or to what extent the law serves its purposes, we need to first understand just what its purposes are. If the purposes of law are clear, easily understood, and logical, then we would expect the formal institutions and processes of the law to follow suit. If, on the other hand, the purposes of law are complex, contradictory, and illogical, we would expect to find the institutions and processes to be embroiled in controversy and conflict.

Actually, the law serves two broad purposes which are closely interrelated. It is sometimes difficult to separate the two, and each is highly complex in its own right. Taken together, they have presented topics of discussion for legal scholars for centuries.

The Need For Order If all people had the unlimited authority to do as they wished, the result would be anarchy. As Bodenheimer points out, "Where anarchy reigns, there are no obligatory rules which each person is bound to recognize and obey. Everybody is free to follow his own impulses and to do whatever comes to his mind."[2] If we were strict hermits, then anarchy might be quite acceptable and appropriate. We are not hermits; we live in close association with one another and each of us is a member of many social groups.

Each group within society serves some purpose and should benefit both the group as a whole as well as its individual members. If these benefits are to occur, there must be some means for establishing *order* so that behavior can be predicted, passions controlled, and reasonable predictability assured. For this reason each group establishes a set of *norms*, rules which goven the conduct of its members. Society itself is a group and the law is but one class of norms which seeks to assure order among all of its members. Law provides an "orderly" framework within which all members of society (individually and collectively) can organize their lives and affairs. Laws (legal norms) are considered so important that their compliance is backed by the threat of force and violence.

Although the need for order reduces individual liberty, it also reduces many of the immediate threats the individual would otherwise face. In its most basic sense, "order" is a trade-off in which the individual is willing to make certain personal sacrifices in return for explicit personal and social benefits. It is clear that the sacrifices should be *necessary* and the benefits should be proportionate. If they are not, the trade-off would be "unfair," and that leads to the second major purpose of law.

The Need For Justice There are obviously many ways of securing order, and order by itself is no guarantee that a given individual or group will achieve benefits which are commensurate with the sacrifices made. There can be order, for example, under tyranny in which a despotic government ceaselessly and ruthlessly regulates every aspect of the individual's life. However, we would consider a society of that type to be "unjust," and we expect our laws to prevent injustice. The second major function of law, therefore, is to achieve justice. Justice is clearly a much more complex issue than order if for no other reason than the fact that there is no universally accepted definition of "justice".

In its broadest sense, justice has been defined in terms of its goals: "To coordinate the diversified efforts and activities of the members of the community and to allocate rights, powers, and duties among them in a manner which will satisfy the reasonable needs and aspirations of individuals and at the same time promote maximum productive effort and social cohesion."[3] What does this mean? The answer is not clear; in fact, Bodenheimer noted that "when we delve into the problem of justice and endeavor to unravel its perplexing secrets, discouragement and despair are likely to befall us."[4] Is justice, as Plato suggested, the obligation of people to tend to their own business and not meddle in the affairs of members of the other classes? Or is its goal some sort of

27

"equality," as Aristotle suggested?* Or is justice, as Herbert Spencer proposed, the freedom of every person to reap whatever benefits his talents would allow, impeded only by the obligation of not infringing on the equal freedom of another? Legal scholars have debated questions of this type throughout recorded history. These questions still underlie many of the issues which are currently brought before judicial and legislative bodies.

In its most basic sense, justice seems to require some kind of accommodation and synthesis between the rights of the individual (however those rights are defined) and the needs of society (whatever those needs might be). "Justice demands that freedom, equality, and other basic rights be accorded and secured to human beings to the greatest extent consistent with the common good."[5] But the most perplexing question remains — who is to decide what those rights are, or what constitutes the common good? Problems in deciding what is "just" and to what extent trade-offs and compromises must be made are at the very root of many of the problems within both the criminal justice system and the community!

The Sources of Law

Although based on moral and philosophical issues, the law as a formal institution is a very real and pragmatic entity. Laws are formal rules — but where do they come from? It is clear enough that actual statutes are enacted by legislative bodies and that courts create law in their decisions; even these formal processes must be based on more fundamental processes. For this reason we will look at both the informal and formal sources of law.

Informal Sources of Law Laws are based on shared values, sentiment, subjective interpretations of what is "right" and experience. There can be little doubt that societies existed before there were formal laws and that laws must actually represent the "formalization" of the processes which preceded them. The kinds of norms which governed early societies were

---

*Aristotle's concept of equality is quite different from contemporary definitions. He apparently believed that equal things should go to equal people — but not all people were equal! He believed that the just distribution of society's benefits should be made according to merit, and the people who exhibited the greatest civic excellence should accordingly receive the greatest rewards. His concept of justice also included a retributive component in which those who violated his notion of distributive justice would be punished according to the nature and magnitude of their transgression. Both Plato and Aristotle were well aware of the value of law, but they were both also aware of its drawbacks; laws, because of their rigidity, could cause numerous hardships. They knew that general, universal rules designed to control complex human behavior had a great potential for actually being counterproductive and accordingly required some means of establishing equity where the law was defective (a concept which subsequently became embodied in English law and which has been carried over to American jurisprudence).

themselves a function of man's understanding of his environment and his place within it, particularly in relation to concepts of man's creator. It should come as no surprise that a great deal of early "legal thought" arose from both superstition and religion — one reason why morality still plays a major role in legal issues.

In fact, among the earliest and most important laws are those embodied in the *Torah* — the first five books of the Hebrew Bible: Genesis, Exodus, Leviticus, Numbers, and Deuteronomy. The Torah is canonical; it is considered to be divinely inspired and is the keystone of three of the world's major faiths: Judaism, Christianity, and Islam, although it is held in highest esteem by Judaism. Originally called the law of Moses, by the second century BC it was called the *Torah* (Hebrew for *law*); from about the third century AD it has also been called the *Pentateuch* ("five books" from the Greek *pente teuchos*). The Torah is not solely law; it also includes other elements such as songs, oracles, prayers, miracles, and history. This book of sacred writings has given the world not only some of its richest and most poignant literature, but it is also a history of the wellspring of law itself. Consider for example, the Decalogue (Ten Commandments) as a source of moral/legal guidance or the terrible threats in Leviticus to those who would break the covenant ("I will even appoint over you terror ....") as the basis for the legitimacy of retribution.[6]

For generation after generation religion *was* law. It was the responsibility of religion to define morality according to revelation or inspiration and to codify behavior accordingly. There were several reasons why this could be done with little difficulty. Religion regulated highly homogenous groups; societies were not nearly as diverse and complex as they are now. In the absence of science, human knowledge was minimal at best. This meant that elaborate stratification within society based on knowledge was impossible; *so little was known* that mastery of all but the most esoteric forms of knowledge was within the grasp of nearly everyone. People were equally ignorant.

Custom was also a basis for what ultimately became embodied in law. Forms of social organization, the distribution of land and other property, rights, duties and obligations all arose from a communal context in which the division of labor produced different rights and responsibilities which ultimately came to be seen as "proper" in their own right. Much of this "proper" conduct ultimately shifted from custom to law.[7] It was not until the time of Henry II (1154-1189) that the ancient tribal system of law based on religion and custom began to give way and a system of formal law emerged to replace it. It is significant that during the reign of Henry II the church and the state were formally separated and that thereafter a system of writs, procedures and common law began to emerge. It was after the establishment of the political state that the *formal* sources of law emerged. The *informal* sources continued — as they still do — to exert a major influence on the nature of the law.

Formal Sources Of Law   There are several formal sources of law in contemporary society probably the most important of which is *legislation*. Legislative bodies include those at the local, state, and federal levels. At the federal level laws are passed by the Congress. State legislatures perform the same function at the state level, while local laws (ordinances) are passed by city councils, boards of aldermen, or county commissions. In each case the intent is the same: to formalize a norm. In fact, legislative power may be defined as the power to establish rules of law. The authority which each state has to pass laws for its internal regulation and to provide for government is called its *police power*. A state must have such powers in order to preserve the health, safety, morals, and welfare of its residents. A state has the duty to protect its citizens and to provide for both public safety and order. States have very few limitations on this power: they must conform to the requirements of their own constitution and may not enact laws which violate or contradict federal law or the United States Constitution.[8] In general, local governments are considered to be creatures of state government and are subordinate to them.

Many of these legislative bodies have enacted laws which merely formalize custom and sentiment. For example, laws which prohibit *mal— um in se* crimes (those have traditionally been considered evil acts in and of themselves, such as murder, rape, and robbery) are simply the codification of ancient sentiment. Legislative bodies also enact *malum prohibitum* legislation – laws which prohibit (or require) some act not because the act (or failure to act) is inherently evil by its very nature, but because the existence of such a law will operate to the benefit of society or some group within society. Examples include laws which prohibit the sale of guns to minors or felons; laws which establish age, safety, and compensation requirements for members of the labor force; and laws which regulate the safe and orderly flow of traffic.

As Chambliss and Seidman have noted, "Regardless of how homogeneous a society may at first glance appear, behind the cloud of consensus and unanimity there always lurks the fact of widespread disagreement on what constitutes the 'right and proper' thing to do."[9]

This means that legislation will frequently be the result of interest-group activity in which various groups will seek the passage of laws that reflect their own particular interests — often in opposition to the interests of other groups. Examples include laws which assure profitable returns to specific industries (such as milk, insurance, and tobacco) and laws which require a percentage of construction contracts to be given to minority contractors. Chambliss and Seidman point out that "every detailed study of the emergence of legal norms has consistently shown the immense importance of interest-group activity, not 'the public interest,' as the critical variable in determining the content of legislation."[10] This means that the output of legislation can mean rags or riches, servility or power, weakness or strength to every interest group in the country.[11] If laws reflect special interests, and if legislation is more "available" to some members of the community than others, then laws may actually contribute to social inequities and foster citizen dissatisfaction.

Another source of law comes in the form of *delegated* or *autonomic legislation*. In this case administrative agencies are created by legislative bodies and are vested with rule-making authority. For all practical purposes, the rules they make carry the weight of law. These agencies flourish under a wide variety of names — they are sometimes called commissions, bureaus, boards, authorities, administrations and so on. Their rule-making powers are of course checked by both the legislatures which created them and by judicial review; yet many of these agencies are extremely powerful and have the authority to regulate some very important aspects of our lives.

A final major source of law resides within the courts. "It is today the prevailing opinion in the Ango-American legal world that a decision of a court of law — especially a court of last resort — which explicitly or implicitly lays down a legal proposition constitutes a general and formal source of law."[12] When a court renders a "holding," that decision carries the impact of law. In general, courts seek to avoid "creating new laws" and prefer to stick with precedent. However, in the case of some controversies, there is either no precedent or existing precedent is inadequate. In such cases the courts make "new law" by their decisions. As in the case of legislation, the law generated by the courts tends to favor certain groups over others: "On the whole, courts have been particularly active in rule-making in those areas of law which affect litigants who are sufficiently wealthy to be able to activate legal processes."[13] Although there are many legal problems affecting the poor which never reach the courts (in spite of the fact that the number of persons who might be affected is very large), this is changing. Legal advocacy for the poor, minorities and others has increased dramatically within the past decade. The courts have been used with great frequency in recent years to hear disputes in the area of criminal justice and have rendered landmark decisions, especially in the area of rights of the accused and prisoner's rights.

It is important to remember that the major formal sources of the law employ formal organizations, such as legislatures, courts, and administrative agencies, which operate in their own unique power settings. Moreover, membership in these organizations is still very much a function of class and status considerations. One does not necessarily become an attorney, judge, or legislator at will — and the process of becoming a functionary within these institutions nearly always involves a socialization process of its own, a process which operates to produce the same end that is sought by law itself: order and predictability.

Types of Law

There are many kinds of law: constitutional law, case law, statute law, treaties, executive orders, the regulations of administrative agencies, and local ordinances. It is convenient to divide law into two major classes: civil and criminal. Before looking at these two areas, it is important to distinguish between *substantive law* and *procedural law*. Substantive law is "That part of the law which creates, defines, and regulates rights."[14] It specifically defines the legal relationship between citizens and the state as well as among citizens themselves. The bulk of substantive law comes to us from the legislative branch of government. A simple way of remembering what substantive law means is to think of it as the *substance* of what our lawmakers require of us. When we state something as "against the law," we are usually referring to substantive law.

Procedural law, on the other hand, is that body of law which sets forth the "methods and means of enforcing substantive legal rights. It provides the machinery to maintain suits to enforce these rights or to obtain redress for their invasion."[15] Perhaps it is easiest to think of procedural law as that body of regulation which provides the mechanisms for bringing substantive law into practice. Both civil and criminal law have substantive and procedural components. All of this simply underscores the fact that the law is not a random, chaotic application of rules of convenience; the law not only regulates and imposes order, it is ordered and well regulated!

Civil Law People consistently engage in certain behaviors. For example, most marry and many divorce; bargains are struck and contracts are entered into; goods are sold or sometimes given away or traded; money is borrowed and must be repaid; the right to enjoy the use of certain chattels is asserted; money is left to heirs, and citizenship is claimed or renounced. These are essentially private or personal matters, yet the state has an interest in how they are conducted; collectively, such transactions have a major influence on all of us. In some cases misconduct in these areas is a crime (bigamy, theft and fraud). For the most part, however, these kinds of transactions are regulated not by criminal law, but by *civil* law.

Civil law has both substantive and procedural components and is designed to assist in the regulation of private affairs and to provide means for settling disputes in cases where conflicts arise. In general, such conflicts arise when there is a dispute between parties over either a breach of agreement or a breach of a duty imposed by law. In these cases the state does not prosecute as it does in criminal cases. The private parties themselves contest the controversy — but they use the courts to do so.

Civil Suits   A controversy between private parties which is heard in the courts is a civil suit. It is an adversary proceeding and must follow certain procedural rules. The party bringing the complaint (doing the suing) is the *plaintiff*. The plaintiff alleges some wrong and asks the court to provide a remedy. These remedies can take a wide range of forms; a partial list is provided below.

- *Mandatory Injunctions*, an order by the court which specifically directs some person to do something;

- *Prohibitory Injunctions*, an order by the court which prohibits some person from doing some specific activity;

- *Reformation*, a court order which changes a written instrument in order to reflect the actual agreement which had been entered into by two or more parties (where the instrument either inaccurately reflects such agreements or omits them);

- *Restitution*, where the court attempts to restore a person to a previous position or status;

- *Declaratory Judgment*, in which the court makes a determination of just what the parties' legal rights are;

- *Compensatory Damages*, in which money is awarded in order to compensate someone for losses they sustained because of the wrongful actions of someone else;

- *Punitive Damages*, in which money in addition to compensatory damages is awarded in order to punish the person doing the harm;
- *Nominal Damages*, in which a trivial sum of money is awarded (in cases where no actual loss resulted as a consequence of the wrongful behavior of another); and,
- *Liquidated Damages*, in which money is awarded according to a previous agreement made by the parties involved.

The kind of remedy sought obviously depends upon the kind of case or conflict which comes before the court. It is also very important to remember that many — perhaps the majority — of conflicts do *not* come before a civil court. In most of these cases, an "out of court settlement" is reached by the attorneys for the parties involved and the matter ends without an actual trial.

It was already pointed out that most of these private controversies arise as a result of a breach of an agreement or when someone suffers a harm because another person has breached a duty imposed by law. The former is a *breach of contract* and the latter is a *tort*. A contract is nothing more than an agreement between two or more parties that creates some kind of obligation. Contracts are voluntarily entered, and once entered into are enforceable by law. A person failing to uphold an obligation created by contract may be sued for his breach and appropriate remedies may be sought. Thus, if A agrees under contract to build a house and sell it to B for a certain sum of money, he has entered into a contract (according to its terms). Let us assume A agreed to build the house and sell it to B for $50,000. However, by the time the house is finished, the price of housing in the area has gone up and C offers to buy the house from A for $75,000, who then tells B he will not sell him the house (or will not sell it at the price previously agreed upon). B may then sue A for breach of contract.

Torts are wrongful acts (not involving a breach of contract) which arise as the result of the tortfeasor's failure to abide by some lawful duty. A tort duty is imposed by law. "Tort law establishes standards of conduct which all citizens must meet. It creates social duties among all members of society."[16] An unintentional tort arises when one accidently breaches a duty imposed by law. Most unintentional torts are based on negligence: the failure to use reasonable care. Most such cases in this country are automobile collision suits in which the plaintiff argues that the defendant was negligent in the manner in which he operated a car, in violation of duties imposed by traffic law. *Intentional* torts, on the other hand, are based on willful misconduct where the wrongful act is intended.

This includes such things as libel, slander and false imprisonment.*

Theoretically, every citizen has the right to prosecute a civil wrong. However, that right is severely limited because most people lack the technical ability to bring such suits and must rely on an attorney to actually handle the case and legal fees can effectively bar those with meager resources from bringing suits. In some cases lawyers will accept "contingent fees" which are a percentage of a favorable judgment and can run as high as forty percent. Even when attorneys are willing to accept contingent fee cases, the client may have to pay for the initial exploratory conference with the lawyer and may be required to pay actual expenses, such as the cost of taking depositions (which can be very expensive). Although legal remedies exist for virtually all legitimate civil wrongs, access to those remedies tends to be limited to those who have money. This is but one more example of how socio-economic, class, status, and power relationships affect how various members of the community are able to influence their environment — or how they are prevented from doing so.

Criminal Law A crime is an offense against the state; it is a *public* rather than private wrong. An act is not a crime unless it is made a crime by law. There are no "secret" crimes (at least not in the United States). Crimes have traditionally been classified as *treason, felonies,* and *misdemeanors.* A treason, previously termed *lese majesty*, is an offense against the duty of allegiance and consists of levying war against the government or giving aid and comfort to its enemies.[17] Felonies are serious crimes for which the state may inflict the death penalty or impose a lengthy term of imprisonment often in excess of a year. Misdemeanors are all other crimes, and may be punished by a fine or a relatively short term of incarceration or both.

The substantive law of crimes defines what acts are prohibited, and criminal procedure governs the actual administration of justice from initial investigation all the way through release from prison as well as parole and aftercare. The guarantees that deal with criminal procedure are defined primarily in the Fourth, Fifth, Sixth, Eighth, and Fourteenth Amendments to the Constitution. These procedural rules define what the state may and may not do in pursuing a criminal case.

We are now ready for a specific definition of crime: *A crime is a legal wrong for which the offender is liable to be prosecuted and, if convicted by a court of competent jurisdiction, liable to be punished by the state.* [18]

---

*The same act which constitutes a tort *may* also be a crime.

A crime is not simply the violation of moral sensibilities (although that may be involved); it violates a specific law, and that law carries with it a specific punishment for the violation. These laws are passed for a number of reasons. For one thing, criminal law seeks to protect the public from violent or dangerous conduct such as assaults, murders, and arson. Criminal laws also seek to protect public health through such devices as pure food and drug laws and other laws which regulate the practice of medicine and pharmacy. Some criminal laws are designed to maintain public order (traffic laws are probably the best example of this). Other criminal laws protect the right of privacy (for example, by making it a crime to unlawfully intercept private communications) or seek to protect public morality (such as laws regulating or prohibiting such things as prostitution, pornography and the consumption of alcohol). In some cases criminal law is enacted simply to advance some kind of public policy, as in the case of backing civil rights legislation with criminal sanctions.

The forbidden act or omission (actus reus) which is the basis of the crime must be spelled out in clear detail. For example, North Carolina General Statute 14-258.3, which makes it a crime for any prisoner to take a hostage, fully defines this crime as one in which,

> Any prisoner
> a. confined in the custody of the Department of Corrections or confined in a local confinement facility
> b. who by threats, coercion, intimidation or physical force
> c. takes, holds, or carries away
> d. any person as hostage or otherwise

is subject to prosecution for violation of this particular law, and if convicted, would be guilty of a felony and could receive a term of imprisonment for up to ten years or a fine (as provided for under a separate section of North Carolina law). In order to convict a person accused of violating this law, it would be necessary for the state to prove beyond a reasonable doubt that each of the four elements set forth above actually took place. Most crimes are composed of such elements, and when the police investigate a crime they are actually trying to determine whether or not each of the elements took place and to obtain evidence to that effect so the prosecution can "prove" the case later. If any one of the elements cannot be established, then the "crime" does not exist (although the elements which are demonstrable may support a conviction for another, related crime).

In some cases it is also necessary to show a criminal intent (Mens Rea).* Criminal intent is a vague concept, and the courts have generally found that it exists along a gradient extending from behavior which was merely negligent to that which was reckless, to that which was done "knowingly" and finally, to conduct that was "intentionally" committed in spite of the knowledge that it was illegal. In the case of *strict liability* crimes there is no need to show intent; proof of the wrongful act is sufficient to earn a conviction. Statutory rape cases are usually strict liability crimes: all the state needs to prove is that the accused had sexual intercourse with a female below the age of consent. What he thought is beside the point; all that matters is what he did. This raises an interesting side issue: the difference between *motive* and *intent*. It is generally of no consequence to the state what a person's reasons were for committing a crime; the state is interested in establishing the fact that the offender intended to commit the crime.

There are, of course, many defenses which a person can offer when accused of a crime. If a defense accords with those which are allowed by law, and if the accused can establish the credibility of his defense, then he may be able to either avoid prosecution or may secure an acquittal. No defendant is required to offer a defense because it is the job of the state to convict him. In fact, all defendants are presumed to be innocent until the state proves otherwise.

The Criminal Justice System

In order to make the laws work, the state has established not only procedures for prosecution and defense, but it has also created an elaborate network of agencies to insure that laws are obeyed. The police, among other things, try to learn exactly what crimes have been committed and who committed them. They use their authority to investigate in order to develop this information. The police, after establishing that a crime has been committed, identifying the offender, and gathering evidence, turn the case over to a prosecutor so that a formal accusation can be made against the offender. The case is heard by a court and if the offender is convicted he is subjected to some kind of lawful punishment. Each aspect of this administration of justice is carefully regulated by procedural law, custom, administrative guidelines, and

---

*From *Actus non facit reum, nisi mens sit rea:* "An act does not make the doer of it guilty unless he intended the act."

precedent. The state is limited in how it may go about this process and hopefully the process will result in "order" that is tempered by "justice." Even at that, there are many ways in which inequities can creep into the administration of justice.

For one thing, criminal justice agencies may be negligent in their duties: police may fail to investigate crimes or may overlook them, depending on the nature of the crime and the status of those who are involved. Some criminal defendants may fare better than others because they can afford better legal counsel. Public policy in a given community can produce an uneven enforcement of the law, favoring some groups over others. Another potential problem is that criminal justice agencies may perform their duties improperly, as when police beat a confession out of a suspect or otherwise improperly and illegally obtain evidence. A prosecutor can be "bought" and refuse to prosecute certain offenders, or courts may disregard procedure in favor of (or against) a defendant. Defense lawyers may literally extort their clients — or fail to provide them with an adequate defense. Citizens themselves can subvert the administration of justice by failing to report crimes, refusing to cooperate with authorities during an investigation, withholding evidence, or by concealing crimes. In short, there are many ways in which the administration of justice can fail. When it does fail, it does not provide the benefits promised by the rule of law, and society moves closer to the grim picture painted by Hobbes.

Another problem is that many people do not understand the administration of justice. They do not understand the distinctions between civil and criminal law. Some think the law can do more than is really allowed and others have absolutely no faith in the law. The law itself has not always been "fair." In fact, court decisions continually change the meaning of law in an effort to keep it abreast of the times; it often seems to lag behind, producing resentment and hostility. There are many ways in which the administration of justice can itself contribute to poor community relations, and this will be discussed in the following chapters.

The Law As A System of Public Control

Criminal law, through the administration of justice process, may be regarded as part of a *public control system*. Criminal laws are intended for the protection and benefit of the public as a whole, even though a given crime may only directly affect the parties involved. For this reason justice is personified as being blindfolded — as seeing neither race nor creed, wealth nor poverty, high nor low status. Although criminal laws may incorporate moral judgments, they are still applied evenly across society as a whole.

The criminal justice system is therefore the mechanism of the public control system. The work of the various criminal justice agencies should be seen as a collective good intended to benefit all citizens, whether they are direct beneficiaries or not. Of course, if these agencies fail in their responsibilities, they reduce the actual worth of the collective good they are supposed to be producing. Their failures can result from many factors, including those discussed in the preceding paragraphs. One reason for studying the issue of community relations is to identify sources of failure within the public control system so that changes can be made which will improve the quality of criminal justice as a collective good.

Private Control

The law is formal and it is administered by agencies of government. However, not all conflict is sufficiently serious that it requires governmental intervention. Actually, it might be helpful to look at social control as extending along a continuum. At the "mild" end, control is simple, personal, and "corrective" in nature. At the opposite end, it is complex, formal, and punitive in nature. At some point along this continuum — as misbehavior becomes relatively serious — the public control system enters the picture (in the form of the criminal justice system) and takes over. But how is an individual controlled up to that point? That is the task of the *private* control system.

The private control system is composed of institutions which are basically intended to shape, nurture, and support the individual. They are *socializing* institutions. Their processes are carried out through personal, face-to-face settings and their relationships with the individual are usually intimate in nature and long-lasting in duration. It might be safe to say that the ultimate goal of the private control system is to produce a "proper" person. A proper person is simply one who is able and willing to function in an acceptable manner according to the normative standards of the group with which he identified and of the community of which he is a part. In American society the private control system is composed of five major elements: the family, schools, religion, the person's work setting, and the individual's social environment.

The Family The family is probably the single most important influence on a person's life. The particular family into which a person is born or in which he is reared is the wellspring from which nearly everything else flows. The first and most basic function of the family is to nurture the infant physically and mentally. This is an integral part of the child's development, and it is likely that much of his or her personality will be shaped through this process. The childrearing process is also the means by which the individual is taught not only basic roles which will guide him through life but it is also the process through which basic values are transmitted from one generation to the next.[19]

The development of the child is an enormously complex process and takes a number of years. It involves not only the development of motor skills and self-awareness, but also a wide range of tasks including sex-role identification, the development of perceptual "sets," and the incorporation of moral precepts. If all goes well, the individual emerges from childhood with a conscience based on the values learned in the home; this conscience is one of the most unique and long-lasting control mechanisms a person can have. It is a powerful regulator of behavior and remains with the individual throughout life. Its importance can be illustrated by imagining a world in which nobody had a conscience!

The conscience is developed as control is imposed on the child and as he accepts and integrates those controls. The controls themselves are based on the use of rewards and punishments. A smile, a frown, a strongly-worded "NO!" or a pat on the head can be powerful instruments for shaping behavior. Of course, what the child is rewarded or punished for is important, for those things will become the basis for his value structure.

Different groups within society have somewhat different child-rearing practices which reflect their unique value orientations. These groups may share certain values and differ on others which may result in considerable diversity within an overall framework of consensus. This is one of the reasons why complex societies are characterized as being pluralistic in their makeup.

Unfortunately, not all children are reared in wholesome environments or by stable, nurturing families; many negative possibilities exist. Some children are unwanted or ignored; others are subjected to physical and emotional abuse, while yet others are chronically neglected. Some children are passed from one caretaker to another and live in a state of chronic emotional deprivation. These conditions also shape the personality, and there is growing evidence which indicates that children raised in hostile or negative environments are more likely to develop a negative self-image and to mirror the hostility which they have faced. Some children are subjected to very little control in the home and fail to develop a healthy respect for either themselves or for others and many of them ultimately develop behavior patterns that are considered anti-social. There is little doubt about the truth of the old adage, "As the twig is bent, so grows the tree."

School   Around the age of five, most children move beyond the narrow world of the family and into the second-most important institution of their lives: school. The schools impose control through both *what* they teach and *how* they do it. Ideally, the schools should reinforce the values imparted by the family and should expand on them. Schools actually do far more than teach subjects to students; they place social and behavioral expectations on children and shape them as socially interactive beings. It is through the medium of the schools that the plurality of our society is (or should be) mediated: children of different races, ethnic, class and status backgrounds are brought together and given common instruction in academic and social skills. In fact, one of the missions of the schools is to prepare young people for responsible citizenship by encouraging students to:

- Show concern for the welfare and dignity of others;
- Support the rights and freedoms of all individuals;
- Help maintain law and order;
- Know the main structure and functions of government;
- Seek community improvement through active, democratic participation;
- Understand the problems of international relations;
- Support rationality in communication, thought, and action on social problems;
- Take responsibility for one's own personal development and obligations; and to
- Help respect their own families.[20]

Schools reward children for conforming and punish them for misbehaving. Good grades and peer approval push the student in the direction of academic and social achievement; bad grades and punitive measures signal the child that his performance is lacking. Children who exhibit serious problems may be referred to school psychologists or counselors, or if the problem is serious enough, they may also be referred to public mental health programs for treatment. All of this is done in an effort to impose social control over the child as he moves towards maturity.

Unfortunately schools can and sometimes do fail to impose this social control. In some instances children who present serious behavior problems may be isolated, ignored, expelled or even promoted. Students in the upper grades (particularly the 8th through 12th) present especially challenging problems because they are nearing physical adulthood and are extremely sensitive to peer pressures. Schools may react to a student's misbehavior by labelling him and isolating him from other students. The miscreant may react to this by accepting the label and acting according to its definition, associating with other problem students. The schools are generally not provided with staff to deal with serious problems and these students soon find themselves becoming outsiders. In fact, it is worth noting that the isolation of students who misbehave is directed as much at conforming students as it is at those who are misbehaving because it shows what will happen to those who don't abide by the rules.

Religion   Religion has played a powerful role in the history of mankind. For one thing, it has provided answers to some difficult questions. It has also provided a framework, a meaning which has allowed people to make sense out of what might otherwise seem a capricious world. Most important for our perspective, religion has been closely related to the whole realm of ethics and morality.[21] By emphasizing morality and ethics, moral laws, as interpreted by clergy, take on the weight of divine commandments and ethical duties become obligations. Thus religions not only explain meaning to their members, they also compel behavior according to the teachings of the religion. Religions also foster a sense of community by providing a common ground for people of similar faith, and they add basic meaning to life by providing rituals for our most significant personal events: births, marriages, and death. For many, religion is a vehicle for travelling through life.

The standards of behavior which most religions expect of their adherents is a direct form of social control. In earlier times the church was able to physically enforce its standards of behavior on people; however, since the time of Henry II, sacred and secular courts have been separate and the church may no longer inflict direct punishment on moral offenders. Since the ethics and morality taught by religion complement that which is taught at home and in the schools, the individual is presented with a relatively consistent set of expectations. If he violates those expectations, he will be punished by these private agencies in a variety of informal and extralegal of ways. These punishments are intended to coerce the person back to correct behavior and to prevent recurrences of the unacceptable behavior.

The Work Setting   After one's formal education is complete, it is normal to enter the labor force. Here the person becomes part of a work setting, and the predominant norms of his particular work setting also act as a control over his behavior. Those who conform are rewarded with privileges, promotions, raises and other benefits. Those who do not often find themselves looking for a new work setting. Few people fully realize the extent to which the work setting imposes control on the individual. Some jobs require specific kinds of clothing; most set the exact hours and place where a person is to work, and some even extend control into the more private aspects of a person's life. Some employers pressure their employees to involve themselves in civic or professional activities within the community and others specify where within the community the individual will actually live.[22] As people adapt to the requirements of their work setting, their lives take on a degree of predictability and stability which they in turn demand of others.[23]

Social Environment A person's social environment is composed of that particular set of associations, residence, work, play, and interpersonal relations which surround him. People have different family backgrounds, levels and quality of education, and occupations, and those whose situations in life are similar tend to cluster together. An individual's social environment is a composite of all of the individual factors noted above — plus many more — and serves as the final major source of private control. Our social environment is our "place." All of us know when we are "out of place" — where we do not belong. One of the interesting things about being "out of place" is that we quickly become confused as to what is expected of us. The usual cues and behavioral signals are different or unfamiliar, and our inability to predict just what will happen next is unsettling. We see this, for example, when we go as a guest into the home of a person whose social standing is quite different from ours or when we visit the ethnic or other enclaves in a city such as Little Italy, Chinatown, or the Bowery.

Each of the components of the private control system work together to influence the behavior of the individual. They collectively teach the individual his way in the world, and they function in a manner calculated to keep the individual within the confines of an orderly and predictable environment. For the most part the private control system shapes the person with an emphasis on *preventing* misbehavior. The sanctions imposed by the private control system are informal and personal. For the most part they center around the acceptance or rejection of the individual.

The private control system can fail in two ways. In the first instance, some or all of the elements of the private control system simply fail to fulfill their responsibilities. This may happen when children are abused or neglected; when they are ignored or rejected by the schools; when they do not come under the influence of a religion; and when they find themselves incompatible with a non-deviant work environment. The second kind of failure occurs when a person comes under the influence of a family or other primary setting which actually teaches or encourages deviant values.

Most people are "controlled" in their day-to-day activities by their moral and ethical values and by their willingness to do what is expected of them. From time to time conflicts occur, most of which can be settled through informal processes. Sometimes conflicts require more formal mediation, and the individuals may use the civil courts. In more serious cases, an individual will behave in such a manner that the private control system either cannot resolve the problem or would be an inappropriate method for doing so. In those cases the criminal justice system may be called upon to invoke formal sanctions against the individual. Were it not for the existence of conflict and the need for control, there would be no need for a criminal justice system — and no concern about how well it relates to the community!

Crime and Disorder: The Economics Of Being Human

The criminal justice system is society's major formal response to problems of crime and disorder. It is the means by which the state exercises its police power to provide for the common good and to assure justice for its citizens. We have already noted that the criminal justice system must work within the framework of substantive law and procedural due process. It must also function in a manner consistent with community sentiment. Part of the difficulty with this is that the criminal justice system must perform its tasks in a continually changing environment in which it must satisfy substantial numbers of people who hold widely varying notions as to just exactly what "law and order" is or ought to be. The problem of crime has been particularly difficult to deal with simply because it means so many things to so many people.

Until approximately 1969 most academic research on crime was done by sociologists.[24] The basic premise they took was that criminals were somehow different from noncriminals, and their major research consisted of looking for the ways in which criminals and noncriminals differed.[25] To be sure, the sociologists/criminologists have added a great deal to our knowledge of crime and criminals. Their theories of crime causation have provided significant insights into the structure and functioning of criminal subcultures and the impact of social culture on crime. However, in 1968 and in the years thereafter a number of articles by economists dealing with crime began to appear, and these works began to provide an important new perspective on crime.[26] These economists argued that criminals are pretty much the same as anyone else: they are rational people who seek to maximize their own self-interest, and their decisions are made on the basis of those self-interests and in the light of limitations in their environment. The basic question, according to this viewpoint, is simply whether or not the individual sees criminal conduct as being in his best interests.

This merely underscores the thesis that all behavior is meaningful, although its meaning may not always be clear to outside observers.* Unfortunately, when we talk about the "meaning" of behavior we run the risk of using definitions that have limited utility. Legal definitions by themselves, for example, tend to be sterile and often strangely out of context because they discount motive. Sociological definitions, on the other hand, tend to be repetitious, and many psychological definitions of crime are simply self-fulfilling. What is needed is a model which allows us to see criminal behavior in context and which also permits us to examine the relationships among criminals, victims, and the criminal justice system. The use of economic theory is helpful in providing us with such a perspective.

Categories of Crime

From an economic viewpoint, criminal offenses may be divided into three categories:

- Crimes against the person
- Crimes against property
- Victimless crimes[27]

The first two are predatory or coercive crimes. Crimes against property, moreover, are nothing more than a transfer of income or assets. Victimless crimes involve the production and consumption of illegal goods. This classification is not inconsistent with crime categories used in law enforcement.

CRIME REPORTING

The FBI publishes its *Uniform Crime Reports* each year in order to "give a nationwide view of crime based on police statistics contributed by state and local law enforcement agencies." The FBI breaks crime into "Part I" and "Part II" crimes, the Part I crimes being the more serious offenses. The Part I crimes include their so-called "Index Crimes" of murder and nonnegligent manslaughter; forcible rape; robbery; aggravated assault; burglary; larceny-theft; motor vehicle theft; and arson. The first four are considered by the FBI to be violent crimes and the last four property crimes.

The crimes reported on by the FBI in the *Uniform Crime Reports* are as follows:

---

*Some psychologists would also argue that the true meaning of a person's behavior might not be clear to the individual himself.

Part I Offenses

Criminal homicide. — a. Murder and nonnegligent manslaughter: the willful (nonnegligent) killing of one human being by another. Deaths caused by negligence, attempts to kill, assaults to kill, suicides, accidental deaths, and justifiable homocides are excluded. Justifiable homicides are limited to: (1) the killing of a felon by a law enforcement officer in the line of duty; and (2) the killing of a felon by a private citizen. b. Manslaughter by negligence: the killing of another person through gross negligence. Excludes traffic fatalities. While manslaughter by negligence is a Part I crime, it is not included in the Crime Index.

Forcible rape. — The carnal knowledge of a female forcibly and against her will. Included are rapes by force and attempts or assaults to rape. Statutory offenses (no force used — victim under age of consent) are excluded.

Robbery. — The taking or attempting to take anything of value from the care, custody, or control of a person or persons by force or threat of force or violence and/or by putting the victim in fear.

Aggravated assault. — An unlawful attack by one person upon another for the purpose of inflicting severe or aggravated bodily injury. This type of assault usually is accompanied by the use of a weapon or by means likely to produce death or great bodily harm. Simple assaults are excluded.

Burglary — breaking or entering. — The unlawful entry of a structure to commit a felony or a theft. Attempted forcible entry is included.

Larcency — theft (except motor vehicle theft). — The unlawful taking, carrying, leading, or riding away of property from the possession or constructive possession of another. Examples are thefts of bicycles, automobile accessories, shoplifting, pocket-picking, or any stealing of property or article which is not taken by force and violence or by fraud. Attempted larcencies are included. Embezzlement, "con" games, forgery, worthless checks, etc., are excluded.

Motor vehicle theft. — The theft or attempted theft of a motor vehicle. A motor vehicle is self-propelled and runs on the surface and not on rails. Specifically excluded from this category are motorboats, construction equipment, airplanes, and farming equipment.

Arson. — Any willful or malicious burning or attempts to burn, with or without intent to defraud, a dwelling house, public building, motor vehicle or aircraft, personal property of another, etc.

46

Part II Offenses

Other assaults (simple). — Assaults or attempted assaults where no weapon was used or which did not result in serious or aggravated injury to the victim.

Forgery and counterfeiting. — Making, altering, uttering, or possessing, with intent to defraud, anything false which is made to appear true. Attempts are included.

Fraud. — Fraudulent conversion and obtaining money or property by false pretenses. Included are larceny by bailee and bad checks except forgeries and counterfeiting.

Embezzlement. — Misappropriation or misapplication of money or property entrusted to one's care, custody, or control.

Stolen property; buying, receiving, possessing. — Buying, receiving, and possessing stolen property, including attempts.

Vandalism. — Willful or malicious destruction, injury, disfigurement, or defacement of any public or private property, real or personal, without consent of the owner or person having custody or control

Weapons; carrying, possessing, etc. — All violations of regulations or statutes controlling the carrying, using, possessing, furnishing, and manufacturing of deadly weapons or silencers. Included are attempts.

Prostitution and commercialized vice. — Sex offenses of a commercialized nature, such as prostitution, keeping a bawdy house, procuring, or transporting women for immoral purposes. Attempts are included.

Sex offenses (except forcible rape, prostitution, and commercialized vice). — Statutory rape and offenses against chastity, common decency, morals, and the like. Attempts are included.

Drug abuse violations. — State and local offenses relating to narcotic drugs, such as unlawful possession, sale, use, growing, and manufacturing of narcotic drugs.

Gambling. — Promoting, permitting, or engaging in illegal gambling.

Offenses against the family and children. — Nonsupport, neglect, desertion, or abuse of family and children.

Driving under the influence. — Driving or operating any vehicle or common carrier while drunk or under the influence of liquor or narcotics.

Liquor laws. — State or local liquor law violations, except "drunkenness" and "driving under the influence". Federal violations are excluded.

Drunkenness. — Drunkenness or intoxication. Excluded is "driving under the influence."

Disorderly conduct. — Breach of the peace.

All other offenses. — All violations of state or local laws and traffic offenses.

Suspicion. — No specific offense; suspect released without formal charges being placed.

Curfew and loitering laws. — Offenses relating to violation of local curfew or loitering ordinances where such laws exist.

Runaway. — Limited to juveniles taken into protective custody under provisions of local statutes.

At the very root of the economic perspective of crime is the concept of "getting and giving" in which a person seeks to get something he wants in return for something which must be given. In the legitimate marketplace there is usually a close relationship between the value of that which is given and that which is received. For example, if you wanted a stereo system worth $1000, that is what you would expect to pay for it in a store. You might be able to get the same stereo from an acquaintance through some kind of barter. In that case, the person giving up the stereo would want something in return worth approximately the value of the stereo. You might swap a used car for the stereo, and if you really did not want the car anymore (or if you saw its continued ownership as a liability), you might feel you had made a "good deal."

However, in looking at criminal transactions we must be careful in order to avoid being seduced by monetary value. Money is, after all, only a medium of exchange. As we will see, there are many others. Returning to our main point, it is fairly obvious that in any given transaction, it is important that the individual get what he wants, in return for which he should give no more than it is worth, and preferably less, if possible. A final, important point is that in the usual business context both buyer and seller have a common means for assigning value (usually monetary worth). In the case of crime, however, this relationship becomes distorted. The *objective* worth of an object or service is subordinated to an idiosyncratic value attached by the criminal. In other words, the value of a stereo is not measured in terms of its fair market value or any other value its owner might place on it, but rather its value may be measured in terms of the risk involved in stealing it or how much the thief wants the stereo.

For some people transactions involve little more than the exchange of things of tangible value, such as money or merchandise. For others there may be intangibles such as reputation, esteem, honor, convenience, or power. For many people a desirable transaction may involve all of these elements, under various circumstances. Different circumstances will determine the value an individual may place on the elements of a transaction. This is why some people are almost never honest, others are honest most of the time, and yet others are almost never dishonest. Not only does crime have a great deal to do with values, it is strongly related to *opportunity* and to factors which correlate with opportunity.

Opportunity Cost   In its most basic sense, opportunity cost is what one must give up in order to get something else. Questions of value can be very important in considering opportunity cost. Someone who places a high value on his own honesty may not be willing to sacrifice self-esteem in favor of getting something by cheating. In that case cheating would not be "economical" to the person, even though he might make a significant financial gain. This underscores the thesis that the worth of an object or act can be measured in many different ways. An action which one person considered rational under the circumstances might be repugnant to a different person under the same circumstances.

In the case of crime, although the "transaction" is illegal, legality may or may not have much of anything to do with the actual situation, at least as it is perceived by the people involved. Gordon points out this difference in perception:

> Only rarely, it appears, can ghetto criminals be regarded as raving, irrational, antisocial lunatics. The 'legitimate' jobs open to many ghetto residents, especially to young black males, typically pay low wages, offer relatively demeaning assignments, and carry the constant risk of layoff. In contrast, many kinds of crime 'available' in the ghetto often bring higher monetary return, offer even higher social status, and — at least in cases like numbers running — sometimes carry relatively low risk of arrest and punishment. [28]

Seen in this light, low income people may give up little or nothing when they go into crime; in fact, they may actually stand to gain. "If all factors were equal, we would predict that people with low opportunity cost (low educational attainment and lack of job experience) would have a greater propensity to engage in crime. Examples would be the young, the poor, and members of minority groups."[29] Available data on crime clearly support this hypothesis — at least in terms of the disproportionate participation of the young, poor, and minorities.

The most prevalent of all crimes are those commited against property:

the various forms of larceny and theft which to economists are nothing more than a transfer of income or assets. A theft devoid of its moral-legal value is the transfer of assets from their rightful holder to the thief. A professional thief may rationalize his crime by claiming that it's the way he makes his living and his "investment" in what he steals is the risk he takes. A good many thefts are committed by "honest" people as well, at least by people who do not see themselves as criminals. However, "honest" people also place a value on their honesty, and this means that they must reconcile their values with their actions. One way of doing this is to manipulate the moral meanings of the illegal act. This allows the individual to violate his principles without having to abandon them.[30] This manipulation may be accomplished through the use of "techniques of neutralization." These techniques involve the creation of justifications for what would otherwise be unacceptable behavior and allows the actor to protect himself from the voice of his own conscience as well as criticism of the larger society. Sykes and Matza discuss five major techniques:

1. *Denial of responsibility* — "I couldn't help it; that's just the way things are done around here."
2. *Denial of injury* — "It doesn't make any difference; they have insurance." "So what? No one got hurt."
3. *Denial of Victim* — "He had it coming." "He should not have been there in the first place."
4. *Condemnation of the condemners* — "Who are they to say it's wrong to smoke grass? They get high on liquor."
5. *Appeal to higher loyalties* — "I didn't do it for myself ! "

The use of techniques of neutralization allows the individual to manipulate moral meanings so he can accept the broad social definitions of right and wrong and still do as he pleases. This kind of manipulation can make an illegitimate transaction "economical" to a person by removing from consideration a moral standard which he may not wish to surrender.

One of the reasons nearly *all* citizens engage in some kind of criminal conduct from time to time is that the "transfer" may be based not on an actual exchange (as in dollars for a stereo), but on the assumption of a low probability risk in return for some gain. That is, the person may "take a chance" on something with the implicit understanding that the probability of getting caught is slim, for if he is caught, the punishment would be tolerable. Traffic violations are a good case in point. Suppose A is following B in a no-passing zone on an isolated country road. A is in a hurry and B is not; B is doing 35 MPH in a 45 MPH zone and there is little traffic. A might reason that if he passed B illegally he might have a head-on collision with another car, or he might get caught by the police. Since the volume of traffic is low and since the odds of a police car being just out of sight are almost infinitesimal, he decides to take the chance. He succeeds in passing B and is pleased: his "gain" (being able to go faster) was purchased at what seemed to be a minimal risk. Nominally honest citizens — at least those who value a public reputation for honesty — can have their public reputation and still steal; however, they must do so in a way that offers them little risk of getting caught and which at the same time preserves their public reputation. There are many ways of doing this, ranging all the way from padding expense accounts and cheating on income taxes to stealing supplies at work and embezzling funds by way of computer manipulation.

Based on an economic perspective, a great deal of criminal behavior can be seen as both relative to the situational context in which it occurs and a function of the values and desires of those involved. Most people elect to commit crimes from time to time. In most cases the crimes are not serious; probably the most "violated" area is traffic law. Exactly why do some people elect to commit crimes — including serious crimes — while others do not? Much of the answer to this question is found in class and power relationships, for those are the variables which probably correlate the closest with opportunity and either the incentives to commit crime or the constraints against such conduct.

Class, Opportunity Cost, and Crime

If the economics of crime is based on "getting and giving," then it is important to know just what kinds of things are received and what must be given for them — and how they are distributed in the first place. The complexity of this set of relationships was alluded to by Gordon when he stated, "The character of crime in America flows almost inevitably from the structure of our social and economic institutions."[32] Gordon says that what a person has is a function of his class and status. A person with high status — those in the upper-class — would presumably have more than those in the lower classes, at least in terms of economic resources.

Not only do the affluent have more than the poor, they also have a stake in maintaining the political and economic institutions which produced and protect their wealth, and for this reason they tend to be politically conservative. They also place high value on their reputations and standing within the community and typically disavow violence as a means for settling conflict (their own lives are closely regulated by negotiations and agreements). They not only espouse the virtues important in their own lives, they also measure the worth of others on the basis of those same virtues. Crimes of violence are inconsistent with their lifestyle, and traditional crimes against property are not only unnecessary but also carry a significant threat to their reputations and community standing. Members of the middle and upper class are, however, by no means exempt from criminal behavior.

The types of crimes committed by middle and upper class people flow logically from their occupations and outlook on life. For example, corporate crime is a very rational response to the expectations of a materialistic society. If the task of the corporation is to augment and protect the capital of its owners, and if those who manage the corporations are rewarded economically and socially for success in doing so, then the goals of getting and protecting capital carry a high value in their own right. The affluent perform these tasks not only on behalf of the corporations which hire them, but they also do it on their own behalf as well — all quite legally. However, if a corporation begins to find it difficult to function successfully in a harshly competitive environment, it may look for ways of "helping things along." A good case in point is the Equity Funding Corporation of America (EFCA) fraud, which was one of the largest single corporate frauds in American business history. [33] This fraud ran from 1964 until its discovery in 1973 and involved a total dollar value of over $2 billion.

The EFCA crime was basically a securities fraud and was pulled off by a group of intelligent and relatively young businessmen whose purpose was "to make EFCA the largest, fastest-growing, most successful financial institution in the world and in the process thereby gain fame and fortune themselves." The fraud was based on a rather complex scheme in which an investor borrowed on mutual fund shares to purchase insurance hoping that the income from appreciation of the mutual fund shares would exceed the interest cost of the loan and would pay for at least part of the premiums of the insurance. The fraud itself was carried out for the most part by inflating the company's reported earnings; personal theft and embezzlement seemed to have played only a minor part in the overall fraud. In other words, intelligent, "respectable" businessmen saw an opportunity to manipulate established business practices in order to enhance the value of the business — and they did so. They certainly did not see themselves in the same league as loan sharks, narcotics importers, or Mafia hit men! They operated within the confines of *conventional* values, making decisions which seemed at the time quite rational and proper.

These kinds of crime are not executed for monetary gain alone; other goals include power (e.g., within the business or financial community), personal prestige, a sense of accomplishment, or even idealistic ends such as keeping people employed and contributing to the local economy. Perhaps in most cases the risk is low, the chance of success high, and the "circumstances" ideal. People who do not understand the power of nonmonetary motives shake their heads and say, "I just don't see why he did it. He seemed to have everything!" They fail to understand the "economics" of the crime by not seeing all that was given in return for what was received.

Of course, this same process operates at the personal as well as the corporate level. Indeed, many dishonest businessmen are basically just extensions of their businesses. It might even be reasonable to ask if it is even possible to separate the people from their businesses. If a corporate executive wants to conduct business with a foreign firm, and if the cost of doing business with them calls for bribes, how long does it take before the businessman sees bribery as just another form of business? Are businessmen who provide hotel accommodations and prostitutes for buyers in town for a convention to be considered pimps — or is that what has to be done in a competitive market? It is easy for many affluent people to rationalize their conduct while at the same time deploring the depravations of "criminals." Techniques of neutralization can soften unethical or illegal behavior in the minds of those who commit it, enabling them to continue their activities with a relatively clear conscience.

The poor, on the other hand, are faced with an entirely different set of circumstances. For one thing, they play virtually no role in "making rules." They have likes and dislikes just as all people do, and they have the same kinds of need for survival and self-esteem; yet they must look for these things in a substantially different environment than that of the middle and upper classes. Again, the situation which confronts them calls for *choices*. To accept conventional social values such as honesty, nonviolence, the Protestant work ethic, and the need to delay gratification implies an exchange. It implies that in subscribing to those values, immediate needs will be tended to and life will be tolerable if not pleasant. The reality of urban slums clearly contradicts this. Where unemployment is more the norm than the exception and where a sense of personal worth is difficult to sustain, the "exchange" seems foolish. That is, the opportunity cost of crime is so low that for many people the choice is virtually made for them. There is so little to be lost and so much to be gained that crime does not seem wrong, it appears necessary. Again, techniques of neutralization play a powerful role. Silberman points this out in his discussion of the social functions of "policy" (numbers) in Harlem:

> ...numbers runners are important community resources, for the numbers is not just a game of chance. Since there are rarely receipts people deal with a numbers runner whom they like and trust — either someone who makes the rounds of the neighborhood each day, imparting information as he collects the bets, or a collector who operates out of a small grocery store, barbershop, beauty parlor, newsstand, pool hall, or bowling alley that serves as a neighborhood hangout. ... When placing a bet in an established numbers station, the bettor has a chance to chat with the proprietor and whoever else may be hanging around. These relationships are solidified everytime someone wins, for it is customary to give the runner a 10 percent tip and, in some neighborhoods, to hold open house so that friends and neighbors can join in the celebrations. This friendly social atmosphere contributes in turn to the important economic and financial functions that numbers fulfill. Betting on the numbers is a form of savings; lower class blacks often refer to their bets as 'investments' ...[34]

Even crimes of violence are at least understandable when viewed in the context in which they take place. We noted earlier that civil law provides a means for correcting private wrongs. Civil processes are also time-consuming, expensive, and require a certain amount of sophistication on the part of those who use them. Many problems, however, do not lend themselves to such solutions. This is especially the case among the poor where disputes are seen as personal matters (not for the courts — *any* kind of courts!) and where solutions are best when they are quick. Thus many a homicide is nothing more than an overly successful aggravated assault, and the assault was an escalation from "killing and cutting" talk. A fist-fight can be a matter of honor among many people, and avoiding a fight in favor of a civil suit is not only inappropriate in some contexts, it is absurd.

Some crimes of violence may represent a complex interplay of social and psychological factors, as in the case of forcible rapes in which the offender may be acting out deeply felt hostility toward women as a means of tension-reduction. For many who commit crimes of violence, the act is not undertaken for its own sake, but rather to advance some other end or to solve what the offender perceives as a problem.[35] Even when attention is shifted to professional criminals, we find that they are people who make choices which appear to be highly rational. In talking about burglars, car thieves, loan sharks, hit men, fences and other "professionals" in crime, Plate has observed that most of them:

- prefer anonymity;
- may well be on speaking terms with the local police;
- are not necessarily members of organized crime;
- in all likelihood are not drug addicts;
- tend to take arrests and even prison in stride;
- do not generally leave fingerprints;
- will, whenever possible, run through a crime before actually committing it;
- may be as familiar with the fine points of the law as the police who arrest them;
- may display surprising prudence in the dispersement of income; and
- may well be family men.[36]

People are, of course, far too complex to be reduced to any single formula — economic or any other kind. However, by looking at criminal conduct as economic transactions we can see a great deal of the "logic" behind much of it. It also brings into stark relief much of what the sociologists and psychologists tell us about poverty, emotional deprivation, differential association, alienation, anomie, and collective behavior. It makes it easier to understand why values cherished by some elements of society seem to have limited meanings in other settings. Finally, it makes it possible to understand why the kinds of crimes committed by the poor are incomprehensible to the affluent — and vice versa.

As long as criminal behavior is personal and meaningful to the person who commits it, *crime* is not seen as a problem; however, when crimes are committed by *others* for reasons that are not clear to those who hear of it, then the crime *per se* is seen as the problem — a perspective that will be made much more clear in the next chapter.

Summary

The diversity of human associations inevitably leads to conflict, and any orderly society must develop mechanisms for preventing or resolving conflict. The formal means for dealing with conflict is through law, which sets forth the rights and duties of all citizens and prescribes the means by which the laws themselves are to be administered. One of the basic functions of law is to establish order, and another is to secure justice. Although these concepts are mutually reinforcing, they also contain some inherent contradictions. One problem is that "justice" is itself very difficult to define.

Many of our ideas of justice arise from informal sources of law —

tradition, religion, and sentiment. The formal sources of law, however, stem from the legislative and judicial functions of government and even those institutions are not completely free of external influence as interest groups and even the socialization process of legislators and judges can influence the kinds of decisions those groups make.

The law itself may be divided into criminal law and civil law. Criminal law concerns itself with the positive rights and duties of all citizens and enforces breaches of those obligations by invoking the criminal justice process. Civil law, on the other hand, deals with the realm of private wrongs and provides a legal forum in which the contesting parties may have their case heard. Civil wrongs generally fall under one of two headings: breaches of contract and torts. Although all citizens have the right to use the civil courts, many cannot do so because of the expense of legal counsel. The criminal justice system (the police, the courts, and corrections) administers the criminal law, and may be regarded as the *public control system*. Obviously, it concerns itself with the more serious cases of conflict.

Along with the public control system there is an informal *private control system* composed of nurturing and socializing agencies: the family, religion, the work setting and the individual's primary social associations. The private control system has the task of nurturing the individual and instilling in him basic values. Ideally, each of the components of the private control system are mutually supportive and collectively serve to prevent the kinds of conflicts which must be handled by the public control system.

Law itself is rather sterile, however, because it does not give much consideration to *why* people commit the acts which have been labelled as crimes. To better understand that, it is important to look at the economic functions of crime. Viewed in this perspective, crime is seen as rational behavior in which the individual engages in certain transactions within his environment. That is, criminal behavior is behavior which has purpose and meaning to the person who commits it, even though it may seem senseless or inappropriate to an outside observer. In some cases crime may be accepted as an illegal necessity, but more often it is rationalized or justified, thus allowing the offender to see himself as a noncriminal while enjoying the benefits of his crime.

A great deal of criminal activity is related to the socioeconomic status of the offender, as class and status play a major role in determining opportunity cost. Crime itself is often a highly complex combination of legal, social, psychological and economic variables closely related to the individual's perception of himself and his needs. This is one reason that the crimes of the poor make so little sense to the affluent, and vice versa.

Discussion Questions

1. Are the goals of order and justice actually conflicting expectations of the law?

2. If sentiment is an informal source of law, can law be objective in a diverse community?

3. Does the police power of the state authorize or justify unpopular laws: Can you give any examples of such laws?

4. How do special interest groups influence legislation to the detriment of the "public interest"?

5. What kinds of acts may be both torts and crimes?

6. In what major ways does civil law differ from criminal law?

7. How can one's social class influence the ability of an individual to secure justice through civil courts?

8. Can an act be a crime if the law does not provide a punishment?

9. Why is the private control system essentially a crime prevention system?

10. Do you think the family of today is as important in the shaping of the individual as the text implies?

11. Does religion really have a role in contemporary society?

12. How can a person's work environment control his behavior?

13. Can justice ever be completely blind (objective)?

14. What is the relationship between the private control system and the public control system?

15. It has been said that a given community gets the kind of justice it deserves. What does this mean and is it true?

16. How do nontangibles play a role in the economics of crime?

17. How would a community go about altering the "opportunity cost" of crime in low income areas?

18. Why do you think low income people frequently see business as having the objective of exploiting the poor?

19. Why can crime almost never be viewed objectively?

20. If the criminal justice system provides for an administration of *criminal* justice, should we support the development of a *civil* justice system which assures all people, regardless of income or status, access to civil remedies?

Glossary

ACTUS REUS   The "forbidden act" which constitutes the basis for a criminal prosecution.

BREACH OF CONTRACT   The wrongful failure to fulfill a promise undertaken at the time the contract was entered into.

CIVIL LAW   That body of law which deals with the regulation of private affairs and which provides remedies in the case of disputes between private parties.

CRIME   A legal wrong against the state, punishable in its name.

CRIMINAL JUSTICE SYSTEM   The aggregate of state agencies which have responsibility for the administration of criminal justice; broadly speaking, it is composed of the police, courts, and corrections (see also public control system).

DEFENDANT   A person against whom an action is brought.

FELONY   A serious crime — one which may be punished by death or a term of imprisonment, usually for a year or more.

INTENT (CRIMINAL)   The "mental state" necessary for the commission of a crime (see also Mens Rea).

LEGAL REMEDY   The legal means to declare or enforce a right or to redress a wrong.

LEGISLATION   The act of establishing statutes; the making of law by a public body who are vested with the authority to make laws.

MALUM PROHIBITUM Acts which are prohibited by law but which are not necessarily wrong in and of themselves.

MALUM IN SE   Acts which are wrong in themselves, whether or not they are prohibited by laws.

MENS REA   Criminal intent; guilty intent; the intention to commit an act.

MISDEMEANOR   A crime less serious than a felony, usually punishable by a fine or a period of imprisonment for less than a year or both.

MOTIVE   The reason why a person commits an act, as distinguished from his *intention* to commit the act.

PLAINTIFF   A person who initiates a lawsuit. The "prosecutor" in civil cases.

POLICE POWER   The authority of legislative bodies to enact laws restraining private rights in the interest of public health, safety, welfare and order.

PRIVATE CONTROL SYSTEM   The network of private, intimate groups which nurture the individual, shape his values, and control his social behavior; broadly, the family, school, religion, work and social setting of the individual. Its primary role in relation to crime is *preventive*.

PROCEDURAL LAW   That body of civil and criminal law which regulates the means and manner by which substantive law is administered and enforced.

PUBLIC CONTROL SYSTEM   Formal agencies of government which enforce standards of behavior required by legislation through the enforcement of the criminal laws.

SUBSTANTIVE LAW   The law of positive rights and duties.

TORT   Any one of various legally recognized private injuries or wrongs which do not arise as the result of a breach of contract.

Notes

[1] Thomas Hobbes, *Leviathan*, I, 13.

[2] Edgar Bodenheimer, *Jurisprudence: The Philosophy and Method of the Law* (Cambridge, Massachusetts: Harvard University Press, 1962), p. 166.

[3] Bodenheimer, *Jurisprudence*. p. 177.

[4] Bodenheimer, *Jurisprudence*, pp. 178-179.

[5] Bodenheimer, *Jurisprudence*, p. 207.

[6] Exodus: 20; Leviticus: 26.

[7] See for example William F. Walsh, *Outlines of the History of English and American Law* (New York: New York University Press, 1926).

[8] See for example *United States Constitution*, Article VI.

[9] William J. Chambliss and Robert B. Seidman, *Law, Order, and Power* (Reading, Massachusetts: Addison-Wesley Publishing Co., 1971), p. 59.

[10] Chambliss and Seidman, *Law, Order, and Power*, p. 73.

[11] Chambliss and Seidman, *Law, Order, and Power*, p. 73.

[12] Bodenheimer, *Jurisprudence*, p. 286.

[13] Chambliss and Seidman, *Law, Order, and Power*, p. 90.

[14] Harold J. Grilliot, *Introduction to Law and the Legal System* (Boston: Houghton Mifflin Co., 1979), p. 13.

[15] Grilliot, *Introduction to Law and the Legal System*, p. 14.

[16] Grilliot, *Introduction to Law and the Legal System*, p. 36.

[17] See for example *United States Constitution*, Article III, Section III.

[18] Thomas J. Gardner and Victor Manian, *Criminal Law: Principles, Cases and Readings* (St. Paul: West Publishing Co., 1980), p. 7.

[19] See for example Muriel Jones and Dorothy Jongeward, *Born to Win: Transactional Analysis with Gestalt Experiments* (Reading, Massachusetts: Addison-Wesley Publishing Co., 1971), p. 65.

[20] Ronald A. Gerlach and Lynne W. Ramprecht, *Teaching About the Law* (Cincinnati: Anderson Publishing Co., 1971), p. 65.

[21] See for example Kenneth E. Boulding, *Beyond Economics: Essays on Society, Religion, and Ethics* (Ann Arbor: University of Michigan Press, 1968).

[22] William H. Whyte, Jr., *Organization Man* (New York: Simon and Schuster, 1956).

[23] Other interesting perspectives on work and its influence on behavior may be found in the following sources: James O'Toole, ed., *Work and the Quality of Life: Resource Papers for Work in America* (Boston: M.I.T. Press, 1974); Louis G. Shaw, *The Bonds of Work: Work in Mind, Time and Tradition* (San Francisco: Jossey-Bass, 1968); Studs Terkel, *Working* (New York: Avon Books, 1975).

[24] Howard Abadinsky, *Social Service in Criminal Justice* (Englewood Cliffs, New Jersey: Prentice-Hall, Inc., 1979), pp. 1-35.

[25] Ralph Andreano and John Siegfried, eds., *The Economics of Crime* (New York: John Wiley and Sons, 1980), p. 13.

[26] See for example Gary S. Becker, "Crime and Punishment: An Economic Approach," *Journal of Political Economy* (March 1968): 169-217; Gordon Tullock, "An Economic Approach to Crime," *Social Science Quarterly* (June 1969): 59-71; Gary S. Becker and William M. Landes, eds., *Essays in the Economics of Crime and Punishment* (New York: National Bureau of Economics Research, 1974); Lee R. McPheters and William B. Stronge, eds., *The Economics of Crime and Law Enforcement* (Springfield, Illinois: Charles C. Thomas, Publishers, 1976); Simon Rottenberg, ed., *The Economics of Crime and Punishment* (Washington, D.C.: American Enterprise Institute, 1973); and Isaac Ehrlich, "Participation in Illegitimate Activities: A Theoretical and Empirical Investigation," *Journal of Political Economy* (May 1973): 521-565.

[27] Morgan O. Reynolds, "The Economics of Criminal Activity," in *The Economics of Crime*, edited by Ralph Andreano and John J. Siegfried (New York: John Wiley and Sons, 1980), pp. 27-69.

[28] David M. Gordon, "Capitalism, Class, and Crime in America," in *The Economics of Crime*, edited by Andreano and Siegfried, p. 103.

[29] Reynolds, "The Economics of Criminal Activity," p. 35.

[30] Gresham M. Sykes, *Criminology* (New York: Harcourt, Brace, Jovanovich, Inc., 1978), p. 308.

[31] See especially Gresham M. Sykes and David Matza, "Techniques of Neutralization: A Theory of Delinquency," *American Sociological Review* (December 1957): 664-670.

[32] Gordon, "Capitalism, Class, and Crime in America," p. 93.

[33] Donn B. Parker, *Crime by Computer* (New York: Charles Scribner's Sons, 1976), pp. 118-174.

[34] Charles E. Silberman, *Criminal Violence, Criminal Justice* (New York: Vintage Books, 1978), p. 136.

[35] For a valuable perspective on the relationship between psychiatry and crime see Seymour L. Halleck, *Psychiatry and the Dilemmas of Crime* (Berkeley, California: University of California Press, 1967).

[36] Thomas Plate, *Crime Pays!* (New York: Simon and Schuster, 1975), pp. 17-21.

CRIMINAL JUSTICE AND THE COMMUNITY: THE INSTITUTION

3

The criminal justice system — the public control system — not only functions within its unique community context, it must do so in cooperation with the other public and private social institutions of the community. Moreover, the criminal justice system will invariably reflect the values of the community of which it is a part. This is one reason why "criminal justice" can vary so widely from one place to another. Some communities obviously expect more of their criminal justice system than do others. The impact of other social institutions, such as education and religion, also varies widely from place to place. Finally, the extent to which behavior is controlled by the *private* control system may differ greatly in different communities.

Communities differ because of variables such as size of the community, its socio-economic makeup, its economic base, and a whole host of similar considerations. Another reason is the distribution of power within the community: who runs what, and what their social objectives are. For these reasons it should be clear that there is no single standard of what constitutes "good" criminal justice. What is "good" is relative to what the community expects, and different communities have different expectations.

Regardless of what the community expects, there is a definite relationship between the respective roles of the private and public control systems. In general, the public control system takes up where the private control system leaves off; however, there is some degree of overlap between the two as demonstrated in figure 3-1.

This area of overlap is the *zone of potential conflict*. Conflict arises when both systems feel they have "primary jurisdiction" in a case and resent the interference of the other. We might expect that in small,

Figure 3-1

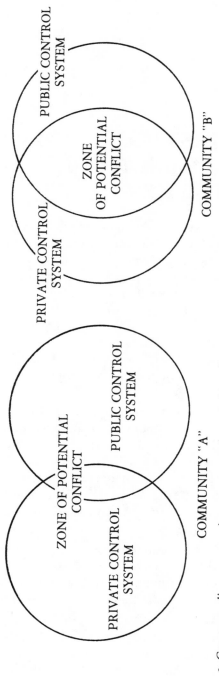

COMMUNITY "A"

- Greater reliance on private means of control/conflict resolution.
- Closer kinship/occupational/religious ties.
- Criminal justice system directed mostly against "outsiders," deviants, and those who commit clearly serious crimes.
- Police tend to be watchman or service oriented.
- Community tends to have a greater degree of consensus on accepted values.
- Community is typically small, rural, and relatively homogeneous.

COMMUNITY "B"

- Less reliance on private means of control/conflict resolution.
- Weak kinship/occupational/religious ties.
- Criminal justice system activities tend to be broadly although differentially spread throughout the community.
- Police tend to be legalistically oriented.
- Community has a multiplicity of value orientations.
- Community is typically large, urban, and heterogeneous.

homogeneous, closely-knit communities the zone of potential conflict would be relatively small. In that kind of community the public control system would be used primarily to deal with outsiders (those who are not likely to be controlled by the private system because of a lack of community ties, community members who violate the consensus of the community, or community members who commit such serious offenses that they cannot be reasonably dealt with by the private control system. In a homogeneous community the public control system is used for the most part to deal with *exceptional* problems. Most routine deviance is handled informally.

In larger, more urbanized communities the picture is apt to be quite different. For one thing, there is likely to be a much larger degree of overlap between the two systems. This is because the larger cities are more pluralistic, the individual is more anonymous, and the ties of kinship, occupation, and religion are looser and less personal. Although the private control system still functions in such a setting, it does so with less efficiency and with greater reservation. For this reason the public control system can and does penetrate the lives of citizens to a greater extent. The police are called upon to deal with many routine conflicts and citizens are more willing to tolerate such interventions. Because of this increased penetration, there is an increased likelihood of conflict. For example, it is not at all uncommon in an urban area for people to call the police on their neighbors because of loud music or some other disturbance. It is also common for the person reported to resent police intrusion into his affairs.

In larger, more anonymous communities the criminal justice system routinely deals with these kinds of minor conflicts and over time develops a formal approach to them. This is reflected in the "legalistic" style commonly associated with big-city police departments in which police services are structured around a legalistic, professional orientation (as opposed to a ministerial, watchman style). This style is, of course, more impersonal and bureaucratic and reflects the separation of the police from the immediate context in which they work. That is, they are agents of government rather than community participants.

The legalistic style of policing is also in part a consequence of the fact that urban police departments tend to be large agencies.* Size is important because small organizations do not usually develop the complex communications and coordination problems that are characteristic of large organizations.[1] Police departments in the larger urban areas accordingly come to embody many of the classic

---

*A good (although informal) definition of "large" is where the highest-ranking members of the organization personally know fewer than half of all the other members of the organization.

characteristics of any bureaucracy: the rigorous use of rules and administrative regulations; careful definition of individual duties and responsibilities; a hierarchical organization of authority; and extensive use of written documentation in the management of the agency.[2]

A major consequence of this process of "bureaucratization" of the police, as well as that of other criminal justice agencies, is that they begin to devote more and more of their resources to maintaining themselves *as an organization*. This means that correspondingly less attention is given to the reason why the organization exists in the first place. This is the classic problem of *goal displacement*. As this process continues, the organization becomes increasingly more impersonal and formal and becomes more of an *institution* and less of an *instrument*. The ultimate consequence of this process, should it be allowed to run its full course, is that the organization eventually insists that it be served by the public, rather than vice-versa. Although criminal justice agencies seldom reach this point, many of the larger agencies *do* become distant from or even hostile toward their clientele, setting into motion a reciprocal relationship which produces disenchantment on the part of citizens and public officials alike, each blaming the other for the problems they perceive.

In many cities, the criminal justice system is highly bureaucratic and is formal in its approach to the public. It often deals with people in matters of conflict which, viewed objectively, do not seem very serious or which perhaps should be dealt with by the *private* control system. The irony of this situation is that although the criminal justice system may be invoked by citizen complaints, it often cannot provide the services which the complainants *really* need. The actual problems behind many complaints are economic, social, psychological or even physical; these problems may manifest themselves in the form of behaviors which are illegal, thus bringing the criminal justice system into the picture. This usually results in treatment of the symptom rather than the problem, an approach which seems destined to fail.

Form Versus Substance

Oddly enough, although all elements of the criminal justice system *need* public support, most neither actively seek it nor even really want it. The courts answer to *concepts of law*, not to the people, and corrections is, for the most part, isolated and self-contained. Until recently, the police likewise answered to no one and considered their work to be "police business" — a domain into which "outsiders" were neither wanted nor welcome. Although this is still the case in many departments, the police have undergone considerable (even revolutionary) change within the past two decades. As public attention has become focused on the police and their methods, objectives, and failures, they have likewise taken an introspective look at themselves. In addition, they have experienced a massive influx of well educated, middle-class recruits and have become very concerned about their image. Many departments have become involved in police-community relations programs of various kinds. Some of these programs have merely been cosmetic whereas others represent a very genuine outreach on the part of the police. It is now becoming clear that the issue of police-community relations is often an issue of *form vs substance*. Thus, it is important at this point to distinguish between programs which emphasize *public* relations and those which involve *community* relations. This extremely important difference is both subtle and distinct.

Public Relations   The concept of public relations first emerged in the world of business and industry. Until the twentieth century, business was largely unconcerned with how the public felt. This sentiment was aptly expressed by William Vanderbilt, head of the New York Central Railroad, when he said, "The public be damned!"[3] Politicians, on the other hand, tended to be exquisitely well-tuned to public sentiment. During the first half of the present century we have seen a reversal of this picture. The arrogance of big business was attacked by journalists who took great pleasure in exposing the wide-ranging dishonesty and corruption in business practices which had often seriously harmed the consuming public; at the same time, government and politics also underwent significant change. The combined pressures of political reform movements and the economic changes wrought by the First World War and the Depression resulted in much more sophisticated political structures and a large, increasingly impersonal governmental bureaucracy.

Private business sensed a need to improve its image with the consuming public. It needed to do this not only to counter the effects of scandals and other exposures, but also as a means of attracting consumers in an increasingly competitive economic marketplace. Government, on the other hand, did *not* concern itself with a need for a better image; after all, government was *government*, not a business which had to compete for clients! Business quickly found the vehicle of *public relations* and seized upon it as a means for managing public opinion. Public relations may be considered one of the major by-products of the era of electronic communications because the extensive use of radio and television could reach into places where print media could not.

Exactly what is *public relations*? According to Bernays, it is "the attempt, by information, persuasion, and adjustment to engineer public support for an activity, cause, movement, or institution."[4] In other words, it is an effort to shape public opinion in some desired direction. *Public opinion* is itself defined as "an aggregate of individual views, attitudes, or beliefs shared by a significant portion of the community."[5] This definition implicitly recognizes the fact that the views, attitudes, and beliefs of *some* portion of the community may *not necessarily* be important because that particular segment of the community is not "significant." Indeed, large segments of our population have traditionally been considered to be insignificant. Minorities, the elderly, females, the poor, youth and others have comprised the "insignificant" proportion of the American community. The thing which they lacked — which made them insignificant — was *power*. These members of the community have traditionally had little or no real power and have accordingly been ignored at best and actively mistreated at worst.

In recent years, however, these groups *have* begun to obtain power. The civil rights movement and changing social values have given power to groups which traditionally had none. These groups have become "significant" parts of the total community and their opinions have likewise become important. Both private and public sector concerns have begun to direct their attention toward these groups and to court their opinion. The problem, however, is that public opinion is based on collectively held attitudes, and many attitudes are formed early in life and often prove resistant to change. An individual's attitudes contain within them a disposition to act in certain ways and over time people become accustomed to acting in those characteristic ways. Thus, behavior is based at least in part on attitudes.[6] A person's attitudes are grounded in *beliefs*, and beliefs are an intrinsic part of the individual's value system. Value systems may vary from group to group (hence the significance of a pluralistic society), and attitudes/values/beliefs provide a ready-made set of cues for interpreting and evaluating new data. In short, they are psychological labor-saving devices which enable the individual to cope with his environment.

Public relations efforts encounter some formidable obstacles when they challenge established values. Basically, two circumstances tend to generate public relations efforts. The first is simply the desire on the part of an organization to improve its image. In the second set of circumstances, public relations may be used to educate the public (or some segment of it) which holds either incorrect or inadequate beliefs concerning the agency. In some cases, the agency may have changed and may wish to inform the public of that fact; in other cases, there may be no change at all, but the agency may wish to cultivate a more positive public image.

Community Relations   Community relations, on the other hand, is not so much a matter of informing or educating the public as it is a set of techniques for working *interactively* with the public. It recognizes the fact that a dynamic relationship exists, which calls for the continuous *management of change*. Walter Lippman recognized this over fifty years ago when he pointed out that in an absolutely static society there would be no problems. Problems, he said, come with change, and although most things do change over time, they do so in different ways and at different rates. Lippman stated that "the disharmonies of uneven evolution are the problems of mankind," and that "a change which constitutes a problem is an altered relationship between two dependent variables."[7] These altered relationships can produce conflict. The process of community relations should be an effort to manage change so that both the community and the agencies which serve it continue to be effective and mutually supportive while conflicts and tensions are resolved.

The difference between *public relations* and *community relations* is largely one of *form* vs *substance*. In public relations *image* is of primary importance, whereas in community relations *conflict resolution* and *mutual growth* are of primary importance. This is not to imply that the former is bad and the latter good; actually, both are important. A good public image must ultimately be based on an agency meeting the purpose for which it was created *and* in doing so, it must be able to change with the times and remain a valid, reliable social instrument. The enormous social change in the United States during the past several decades has called for more flexibility than many criminal justice agencies have possessed, and considerable conflict has resulted. There have also been tremendous changes *within* criminal justice agencies during this period, and these internal changes have wrought considerable internal organizational conflict.

The Impact of Communications

The most fundamental *process* of community relations is *communication*. In addition, communication is also a desirable objective in its own right. Just what is "communication" and why is it so important? Basically, communication is the means by which people and groups interact with one another; it is a device for sharing meaning, reaching consensus, obtaining information, and for facilitating relationships of all kinds. It is accomplished through the use of shared

71

symbols, including words, gestures, and even styles of clothing and behavior. People communicate with one another *directly* in their face-to-face interactions and *indirectly* through various media forms, including books, movies and posters.

Quite obviously, we communicate most effectively with those who share our symbols and who also interpret them the same way we do. We see this when we encounter strangers. If contact with a stranger is going to be sustained, we seek to incorporate the person into our lives by looking for commonalities. Thus, if it turns out that the stranger is about the same age, went to the same college, has a similar interest in sports and politics, then we find him "easy" to communicate with; if his attitudes, values and beliefs are consistent with our own, then communication becomes much easier. On the other hand, when we encounter individuals or groups who are substantially different from us, our communications tend to be more formal and cautious (according to the circumstances under which contact is made). If the differences are great enough, we may even seek to avoid establishing or continuing communication.

Communicating is far more than just using shared symbols: it is a process whereby information is transmitted, opinions are formed, and beliefs are either confirmed or confronted. Through the process of communication, people *learn* things and react to their social environment. If an individual is given erroneous information, the responses he makes based on that information are likely to be incorrect. If a person misinterprets what he is told, the same result usually occurs. If there is *no* communication, then information must be obtained from other sources or opinions must be made and decisions formed on the basis of missing data. The possibility for error in such cases should be apparent. Individuals or groups who are isolated are likely to both give and receive information inefficiently or inadequately, increasing the likelihood of error. This can produce a variety of problems.

It has already been pointed out that ours is a very pluralistic society. Americans differ on the basis of many variables: geography, ethnicity, age, race, education, occupation, class, status, and power — to name but a few. Indeed, this is the basis for the motto on our currency — E PLURIBUS UNUM (From Many, One). We are a single nation made up of many different parts. Although this pluralism has undoubtedly contributed to our national strength, it has also produced an enormous array of problems. Communication among these diverse groups has not always been either open or effective.

Until recently, government ignored the consequences of diversity and sometimes even exploited these differences. For example, entry into the Foreign Service has traditionally been the prerogative of the well-educated scions of upper class families; executive positions in government have been available to well-connected white, Anglo-Saxon, male Protestants, and the career officer corps of the military and naval establishments was largely limited in peacetime to the "right" people, via entrance to the service academies and other commissioning sources. State and local government has been no exception, and the services provided by government have likewise been unevenly distributed.

Criminal justice occupations have followed a similar pattern. Policing has been a working-class occupation and in some metropolitan areas has been heavily influenced by ethnic politics (e.g., the Irish in New York and Boston). For generations in many cities, entry into the police called for at least the tacit approval of politicians, meaning the would-be applicants had to have "contacts" in order to get and keep their jobs. Although this has changed dramatically in the last several decades, police departments are now faced with its lingering consequences: no significant numbers of Blacks or other minorities in command or executive positions. Judges, lawyers, and prosecutors likewise represent a thin slice of American culture. They are usually graduates of law schools and many come from upper-middle class backgrounds. As elected or appointed officials, they are part of the dominant political power structure and certainly ought to be sensitive to its moods. Those who work in corrections are also usually working-class people, except for those at the highest levels, who have often been political appointees. The main point is that criminal justice occupations are *not* filled with people who represent our society as a whole; these occupations are themselves a part of the great filtering process which has traditionally guided and structured society, and which has perpetuated numerous inequalities.

Accordingly, each of these occupational groups had its own frame of reference based on the values, beliefs, and attitudes of the majority of its group members. The *clientele* — those who receive the services of the criminal justice system — have likewise been varied and have generally been treated according to their differences, with those having the least power getting the shabbiest treatment. Each group, both inside and outside the criminal justice system, has for the most part been concerned only with itself. Police officers, for example, don't concern themselves with the world of lawyers and judges or that of prosecutors, correctional officers, or social workers — and vice-versa. Traditionally, the criminal justice system as a whole has also ignored *groups* as such.

Although adjustments are made in individual cases, the system simply has not concerned itself one way or another with the broader social context of Blacks, Hispanics, the poor, the rich, or any other group. In other words, criminal justice has been largely interested in *ad hoc* events and has dealt with issues and people pretty much on a case-by-case basis, in accordance with the status of the individual.

It is now becoming clear that the traditional approach has resulted in many problems, not the least of which is that it has fostered inadequate communications among and between groups. This has forced the participants to deal with one another on the basis of inadequate or inaccurate information, and the results have been costly — riots, lives lost, communities disrupted, and opportunities for social growth thwarted. It has also resulted in a denial of justice, a diminution in the quality of life, and a hardening of positions. The inequalities within our society have always been there, and it is not unreasonable to assume they would be reflected in our social institutions (including the criminal justice system). The massive social upheaval of recent decades has made these inequalities much more visible and has drawn attention to connections and relationships that had previously been overlooked. It has become clear, for example, that the criminal justice system — in all of its components — is faced with a very urgent and serious need to *communicate* with the many elements which comprise our society. It is equally clear that many elements of society have an imperfect and inaccurate view of the criminal justice system as well as the role of the individual citizen in securing a fair and just society. At least within police departments, this need became clear and a substantial community relations movement evolved in the aftermath of the disturbances of the 1960's and early 1970's. This movement, however, has not been without its difficulties.

Police-Community Relations   As Lippman has noted, the prevailing system of rights and duties at any time is at bottom a slightly antiquated formulation of the balance of power among the active interests in the community.[8] Within the last two decades the balance of power has shifted, and the criminal justice system has been caught off guard. The brunt of this shift has fallen on the police, and for that reason the police have made the greatest adaptation of any of the elements of the criminal justice system.

When it became clear that the relationship between the police and the public was not as good as it should be, many departments began to look for ways to improve that relationship. Intensive public criticism of police procedures along with increasingly strident demands by civil rights groups for more community-oriented policing practices set the stage. This was part of a sequence of events which also saw the creation by President Lyndon B. Johnson of the President's Commission on Law Enforcement and Administration of Justice, which conducted a detailed inquiry into the relationship between "crime and a free society," with emphasis on the workings of the criminal justice system.

The Commission issued a series of reports which ultimately led to the Omnibus Crime Control and Safe Streets Act of 1968, which in turn created the Law Enforcement Assistance Administration (LEAA). The LEAA provided massive funding to criminal justice agencies in an effort to upgrade them and to improve the scope and quality of their services. One area in which they placed a major emphasis was on police-community relations. Thus, not only was a need articulated, but funding was also made available for the development of new programs.

Within a relatively short period of time, police departments throughout the nation were initiating police-community relations programs. The type and quality of these programs have varied widely, and Lee P. Brown has created a typology of police departments based on their respective community relations orientation.[9] Those departments which are *externally oriented* tend to use specialists who work out of a police-community relations unit which develops specific programs directed toward the community as a whole or at specific segments of the community. The programs which these specialists operate are typically external to the routine day-to-day operations of the department and include, but are not limited to, the following types of programs:

> **Officer Friendly** These programs generally use older, non-threatening police officers who set up programs for children, including bicycle inspections, school lectures, and the distribution of comic books, toy badges, and pro-police literature. Although sincere and well-meaning, many of these officers present a substantially different image of the police from what a juvenile is likely to encounter on the street — an image which is likely to burst the first time a youth encounters an officer who is not (and does not want to be) "officer friendly."

> **Store Fronts** These are facilities leased by the police department, usually in high-crime areas. The store front may be staffed by one or more officers who are there to answer questions, listen to complaints, and perhaps to make referrals to other agencies. The store fronts often contain literature on narcotics as well as police recruiting information. In some cities the officers who work in the store fronts have been

instructed not to take enforcement action in the event an offense takes place in their presence, but rather to "call the police."

Crime Specific Programs. Many departments offer special programs designed to improve community relations and at the same time to prevent crime. Such efforts include anti-rape seminars; loss-prevention programs; identification programs (for marking personal property); bicycle safety courses, and so on.

Police Advisory Councils. In this effort, the police department creates advisory councils in various parts of town and has officers meet with council members at regular intervals. These have been especially popular with many police departments in recent years.

Many of these programs have been imaginative, resourceful and helpful; some have not. The problem with many of them is that they have been the domain of *specialists*, leaving the bulk of the police department to go about its business as usual. Second, they have a tendency to attract people who are already favorably disposed toward the police and thus have little impact on the disgruntled. Third, they tend to dry up when federal funding ends. Finally — and perhaps worst of all — "When the police make a half-hearted attempt at community relations, they not only do not fool anybody, but they make survival-oriented people (those who must constantly struggle simply to survive) even less likely to trust them in the future. The officers, too, sense the phoniness of such programs. Many become cynical and defensive."[10]

A second type of approach in Brown's typology is the *youth oriented* department. In this type of department the major emphasis is placed on directing efforts toward young people. Typically, it involves a community relations unit which spends most of its time working with juveniles in such enterprises as police athletic leagues, sporting events and summer recreation projects. Although these programs may be popular among their participants, their long-term worth is not clear. In fact, sometimes their short-term consequences may not be what the police department had in mind: in one Southern community, city-sponsored activities have even led to trouble. In one incident the police-community relations unit showed a movie for young people — who refused to go home afterwards. The "regular police" had to be called to disperse the crowd.[11] Of course, the major problem with youth-oriented programs is that they may not reach the juveniles who are most likely to be involved in crime or disruptive activities; that is, their target population may be too general to produce any really valuable long-term outcomes.

Third, according to Brown, a department may be *internally oriented*. "Such departments operate on the premise that every officer is a police-community relations officer and attempt to involve all members of the department in promoting good community relations."[12] This approach should not leave the initiative to the individual officer, however. To be effective, the department should actively support its philosophy by providing training, encouraging education, and establishing an operational/administrative environment which helps to create both the attitudes and skills needed by the individual officers. These kinds of departments have shown subtle but dramatic results. For example, the use of hostage negotiation instead of guns and gas grenades; low-key, non-confrontive tactics dealing with dissidents; and careful recruitment of new officers have gone a long way towards shaping these kinds of police departments into agencies which inspire both confidence and trust where there had previously been animosity and distrust.

Finally, a department may adopt a *service orientation*. This kind of department places a strong emphasis on the alleviation of social problems which are believed to contribute to both crime and unrest. "The essential characteristic of a service oriented program is its concern and involvement in the socioeconomic problems of the community. Such a unit acts as a discovery and referral agency for ridding the community of various problems."[13] This represents a rather significant departure from the traditional law enforcement orientation and calls for the use of police officers who are in fact sensitive to the socioeconomic needs of the community. In theory, the approach has considerable merit, but in its practical application there are apt to be many problems, not the least of which is the matter of overcoming traditional police attitudes. Second, very few police departments have either the manpower or the training to develop this kind of approach. Finally, this approach actually places the police in the position of doing someone else's work, and it is doubtful that the inability or unwillingness of social welfare agencies to do their own job constitutes adequate justification for the police doing it for them. Certainly the police should cooperate fully with such agencies and should make proper referrals when necessary, but they should also remember that they are *police* departments.

Brown's typology is broad in its scope, and in all likelihood many departments have community relations programs which overlap the various typologies. In retrospect it is clear that many of the police-community relations programs which sprang up in the 1960's and 1970's were poorly conceived and executed. There is some evidence which indicates many of them were undertaken simply because the money was there and because police executives saw them as a way of increasing police manpower. There was great resistance within many departments to these programs because many officers thought them a waste of time. Many officers regarded them as not being a legitimate part of the police function and many officers also saw them as concessions to the very people who were the most likely to give them problems. In many departments the community relations unit became a dumping ground for officers who were part-time ministers, semi-retired men who wished to avoid street work, and blacks who, it was hoped, could work some kind of magic within the Black community.

One of the initial (and continuing) problems with police-community relations efforts is that police officers and police departments in general feel that they *are* doing what they are supposed to be doing; there is no real need for them to change. The assumption is that the *community* must be made to accept the police essentially as they are and to cooperate more fully with them. Thus, "most police departments regard community relations as public relations — as efforts to sell the organization."[14] By the same token, critics of the police see them as repressive, insensitive, non-responsive — and sometimes even incompetent. This emphasizes the fact that different groups have different frames of reference and that they tend to interpret the same event in different ways. To complicate matters, people and groups routinely protect their perceptions of events from contradictory evidence.[15] This means that not only do groups see what they want to see, they make their interpretations according to their own psychological needs. It also means that police performance is probably not as good as the police think it is, nor is it as bad as their critics claim — yet too often neither camp is willing to alter its position substantially. Police community relations have therefore not been extremely successful in shaping public opinion.

The problem of police community relations is far more complex than it appears because how the police department relates to the community is significantly influenced by how the police department is organized in the first place. In urban areas the department is usually divided geographically by districts, and within districts it is divided by time (e.g., shifts) and specialties such as patrol, investigations and traffic. Most officers work their beat, performing their respective functions, and in many cases have very little contact with the community other than in answering calls or making traffic stops. Officers spend a considerable amount of time in their cars patrolling or actually working calls. They have little opportunity to become acquainted with the *full range* of citizens within their areas.

Because they recognized this problem, a number of departments began an alternative approach. Known under the general rubric of *team policing*, this effort tried to decentralize police operations by giving individual officers and teams of officers greater responsibility, including a team responsibility for providing police services to relatively small areas. The technique attempted to combine job enrichment with community relations. Each team was expected to learn its neighborhood and to become familiar with its people and problems. Patrol officers were given wider latitude in conducting follow-up investigations and the control of officers in the field was decentralized. The team approach encourages — even requires — team participation in decision-making: goals are set, performance criteria established, and operational procedures ironed out by the team rather than by police headquarters. Although well over 100 police departments experimented with team policing, most have dropped the concept. Administrators are very reluctant to surrender control to lower levels within the hierarchy. One writer noted:

> If police administrators are serious about giving captains and
> lieutenants full authority over a neighborhood, if they are
> serious about giving sergeants and patrol officers the right to
> participate in decision making, then they are talking about
> taking power away from some people and granting it to
> others. And that rarely happens without a battle in
> organizations like police departments. 'If it's done right, team
> policing amounts to a major revolution,' declares police
> researcher Lawrence Sherman. 'And it's not surprising that
> many attempts at revolution fail.'[16]

The police, of course, must operate with limited resources and this means they must allocate those resources most "economically"; in a way which gives them the best return on their investment in manpower and effort. They must also allocate their services in accordance with a sense of equity which satisfies a fundamental need for fairness. In doing this, the police do not usually look at crime from the perspective of the criminal or the victim. Instead they look at crime in terms of: (a) its legal definitions; (b) the demands it places on human and physical resources within the police department; (c) the amount of discretionary latitude the crime allows; (d) the threat the crime poses to good order; and (e) the seriousness of the crime from the police perspective. In short, the police want to do a good job according to their own criteria.

The problem in approaching their work from this perspective is that what they think is important might be at variance with what others within the community think is important. For example, a poor person might complain to the police about what he considers a serious problem only to discover that the police are not interested. Perhaps the problem is civil in nature (as many domestic complaints and landlord/tenant disputes are) and falls outside of police authority. The person making the complaint may not understand the distinction between private wrongs and public wrongs and might simply conclude the police are indifferent — or worse yet, the system is against him. By the same token, many citizens call the police and insist that they arrest some real or imagined wrongdoer and when the police refuse to do so because the arrest would violate procedural due process, the complainant is usually dissatisfied and resentful. Differing perspectives on crime and the propriety of police conduct lead to different expectations and increase the likelihood of conflict and citizen dissatisfaction, making police-community relations all the more important.

Converting Institutions Into Instruments

The basic objective in criminal justice-community relations should be one of transforming themselves as *institutions* back into *instruments* in an effort to make criminal justice agencies genuinely responsive to the actual needs for which they exist. It should also be clear from the outset that this is not the responsibility of the criminal justice system alone — *all* of society's basic institutions need to be responsive to the legitimate needs of their members and must also be willing to support the service objectives of other basic social institutions.

Given the inevitability of self-interest in the structuring of human affairs, this objective seems more utopian than realistic. The improbability of achieving a goal is no reason for not trying; if we could improve the responsiveness of basic social institutions by even a small percentage, the consequences to society in terms of improvement in the quality of life would be significant. How then is an institution to go about reversing its trend toward goal displacement and non-responsiveness?

Altogether too many institutions have a *stated purpose* — but pay little attention to it. Bureaucratic ideologies notwithstanding, the *actual* (as opposed to *theoretical*) purpose of an organization is what its people accomplish; if what its people accomplish is not in harmony with the theoretical goal of the organization, then something is wrong. One or the other needs to be changed, and most often, what needs to be changed is what actually is being done. Thus we can see that many of the reforms called for in criminal justice such as improvement of police services, bail reform, and prison reform are really nothing more than calls for the organization to do what it is *supposed* to do; calls for reform urge the organization to tailor its *practices* so they conform to the organization's *purposes*!

The police have little trouble in dealing with *real* emergencies such as serious accidents or crimes of violence. When they deal with real emergencies both the public and press generally support them. However, when they "create" emergencies (using the term loosely) and then develop strategies for dealing with those emergencies, they tend to have problems. Police response to commercialized sex, drugs, gambling and other status offenses are good examples. It is in these areas that the police have been most frequently and seriously rebuked by the courts and the public. Interestingly enough, the courts never determine their own emergencies, for they neither call for cases to be brought before them nor do they decide theoretical problems. Prisons, on the other hand, have been allowed to declare their own emergencies and to develop strategies for responding to them, many of which the courts have subsequently ruled unacceptable.

The Need To Establish Policy And Set Priorities

Although an agency may be technically capable of many things, it may experience problems if it tries to do them all at the same time. Furthermore, simply because an agency *can* do something does not necessarily mean that it *ought* to. Figuring out just *what* an agency should do and *how* it should be done is a matter of establishing policy and setting priorities.

Policy Agencies that routinely deal with recurring activities or problems usually establish guidelines to carry out such work. These guidelines are *policies* and they take advantage of corporate memory and the organization's past experience. *Rational* policies are based on some principle, along with guidelines for meeting the principle. For example, if a prison has a policy based on the principle of *rehabilitation*, then it must also have some guidelines which direct institutional resources toward achieving that goal. If the police department has a policy of strict law enforcement based on the rule of law, then it must establish guidelines on such things as the use of force and arrest procedures. It is important to make sure that the policy is clear and that the operational guidelines support it. If a department espouses a set of principles, but lacks operational guidelines to carry them out, then its policies are hypocritical and pointless.

The use of rational policy benefits an organization in several ways. First, policies and their attendant operational guidelines keep members of the organization from acting in an arbitrary manner: the policies establish guidelines for action which all are obliged to follow. Because of this, policies make it possible to predict the behaviors of members of the organization. This latter point is important because decentralization is facilitated, and decentralization allows the top executives to concentrate on matters which involve exceptions to policy. Policy also provides a basis for evaluating performance and this strengthens accountability.

Unfortunately, many criminal justice agencies do not operate under rational policy. Many of them function under policies based on tradition, and factors which determine such policy include history, tradition, and precedent. This results in rigid, static organizations. Yet other agencies are governed by "policy by fiat," or the arbitrary pronouncements of one man: an autocratic police chief or sheriff, prosecutor, or warden. If an organization does not base its operations on rational policy, it is likely to be out of touch with not only its own members' needs, but also with those of the community it serves.

Priorities   The establishment of rational policy should also involve the structuring of operational priorities, the listing of what the agency will attempt to do and under what circumstances it may be accomplished. With limited resources of money and manpower, criminal justice agencies must establish a hierarchy of tasks they wish to accomplish. This hierarchy should be based on the importance of the task to the public, not the convenience of the tasks for the agency or its administrators. Some tasks may be mandated by law; for example, sheriff's departments are normally required to maintain the security of the courthouse, and prisons are required to accept prisoners committed to them by the courts. Mandated priorities may in turn establish a rough order of priorities for the agency (e.g., prisons must place a high priority on custodial security even though they might rather spend the money on inmate services).

If an agency can set at least some of its priorities, it ought to do so in conjunction with community wishes. A police department may place a high priority on narcotics operations and a low priority on minor public order violations; yet residents of an area may be much more concerned with the drunks and prostitutes they can see in their neighborhood than with clandestine drug operations which they cannot see. This kind of discrepancy can lead citizens to conclude that the police are not doing anything and do not care about the residents' concerns. The department's priorities in this case might be quite legitimate, but the lack of communication can also be costly in terms of citizen attitudes toward the police. Priorities should be carefully thought out and should represent the interests of both the department and the community, even though that may well involve having to make some compromises. It should be clear by now that the creation of rational policy and the development of priorities cannot be made in a vacuum and that they must be part of an on-going process of communication with other major elements of the community.

Economic Problems

There are important economic factors concerning criminal justice which play an important role in the relationship between the quality of the output of the criminal justice system and the opinion of the public toward the system. Like many other aspects of the criminal justice system, economic factors generate some very perplexing inconsistencies and contradictions which clearly keep the system from operating at full efficiency — and it is highly unlikely that these factors can be changed to any significant degree. Understanding some of these inconsistencies and contradictions is important if expectations are to be matched with reality, for any enterprise must learn to live within its limitations.

First of all, *economics* is the social science which deals with the production, distribution, and consumption of goods and services. Crimes must be thought of as economic entities, for they also involve goods and services. Some of the goods and services are *illicit*; they violate law. Included in this category would be such things as proscribed narcotics, pornography, murder-for-hire and prostitution. Other goods and services may be *licit*, but the means of their production, distribution or consumption might be illegal, as in the embezzlement of funds or other forms of the theft of property or larceny. The relationship between criminal justice, consumers, and producers becomes complex because many people in society want to have their cake and eat it too: they want a just and orderly society, but they also want illicit goods and services. Matters would be much simpler if only deviants provided and consumed illegal goods and services and only "decent" citizens sought a just and orderly society. However, this is not the case at all. Many "decent" people — people who quickly proclaim their support of "law and order" — also want to consume, produce, or distribute illegal goods and services. In some cases it is quite innocuous: the couple who periodically hold a garage sale and do not report their income; merchants and professional people who trade services or who provide services "off the books" so as to reduce tax liability; and people who take home from work "odds and ends" such as pens, pencils and paper. Many otherwise respectable people avail themselves of illicit sex, drugs, and gambling, to say nothing of nominally honest citizens who profit from economic crime: insurance frauds, employee thefts, price-fixing, overcharging customers or failing to properly provide a service already purchased. In addition, a great many "conventional crimes" — larcenies, assaults, frauds — are routinely committed by very conventional people. Although these people support the criminal justice system in theory, they have no desire to be one of its victims; they usually are quick to defend close friends and relatives who get caught with their fists in the cookie jar. Although many, if not most people, want justice and order and support the criminal justice system in theory, they actually place many restrictions on their support in practice. They are eager to see strangers with whom they have little in common prosecuted for *crimes of violence*. However, if one were to consider society as a whole, this attitude amounts to a massive resistance to criminal justice and a strong public support of illicit markets.

If the efficiency of criminal justice depends in part on citizen cooperation, when citizens withhold their *individual* support of the system, their collective resistance will cause the justice system to fall short of achieving its ultimate objectives. This goes well beyond citizens who do not want to be charged with crimes; it also includes unwillingness to act as a witness, to serve on a jury, to report crimes of which they are aware, and a reluctance to support proposals for increased expenditures in the local budget or bond issues.

Another economic factor of importance to the criminal justice system involves constraints on the resources available to the various elements of the system. It costs money to provide services, and because they are public agencies, criminal justice units are tied to public budgets. Public revenues are subject to fierce competition in what is clearly a zero-sum game: what money one part of government gets, another does not. Plainly put, there are just so many ways to slice the pie, and after it's sliced, each agency must live with its share. Its operations will be limited by the amount of money available. Heavily burdened taxpayers are increasingly unwilling to authorize any major growth in public budgets, and many cities routinely increase their revenues by reassessing property values so they can squeeze additional property taxes out of residents without having to raise actual tax rates, which are already at the maximum allowable limit in many cities. Taxpayers are much more resentful of the burden they must carry and give every indication of wanting to hold back the rate of growth of an already highly expensive public bureaucracy. Public finance officers have had to be very creative and astute in the managing of public revenues; many cities have been forced to cut back on the services they provide, including emergency services. This means that criminal justice agencies have to do as much or more, but with less funding. It is inevitable that this will involve a cutback in either the scope or quality of services, and this is bound to have an adverse impact on public opinion. There seems to be little that public agencies can do about the problem.

One answer, in theory, is to increase *productivity*, or to try to get more out of every dollar spent. One way of doing this is through the use of advanced technologies which produce increased outputs per measure of input. However, that calls for the shifting of resources from one type of technology to another. This is referred to by economists as "malleability of capital," but is difficult for criminal justice agencies to do, because many of them are heavily committed to existing technologies and equipment. Not only is *technology* in criminal justice rigid, so is *labor*. Existing labor resources are heavily committed to traditional labor-intensive practices, and this is unlikely to change in the near future. There are a number of factors which act as limitations on the increase in criminal justice productivity and may seriously hamper criminal justice outcomes in the near future.

We therefore see a basic economic problem which stems from a strong commitment to sunken cost and established procedure. Although a tremendous amount of money is spent on criminal justice in the United States each year, there are still no assurances that any real worthwhile results come from those expenditures. There are basically no *effective* means of measuring the quality of criminal justice outputs, and there are simply too many competing objectives within the system. Another related problem is that there may be some long-range harmful effects in the ways the system operates, and these detrimental effects may only compound the overall cost of justice while at the same time detracting from the overall effectiveness of the system.

These are problems which many criminal justice managers simply do not see because they are so deeply involved in routine day-to-day problems. Moreover, some of these problems require a degree of sophistication which many criminal justice managers do not possess. Thus, internal limitations on the actual ability to see, understand, and deal with complex macroeconomic problems is a problem itself in addition to all of the other problems. The situation is not as hopeless as it might seem at first glance. In fact, there are several key steps criminal justice agencies can take which would assist them in the management of productivity.

First, *each* element — police, courts, and corrections — needs to keep in mind that none produces a *final product*, but rather only produces an *intermediate* product in the process of "justice." Justice is not served by an arrest alone; nor is it served by a criminal prosecution or some kind of court-imposed punishment. Each agency must bear in mind that its effectiveness is enhanced or limited by the effectiveness of all other agencies, and it is only through the efficient operation of all of the elements within the system that justice is served.

Second, each criminal justice agency must be mindful of the need to establish measures which would be helpful in both evaluating the effectiveness of the agency's personnel and which would also give the agency some idea of the impact of its services. These are *output measures*, and they should attempt to focus on the cost-effectiveness of the agency and its operations. Quite obviously, benefits should be compared to costs, and the cost-benefit criterion is that if the benefits of a program exceed its cost, it is effective. One way of working toward this end is through the integration of public services for the provision of collective goods.

Integration of Public Services

The integration of public services does not mean the consolidation of agencies, as in the consolidation of fire and police departments. Rather, it means the integration of *service objectives* and programs so that coordinated and cost-effective services can be delivered with a minimum of delay and cost. Perhaps several simple examples would make the concept clearer. In most cities the police perform the traffic law enforcement function. They investigate accidents, issue tickets, and generally facilitate the flow of traffic. At the same time, there is usually another department belonging to the city, county or state which concerns itself with traffic engineering. Experts in this field keep tabs on traffic volumes: this might indicate a need for more or wider streets or a change in speed limits or control devices. They also monitor accidents at the intersections and mid-blocks. They do this to see if there are any engineering flaws, such as inadequate sight distance or improper signals which contribute to accidents at a given location. In many cases, these traffic engineers know more about the actual traffic law enforcement needs of the community than does the police department. For instance, the police may issue a great many tickets for speeding, but engineering studies indicate that other violations, such as unsafe turning movements, are much more closely related to accidents. The police may randomly patrol their districts looking for any violation, but engineers know that a few high accident locations provide the greatest risk during specific hours of the day. In most of these cities the police traffic division and the traffic engineer almost never meet and almost never coordinate data. Each is realistically an extension of the other, but each works in isolation. Another example would be the police department and the parks and recreation department. The police, especially through its youth division, may have a very good idea of where bored and idle children congregate and become involved in various kinds of mischief or vandalism. A solution to the problem could be youth activities sponsored by the parks and recreation department, if only they knew where they had to concentrate their resources. Again, the two seldom work closely together in this kind of planning.

The same is true with the police, the courts, local jails and the various social welfare services. Many mental health resources exist for helping people under stress, ranging all the way from women's shelters to child abuse prevention councils — all of which could provide a valuable service to the police, the courts, and jails — if only the services of those agencies could be more effectively coordinated. Although each kind of agency may have a different perspective on the problems which they treat, they all deal with the same *basic* problems. Often the problem with public agencies is not that they are incapable of providing effective services, but that they are not properly organized to do so. By integrating public services toward the accomplishment of some clearly defined objectives, it should be possible to make the work of each agency easier and more cost effective, and in the long run should result not only in a better overall product, but a more supportive public as well. Fortunately there is some evidence that this kind of integrated effort is being recognized and some efforts are underway to more fully coordinate public services — yet a great deal more progress needs to be made, especially in urban areas.

Images and Realities

One of the consequences of inadequate or erroneous communications is that there is apt to be a substantial difference between *reality* and what appears to be reality. Problems tend to be magnified or diminished depending on the viewer and his perspective.

The difference between images and their corresponding realities is the zone in which criminal justice agencies need to focus serious attention if they are genuinely interested in the issue of community relations. Of course, one of the problems is that most criminal justice agencies themselves have a great deal of difficulty in distinguishing between images and realities. The view an agency has of itself, its work, its employees, and its clientele is shaped by its routine operations, and the nature of those operations may distort reality. The very nature of bureaucratic organization can impede objectivity. Downs has pointed out that the larger a bureaucracy is, the more reluctant it will be to adopt any given change.[17] Organizations which refuse to change over time become increasingly unrealistic in their orientation.

Downs also points out that in any large, multi-level bureaucracy, a very significant portion of all the activity being carried out is completely unrelated to the bureau's goals, or even to the goals of its highest officials because in order to accomplish its *formal* goals, every organization must undertake many activities that have no direct connection with those goals, but which are aimed at maintaining the coalition of individuals necessary to achieving them.[18] This problem also exists for criminal justice agencies, and it creates a rift between images and realities. This is one reason why criminal justice agencies cling so tightly to bureaucratic ideologies (eg., "to protect and serve") while at the same time they go about doing other things.

There are also many problems at the "delivery level" which result in a discrepancy between images and realities. The highest volume of police "street work" takes place in neighborhoods that are poor. These neighborhoods tend to have concentrations of ethnic or racial minorities and experience very high rates of social disorganization and criminal activity. These are what the police typically refer to as "hot districts" — areas where most of the shootings and cuttings take place and where there are continued demands for service. It is easy to associate social disorganization and crime in these neighborhoods with the race or ethnicity of their residents and to conclude that race or ethnicity *causes* crime. It is very easy to overlook the roles played by more important factors of education, economics, and social class. It is also easy to overlook the fact that many, if not most of the people who live in these areas are law-abiding citizens. Police attitudes can and do harden on the basis of repeated experiences with a small proportion of the population, leading to incorrect overall judgements.

By the same token, ghetto hostility toward the police can be equally faulty in its origins. There is a popular and enduring conventional wisdom among many ghetto residents that the police routinely mistreat Blacks. Much of this belief arises from rumor, past practices no longer employed, and even a need to appear a victim of "the system" as a means of coping with personal failure or inadequacy. To feel oppressed is easy when one is poor in the midst of affluence, but the mere presence of the police does not constitute evidence that the criminal justice system is oppressive and that, as some radical writers have claimed, the police are an "army of occupation." Yet these images persist, and efforts to change them meet with spirited resistance.

There is also a serious discrepancy between the image and reality of the courts. Courtrooms and judicial procedings, despite their physical impressiveness and complex jargon, are in reality little more than social machines for processing cases. In too many courts the needs of all parties — the victim, the offender, and the state — are routinely disregarded in favor of judicial or prosecutorial convenience. Many who have had first-hand experience with the courts have left them disappointed or embittered. Whether the courts are unaware of this or simply do not care is hard to say: there is, however, a substantial gap between the images and realities of the courts.

Perhaps the one area within criminal justice where images and realities come the closest to being in harmony with one another is in the area of corrections, especially jails and prisons. Little is expected and little is delivered. Interestingly enough, there are *many* professionals within corrections who are concerned about this problem, yet conventional wisdom does not recognize either the existence of these people or the work they are doing. It seems that corrections can only fulfill public expectations by failing. In addition, the use of probation and parole is often erroneously interpreted as constituting a *failure* within the criminal justice system because many regard it as letting offenders go free. In this case, public misunderstanding of the theory and practice of probation and parole is not in harmony with its reality.

Reconciling images with reality is one of the many basic (but nearly impossible) problems faced by the criminal justice system. In reality, what we have done is to take a wide range of interrelated but separate functions and call them a *system*, because in theory, they should function as a system. In spite of the rhetoric, the criminal justice system is a system in name only and remains plagued with inconsistent and contradictory objectives and methods, a fragmentation of effort, and a wide gap between its images and realities. Community relations cannot be effectively served simply by engaging in public relations efforts; root problems in communications, policy formation, and service integration must receive serious attention across the board. Until this happens, adequate criminal justice community relations will continue to be wishful thinking.

Summary

Criminal justice is essentially a community process because in one way or another it involves the entire community, both individuals and groups. How a community is organized as well as its size and complexity play a major role in both the demands for and expectations of criminal justice services. The larger and more complex the community, the larger and more bureaucratic the agencies of criminal justice, and the larger agencies are, the more likely it is that they suffer from the problems which plague most complex agencies. Ultimately, this means that they will begin to shift from being instruments which deal with problems to institutions which seek to aggrandize and maintain themselves.

In dealing with the public, community relations programs must remain mindful of the difference between "public relations" and "community relations." Public relations simply tries to shape public opinion in favor of the agency whereas community relations tries to generate an atmosphere of cooperation within the community by engaging in activities which make the organization more responsive to the needs of the agency and vice-versa. Criminal justice community relations should be concerned with the management of change so that all elements of the community (including its various subgroups) can remain aware of evolving needs and meet them in a manner which is both responsive and timely. Thus, community relations is a process through which the agencies involved avoid institutional isolation and seek to serve the public to and for which they are responsible.

The principal vehicle for effective community relations is communications. The problem with effective communications, however, is that in a pluralistic society different groups tend to perceive different needs and communications among these groups are often strained, incorrect, or nonexistent. As public agencies, criminal justice organizations are constantly confronted with the consequences of these communications failures and to an extent even contribute to them. The problem then becomes that of establishing accurate communications with the various groups and then using them in the management of differences in perception. In the final analysis, groups which do not communicate with one another have no realistic hope of being able to deal effectively with one another.

Within the criminal justice system, the idea of community relations is relatively new, and thus far only the police have made a serious effort to establish community relations programs. Although the efforts by the police have been halting and in some cases poorly thought out, their efforts still represent a major move forward on behalf of the entire criminal justice system. As time goes by, it is likely that these programs will become more sophisticated and that other elements of the criminal justice system will recognize their value and will also initiate community relations programs.

What is needed on both sides of the fence is organizational renewal — the converting of institutions back into instruments. In order to do this, the institutions must re-orient their work so it conforms with the actual objectives of the organization. In addition, there is a strong and continuing need for the development of rational policy and for the creation of corresponding operational guidelines so those who work for the agencies not only know what they ought to be doing, but also why they should be doing it. The use of rational policy serves to prevent arbitrary and capricious behavior by individuals and makes the functions of the organization predictable. They also produce performance standards against which the actions of the institution's members can be evaluated.

There are other impediments to effective community relations, and perhaps one of the most important is that of economics. Although the public generally supports the criminal justice system in theory, that support is qualified in practice. For example, the public also demands many illicit goods and services and often resents interference by the criminal justice system in the delivery or consumption of those illicit goods and services, at least at the individual level. Second, a great deal of crime is committed by conventional people, yet many of these same people see "criminals" as being different from them in kind rather than degree and thus expect the criminal justice system to concentrate its efforts "elsewhere." Economic factors also limit the resources which are available to the criminal justice system and further lock its agencies into conventional techniques and approaches because of the large sunken cost in both manpower and technology.

Finally, there is a significant difference between images and realities, and much of what the criminal justice system (and the public) does is intended to maintain the images rather than to bring them into line with realities. The criminal justice system is rife with inconsistencies and contradictory expectations — and so is the public. These inconsistencies and contradictions only serve to perpetuate the problems which have made community relations necessary in the first place.

Discussion Questions

1.   Why would it be impossible to carry out the administration of justice consistently from one community to another? Is this necessarily bad?

2.   Is it possible to have a community relations program without also having a public relations program?

3.   In what ways do public opinions become "fixed? "

4.   Granted that a community is always in a state of change, how can you tell the *kind* or *direction* of that change? Must the interested observer always be "behind the times?"

5.   How do people generate contradictory communications when they relate to the criminal justice system?

6.   How can the various formal social institutions within the community support one another?

7.   What do you think would be the most formidable barriers to converting "institutions" back into "instruments?"

8.   What happens to an organization when its operations are not the result of "rational policy?"

9.   How do "honest" citizens add to the cost of providing criminal justice through their tacit support of illicit markets?

10.   Do the images that the criminal justice system generate concerning the nature of their work help or hinder them in getting their job done?

Glossary

COMMUNITY RELATIONS   The management of mutually beneficial change through a process of cooperative interaction between a public agency and some element of the community.

GOAL DISPLACEMENT   The substitution of internal for external objectives within an organization.

PUBLIC OPINION   An aggregate of individual views, attitudes, or beliefs shared by a significant portion of the community.

PUBLIC RELATIONS   The attempt to shape public opinion in some desired direction.

ZONE OF POTENTIAL CONFLICT   The area in which both the private and public control systems may reasonably believe each has primary responsibility for a problem or conflict.

Notes

[1] Anthony Downs, *Inside Bureaucracy* (Boston: Little, Brown and Company, 1967), p. 27.

[2] See Max Weber, *Bureaucracy* in Jay N. Shafritz and Philip H. Whitbeck, eds., *Classics of Organizational Theory* (Oak Park, Illinois: Moore Publishing Co., Inc., 1978), pp. 37-42.

[3] Irwin Ross, *The Image Merchants* (Garden City, New York: Doubleday and Co., Inc., 1959), p. 33.

[4] Edward L. Bernays, ed., *The Engineering of Consent* (Norman, Oklahoma: University of Oklahoma Press, 1955), pp. 3-4.

[5] Jack C. Plano and Milton Greenbery, *The American Political Dictionary*, 2d ed. (New York: Holt, Rinehart and Co., 1967), p. 116.

[6] See Marie Jahoda and Neil Warren, eds., *Attitudes* (Baltimore, Maryland: Penguin Books, 1966).

[7] Walter Lippmann, *The Phantom Public* (New York: Macmillan Co., 1927), pp. 84, 88-89.

[8] Lippmann, *Phantom Public*, p. 100.

[9] Lee P. Brown, "Typology," *The Police Chief*, March 1971, pp. 16-21.

[10] Robert Shellow and Morton Bard, *Issues in Law Enforcement: Essays and Case Studies* (Reston, Virginia: Reston Publishing Co., Inc., 1976), p. 63.

[11] "Disturbance Spurs Recreation Effort," *Greensboro Daily News*, 2 August 1980, p. B2.

[12] Brown, "Typology."

[13] Brown, "Typology."

[14] Shellow and Bard, *Issues in Law Enforcement*, p. 66.

[15] John P. Hewitt and Randall Stokes, "Disclaimers," *American Sociological Review* 40 (February 1975): 1-11.

[16] David C. Anderson, "Getting Down with the People," *Police Magazine*, July 1978, p. 12.

[17] Downs, *Inside Bureaucracy*, p. 274.

[18] Downs, *Inside Bureaucracy*, p. 270.

CRIMINAL JUSTICE AND THE COMMUNITY: THE PEOPLE

4

Most analyses of the criminal justice system examine its major components: the police, the courts, and prisons. More detailed analyses subdivide the major areas into logical subcomponents. Although this kind of analysis may be technically correct, it is still much like describing transportation by analyzing motor vehicles: something is clearly missing. Just as understanding transportation requires an analysis of road systems, understanding the criminal justice system requires knowledge of the role of the *public as a component* of the overall criminal justice system.

With the exception of traditional custodial prisons (which are closed, isolated institutions), criminal justice agencies are in constant contact with the public. In fact, *without* close and continuing support from citizens the criminal justice system simply could not function: most police activities are initiated by citizens, and the courts require citizen participation and cooperation to fill juries, file complaints, and serve as witnesses. Prosecutors and judges are elected by the citizens they serve. Finally, citizens *pay* for the system through a variety of taxes. If the citizens of a community were to completely withdraw their support, the criminal justice system would soon collapse; it simply could not function.

Just as the community depends upon and needs the criminal justice system, the system depends upon and needs the community. This is a classic symbiotic relationship in which each benefits from the other and in which the whole is greater than the sum of its parts. One way of looking at this relationship is to take the position that criminal justice is a *citizen* responsibility, although most aspects of that responsibility are carried out by relatively few people. It is the work of those few people who are involved in criminal justice as a profession which makes criminal justice a reality. This is not just idle talk; citizens *may* make arrests and initiate prosecutions, although most people prefer that these tasks be carried out by police officers and prosecutors. In a very real sense we delegate our responsibilities to the system, but in order for its employees to carry out their tasks, they must have our cooperation.

We would expect that given this mutual dependence there would be an easy and open flow of information and cooperation between citizens and the system. Unfortunately, this is not always the case. As many as half (or more) of all the crimes committed are never even reported to the police. A great many citizens actively seek to avoid jury duty or to act as witnesses in criminal cases. There is widespread distrust of lawyers, courts, the police and prosecutors. Altogether too many people want justice (as *they* define it) without playing an active role in securing it.

On the other side of the coin, many criminal justice agencies and their employees hold the public in contempt. Some services are delivered with indifference or even outright hostility. In some places there are many levels of justice, depending on how much money or power a person possesses. In some communities citizen-agency relationships are characterized by misunderstanding, stress, and dissatisfaction. This dysfunction is not without its cost. People lose confidence in government and withhold their support. Crimes remain unsolved and criminals go unpunished. The morale and effectiveness of criminal justice agencies suffers and manifests itself in sloppy work and bad attitudes, setting up a self-perpetuating cycle. In some communities, the police and court officials have themselves become criminals — fortunately this is a rare occurrence.

Clearly, the point of interface, the point where the public and the criminal justice system meet, is an important place, for it is there that changes need to be made and citizen-system alliances strengthened or cemented. Problems between citizens and the system in what they expect of one another and how those expectations are to be met need to be clarified and resolved.

The Public As A Consumer Of Criminal Justice

The criminal justice process is supposed to be *instrumental*; it is supposed to accomplish some desired result. What is that result? Most persons would say either "justice" or "a just and orderly society;" however, such answers would be inadequate. Justice is a highly abstract concept and any attempts to define it are bound to be either too broad or too narrow. Instead of defining justice, it would probably be more constructive to look at the basic psychological needs of humans. In fact, our collective social institutions are, to a large extent, shaped around these individual needs. Psychological needs can be very complex and even contradictory; they can and often do come into conflict with the law, as noted in Chapter 2.

TABLE 4.1

∧

MASLOW'S NEEDS HIERARCHY

/ \

Self-Actualization

The need to reach one's ultimate potential as a creative, fulfilled person; becoming the most that one is capable of becoming.

/ ↑ \

Esteem (Status) Needs

The need to feel important and to be respected; the need to have feelings of self-worth and self-respect.

/ ↑ \

Belongingness/Love Needs

The need to give and to receive affection; to associate with others; to enjoy social interaction, acceptance, and group membership.

/ ↑ \

Safety Needs

The need to protect the organism from harm, both physical and psychological; the need to avoid pain and suffering.

↑

Physiological Needs

The needs associated with the most basic biological necessities; e.g., eating, sleeping, breathing, etc.

Abraham Maslow perceived the individual as having five levels of needs which are arranged in a hierarchy going from low to high (see Table 4.1). Maslow argued that lower level needs must be satisfied before the higher level needs can motivate behavior. Maslow's needs hierarchy rests on two important assumptions. The first is that *unsatisfied* needs motivate behavior, and the second is that each level of need must be satisfied before the next level can serve as a motivator.

According to the theory of Maslow's hierarchy, if a person is having difficulty breathing, he will concentrate his efforts on getting air: nothing else would be important enough to motivate him to do anything else. People who are hungry think of little other than food. People who are secure in their physiological and safety needs seek out companionship and the association of others, and so on through the entire hierarchy. Viewed in this light, it is not hard to see how easy it would be for a starving person to steal in order to eat. It is also easy to see how a Supreme Court Justice (appointed for life at a high salary to a job with considerable prestige) can leisurely and comfortably mull over the fine points of legal philosophy and render a decision having a profound impact on the lives of countless people; he does not have to worry about the consquences of those decisions. The question of what constitutes justice also involves another issue — different people have different ideas concerning what justice is and how it should be applied. The law does not usually make such distinctions. Of course, all of the foregoing assumes we are talking about the psychological needs of *normal* people. There is a whole spectrum of problems associated with those who are *not* psychologically normal.[2] The criminal justice system comes into frequent contact with disordered individuals and disordered groups. These people range from the disoriented and confused to the violently destructive. Much of the study of deviance concerns the mentally and emotionally disturbed. This chapter will not concern itself with either mental illness or the private control system, but will look at the criminal justice system and will explore the ways in which it interfaces with the public as a whole. It will discuss the broad responsibilities of the criminal justice system as well as what the public expects of the system. Finally, the chapter will look at *public* responsibilities and contradictory expectations between the public and the system. First, let's look at some of the major, broad expectations of the public.

Crime Control

The public as a consumer expects the criminal justice system to control crime. People do not wish to be victimized by criminals; they wish to be secure in their persons and places. They want to be able to go about their business without having to be afraid of being hurt or exploited, and they expect the criminal justice system to see to it that crime is kept within acceptable limits (which usually means in someone else's neighborhood). Crime control is a vague term, whether viewed either as an end in itself or as a means to an end. The criminal justice system is expected to "adequately" define the concept and to implement measures to meet the requirements of that definition.

Crime is in fact a serious problem: many people suffer personal hardship as a direct result of crimes committed against them, and perhaps *the* principal task of the criminal justice system *is* the control of crime. Overall, this is done through law enforcement (the police function); adjudication (the court function); and finally, through punishment (the corrections function). The question of the efficiency and effectiveness of these agencies will be dealt with in subsequent chapters; suffice it to say here that one of their most important tasks is the control of crime.

Public Order

Crimes are violations of statutes and are typically thought of as more serious cases of deviance, especially when they involve felonies. Other forms of deviance, including minor crimes, arise out of the situational context of human interaction. People are constantly going places and doing things, and this requires external intervention in order to see to it that routine problems are kept to a minimum. We see this most readily in the control and regulation of traffic; however, that's only the tip of the iceberg. All communities have various devices for protecting health and safety and for facilitating the pursuit of commerce and pleasure. For example, regarding *health* matters, food products are inspected; medical and dental practices are licensed; restaurants (and their employees) are inspected and certified; the sale of alcohol and tobacco is restricted, and so on. In the case of *safety* matters, building and fire codes are established and enforced; plumbing and electrical contractors are licensed; firearms are restricted through various licenses and permits; and, standards for the safe flow of traffic are established and enforced. The public welfare is advanced through precautions such as the regulation of utilities, the licensing of such occupations as undertaking and cosmetology, and regulation of the manufacture, sale and possession of dangerous substances.

Assistance

The criminal justice system also provides assistance to people who are in need of help. This is done for the most part by the police because of their ready availability. People who become lost, hurt, confused, frightened or desperate often call upon the police for assistance, even though their immediate problem may have nothing to do with crimes or law-breaking. In fact, such activities may well constitute the bulk of a working police officer's duty time. Activities such as rendering first aid, locating missing persons, and recovering lost or stolen property are typical examples of how the police assist citizens.

District attorneys' offices may operate consumer fraud sections and may provide legal assistance or advice to persons who feel they may have been mistreated by unscrupulous merchants. Small claims courts provide an easy and inexpensive way whereby citizens are provided with legal assistance in settling disputes, and public defenders provide valuable assistance to those who are charged with crimes but who lack the money to hire private counsel.

—Item: A police officer saw a car stopped on a busy street and decided to investigate. He found a father desperately trying to revive a small child who was in respiratory arrest (the father had been on the way to the hospital with the child who was having seizures). The officer put the child in his police car and rushed him to the emergency room of a nearby hospital.

—Item: In 1971 the Night Prosecutor Program was initiated in Columbus, Ohio to provide an out of court method of resolving neighborhood and family disputes through mediation and counseling. In 1976 it heard 3,478 cases, not including 10,196 bad check disputes with criminal affidavits filed in only 2 percent of the cases.

—Item: In 1974 a group of Baton Rouge, Louisiana women, representing a cross section of the community, mounted an offensive against rape. They identified two key problems: the low priority given rape cases by the community's law enforcement agencies and the lack of supportive social services for rape victims. They brought their findings to the District Attorney who helped them design a comprehensive program to improve enforcement and prosecutorial techniques while minimizing the victim's trauma.[3]

Crime Prevention

One of the major tasks of the criminal justice system is the *prevention* of crime. This is attempted in a number of ways; for one, it is hoped that by effectively and efficiently discharging their basic enforcement/adjudication/punishment functions, the system will generate *deterrence*. Other programs more specifically directed toward the prevention of crime include those which diminish opportunities for crime through such tactics as neighborhood watch programs and various kinds of environmental designs. Other programs seek to divert those who are most likely to commit crimes into more socially acceptable forms of behavior by using devices such as youth or athletic programs. Sometimes after a crime has actually been committed, the system intervenes in a manner designed to reduce the likelihood of repeat offenses — but without actually punishing the offender (as in the case of many of the so-called "first offender" programs).

—Item: In Lincoln, Nebraska, lay volunteers are successfully counseling high-risk probationers - misdemeanants aged between 16 and 25 with an average of 7.3 previous arrests and convictions.[4]

—Item: Project New Pride in Denver, Colorado is a successful attempt to help juveniles, most with lengthy records of prior arrest and conviction, to break out of what could be a life-long pattern of crime by instilling a sense of self-pride. The project integrates education, employment, counseling, and cultural education — services which are usually highly specialized and fragmented. Intensive application of this service integration is regarded as the key to the success of the program.

The total criminal justice system thus provides an incredible array of services and opportunities to its clientele. The consumers of the system's services include virtually all citizens, although some of them are only indirect beneficiaries. Although some people and groups of people come into direct contact with the criminal justice system more frequently than others, the kind and quality of services provided by the system plays a major role in the *overall* quality of life within the community for everyone.

The Citizen's Perspective Of The System

What the criminal justice system *says* its goals are is one thing; what the public — the consumers — *think of the system* is something else. Citizen perceptions and expectations are important because they ultimately play a role in the shaping of the policy environment of the agencies themselves. If people do not expect certain things of the system, they won't ask for them — and most likely won't get them. If citizen perceptions are wrong, then their evaluation of the system is also likely to be wrong. This can lead to dissatisfaction, disenchantment, alienation or even outright hostility. When citizens and representatives of the system see themselves in *adversarial* roles, the effectiveness of the system will surely diminish. If there are differences between what the system *is* and *does*, and what it is *perceived* as being and doing, then corrective efforts need to be initiated as soon as possible.

Perceptions of Crime

Crime has been a major public concern since the 1960s; in May of 1978 the American Institute of Public Opinion reported in its *Gallup Index* that "For the first time in the decade, public concern with and perceptions of crime are leveling off, if not subsiding."[5] In spite of this trend, a substantial number of Americans *are* afraid of crime.

Prior to its disestablishment, the Law Enforcement Assistance

Administration (LEAA), in conjunction with the Bureau of the Census, conducted a series of victimization surveys (NCS - National Crime Surveys) in selected cities. Eight cities selected for participation in the LEAA's High Impact Crime Reduction Program (Atlanta, Baltimore, Cleveland, Dallas, Denver, Newark, Portland, and St. Louis) were subjected to a carefully controlled survey. In each of these cities about 10,000 households (involving about 22,000 people) were interviewed. These residents were questioned about victimization and also answered an attitude questionnaire. Based on the results of these questionnaires, it has been possible to measure at least some of the public's opinions and concerns as they relate to crime.[6]

Eight out of ten of the respondents thought that crime had increased in the preceding year or two — although only about *half* that number thought crime had increased in *their own* neighborhood. In terms of actual *fear* of crime, the majority of the respondents (53 percent) said they felt very safe being out alone in their own neighborhoods during the *day*; however, only 18 percent said they felt very safe being out alone in their own neighborhood at *night*. Females were much more concerned about their safety than males, regardless of time of day. Interestingly enough, although there was a great deal of concern about safety in one's neighborhood, most of those who expressed concern did not translate their fear into a desire to move from their neighborhood. In fact, the majority (about 60 percent) of all the respondents of each age and race group had no complaints about their own particular neighborhood, and those who did have complaints were more worried about trash, noise, and overcrowding than about crime.[7] Another interesting result was that respondents showed a tendency to rate their own neighborhoods as less dangerous than others in the metropolitan area.

Although many people are concerned about crime, and although a large number of them believe *other people* have limited or changed their activities because of crime, most of the respondents said *they* have not limited or changed their own activities! In other words, there was a trend for respondents to perceive crime as less serious as the frame of reference moves closer to themselves. These findings have been generally confirmed by independent organizations.[8]

Just how real is the fear of crime? Although many people *are* afraid of crime, it may well be the case that their fear — although *real* — may not be *realistic*. For one thing, fear of crime is highly subjective. As other threats intrude on the individual, his priorities are likely to change accordingly. For example, a Gallup survey of a representative cross-section of the nation's adult population asked, "What do you think is the most important problem facing this country today?" The results were as follows:[9]

Inflation/High Cost of Living	61%
Unemployment	16%
International problems	15%
Dissatisfaction with government	6%
Energy	4%
Government spending	3%
Moral decline	3%
Crime	2%

NOTE: Totals to more than 100% because of multiple responses.[9]

Silberman noticed this lack of reality in fear of crime and made the comment that "Ultimately, the whole fabric of urban life is based on trust: trust that others will act predictably, in accordance with generally accepted rules of behavior, and that they will not take advantage of that trust."[10] He goes on to state that "Crime does more than expose the weakness in social relationships; it undermines the social order itself, by destroying the assumptions on which it is based."[11] People need to be secure in their perceptions of their environment; they need to be able to *predict* what will happen to them, based on their own actions (remember, the *inability* to predict outcomes is one basis for alienation). People normally predict what their environment holds for them through the use of a complex network of sophisticated cues which enables the individual to meet what Maslow would consider basic safety needs. Crime, however, interferes with this process by reducing the individual's ability to predict and this absence of effective warning cues is what is especially frightening about stranger-to-stranger crimes. As Silberman said, "Thus the emotional impact of being attacked by a stranger transcends the incident itself; it reaches a primordial layer of fear unlike anything evoked by an equally damaging encounter with an automobile or other inanimate object, or even by a crime that does not involve a direct encounter with another person."[12] What makes this especially interesting and significant is that what the individual fears the most by way of crime is precisely the kind of crime he is least likely to encounter. Although the fear of crime is a personal safety measure, it is often unrealistic.

The *fear* of crime renders a person impotent because the individual doesn't know what to expect or when it will come. He really doesn't know what to do to prevent it, and he doesn't know exactly what its consequences will be. This is not the case with *accidents* because most accidents are comprehensible. For example, we appreciate the fact that to operate an automobile carries with it a certain amount of risk, and most of us understand that risk and know how to cope with it. We also know how easy it is to slip in the shower or to fall on icy steps, and we know how to take basic precautions against such dangers. However, many people do *not* know what awaits them in the dark or in strange neighborhoods: these are events for which our repertoire of cues and responses is inadequate, and therefore we fear them without really knowing what it is that we fear. Many people have given that unknown fear a convenient label: crime. This is why people who live in high crime areas see their own neighborhoods as safer than those with which they are unfamiliar.

Perceptions And Expectations Of The Police The police are the most visible component of the entire criminal justice system — the only part that drives around town and makes house calls. A greater part of the public has some kind of contact with the police on a regular basis, even if that amounts to nothing more than seeing officers directing traffic or conducting their patrol duties. Most people are also brought into contact with the police through the news and entertainment media. As a result of this, most people have "feelings" about the police. However, the level of public confidence in the ability of the police to protect citizens from violent crime is low. A *Newsweek* survey reported that 42 percent of those surveyed had "not very much" confidence in the ability of the police to protect them from violent crime. Eight percent had "none at all." Only 15 percent had "a great deal" of such confidence.[13] The people who are *least likely* to have actual direct contact with the police (those who are older, have high incomes, and who have high levels of education) tend to be the *most likely* to say the police are doing a good job.[14] There is a clear and consistent relationship between race and citizen perception of the police. In one survey which dealt with the issue of discrimination, 61 percent of the Black respondents said they felt Blacks *were* discriminated against when it came to being protected against crime while only 23 percent of the Whites surveyed thought that Blacks were discriminated against in crime protection. In addition, 71 percent of the Black respondents felt that Blacks were discriminated against in the way they were treated by the police, although only 28 percent of the white respondents thought Blacks were discriminated against by the police. Finally, 69 percent of the Black respondents thought that Blacks were discriminated against in the way Blacks were treated if they were arrested for a crime, but only 28 percent of the Whites thought this was the case.[15] What is really interesting, however, is that when asked, "In what ways could they (local police) improve," only 9 percent of Black males and 6 percent of Black females said "don't discriminate." In fact, their most frequent response to that question was "Need more policemen."[16]

In general, Blacks are about three times more likely than Whites to believe the police are doing a poor job and the younger the age group, the more likely its members are to have a negative attitude. Although there is some tendency for people who have been victims of more serious (or face-to-face) crimes to evaluate the police more negatively than others, the differences are generally not as great as those associated with the race and age of the individual. Interestingly enough, most citizens do not blame the police for high crime rates. Citizen attitudes toward the deterrent effect of the law enforcement system is not, however, particularly supportive. When asked if they felt the system of law enforcement works to really discourage people from committing crimes, only 16 percent of the respondents felt that the system did discourage crime, while 79 percent felt that it did not![17] This would imply that many people do not necessarily see the police as part of the problem, but also that they do not see them as part of the solution! This is supported in part by the fact that a large proportion of the crimes that are committed are never reported to the police:

ESTIMATED PERCENT OF VICTIMIZATIONS NOT REPORTED TO THE POLICE

PERSONAL VICTIMIZATIONS

Rape and attempted rape 48%
Robbery 42%
    Attempted robbery, without injury 67%
    Robbery (or attempt), with injury 35%
    Serious assault 32%
    Minor assault 38%
    Robbery, without injury 34%
Assault 54%
    Aggravated assault 44%
    With injury 36%
    Attempted assault with a weapon 49%
    Simple assault 59%
    With injury 46%
    Attempted assault without a weapon 64%
Personal larceny with contact 64%
    Purse-snatching 40%
    Attempted purse-snatching 76%
    Pocket-picking 70%
Personal larceny without contact 74%

HOUSEHOLD VICTIMIZATIONS

Burglary 51%
    Forcible entry 27%

Unlawful entry, without force 60%
Attempted forcible entry 67%
Larcency 74%
   Under $50 .... 86%
   $50 or more 55%
   Amount not ascertained 77%
Attempted larcency 75%
Vehicle theft 30%
   Completed 13%
   Attempted 63%

[18]

There are many reasons why people do not report crimes to the police, just as there are a number of reasons why people do report them. One reason crimes are reported to the police is because it is necessary to do so in order to file an insurance claim in the event of a loss. Another reason is to minimize the impact of what has been lost (as in reporting stolen credit cards). Of course, many people do notify the police because they want something done about the crime — either to have the offender punished, to recover stolen property, or to impose control over the offender. Among the reasons for not reporting criminal victimization to the police is the belief that the police cannot or will not do anything about it anyway; to avoid reprisals; because it is too much bother, or to avoid embarassment to either the victim or the offender (who may very well be a "friend" or a relative). Many victims claim that the crime committed against them wasn't important enough to report in the first place or that they lacked "proof." In the case of unreported assaults, a large number of victims said they did not report the assault to the police because they thought that the offender, even if caught, would not be punished.[19] These reasons do not generally constitute an indictment of the police; they simply underscore the contention that a great deal of crime is seen more as a personal than as a public problem.

Just what do citizens expect of their police? This question is more complicated than it seems at first, because in order to answer it, we must also inquire into *how* citizens expect police to do their job. Probably the most important thing citizens expect of the police — according to conventional wisdom — is to arrest criminals. However, in expecting the police to enforce the law, it is apparent that citizens also have certain expectations regarding whom the law should be enforced against. In other words, there may be a problem in defining just who is a criminal and who should be arrested. Illegal acts by the individual himself, his relatives or friends (unless it involves a very serious crime) are typically viewed as problems that ought to be dealt with by the private control system. The offenders whom most citizens want arrested are probably the perpetrators of stranger-to-stranger crimes or those whose offenses are clearly too serious to be handled by the private control system.

Although citizens want the police to make arrests, they are reluctant to give them extraordinary powers to do so. For example, the majority of respondents in one survey disapproved of allowing the police to stop and search anybody on suspicion, or of allowing the police to tap the telephone of anyone they suspected or of allowing them to search a home without a warrant.[20] In spite of expecting a great deal from the police, the public continues to view them with reservation, especially in matters concerning the use of force.[21] This seems to indicate that the public wants the police to enforce the law but at the same time it does not wish to confer too much authority upon them.

Perhaps a better way to see what the public expects of the police is to look at what the public *actually* asks them to do. Research has consistently disclosed that most calls to the police ask for some kind of *service*.[22] These typically involve situations in which the police are *not* expected to make an arrest, but rather to provide some kind of assistance — often nothing more than just listening and offering advice. What problems result in these calls for service? Bittner says they are incidents which involve *"something-that-ought-not-to-be-happening-and-about-which-someone-had-better-do-something-now."*[23] In other words, many citizens expect the police to help them with their safety needs, as Maslow would say, but not necessarily by invoking the criminal justice process. This is not a new development; according to Whitehouse,

> The police of yesterday performed a variety of health, welfare, and other social service functions. These duties were considered commonplace and essential ... The police officer's dual function of performing law enforcement duties and peacekeeping community services has apparently been present as long as there have been municipal police departments.[24]

Another key question with respect to citizen expectations is *"Who expects what?"* There are probably some very major class distinctions to be made in answering this question. For example, it is highly likely that middle and upper class people are apt to call the police for *crime* related problems, whereas lower class people are more likely to call the police for both crime and *service* related problems. The reason for this is that middle and upper class people are much more concerned about their public reputations and are much more likely to keep family problems private; in addition, they are aware of the services available through such professionals as attorneys, psychologists, marriage counselors and so on, and are more likely to be able to afford those services. Middle and upper class people are more likely to see the police as *crime specialists* and to use them in that capacity. Lower class people typically have fewer coping resources and cannot afford specialized professional help for personal and family problems. They are much more likely to call the police for assistance in minor, routine, or even family problems. The police, after all, are "free" and are available at any time of the day or night.

An interesting insight into citizen calls for police assistance emerged from a study conducted in Kansas City, Missouri. This study was done to assess the value of rapid police response, and it sought to analyse the relationship between police response time to calls and such outcomes as arrests made, witnesses identified, citizen satisfaction and to identify problems or patterns in citizen reporting of crimes or requests for police assistance.[25] The target area for this study was one in which it was expected there would be many calls concerning serious (Part I) crimes. The final sample of calls studied consisted of 949 calls to the police. By type of crime they were categorized as follows: 10 rapes, 127 robberies, 84 aggravated assaults, 352 burglaries, 297 larcency-thefts, and 79 motor vehicle thefts.

What was enlightening was that in many of these cases there was a significant delay in reporting even serious crimes to the police. It was discovered that in 448 of the cases (47.7 percent), the person reporting the crime talked to someone else first. In 10.3 percent of the cases the complainant either telephoned someone else first or received a call from someone else before calling the police. Of course, the classic case of delaying a report to the police in a serious crime was the Kitty Genovese case. For more than an hour in the early morning hours of March 14, 1964, a killer stalked and repeatedly stabbed the 28-year old woman as she screamed for help. At least 38 people saw and heard the attack; after the woman was dead, one of them called the police — who arrived less than two minutes after receiving the call. Sometimes it is hard to tell just what the public expects from the police. Consider the following news item.

> Nashville, Tenn. (AP) Two children found beaten early Thursday begged for food and went without coats and shoes during the winter, neighbors said Friday. Rhonda Hyde, 4, was listed in critical condition in Hubbard Hospital where doctors said she had a 50-50 chance of survival. Her sister, Ruby Hyde, 12, was in fair condition.
>
> James Kennedy, 64, was jailed on two counts of child abuse in lieu of $5,000 bond. The charges carry maximum sentences

of 11 months, 29 days in jail and $1,000 fines.

Neighbors said the children frequently were seen at a market, buying cigarettes for Kennedy's wife and begging for food. "You should have seen Ruby Jean two months ago — her nose was where her jaw should have been," Margaret Hall, owner of the market, said. "She was scared to death, and told me to please not tell anybody that she was being beaten. She hadn't been to school in two years."

Mrs. Hall said she never reported the matter to authorities because she didn't want to have to go to court and miss work.

The police said the two girls were abandoned by their mother three years ago and have lived since then with Kennedy and his wife. Police Major George Currey said the younger girl had lacerations so deep that bones were visible. "I knew it was going to be bad when I came in and saw some of the resident doctors and nurses crying," he said.

Rhonda also had a hole in her right hip, a missing toe, and numerous sores, the police said.

Perceptions And Expectations Of The Courts The courts are not nearly as visible to the average citizen as the police; moreover, the courts are governed by a different set of rules. Even if a citizen visits the courts, he is not likely to understand all of what is going on or why. As a result, familiarity with the courts — federal, state, and local — is low. In a study commissioned by the National Center for State Courts, it was disclosed that "three out of four claim that they know very little or nothing at all about state and local courts. This *self-perception* of low knowledge is matched by a low level of correct actual knowledge."[26] The study discovered that the public is misinformed about many topics related to court jurisdiction, operation, and procedure and illustrated this by giving the following examples:

—72% incorrectly believe that the U.S. Supreme Court can review and reverse any decision made by a state Court.

—37% incorrectly think it is the responsibility of a person accused of a crime to prove his innocence.

—30% incorrectly believe that a district attorney's job is to defend an accused criminal who cannot afford a lawyer.[27]

—Perhaps the most compelling specific gap in knowledge relates to rights. Blacks, Hispanics, and the poor are often unaware that a person is innocent until proven guilty.[28]

The relative "invisibility" of the courts has had three important consequences:

1. By and large, the public is unable to distinguish one court from another.

2. Recent court reforms have gone largely unnoticed by the public; and,

3. Evaluation of the courts are more favorable than they would be if more people knew about them; the higher a person's familiarity/knowledge, the more likely he is to have an unfavorable attitude toward the courts![29]

In the matter of actual experience with the courts, only about 17 percent of all Americans have been defendants in a case — and about half of those cases involved minor matters (traffic cases, minor civil or criminal matters, or juvenile cases). A person's reaction to the courts seems to be affected by three factors: (1) the type of case; (2) the role played — victim, witness, defendant, juror; and (3) the outcome of the case. In general, those involved in civil cases tend to have more favorable evaluations of the courts than those whose experience was in criminal cases; juvenile cases produced the highest levels of dissatisfaction.[30]

G.K. Chesterson, in an essay entitled "The Twelve Men," described a jury trial through the eyes of a layman, and had this to say:

> And the horrible thing about all legal officials, even the best, about all judges, magistrates, barristers, detectives, and policemen, is not that they are wicked (some of them are good), not that they are stupid (some of them are quite intelligent); it is simply that they have gotten used to it. Strictly, they do not see the prisoner in the dock; all they see is the usual man in the usual place. They do not see the awful court of judgement; they see only their own workshop.[31]

Worse yet, the public neither sees nor understands this workshop, and the nation's courts are beset with problems.[32] Thirty-seven percent of the public reports low confidence in the courts (48 percent of the general public and 71 percent of community leaders perceive a moderate to great need for court reform).[33] In a survey conducted for the American Bar Foundation, 57 percent of the respondents agreed (33 percent strongly and 24 percent slightly) with the statement that the legal system favors the rich and powerful over everyone else, although 85 percent agreed that, if accused, they would get a fair trial.[34]

Thus, it is clear that citizen perceptions of the courts are cloudy and are based on inadequate knowledge. Unlike the police, the courts do not deal with citizens at the "street level" nor do they communicate with them informally. The courts are a specialized arena in which the game of justice is played out according to lawyers' rules, and the non-lawyer is little more than an "incidental" to this process.

Citizens in general are not well-informed about the courts and many would like to see significant reform. But just exactly *what* do citizens expect of the courts? According to the National Center for State Courts, the public has three expectations: (1) the protection of society; (2) equality and fairness; and, (3) quality performance (responsiveness, accessibility, and competence).[35]

The expectation that the courts should *protect society* underscores the public's fear of crime. The perceived inability of the courts to reduce crime rates was regarded as the most serious of all the problems studied by the National Center for State Courts.[36] This concern was shared by rich and poor, black and white alike. Another indicator of the feeling that the courts were not doing enough to protect society was the reported view that sentences are not tough enough.[37] The National Center for State Courts' findings were supported by a number of other sources. For example, data from the National Opinion Research Center indicate that a substantial majority of citizens (between 75 and 80 percent, both white and nonwhite) agreed that the courts do *not* deal harshly enough with criminals.[38] A Harris survey conducted in 1977 found that 77 percent of its respondents felt that "generally, the courts have been too lenient" in dealing with criminals.[39]

As to the issue of *equality* and *fairness*, citizens have some very explicit expectations. For one thing, most people think there are some factors which ought *not* to bear on court processes (but which they feel never the less *do* have an influence). These include political considerations, affluence or poverty, and race.[40]

It appears, however, that most citizens believe the courts are doing a better job of being fair than of protecting society, although Blacks and the poor are still concerned about the fairness of the courts.[41] The National Center for State Courts has noted that "...the problem with courts, people say, is *not* that they are grossly unfair or inequitable. Rather, despite their reasonably sound performance on this count, courts are not fair or equitable enough."[42]

With respect to *quality performance*, the National Center for State Courts states that there are four indications of public concern about the quality of court performance: *delay, cost, lawyers,* and *judges.* On the issue of delay, about one third of the American public believes that there is too much time spent between the time of a person's arrest and when he is brought to trial. About the same proportion of the public believes that court expense is a major problem. The problem of cost is also the basic complaint against lawyers: 44 percent believe they are too expensive. Another concern many people have about lawyers is that they feel lawyers are more interested in themselves than their clients (nothing new about this: Shakespeare said, "Adversaries in law strive mightily, but eat and drink as friends"). Finally, on the issue of judges, the public's principal concern is that there simply are not enough of them. People tend to have a basic respect for judges — although that esteem *is* somewhat guarded.[43]

An important finding raised in the National Center For State Courts' study was that there is an incongruence of opinion among judges, lawyers, community leaders, and the public, with differences of opinion between judges and the public the most pronounced. Community leaders' views approximate those of the public and lawyers' attitudes, although closer to those of judges, represent sort of a middle ground. These gaps are persistent, regardless of issue.[44]

The basic question is this: who "owns" the courts — the people or the legal profession? Are the courts *instruments* for justice and equity, or are they *institutions* which enable those in the legal profession to earn a living? The answer is probably that the courts are a combination of both, and whether the courts are an institution or an instrument in any given case depends on the circumstances of the case itself as much as anything else. It should also be noted that courts are not static institutions; they *do* change over time, and they *do* become more responsive to consumer needs. Indeed, American courts have been shaped and continue to be shaped by a wide range of social movements, including such major areas as environmental litigation, consumer protection, civil rights, and social welfare.[45]

Perceptions And Expectations Of Corrections If citizens have a limited opportunity to view the courts, they have almost *no* opportunity to look at corrections. The incarceration of offenders, whether in a county jail or a state prison, is hidden from public view. This is done primarily for security/custody reasons, but it does have the effect of denying the public the opportunity to see what happens within correctional systems. In fairness, however, it should be pointed out that very few people would want to "look", even if they had the chance. What the public does know of corrections, it learns through the news and entertainment media.[46] The public did become more aware of corrections — especially prisons — in the 1960's and 1970's as a result of the publicity given to riots in prisons, the Black Power movement, and increased concern over the issue of prisoner's rights.[47] In spite of coverage of corrections by the media, the public's perceptions of prisons remain vague and incomplete. Perhaps most people prefer *not* to think about jails, prisons, and criminal offenders; that could certainly account for what has been termed our "callous neglect (which) has produced a debacle of major proportions in the nation's misguided and under-funded correctional efforts."[48]

If citizen *perceptions* of corrections are vague, the same can hardly be said of their *expectations*. People expect corrections to accomplish three objectives:

1. To protect the public.
2. To punish criminals.
3. To rehabilitate offenders.

Protecting the public is supposed to be accomplished by (1) *incapacitating* criminals; that is, by keeping them locked away; and (2) through deterrence, a process whereby in theory offenders are prevented from repeating their crimes and through which non-offenders are pursuaded to *remain* non-offenders. This expectation is both basic and reasonable: society wants and expects to be protected from those who would harm them. The problem arises in trying to figure out the best ways of accomplishing this objective. Traditionally, *punishment* has been seen as the answer. Offenders are punished for their crimes by having their liberty restricted, either through actual confinement or through some kind of community-based corrections. This punishment is intended to serve as a liability which offsets the benefits of the crime; thus, the person being punished is given a taste of the "cost" of his deviance and is supposed to logically conclude that more crime would be counterproductive ("special deterrence"). Non-offenders are supposed to be deterred by seeing offenders being caught and punished ("general deterrence"). Punishment also satisfies a darker side of the human psyche: the wish for retribution. Quite obviously, "being good" is not as much fun as "being bad," but most people accept their social responsibilities and behave in the normative fashion. Many people resent seeing others deviate and simply want them punished for it. Moreover, if punishment were idiosyncratic — that is, varied from offense to offense or from offender to offender — then in some cases the retribution might be disproportionate to the crime. Retribution should be consistent and fair and this is one reason why state-inflicted punishment is regulated by the criminal justice system rather than by victims. There are very strong public sentiments regarding the whole matter of corrections; for example, a priest writing in a national magazine made the following observations (based on his experiences with parishoners who had suffered at the hands of criminals):

We must listen to the experts who tell us that most crimes are committed by persistent offenders. And when a persistent violent offender is convicted, he must be contained like nuclear waste, so that his lethal influence will stop. Our society needs swift and certain justice for violent criminals and their prompt and enduring containment. Now the criminal gets a lottery ticket in the justice casino; and the odds, according to statistics, are all in his favor. Our society needs a terrifying sentence incumbent on the possession of a gun or knife in the commission of a crime. For deterrence, yes; but more to contain the violent criminal and to protect others against his repeated violence. Too strong? Too expensive to build prisons? Talk to the man who lost an eye, the blind girl tearfully seeking a safe residence. See the bodies of the elderly who have been slain. Sense the fear of people on the streets and in the elevators.[49]

The public is also quite aware of the fact that most people who *are* locked up eventually get out, and they expect corrections to tame them and to make them useful members of society. In other words, corrections is also supposed to *rehabilitate* offenders. This is supposed to be done through a wide variety of approaches: vocational training; educational programs; psychological treatment; alcohol and drug counseling; and through early release or community-based correctional programs which place offenders in jobs and keep them under close supervision.

The one issue which remains strong among members of the public, however, is the issue of punishment. There seems to be a general sentiment that the punishments meted out to criminals are *not harsh enough*. According to the Roper Public Opinion Research Center, 83 percent of a national sample indicated that they did not think the courts dealt harshly enough with criminals; this feeling cut across all lines and was the same, regardless of the age, sex, race, income, education, religion, politics, or geographic location of the respondent.[50] Americans also favor capital punishment, and in some cases, favor it very strongly.[51] A substantial number of people *do* feel that capital punishment deters crime.

It is clear that many people are afraid of crime (however they define it); that they want criminals, at least those criminals who are not acquaintances or relatives, caught and punished; and, in some cases, they want very harsh punishments. The public is *not* clear about the mechanics of how this is done, and does not seem to care, as long as the procedures used are fair, equitable, and efficient!

The Problem of Plurality

How people perceive the criminal justice system and what they expect of it can and does vary according to individual frames of refernce. To the poor and ignorant, the system may seem capricious and frightening. Since they do not understand the rules of the system or those of its subcomponents, they may assume that there *are no* rules or they may believe that the rules are designed to snare the weak and the poor. This is by no means a new sentiment: Anacharisis said, "The written laws are just like spiders' webbs; the small and feeble may be caught and entangled in them, but the rich and the mighty can force their way through, and despise them." There is, unfortunately, some very real truth to this fear. As Blumberg has stated, "To ignore the differential allocations of power in the American social structure as it permeates and affects all institutional arrangements, including criminal justice, would be naive and irresponsible."[52] This is an important point, because the poor and the inadequately educated are the very people who have the most frequent contact with the system and whom the system *needs* as advocates and supporters. The plurality of our society has placed a disproportionate exposure of the criminal justice system on the levels of society which understand it the least.

At this time it might be good to point out the fact that there is a relationship between *perception* and one's *needs*. In fact, perception is itself *instrumental* to other needs. In one classic experiment, for example, research subjects were shown vague pictures that might or might not suggest food. Hungry subjects identified the pictures as food-related significantly more often than did subjects who were not hungry. In addition, food words were selected from a list of words which contained both food-words and non-food words by hungry subjects more frequently than they were selected by subjects who had just eaten.[53] People do perceive what they *need* to perceive. What if their needs are not simply basic needs (e.g., hunger) but are higher order needs? What about safety needs? How will a person perceive a social institution — such as the police — in relation to his needs? If a person is ill-educated and insecure, will he see the police as friendly helpers and guardians of the public welfare? Probably not. Also, by perceiving the criminal justice system as a threat, an individual can develop countermeasures against that threat: non-cooperation; avoidance; passive aggression; and the structuring of peer approval through selective differential association.

Why do many Blacks and Hispanics so persistently view the criminal justice system as discriminating against them as a group? Could it be that the experiences of *past generations* have conditioned the present generation to see the system as discriminatory *by its very nature?* If so, is this an adaptive *defense* mechanism? These are by no means flippant or easy questions; Davies has pointed out that "our associations with people has much to do with the style and content of all our perceptions and actions..."[54] He also notes that in politics we tend to organize our perceptions in three ways. First, there is a tendency toward completeness and simplicity, and this means that people both seek out and accept simple, categorical solutions to complex problems. Second, people tend to categorize and classify things into coherent and consistent entities. Finally, there is a strong tendency to persist in established views.[55] This supports the contention that people tend to organize their perceptions around what they *need* to perceive, and those needs reflect the normative value structure and history of the individual's reference group. This also means that there are at least as many criminal justice systems as there are groups with different perceptions of them. Although there *is* a great deal of overlap in needs and perceptions within our society, our pluralistic structure guarantees differences as well. It is out of this conflict in perception among the various groups that we both cement consensus and assure dissent.

The Role Of The Media In Citizen Perceptions The average person's most probable contact with the criminal justice system is likely to be through the entertainment media including the "news". Most of us are certainly more likely to see a crime on television or at the movies than "in the flesh." People who will never see the inside of a prison or a courtroom become spectators to prison and court dramas in the comfort of their own living rooms. How do people react to these vicarious experiences? Research conducted at the Annenberg School of Communications of the University of Pennsylvania indicates that many viewers accept what they see on television as being representative of the "real world."[56]

If people believe what they see in the entertainment media, just how accurate is what they see? According to Altheide and Snow, the media have a particular perspective which "...consists of a set of norms or criteria for presenting and evaluating behavior."[57] The entertainment media employ a number of specific elements, including behavior that is extraordinary; a distinct timing of interactions; and a set of "ideal" norms. The result has become what has been called a "pseudo event"; a creation that "not only appears believable, but is attributed more importance than it deserves."[58] To put this more plainly:

> Television takes topical subjects and presents them through the entertainment perspective and formats ... In doing so, certain aspects of the way in which the subject is presented are emphasized over others; thus, the subject is significantly altered. For example, in dealing with the victim of a crime, television programs emphasize the aspects of police work that are entertaining.[59]

For many people, television *is* reality. As Littlejohn noted, "TV has become a reality for many people because it is more tolerable than any other. Real reality is too impossibly complex to deal with..."[60] If the point of interface between the public and the criminal justice system is the entertainment media, then there is a serious threat that misinformation will be received and reinforced. Stereotypes may be played upon and perpetuated, and totally unrealistic scenarios may be presented to the public as representations of fact. The constant reporting of relatively rare events, such as murders (especially stranger-to-stranger murders) can heighten an already unrealistic public fear of crime and may create corresponding expectations that a TV-like criminal justice system will send forth hordes of inspectors, lieutenants (and even chiefs!) to solve these crimes within 30, 60, or 90 minutes! People may expect brilliant trial lawyers who can win seemingly impossible cases only to be shocked by the banal reality of courts, should they ever find themselves in a *typical* courtroom. Proper public support of the criminal justice system requires a realistic understanding of what that system is and what it does. Without support, the system cannot function optimally, and the entertainment media offers a view of the system which is both unrealistic — and insupportable.

Contradictions In The Criminal Justice System

In Charles Dickens' classic *Bleak House* there is a bizzare character by the name of Krook, a junk-peddler who constantly searches for a particular piece of paper. The paper he is looking for is the key to a major law suit (which forms the basis of the book). Unfortunately, Krook can't read, so he can't tell if a given piece of paper is the one for which he is hunting. On top of that, he won't let anyone teach him to read because he doesn't trust anyone! Thus, although Krook knows what he needs, all of his efforts are counterproductive.

Fortunately, the criminal justice system is not quite as bizzare as Krook, but it *does* have a large number of contradictions, inconsistencies, and mutually incompatible objectives. These collective contradictions produce an enormous amount of difficulty for the system; yet it is virtually *impossible* to weed out many of these contradictions. In some cases they have taken on an institutional character in their own right, and as such constitute a part of the "sunken cost" of criminal justice in America.

One of the most fundamental contradictions is between the desire for "criminal justice," which is an indivisible public good, and the incredible range of self-interests which motivate both individuals and organizations. Not all self-interest is counterproductive; in fact, many people achieve their goals in life (including power, prestige, and income) by doing things that advance the common good. Others, quite obviously, work solely for their own self-interest, regardless of the costs to society. Institutions have self-interests, and many of their actions are designed to advance those interests rather than to do what the institution was created to do in the first place. This is a fundamental and basic contradiction and it will be seen again and again as we look at both people and their settings.

Basic psychological needs may themselves create contradictions that involve the criminal justice system. For example, the need for *achievement* may lead a person to go beyond the legitimate restrictions established by society, just as the need for *autonomy* may cause a person to reject proper authority and convention. In fact, an examination of psychological needs points to an interesting contradiction in that many of these needs are polar extremes on a continuum. For example, *affiliation* and *autonomy* contradict one another, as do the needs to *defer* and be *aggressive*. All people have such contradictory needs and they take on varying degrees of potency, depending on the specific situation. In other words, specific needs arise under specific circumstances. As they are called forth they push the others into the background, only to be pushed back themselves as circumstances change and new needs become prepotent. We recognize these shifts in our many moods and in our changing feelings. Over time, most of us learn the proper responses to our needs; indeed, we learn to respond through our socialization process.

At a more sociological level, we have seen that there is a wide range in the definitions of "proper" conduct, and this makes a consistent definition of *deviance* very difficult. This in turn produces inconsistencies and contradictions which then require the existence of both private and public control systems to mediate those differences. However, there is conflict between the private and public control systems! Although the two complement one another, they may still be pitted against one another. For example, some parents (or other relatives) may go to great — and expensive — lengths to shield their children from the public control system. Lawyers might be hired, psychologists employed, or the help of other professionals sought in order to avoid having to face the operations of the public control system. The cases of Patty Hearst and John W. Hinckley, Jr. are excellent examples.

Crime itself is beset with conflicts and contradictions, not the least of which is the difference between what crime *really* is and what people *think* it is. The key to understanding the real, *practical* meaning of crime is to be found in the relationship between the event and its participants — not in what the laws say, and that is a contradiction! The "administration" of justice is supposed to be "blind" to such subjective factors, and for this reason the law is as unrealistic as the perceptions of those to whom it is supposed to apply! These kinds of contradictions cannot be eliminated or even significantly altered. Although they *are* a large part of the sunken cost of the system, that certainly does not mean that we should not try to understand the role they play.

A major contradiction is in the very concept of a criminal justice "system." The idea grew out of the systems approach which dates from the 1920s.[61] The idea took on significance in the 1960's, especially in defense planning, where highly complex engineering and production requirements had to be programmed so that each element fell into place just when and where it was supposed to. It became rather fashionable in the 1960's to look at the police, the courts, and corrections as integrated components of a "system" of criminal justice. In this scheme of things one agency's *output* became another's *input* and each was seen as depending on and complementing the other. The approach obviously makes good sense, and it assumes that each of the major components has a set of common objectives. It is an approach which emphasizes *instrumental* and *rational* relationships. However, it did not give adequate consideration to *institutional* and *irrational* factors, most of which are based on the application of self-interest rather than purely public goals.

Each component of the criminal justice system is an independent institution and each has its own internal goals. Some of these internal goals *do* facilitate interaction with the other agencies in the system — but many do not. To a certain extent, the police, courts, and corrections are *closed systems* which don't depend on the others so much as they *use* them for their own purposes. This quite naturally produces tremendous conflict among the agencies and often causes the several elements of the system to accuse one another of being structurally unsound and administratively inept. The police complain about what the courts do with the criminals that are sent to them, and the courts complain about the inadequacy and unresponsiveness of the police and both agree that the prisons are a mess. The prisons say they do the best with what they are sent, and so it goes.

Even within the components of the system we find contradiction and confusion. The police, for example, see their primary task as being *law enforcement* when in reality most of what they do is to provide order maintenance. Individual officers are willing to put up with what their job is really all about in order to perpetuate the myth that their job really is what it *is not*, at least what it isn't 80 - 90 percent of the time. Police officers often refer to routine service calls as "garbage calls" and many strive to get into assignments which allow them to do more "real" police work (hence many of them request assignment to such units as tactical squads, the detective division, or traffic). On top of that, the police are superbly trained to do what they are called upon to do the least often while they are poorly trained, equipped, or supported to perform those tasks for which they are most frequently summoned.[62]

Organizationally, many police departments continue to be organized and managed by people who see themselves as high-ranking police officers rather than as managers of highly complex and expensive public enterprises. These organizational and administrative contradictions have produced police agencies which are at best only marginally effective — although they may be *very* efficient.

No less is true of the courts. Virtually all Americans agree that an accused person has a right to trial by his peers — although *very few* ever receive such a trial. The overwhelming majority of people convicted of crimes are convicted on the basis of their own plea of guilty, which was given in consideration for some kind of judicial payoff (e.g., a reduced charge, a probated sentence, a reduction in the number of charges, etc.). Most officers of the court — judges, prosecutors, defense attorneys — do their best to *minimize* the actual amount of time they have to spend in court. Although courts are probably *the* symbol of justice, many (if not most or even all) of them operate on the basis of expediency, convenience, or time-weary and expensive tradition. Even in a litigated case, contradictions arise. The courts hold the work of the police against complex legal standards, but the police (who are not lawyers) must make what they consider to be the best decision at the time, often under very difficult or ambiguous circumstances. Of course, the police *do* make mistakes, and when they do, the courts neither train them nor punish them. What happens? As Justice Cardozo said, "The criminal is to go free because the constable blundered."[63] Many believe that this contradicts the goal of justice.

Lawyers are by no means exempt. They are the gate-keepers of justice, for the courtroom is the lawyer's domain. Yet the actual *practice* of lawyers has produced some of the bitterest criticism of the entire system:

> The truth about the legal profession contradicts the image of Daniel Webster selflessly trying to save the Union or Abraham Lincoln, the country lawyer who helps all comers at

modest fees. In fact, most lawyers have been rather singularly interested in getting as high an income as possible, and the profession as a whole sells its services to the highest bidder.[64]

The contradictions within corrections are no less discomforting. Prisons may protect those on the *outside*, but they certainly don't protect those on the *inside*: prisons are very dangerous places. Moreover, what happens when an offender is released? Ours has not proven to be a forgiving society; and often prisoners are barred from many occupations; this sometimes forces them back into crime.[65] There is a large and growing body of evidence which suggests that programs of rehabilitation don't work, and American prison sentences tend to be among the harshest in the western world — yet the public clearly wants even *harsher* sentences! Criminals wind up in the arms of correctional facilities because they violated the normative order of their communities, yet we deal with them by putting them in totally abnormal and unrealistic communities (prisons) — and expect them to come out better people! And when this whole process doesn't work, we insist on even more of it! Finally, regardless of the social philosophies behind corrections, the *reality* of custodial facilities is based on *custody* and *security*.[66] Everything else is secondary. This clearly contradicts the rhetoric of rehabilitation.

These inconsistencies and contradictions merely scratch the surface, and will be dealt with in greater detail in subsequent chapters. The main point is that both the public and private control systems are beset with problems and dilemmas, many of which cannot be resolved. Each problem area contributes to the complexity of trying to assure justice for all in a pluralistic society, and all of them generate problems of interface.

Public Responsibility

The public control system is an important part of our society. In spite of the contradictions and inconsistencies which have been mentioned, the system is still an essential ingredient in the establishment and maintenance of a safe and democratic social order. The system should recognize the diversity of the total society it serves and should constantly strive to remain both flexible and *truly* instrumental — at least as much as possible. However, in the final analysis, the system will be essentially a *human* organization. It will be composed of people in certain roles dealing with other people in different roles. This calls for a reciprocal relationship in which all parties must be willing to make a cooperative effort. The prestigious Committee for Economic Development correctly noted that "The Declaration of Independence advanced the proposition that governments derive their just powers from the consent of the governed. But great numbers of Americans do not now consent, at least

121

to many of their laws nor to the manner of their enforcement."[67] They go on to suggest that criminal codes must be made to conform to the prevailing public consensus on what conduct should be forbidden by law and on what the most appropriate penalties ought to be. They also call for nondiscriminatory, fair, and equitable enforcement of the law. Finally, they urge businessmen, as community leaders, to recognize their own responsibility to observe the law and to offer support to the criminal justice system.[68]

The system requires far more than simple support. It requires nothing less than a willingness on the part of all segments of society to accept the rule of law and to *insist* that the law be fair in its intention and that it be administered with intelligence, sensitivity, and care. Citizens must make themselves aware of the dual responsibilities which both they and the "system" enjoy. To the extent that citizens abandon their own responsibilities, they make it difficult for the system to function and create a very real risk that the system will get more power than it should. Citizens should recognize the fact that *primary crime prevention* is one of the most basic responsibilities of the *private* control system — not of the police or the courts. Families, churches, and schools must accept their responsibility and develop more effective strategies for instilling positive values in their members; they can no longer afford to rely on using the criminal justice system as a threat to ensure proper behavior on the part of children. In fact, the existence of the public control system represents at least a partial *failure* of the private control system.

There is evidence that the public is in fact doing this. For one thing, there has been a dramatic growth in tolerance during the last quarter century: "One of the most dramatic trends in the 44-year history of the Gallup Poll has been the growth in tolerance toward persons of different religions and races.[69] People are showing a very global tolerance, and the Gallup people believe that one of the key factors in the growth of racial and religious tolerance in the United States has been the increase in the proportion of the population with a college education which has more than tripled since the Gallup Poll was founded in 1935.[70] This tolerance has been especially strong in the area of race relations. According to the Gallup Poll, at the time of the 1963 demonstration when Blacks from all around the country converged on Washington, D.C., nearly half of White Americans (45 percent) were "ready to pack the moving van and leave if a Black family moved in next door."[71] Today, that figure has dropped to just 13 percent. There are, however, still differing perceptions:

> About three Whites in every four, 73 percent, think Blacks have the same opportunity as members of their own race to get

any job for which they are qualified .... However, only 38 percent of Blacks, nationwide, share this view .... Other Gallup Polls have shown that the last 15 years have been a time of tremendous improvement for Blacks in terms of their satisfaction with the basic circumstances of life, including income, jobs, and their children's education. Yet the gap between Whites and Blacks is still a wide one.[72]

The important point is that society does seem to be moving more toward a fundamental and fair consensus. It is probably safe to assume that this positive shift has resulted at least in part from the demands made by many segments of the public for improvements in the delivery of criminal justice. Although some of those demands have taken violent and distasteful forms, the *outcome* seems to be a better criminal justice system and a more unified population. If this is true, then it is important for *all* citizens to recognize the fact that they must do the best job they can within the private control system and to expect the public control system to do *its* best.

Summary

"Criminal justice" is everyone's responsibility, but the actual duties of operating a criminal justice system are carried out by relatively few; however, those who are employed full-time within the criminal justice system still depend on all others in society for their continuing support. Without that support, the system cannot function. In addition, the public is the *consumer* of criminal justice and as such has many perceptions and expectations of the system. These perceptions and expectations play a major role in determining the kind of support they will give; thus, an understanding of the consumer's perspective is important to those who work within the system.

People's perceptions and expectations are based in part on their *needs*, both social and psychological. These needs can be highly complex and even contradictory; yet these needs shape behavior. The behaviors which arise out of individual and collective needs can easily come into conflict with the law and its agencies. The criminal justice system is supposed to assist in moderating these conflicts and this is done in four major ways. First, the criminal justice system is supposed to *control crime*. Its second major task is to provide *order maintenance*. Third, it is supposed to *provide aid and assistance* to those who are having problems and don't know what to do. Finally, the criminal justice system is expected to help *prevent crime*. The criminal justice system attempts to fulfill these mandates through the actions of its principal agencies: the police, the courts, and corrections.

The public, as consumers of criminal justice, perceive the operations of these agencies and expresses certain expectations of them. The public, which has a substantial fear of crime expects the system to deal with the crime problem; however, there is some reason to believe that the public fear of crime is not as realistic as it is real. The police are expected to deal with the problem of crime through the law enforcement process, but the public has contradictory expectations of the police. Although most people do not see crime as being the fault of the police, neither do most of them see the police as part of the solution to the problem, even though they expect them to enforce the law. Public perceptions of the police are very favorable, especially among that segment of the population which has the least to do with them. There is a deep suspicion among Blacks that the police discriminate in their work, that the entire criminal justice system is discriminatory, although there is probably much less of a basis for such a belief than there has been in past generations. The public likewise is not consistent in how it expects the police to enforce the law and is generally unwilling to give them extraordinary powers to do so. At a very practical level, the public expects the police to help them when they have problems and they see the law enforcement aspect as being only one part of what the police are supposed to do.

Citizens have a very limited opportunity to observe the courts, and the public's knowledge of the courts is generally inadequate. The courts are generally held in lower esteem by the public than are the police. Although most people feel they could get a fair trial, most still believe the courts favor the rich and powerful. However, the public does expect the courts to protect society, to be fair, and to operate efficiently. The biggest failing on the part of the courts, according to many citizens, is that they are not harsh enough on criminals.

The public has virtually no opportunity to observe correctional systems. In spite of that, the public does have very explicit expectations of corrections. They expect correctional systems to protect society, to punish offenders, and to rehabilitate criminals.

Public perceptions and expectations may vary considerably according to such variables as income, education, occupation and class/status. Middle and upper class people are much more likely to see the police, for example, as crime specialists whereas lower class people not only view them as crime specialists but also look to them for non-criminal services as well. Public perceptions of the criminal justice system are also shaped by the entertainment media, and this can have considerable importance in the development of misperceptions and unrealistic expectations!

The entire criminal justice system is plagued with inconsistencies and contradictions which constitute part of the "sunken cost" of the system. Many of these contradictions are based on conflicts between the public interest and the self-interests of those who demand (and those who provide) criminal justice services. Some of the contradictions arise from the basic psychological needs shared by all people and the means by which society meets those needs. For example, definitions of crime and deviance are themselves often contradictory and inconsistent, as are the techniques for dealing with them. Criminal justice agencies may be part of a bigger justice system, but they still tend to be relatively closed systems which operate on the basis of institutional self-interests.

The effective operation of any criminal justice system requires the full and cooperative efforts of all citizens and this means the general public must not only be aware of its role, but it must be willing to play that role as well. The public cannot be a passive consumer of criminal justice, because the public shapes the policy environment which determines which services will be provided to what groups under what circumstances.

Discussion Questions

1. Give some examples of how conflicting psychological needs can bring an individual into conflict with the law.

2. Why are citizen perceptions of the goals of the criminal justice system so important?

3. Why are so many citizens willing to rate neighborhoods other than their own as being more dangerous?

4. Why is the widespread fear of crime unrealistic, and what impact does this fear of crime have on citizen expectations of the criminal justice system?

5. How would you distinguish between crimes people are likely to see as being *personal* rather than *public*?

6. Most of the calls the police receive are service calls. Do you think if another (non-police) agency were available to handle such service calls the public would use them — or would they still call the police?

7. Exactly why do citizens have such a limited perception of the courts? Is this really bad?

8. Why do you think the public wants harsher punishments for criminals? Is this desire sensible or do you think it is counterproductive? Why?

9. How does the entertainment media distort public perceptions of crime and the criminal justice system?

10. How are contradictions "built into" the criminal justice system?

Glossary

ACQUITTAL   The decision by a judge or jury that a defendant is not guilty of a crime with which he has been charged.

ADJUDICATION   A judgment or decision.

ALLEGATION   An assertion made in a legal proceeding.

APPEAL   An application to a higher court to correct or modify the judgement of a lower court.

ARRAIGNMENT   The post-indictment stage at which the defendant is brought before trial court, hears the charges in the indictment, and is asked to enter a plea.

CHARGE   (1) The instructions given by the court to a jury at the close of a trial as to the law which should be used in reaching a verdict. (2) An allegation accusing a person of a crime.

CIRCUIT COURT   Various courts in different jurisdictions which are inferior to supreme courts. Some of them are intermediate appellate courts and some of them are trial courts.

CITY ATTORNEY   The legal officer of a municipality. The city attorney is often the prosecutor in cases involving violation of city ordinances.

CONVICTION   A decision by a judge or a jury that a defendant is guilty of the allegations made against him.

CORPORATION   An artificial person composed of individuals. It usually has a corporate name and a perpetual duration. Sometimes its duration is for a fixed term of years. A corporation substitutes for the individuals who compose it and limits their personal liability.

COUNTY ATTORNEY   The legal officer of a county. The county attorney is often the prosecutor in cases involving violation of county ordinances.

DISTRICT ATTORNEY   A State officer who is the prosecutor within a given judicial district. The district attorney is responsible for prosecuting all crimes against the state which are committed within his judicial district.

DIVERSION   Giving offenders a break by not making a formal arrest when the circumstances justify doing so, or by suspending prosecution for persons who have been arrested so they might be given the opportunity to receive more appropriate treatment. In general, a more lenient, treatment-oriented administrative procedure for handling and disposing of criminal cases without resorting to formal prosecution.

FELONY   A crime punishable by death or incarceration in a state correctional institution for a term of greater than one year.

INDICTMENT   The decision by a Grand Jury that there is probable cause to arraign a defendant on one or more criminal charges. Such a decision takes the form of a "true bill" which is filed with the trial court.

JUDICIAL DISTRICT   A geographic area within a state within which the state's judicial functions are discharged. Each judicial district has its own prosecutor (district attorney) as well as its own civil and criminal courts.

JURISDICTION   The court's legal authority to preside over a case or to decide an issue at law. Also, the geographic area within which police agencies are empowered to act.

LITIGATION   A lawsuit; a contest in court.

MUNICIPALITY   A city. The term is usually used when refering to cities which are incorporated.

NOLLE PROSEQUI (NOL PROS)   The declaration by a prosecutor that he will proceed no further with a case; declining to prosecute.

ORDINANCE   A law, statute, or legislative enactment particularly by a city or county government. Ordinances which impose criminal sanctions are laws which make their violation a misdemeanor.

PLEA BARGAIN   To plead guilty to a criminal charge in consideration for some benefit.

PROSECUTOR   The state's legal representative whose primary responsbility is to convict offenders.

SCREENING   The means by which a prosecutor reviews criminal allegations and decides how they are to be handled.

Notes

[1] Abraham H. Maslow, *Motivation and Personality* (New York: Oxford University Press, 1938).

[2] See for example Samuel Yochelson and Stanton E. Samenow, *The Criminal Personality* (New York: Jason Aronsen, 1976); Curt R. Bartol, *Criminal Behavior: A Psychological Approach* (Englewood Cliffs, New Jersey: Prentice-Hall, Inc., 1980).

[3] Office of Development, Testing, and Dissemination, National Institute of Enforcement and Criminal Justice, *Exemplary Projects* (Washington, D.C.: U.S. Government Printing Office, 1979), p. 4.

[4] *Exemplary Projects*, p. 6.

[5] George H. Gallup, *The Gallup Opinion Index*, Report No. 154 (Princeton, New Jersey: The Gallup Poll, May 1978), p. 24.

[6] National Criminal Justice Information and Statistics Service, *Public Opinion About Crime: The Attitudes of Victims and Nonvictims in Selected Cities* (Washington, D.C.: U.S. Government Printing Office, 1977).

[7] *Public Opinion About Crime*, p. 21.

[8] See for example *The Figgie Report on Fear of Crime: America Afraid* (Willoughby, Ohio (A-T-O Inc., 1980), pp. 65-66; see also: Dave Kalinich and Jon Karr, "The Impact of Violent Crime Rates on Community Members: Perceptions of Safety From Criminal Victimization," *Police Studies* 4 (Fall 1981): 20-34.

[9] George H. Gallup, *The Gallup Opinion Index*, Report No. 181 (Princeton, New Jersey: The Gallup Poll, September 1980), p. 10.

[10] Charles E. Silberman, *Criminal Violence, Criminal Justice* (New York: Vintage Books, 1978), p. 13.

[11] Silberman, *Criminal Violence, Criminal Justice*, p. 16.

[12] Silberman, *Criminal Violence, Criminal Justice*, p. 18.

[13] "The Plague of Violent Crime," *Newsweek*, 23 March 1981, p. 49.

[14] See for example Louis Harris, *The Harris Survey* (New York: *The Chicago Tribune* - New York News Syndicate, February 26, 1981), pp. 3-4.

[15] Nicolette Parisi, Michael R. Gottfredson, Michael J. Hindeland and Timothy J. Flanagan, eds., *Sourcebook of Criminal Justice Statistics - 1978*, U.S. Department of Justice, Law Enforcement Assistance Administration, National Criminal Justice Information and Statistics Service (Washington, D.C.: U.S. Government Printing Office, 1979), Table 2.46, p. 309.

[16] *Sourcebook - 1978*, Table 2.36, p. 301.

[17] *The Harris Survey*, p. 3.

[18] Timothy J. Flanagan, David J. Van Alstyne and Michael R. Gottfredson, eds., *Sourcebook of Criminal Justice Statistics - 1981*, U.S. Department of Justice, Bureau of Justice Statistics (Washingdon, D.C.: U.S. Government Printing Office, 1982), Table 3.1, p. 232.

[19] See also Gerald D. Robin, *Introduction to the Criminal Justice System: Principles, Procedures, Practice* (New York: Harper and Row, Publishers, 1980), pp. 21-22.

[20] "The Plague of Violent Crime," *Newsweek*, p. 52.

[21] *Sourcebook - 1981*, Figure 2.10, p. 199.

[22] Thomas E. Bercal, "Calls for Police Assistance," *American Behavorial Scientist* (May-August 1970): 682; James Q. Wilson, *Varieties of Police Behavior* (Cambridge: Harvard University Press, 1968), p. 19; Albert J. Reiss, Jr., *The Police and the Public* (New Haven: Yale University Press, 1971), p. 75.

[23] Egon Bittner, "Florence Nightingale in Pursuit of Willie Sutton: A Theory of the Police," in Herbert Jacobs, ed., *The Potential for Reform in Criminal Justice* (Beverly Hills, California: Sage Publications), p. 30.

[24] Jack E. Whitehouse, "Historical Perspectives on the Police Community Service Function," *Journal of Police Science and Administration* (March 1973): 92.

[25] National Institute of Law Enforcement and Criminal Justice, *Executive Summary: Response Time Analysis, Kansas City, Missouri Police Department* (Washington, D.C.: U.S. Government Printing Office, 1978).

[26] Yankelovich, Skelly, and White, Inc., *The Public Image of Courts: Highlights of a National Survey of the General Public, Judges, Lawyers, and Community Leaders* (Williamsburg, Virginia: National Center for State Courts, 1978), pp. ii-iii.

[27] *Public Image of the Courts*, pp. ii-iii.

[28] *Public Image of the Courts*, p. 1.

[29] *Public Image* of the Courts, p. 2.

[30] *Public Image of the Courts*, p. 15.

[31] G.K. Chesterton, *Tremendous Trifles* (New York: Dodd, Mead and Company, 1913); see specifically Chapter XI, "The Twelve Men," pp. 85-86.

[32] See Howard James, *Crisis in the Courts* (New York: David McKay, Inc., 1977); Amy K. Rausch, "The State of the Judiciary: An Agenda for Change," *State Court Journal* 5 (Summer 1981): 23-25.

[33] *Public Image of the Courts*, p. ii.

[34] Barbara A. Curran, *The Legal Needs of the Public: The Final Report of a National Survey* (Chicago: The American Bar Foundation, 1977), p. 255.

[35] *Public Image of the Courts*, p. 27.

[36] *Public Image of the Courts*, p. 27.

[37] *Public Image of the Courts*, p. 27.

[38] *Sourcebook - 1981*, Figure 2.11, p. 206.

[39] *Sourcebook - 1978*, Table 2.57, p. 322.

[40] *Public Image of the Courts*, p. 27.

[41] *Public Image of the Courts*, p. 28.

[42] *Public Image of the Courts*, p. 28.

[43] *Public Image of the Courts*, p. 28.

[44] *Public Image of the Courts*, p. 45.

[45] See Joel F. Handler, *Social Movements and the Legal System: A Theory of Law Reform and Social Change* (New York: Academic Press, 1978).

[46] See Kathryn W. Burkhard, *Women in Prison* (New York: Popular Library, 1976); Malcolm Braly, *False Starts* (Boston: Little, Brown and Company, 1976); Jessica Mitford, *Kind and Usual Punishment* (New York: Alfred A. Knopf, 1974).

[47] Leonard Orland, *Prisons: Houses of Darkness* (New York: The Free Press, 1975), pp. 4-5.

[48] Committee for Economic Development, *Reducing Crime and Assuring Justice* (New York: Committee for Economic Development, 1972), p. 39.

[50] *Sourcebook - 1978*, Table 2.56, p. 321.

[51] *Sourcebook - 1981*, Table 2.36, pp. 210-211; Table 2.37, p. 212; Table 2.38, p. 212.

[52] Abraham Blumber, *Criminal Justice: Issues and Ironies*, 2d ed. (New York: New Viewpoints, 1979), p. 7.

[53] R.N. Sanford, "The Effects of Abstinence from Food Upon Imagination Processes," *Journal of Psychology* 2 (1936): 129-136.

[54] James C. Davies, *Human Nature in Politics: The Dynamics of Political Behavior* (New York: John Wiley and Sons, Inc., 1963), p. 10.

[55] *Human Nature in Politics*, pp. 112-114.

[56] G. Gerbner and C.P. Gross, "The Scary World of TV's Heavy Viewer," *Psychology Today*, April 1976, p. 41.

[57] David L. Altheide and Robert P. Snow, *Media Logic* (Beverly Hills, California: Sage Publications, 1979), p. 19.

[58] *Media Logic*, p. 47.

[59] *Media Logic*, p. 47.

[60] D. Littlejohn, "Communicating Ideas by Television," in D. Carter and R. Adler, eds., *Television as a Social Force* (New York: Praeger Publishers, 1975), pp. 63-79.

[61] Kenneth L. Karemer, *A Systems Approach to Decision Making: Policy Analysis in Local Government* (Washington, D.C.: International City Management Association, 1973), p. 15.

[62] See Tom Denyer, Robert Callender, and Dennis L. Thomson, "The Policeman as Alienated Laborer," *Journal of Police Science and Administration* 3 (September 1975): 251-258.

[63] *People v. Defore*, 242 NY 13, 150 NE 585.

[64] James P. Levine, Michael C. Musheno, and James J. Palumbo, *Criminal Justice: A Public Policy Approach* (New York: Harcourt, Brace, Jovanovich, Inc., 1980), p. 201; see also Florynce Kennedy, "The Whorehouse Theory of Law," in Robert Lefcourt, ed., *Law Against the People: Essays to Demystify Law, Order, and the Courts* (New York: Random House, 1971), pp. 81-82.

[65] See Andrew D. Gilman, "Legal Barriers to Jobs Are Slowly Disappearing," *Corrections Magazine*, December 1979, pp. 68-72.

[66] See Ernest van den Haag, "Prisons Cost Too Much Because They Are Too Secure," *Corrections Magazine*, April 1980, pp. 39-43.

[67] *Reducing Crime and Assuring Justice*, p. 57.

[68] *Reducing Crime and Assuring Justice*, p. 57.

[69] *The Gallup Index*, Report No. 169 (August 1979), p. 29.

[70] *The Gallup Index*, Report No. 169 (August 1979), p. 30.

[71] *The Gallup Index*, Report No. 160 (November 1978), p. 21.

[72] *The Gallup Index*, Report No. 160 (November 1978), p. 24.

CRIMINAL JUSTICE AND MINORITIES

5

Diversity within the American community has shown no sign of fading away. If anything, changes in the economic and social fabric of the nation point to an even greater degree of diversity in the decades to come. Approximately three out of every four Americans live in a metropolitan area, and this places all kinds of people close to one another. Even though these different people may live close to one another in terms of *geographic* proximity, many of them remain widely separated by social, psychological, and economic distances. It might be accurate to say that urban areas have become highly heterogeneous mosaics because of both the ways in which their populations distribute themselves socially and economically and in the ways in which they are scattered among residential, commercial, and industrial suburbs and central cities. It is clear that cities have become complex interdependent working and living environments whose residents have been caught up in an accelerating rate of change, throwing both the cities and their populations off balance.[1]

The cities themselves as well as the people who live within them are experiencing numerous problems. However, it is important to remember that a problem is always a relationship between two or more factors. Traffic is not a problem just because there are too many cars; it is also a problem because the roadways cannot adequately handle the volume of traffic to which they are subjected. Unemployment is not a problem simply because people are out of work; it is also a problem because mechanization and other technological advances have altered the very nature of the job market, making some skills obsolete and creating entirely new types of jobs. Not only do problems have multiple "sides", people who have problems tend to see them in relative terms according to the kinds of relationships which they perceive. If each major group within the community had to describe its own particular problems and the perceived causes as well as offer suggestions for solving those problems, the diversity of responses would probably match or exceed the diversity of the community itself!

What is even more important, some groups within the community may view their problems as a result of the policies and practices of other groups within the same community. For instance, many middle-class citizens blame their high tax burden on the lower class, claiming that welfare supports the lazy at the expense of those who are willing to work. Many of the chronically poor see themselves as being trapped in a state of dependence created and maintained by those who control the system. The young feel exploited by the old, and the old feel exploited by the young; educators blame their failures on parents while the family blames government in general and the schools in particular. Those hard hit by rampant inflation blame the oil companies, the oil companies blame the Arabs, and the Arabs blame the consumers! To be sure, there are significant economic and social problems, and they do divide and polarize groups. However, the causes and cures for these problems are usually far more complex than most critics realize — but then again, many of the critics are much more concerned with images than they are with realities!

It is difficult for the diverse components of a community to unite against common problems when so many view their neighbors as being responsible for those problems in the first place. The criminal justice system is not exempt from these passions, either within its own institutions or in its relationships with the public.[2] Yet in spite of this multitude of problems, the criminal justice system must still do the best that it can to serve the public as a whole. In this respect it is worth noting that a good deal of the criticism of the system comes from people who feel they have special needs, especially when those needs are not being met. In recent years we have seen the development of the single-issue interest group which loudly proclaims its interests — and only its interests. If this trend continues, more and more demands will be placed on already overburdened resources; this will intensify already keen competition for what these groups hope will be uniquely responsive services.

Special Needs Of Minorities

Perhaps because of the clamor of special interest groups, we have become increasingly aware of the fact that certain groups *do* have different needs, and these needs relate directly to the criminal justice system. We should therefore at least be aware of the needs of these groups, and if possible take them into consideration when planning or delivering criminal justice services. It might be worth keeping in mind that special needs also provide special opportunities. By taking advantage of opportunities to improve the quality of the criminal justice system, we do far more than improve the lot of special interest groups: we improve the quality of the rest of society as well.

The Poor

When one mentions "the poor", most people would probably think about people who have little or no money. While this is correct, it is not nearly inclusive enough. The poor lack a great deal more than money: they are also deficient in power, status, material goods, and influence. They are typically ill-educated, live in undesirable locations, work at demeaning jobs (when they work), and often must suffer the contempt of those who are more fortunate. As Radelet has noted, "Poverty is mean, it is brutal, it is frustrating, it is painful, and it blights the spirit. There are few things in this world that are worse than being caught in the grip of poverty."[3]

Poverty has never been the exclusive domain of any particular group. Poverty ignores differences of race, sex, ethnicity, age, and geographic location. Poverty is an especially persistent social ill because it feeds upon itself: poor education leads to diminished work opportunities, unemployment or underemployment, and the low income which results from underemployment restricts social advancement and continues to fuel the cycle. Poverty is often regarded as a trap from which escape is extremely difficult. Although poverty is relative, it is closely tied to class and status. Those who are in the lower class and enjoy the least status usually comprise the poorest segment of the community.

Poverty tends to produce its own "culture," a proposition first set forth by the sociologist Oscar Lewis.[4] Lewis believed that the "culture of poverty" exists because it provides rewards that enable the poor to adjust to their chronic condition of poverty; this set of attitudes and responses is passed on from one generation of poor to the next. Perhaps the "culture of poverty" with its peculiar social, psychological, and economic aspects is in part responsible for the ambivalent attitude many people have about poverty. Although most people recognize the fact that the conditions which produce poverty are beyond control of the poor, they nevertheless are inclined to blame the poor for their own poverty, ascribing it to laziness, reluctance to work, or even God's will. In a sense, many people tend to equate affluence with "goodness" and poverty with "badness," although this relationship is seldom expressed in such blunt terms. The affluent typically expect the poor to show them the proper deference and gratitude which they feel they deserve, and certainly deny any responsibility for the plight of the poor — even though a large proportion of poverty is a direct function of our economic system, the same system which rewards the affluent for not being poor![5] There is, of course, a long social heritage behind this attitude toward the poor; it is firmly rooted in the rigid class systems of Europe (from which we derive much of our cultural heritage) and in such things as the Elizabethan Poor Laws and subsequent vagrancy laws which virtually made it a crime to be poor.

The poor are placed in an extremely difficult position. They are expected to accept and live by the rules imposed by the larger society; they are expected to be honest, hard-working, and responsive citizens, and they are expected to suffer with patience. Many of them feel caught in a web of humiliation, self-denigration, and dependency, and find the situation hard to accept. In economic terms, there is no significant opportunity cost for rejecting the values of the dominant society in favor of activities which are illegal but more profitable. When the poor see the dominant society as either being responsibile for their poverty or taking advantage of it, their despair turns to resentment or even hatred. The consequences of this type of attitude are not difficult to imagine.

One aspect of poverty which is especially important is that of the involvement of minorities in poverty. Some people equate poverty with minority status, which is a significant error. Although some minorities may be heavily represented in the ranks of the poor, that by no means indicates that members of a given group are all poor. There are some aspects of minority status which make poverty more likely, however, and which make escape from poverty more difficult. Before looking at minorities per se, it is important to note that ours is a harshly competitive society in which the ability to compete has never been equally distributed among all citizens. This has not been the result of any historical accident, for the history of American social and economic relations has been based on carefully enforced patterns of economic and social dominance and the enforced submission of some groups to the will of others. In its most basic form, it has been a question of *power*, and the uneven distribution of power has been clearly reflected in our system of social stratification — a system which has traditionally hindered the advancement of some persons while facilitating that of others. From the beginnings of the Republic until well into the twentieth century, this chasm has reflected racial and ethnic differences, with white Anglo-Saxons being the dominant group. The settlers regarded Indians as savages unworthy of their property and Orientals were brutally exploited for cheap labor. Blacks were seen as property to be used at the pleasure of their owners. Inequality was institutionalized, respected, and even protected by law. We are now living with the long-term consequences of that inequality; it presents some of our most difficult and enduring social problems, and nowhere is this more clear than in the interrelationship of poverty and minority status.

Although the sociology and history of race and ethnic relations is far too complex to summarize here, it is important to remember that contemporary minority problems are firmly rooted in the nation's history, and contemporary problems are so complex that no simple solutions will cure them. Although society has started to bring minorities into full participation within the mainstream of society, for many people the change has come too late and offers too little. Residual effects, hardened attitudes, alienation, and the institutionalized effects of poverty continue to play a major role in contemporary society.

Minorities

The current population of the United States is about 226.5 million; of that total, 31 million are members of minority groups. Fully 26.4 million Americans (about 12 percent of the population) are Black, and the remainder of the minority population consists primarily of Native Americans (Indians), Hispanics (usually Puerto Rican or Mexican heritage), and Asian-Americans. Many of these people are in a double bind: they suffer from the problems of both poverty and racial discrimination. The nature of discrimination varies with the group under consideration, geography, and the cultural characteristics of the group itself. Where poverty and discrimination co-exist, the problems of each are magnified by the other.

Blacks Ironically, the situation of Blacks in America has both improved and worsened. It has improved to the extent that greater opportunities exist than ever before, and that average levels of income and education have risen. Blacks are participating more and more in all fields of endeavor, and the near future promises even greater opportunity. The situation of Blacks has worsened, however, in some other critical aspects; one of these is the accelerating disintegration of the Black nuclear family.[6] This particular trend contains within it some highly negative implications for the future. Let us examine some of the current problems which Black Americans face and see how they relate to the criminal justice system.

Of the 26.4 million Blacks in the United States, approximately 53 percent still reside in the South; of those who have left the South, most

137

have moved into the crowded and disintegrating central cities of the Northeast and Midwest. This Black population consists in part of some 8.4 million families with an average size of 3.01 persons; about 46 percent of these families are headed by a female.[7] The economic situation within many of these families is not good. If one were to subtract cash transfers* and in-kind transfers** from the sources of family income, then 43.8 percent of all Black families have incomes below the poverty level.[8] Blacks and their families have been and continue to be plagued by very real poverty within an affluent society. For example, from 1975 to 1979, the percentage of white persons in metropolitan areas who were below the poverty level dropped from 8.2 percent to 7.8 percent; however, for Blacks it rose from 27.6 percent to 28.3 percent. In the central cities the picture is even worse: whites below the poverty level dropped from 10.8 percent in 1975 to 10.7 percent in 1979; but for Blacks in the central cities, the proportion whose incomes fell below the poverty level increased from 29.1 percent in 1975 to 31.1 percent in 1979. For Blacks outside the metropolitan areas the situation was no better: 39.5 percent had incomes below the poverty level.[9]

Families with female heads of household are much more likely to be below the poverty level, and a high and growing proportion of Black families are headed by a female; the proportion of female-headed households among Blacks has increased from 22.4 million in 1960 to 38 million in 1980 — over a 60 percent increase! There are glaring contrasts: in 1979, for example, 8.9 percent of all white women with children were below the poverty level, but for Black women with children, the figure was 30.9 percent. This very real poverty among Black families has produced a great deal of dependency. As a result, in 1977 about 77.1 percent of the Aid to Families with Dependent Children (AFDC) went to metropolitan areas; of this total, 43 percent of the recipients were Black families.[10] The problems associated with poverty and dependence in turn produce vicious cycles which tend to perpetuate the problem. For example, in 1979, 48.8 percent of all Black births were illegitimate (as compared to 9.4 percent of white births) and in 1980, according to census data, almost 60 percent of all Black children under the age of 18 were living with only one parent or with someone else.

---

*Cash transfers include social security, railroad retirement, government pensions, unemployment insurance compensation, workman's and veterans' compensation, veterans' pension, supplemental social security, and Aid To Families with Dependent Children.

**In-kind transfers include food stamps, child nutrition, housing assistance, medicare, and medicaid. Recent cutbacks in these programs have been acutely felt by the poor, especially among urban Blacks.

These statistics paint a bleak picture, but they do not address the despair, alienation, and resentment which seethes just beneath the surface in many cities, as demonstrated by riots in Miami and Orlando during the summer of 1980. Another set of depressing statistics deals with Black involvement in crime. In city arrest trends in 1981, 28.3 percent of the arrests in urban areas involved Blacks. (See Fig. 5.1)

Although these figures should be interpreted with care, they do point to an involvement by Blacks which is significantly out of proportion to their numbers in the general population. This disproportionate relationship between Blacks and crime has led Charles Silberman to state: "In the end, there is no escaping the question of race and crime."[11] It is a relationship which simply will not go away, and it has serious repercussions throughout the entire criminal justice system: a disproportionate number of Blacks appear before the courts, and a disproportionate number to go to prison (in 1979, approximately 46 percent of the inmates in state and federal correctional facilities were Black).[12]

FIGURE 5.1
URBAN ARRESTS BY CRIME AND RACE (1981)*

CRIME	PERCENTAGE OF ARRESTS BY RACE	
	WHITE	BLACK
Murder and non-negligent manslaughter	42.4	56.3
Forcible rape	44.2	54.1
Robbery	35.9	63.0
Aggravated assault	57.0	41.6
Burglary	64.3	34.5
Larcency-theft	64.4	33.6
Motor Vehicle theft	64.1	34.2
VIOLENT CRIME	48.2	50.5
PROPERTY CRIME	64.5	33.8

*SOURCE: U.S. Department of Justice, Federal Bureau of Investigation, *Uniform Crime Reports - 1981*. (Washington, D.C.: U.S. Government Printing Office, 1982); adapted from Table 43, "City Arrests, Distribution by Race, 1981," p. 191.

The reasons for this human tragedy are extremely complex; the point is, however, that Blacks as a group do have a crime problem and they do come into frequent contact with the criminal justice system. This contact has certainly played a role in shaping Black opinion about the nature of the system. This author (and others who remember how the system was some twenty years ago) has seen incredible advances in the quality of treatment received by Blacks - but neither he nor Blacks have forgotten what it used to be like:[13]

ITEM: In 1959 an automobile driven in a Southwestern city by a Black man struck a utility pole, seriously injuring the driver. Upon arriving at the scene, the police (who were following departmental directives) radioed for a Black ambulance. They were advised that there would be a delay as none of the Black ambulances (operated by a local Black funeral home) were in service. A white ambulance passing by offered to take the victim to the hospital but was told by the police that it could not be allowed to do so.

ITEM: In 1959 the police in the same city stopped a Black male who was carrying two suits in a laundry bag. They placed the well-dressed, soft-spoken man in the car while they radioed their dispatcher to see if he was "wanted" for anything. They did so by giving the dispatcher the man's name and date of birth and by describing him as a "nigger male." He was a surgeon.

Although such practices are now rare and are no longer tolerated in any urban police department, their memory lingers on and will continue to do so as long as those who were victimized have memories. Perhaps such treatment will become part of the folklore of a different era in the future, but the incidents are still too recent to have lost their cutting edge. It is not just the insults and indignities that fuel unpleasant memories. In addition, Blacks were often denied the protection of the law. Crimes by whites against Blacks or crimes by Blacks against other Blacks were routinely minimized or even ignored:

ITEM: In 1943 a Black man killed another Black man in a dice game. He was duly arrested and charged with "misdemeanor murder" and fined $22.50 in court costs and fines. Interestingly enough, almost 30 years later this man's son was one of the first Blacks to be admitted to his state's Highway Patrol.[13]

ITEM: In 1960 (in a rural Southwestern town) the police chief interrogated a man who he suspected had poisoned his wife. The man trapped himself in a series of contradictory statements and then admitted to killing her. He was released and never charged. When the chief was asked why by a naive young college student, he said, "Why? They're just niggers."[13]

It has hardly been a wonder that generations of Blacks have come to view the entire criminal justice system with distrust and fear; too often, it has been a system which worked against them, but not for them. In some places it still works that way. Unfortunately, the beneficial impact of scores of positive police contacts can be wiped out by one surly, arrogant, or brutal encounter and such encounters, rare though they may be, only reinforce the negative folklore which many Blacks (especially the young ones) associate with the police in specific and the criminal justice system in general.

Black attitudes toward the criminal justice system were further shaped by events during the 1960's, especially the civil rights movement, which often placed Blacks in direct confrontation with the law concerning acts of civil disobedience. So many protestors were set upon by police dogs, beaten by law enforcement officers, or knocked down by fire hoses that the perception of mistreatment by law enforcement authorities took on a dimension that transcended its reality. Eventually Black efforts at "integration" dissipated somewhat and were replaced by a new militancy. Black awareness included demands for autonomy and participation — including input concerning how their communities were to be policed (a demand that has not been very popular with authorities). For many whites, the civil rights movement was hard to distinguish from the riots which raged throughout the country in those "long, hot summers," and many police officers were appalled by the tremendous property destruction and violence resulting from the riots. Many officers found previously hostile attitudes towards Blacks reinforced as a consequence of their experiences in the riots. In the minds of many officers, the idea of civil rights simply was not congruent with the reality of arson, looting, and assault.

The growing sense of Black awareness included the suspicion that the situation facing Blacks was part of a larger social phenomenon. One result was that many Blacks in jail came to see themselves not as criminals, but rather as victims of a criminal society. One survey of 150 Black males of various social classes reported that they commonly attributed Black crime to what they perceived as an oppressive social system.[14] A related view was that crime is necessary for survival when people are systematically denied access to institutional participation. Lillyquist has noted that "Another belief given frequently was that black-white interests are incompatible and that blacks, in order to look out for their own interests, must necessarily violate white interests, which tend to be protected by law."[15]

Hispanics   Another major minority group in the United States consists of Spanish-speaking people. Hispanics are an extremely diverse group and represent many different cultural and ethnic backgrounds. Perhaps the largest group of Hispanics in the United States is composed of Mexican-Americans (Chicanos) who number about six and one half million and who reside primarily in the West and Southwest. Many Chicanos are descended from families who occupied their land before it was acquired by the United States and who were annexed along with the land they owned![16] Most Chicanos, however, either migrated to the United States during the present century or are descendants of those who have done so.

Chicanos do not represent one single cultural, ethnic, or historical background. Many Chicanos in the barrios of the West and Southwest differ from the Anglo society in culture, language and ethnicity, and often differ among themselves as well.[17] This produces a degree of complexity which many outsiders find surprising.

Economically, Chicanos have not fared well as a group. Many work as laborers, and a substantial number of Mexican-Americans work in seasonal agricultural industries, often under very harsh conditions. Many agricultural workers are nomadic and follow the various growing seasons. This means that they must live in migrant labor camps which have been criticized for their dehumanizing conditions:

> . . . the camps in which the farm laborers were put up were often horrible collections of unshaded tents and shacks, inadequately supplied with water and open-ditch latrines. Moving from one such camp to another in boxcars, trucks, or rusted jalopies piled high with bedsprings, chicken coops, and children, the Mexicans knew they were in no promised land.[18]

The permanent settlements — the barrios — in the cities are likewise typically substandard in the quality of housing, although in recent years substantial progress has been made in both migrant labor camps and the urban areas in which Chicanos live.

Chicanos have had to endure prejudice and animosity for generations:

> Race prejudice was circulated as scientific dogma in the early decades of the century; R.L. Adams of the University of California, in his text *Farm Management* stated that Mexicans were 'childish, lazy and unambitious.' He argued that as farm laborers they should be segregated from the Japanese who were 'tricky' and both should be kept separate from Negroes given that they were 'notorious pervaricators ... constantly annexing to themselves such minor things as chickens, lines from harnesses, axes and shovels.'[19]

Long considered an "invisible minority," Mexican-Americans are now a highly visible component of many American cities, and their problems are now matters of legitimate and proper concern to state and local government. Schools are beginning to offer bilingual instruction and a cultural blending seems to be taking place which was eloquently summed up by Dr. Manuel Guerra, an educator of Mexican descent, when he said,

> We do not want to give up the Spanish language, pray to God in English, substitute mashed potatoes for *frijoles* or 'junk' our

piñantas. Rather we want to bring all of these values to American society as our contribution to the diversity and wealth of our country. Rather than the melting pot, we believe in the heterogeneity of American society, including the give and take with other peoples and other cultures.[20]

Another major group of Hispanics consists of Puerto Ricans. The United States acquired Puerto Rico in the aftermath of the Spanish-American War (1898), and during World War I the residents of Puerto Rico were granted American citizenship. At the beginning of the twentieth century, there was already some migration of Puerto Ricans from the islands to New York City (the ultimate destination of most emigrating Puerto Ricans), but it was not that great: by 1910 New York City had only about 500 people of Puerto Rican birth. In 1924 the Immigration Act shut off the influx of immigrant labor from Europe, and this created a demand for a new source of labor — a need which was quickly filled by Puerto Ricans. By 1930 there were about 45,000 Puerto Ricans in New York City, and after World War II immigration reached 50,000 per year. By 1970 the Puerto Rican population of New York City had reached 1,000,000.

The Puerto Ricans came to New York City in search of opportunity and also to escape the crowded conditions of the islands and the economic pressures which stifled any hope for the future. They encountered resentment, hostility, and prejudice, as has virtually every large group which has moved to the city. Perhaps one of the reasons Puerto Ricans have faced so much hostility is because they are the first group of newcomers to bring a cultural practice of widespread intermingling and intermarriage of peoples of many different colors.[21] In addition, Puerto Ricans were seen as an economic threat by the already hard-pressed Blacks in New York City — it is worth remembering that New York City has the highest Black population of any city in the world. Puerto Ricans had great difficulty entering the skilled-labor unions and relatively few were able to move into white-collar occupations.

Puerto Ricans crowded into Morrisania in the Bronx and into East Harlem (also known as Spanish Harlem or El Barrio); they lived in run-down tenements and entered into a subculture of poverty. The Puerto Ricans, like the Chicanos, have had to face a multitude of problems ranging all the way from questions of self-identity to basic survival. They are slowly changing the face of New York City and are now beginning to develop the political and economic participation which is a necessary step in entering the mainstream of American life.

The final group of Hispanics to come to the United States are Cubans who fled the Castro regime in the years following 1959. When the first batch of Cubans fled their homeland they were allowed to take with them only five pesos, one watch, one ring, and the clothes on their backs. About 300,000 Cubans arrived in the United States, most of whom settled in the Miami-Dade County area of Florida. The refugees have been described as "the cream of a nation in exile" because so many of them were middle and upper-class men and women who brought with them a great many skills and a strong sense of pride and dedication.

> By the end of Castroism's first decade, the Cuban community in Miami showed a respectable top layer of affluence. Many of the Cubans still eagerly awaited the day when Castro would be overthrown and they could return to their rightful homeland. But thousands were discovering that children born in the house of strangers create blood ties to those strangers and their house. Increasingly, Cubans who had children enrolled in American schools were applying for citizenship papers and settling in for good.[22]

Unfortunately, this sanguine outcome does not seem to have been repeated with the refugees who fled Cuba during the summer of 1980 in the so-called "Freedom Flotilla." Many of the new refugees came without job skills; some were mentally ill and it was rumored that others had been cast out of prisons and jails. It is too early to predict their fate, but their presence will undoubtedly be felt and they will face many of the difficulties with which Chicanos and Puerto Ricans have been confronted.

Although the crime rate of Hispanics does not come close to that of Blacks, it has been a problem.[23] In addition, Hispanics have long complained of discriminatory treatment at the hands of law enforcement officials whom they have traditionally seen as representing the interests of the dominant power structure. It would be naive to assume these complaints are anything other than true, but it is also important to remember that our current social awareness is a relatively recent phenomenon. Much crime involving Hispanics may be considered a natural consequence of the poverty in which they lived, the economic system which exploited them for cheap labor, and the virtual absence of effective legal remedies for the problems which they faced. All of this has no doubt been exacerbated by the conflicting expectations of two cultures operating in the same environment, langugage difficulties, and long-standing patterns of discrimination.

Other Minorities   The United States also has a substantial number of other minorities, including those of Asian extraction (Chinese, Japanese, Filipino, Vietnamese, etc.) and American Indians. There is no statement which can summarize these groups since they represent a wide range of linguistic, ethnic, racial, and cultural backgrounds. Each group poses its own problems and has its own particular set of needs; however, the American community in nearly every part of the country has some of these minority group members as a part of its population. All of these people are guaranteed the same rights and have the same obligations as do all other citizens, yet many of them do not understand their rights and obligations. Some face severe social problems and many come into contact with the criminal justice system, often under conditions which pose great difficulties for the system.[24] It has been somewhat easy for the criminal justice system to ignore the special needs of these minorities, and it has done so until those needs emerged in the form of a crisis. As we will see, an effective community relations program takes the needs and problems of such groups into consideration well before they reach crisis proportions.

Perhaps the key to understanding the relationship between minorities and the criminal justice system is an appreciation of the fact that many members of minority groups have found themselves regulated by laws which were shaped without their participation and were, in some instances, targeted against them; these laws often ignored their unique problems and requirements. Many times the laws have operated against them, but not for them; indeed, many minorities have even been excluded from entry into criminal justice professions. Obviously "If one feels disenfranchised, alienated from the forces that make the decisions which govern one's life, there is greater likelihood that one will feel no obligation to conform to the system created by such decisions."[25] In other words, for many urban Blacks and Hispanics, there has been no social contract which binds them to the rules of the dominant society in any significant way; there is only survival, and survival is defined in very narrow terms which center around the individual's own self-interest. Certainly not all minorities feel this way, but enough do to present a very serious problem to the social fabric of society; as Lincoln suggested over a century ago, a house divided against itself cannot stand.

Perhaps the old idea that it was the obligation of minorities to adapt to the larger society needs to be re-examined; perhaps the idea of America as a "melting pot" is too simplistic. It might be more desirable to bring minorities into full participation within the larger society by incorporating their cultural heritage into the mainstream of society and by seeking areas of commonality that can be used to tie the majority to the minorities. Minorities must bear in mind that they cannot be islands unto themselves and expect the support of a larger society which they themselves reject; the obligation for finding mutual grounds for accommodation is a reciprocal responsibility.

In addition, the needs of all groups within society might be better served if civil remedies for private wrongs were more accessible to all citizens. For example, the exploitative practices of landlords in some cases are grounds for bitter resentment on the part of minorities who feel there is "no justice" to be had. Consider for example, the results of a questionnaire circulated among 1,000 tenants in a Puerto Rican neighborhood in East Harlem asking about housing problems:

> There were 721 cases of defective wiring, 612 of inadequate plumbing, 571 of broken windows, 895 of rats in the building, 696 of gas leaks, 778 of no heat, 553 of no hot water, and 308 of leaks in the roof. It went without saying that the victims of these housing-code violations, lacking political influence, lacking command of English, without money for lawyers, and having no comprehension of bureaucratic byways, were almost powerless to compel landlord to make repairs.[26]

Resentment against exploitative practices and what appear to be obvious injustices calls into question the credibility of the *criminal* justice system, although such inequities may well be a function of flaws in the *social* justice system. Because they do not understand how the system works, many of the poor have inaccurate ideas of exactly what their rights are and how they can be secured. When they complain to the police about the mistreatment they receive and are told there is nothing the police *can* do, many interpret that as meaning there is nothing the police *will* do. For this reason it should be clear that the criminal justice system alone cannot reasonably expect to generate positive and productive community relations without involving a substantially larger segment of the city's government.

The Elderly

We each are inclined to see the world from a perspective based not only on who and what we are, but also *how old* we are. The typical undergraduate college student has his career *ahead* of him; most feel that there is no need to worry about those a generation behind them, much less those who are older. Ours is a relatively young society and the perspective of the elderly is something to which too few of us give any thought. However, people in different age groups do have different needs and to a certain extent even have differences in their relationship to crime and the criminal justice system. The elderly are no exception, and there are presently about 25 million people in the United States who are 65 or older.[27]

Aging can be a difficult process, and in some respects society may even inflict frustrations on its senior citizens which are more harmful to them than biological decline.[28] Social and economic isolation, the loss of power through retirement, and a loss of self-esteem all contribute to the plight of the elderly. The fact that many people consider older citizens to be "useless" has not escaped the awareness of the elderly and it is very difficult for many of them to adjust to such attitudes.

The Elderly As Offenders   One little-explored area in criminal justice is that of the participation of the elderly in crime — a situation which poses unique problems for both the elderly and the criminal justice system. Shichor and Korbin have pointed out the fact that a number of possible trends involving the elderly might be identifiable.[29] For one thing, although the proportion of all arrests of elderly persons for all crimes has shown a decline in recent years, their share of arrests for *index crimes* has risen steadily. Within the index crimes, most elderly persons arrested are charged with aggravated assault, and the second-ranked offense is murder. The elderly may also come into contact with legal authorities through such problem areas as sexual misconduct (especially involving offenses against minors) and offenses associated with alcohol abuse.

Crimes of the elderly are often both pathetic and tragic, and many of them can be attributed to the aging process itself. Significant decline in brain functioning often begins after the age of 65, and this decline is most often the result of either cerebral arteriosclerosis or senile brain disorders. These are physical problems which can be exacerbated by many of the social problems which face the elderly: retirement, reduced income, the loss of one's spouse and friends, and a reduction in social status.[30] The behavior of an elderly person may gradually alter; he may become reclusive, irritable, suspicious, anxious, agitated, and subject to periodic outbursts of rage. Suicide among the elderly is not uncommon. The declining years contain a potential for behavior which may bring the elderly into conflict with the law.

Although many crimes committed by the aged do reflect a diminished responsibility on the part of the offender, many of these crimes still must be dealt with by the criminal justice system. Unfortunately, the management of the elderly offender can be difficult.

The Elderly As Victims   The other side of the coin involves the elderly as *victims* of crime, a problem which has received considerable attention in recent years. Some of the crimes against the elderly are part of the broader spectrum of family violence.[31] However, much of the crime against the elderly is part of the stranger-to-stranger street crime syndrome in which the elderly are particularly "easy" targets.[32] Although some commentators have claimed that criminal abuse of the elderly has reached crisis proportions, a more objective review of the problem does not support such a conclusion.[33] Actually, the victimization rates for the elderly are rather low, as the data in Table 5.2 indicate. Although victimization tends to decrease with age, this is by no means an indication that the problem is not serious. Old people *are* victimized, and some evidence indicates that they are disproportionately the victims of certain forms of crime, among them robbery and grand larceny when the victim was present and force was used.[34] The major problem among the elderly, however, seems to be the *fear* of crime.[35] Victimization studies show that the elderly are *more fearful* of personal crimes than any other age group, and neighborhood-based studies suggest that the fear level of the typical elderly urban resident is based on a fairly realistic perception of the *risk* of crime.[36] Although many of the crimes feared by the elderly are not seen as serious by younger groups (such things are purse-snatching,, burglary, vandalism, consumer fraud, etc.), they *are* frightening to the elderly because their potential impact is more serious on old people and because older victims often suffer more severely than other age groups because of their greater economic, psychological, and physical vulnerability.

Unfortunately, although the elderly tend to be very supportive of the criminal justice system, they also tend to avoid personal contact with it because they typically lack knowledge about the system and how it works.[37] Many fear going out, and the fear of being criminally victimized can itself create barriers to the use of services, especially for the elderly urban poor who are most likely to be in need of such help. A related problem is the reluctance of physicians, nurses, social workers or even repairmen to make home visits in high crime areas, especially in the inner cities.[38]

The elderly are easy for the criminal justice system to overlook. Police tend to be less concerned with minor acts of vandalism simply because they are minor, and often overlook the fact that such incidents may truly terrorize an older person. Police in some areas have taken steps to deal with the problems of the elderly. For example, Philadelphia conducts a decoy operation known as the "grandpop patrol" in which volunteer officers disguise themselves as elderly citizens and walk around in areas where old people are likely to be attacked or intimidated.[39]

Other programs include personal escort and transportation services, the establishment of "safe corridors," training sessions on how to carry wallets and pocketbooks to avoid theft, "post-incident" counseling sessions, court actions which limit the number of appearances elderly victims must make, and in some cases even financial assistance programs for elderly victims. The elderly *do* have special needs, although they are often overlooked. It is important to remember that the quality of criminal justice in the community is not just a function of being able to deal with such serious crimes as rape, robbery and murder; it is also an issue of having the capacity and compassion to reach out to the silent victims. No one should be forced to face their declining years alone, uncared for, and in constant fear.

TABLE 5.2

ESTIMATED VICTIMIZATION RATES PER 100,000 PERSONS 12 YEARS OF AGE OR OLDER, BY AGE OF VICTIM AND TYPES OF VICTIMIZATION

Age of Victim (Both Sexes)	Rape and Attempted Rape	Robbery		Assault		Personal Larcency with Contact
		With Injury	Without Injury	Aggravated	Simple	
12 - 15	133	238	387	1325	2941	291
16 - 19	316	383	405	2018	3585	270
20 - 24	261	437	515	2222	3505	429
25 - 34	126	217	227	1349	2307	279
35 - 49	55	147	246	598	965	210
50 - 64	11	132	171	231	443	250
65+	4	103	85	108	232	353

*SOURCE: Adapted from *Sourcebook of Criminal Justice Statistics - 1981*, Table 3.10, "Estimated Rate (per 100,000 persons 12 years of age or older) of Personal Victimization, by Age of Victim and Type of Victimization, United States, 1979." p. 253.

The Young

At the other end of the age spectrum are the young; like the elderly they have special needs — especially concerning their dealings with the criminal justice system. Like the elderly, young children are especially vunerable to certain kinds of offenses. Child abuse and neglect, for example, are offenses typically committed against very young children, including new-born infants. Somewhat older children may be sexually abused as well. These cases often escaped official notice until recent years; many police departments have begun to give them special attention and to co-ordinate their efforts more closely with local medical and social service agencies. The results have been very encouraging.[40]

The problem with young people and crime is more likely to be one of young people as *offenders* rather than as victims. Young people below the age of 21 account for a significant proportion of all arrests. This is even more alarming when one considers the fact that people under 21 comprise only about 35 percent of the total population. In addition, since about 85 percent of all arrests are of *males* (and they are about half the population), then only about 18 percent of our population accounts for a disproportionate amount of these arrests. It should not be surprising to learn that according to 1981 *Uniform Crime Report* data, 41 percent of those arrested for robbery and 69 percent of those arrested for burglary were under eighteen years of age.[41]

None of this is new. Criminologists have known for a long time that a significant proportion of the total crime picture is accounted for by juveniles and young adults. Criminologists have pointed out that age-cohort patterns are an important component of the overall crime picture; in general, the age group of 16 to 24 is the most crime-prone age group in the United States.[42] Even this finding is conservative because many, if not most, offenders below the age of 16 are not even processed by the criminal justice system, but by juvenile authorities. These juveniles are usually granted a protected status because of their young age.

Youth crime has long presented a dilemma to those who must deal with it. Criminal acts cannot be ignored, but juveniles are believed to be malleable and more in need of supervision, education, and counseling than punishment. The result has been that the *criminal* and *juvenile* justice systems have a shared responsibility in dealing with youth crime, and a bureaucratic jungle has emerged in which the juvenile gets the worst of both worlds.[43] Often when a youthful offender should probably be punished, he evades it; on occasions when he should not be punished, he is![44] Part of the problem lies in the distinction between crimes (such as robbery, burglary) and *status offenses* which are offenses particular to children (e.g., truancy, runaway, etc.). Many youths who repeatedly commit serious crimes avoid punishment, but many other youths are often punished for less serious status offenses.

Internal Administrative Problems

Members of the community who have special problems or needs may be either individuals or members of groups. Their problems may be social, economic, psychological or political, or some combination of those categories. It is unlikely that their problems are *caused* by the criminal justice system, although the way the system works may certainly contribute to their problems. This is an important point, because if the criminal justice system were the cause of those problems, then changes within the system would eliminate the problems. This is clearly not the case. If the criminal justice system is not the cause of these problems, then it cannot be the sole source of their cure. There is a great deal the system can do to reduce the magnitude of these problems and specific strategies will be discussed in the chapters dealing with the various elements of the criminal justice system.

Certain general problem areas which touch upon all elements of the criminal justice system (and which are common to all bureaucratic organizations) can be identified and can serve as a springboard for looking at strategies within specific agencies. There are a number of generic problem areas which can influence the nature of the relationship between an agency and its "clientele." These problem areas differ in any given setting, but nearly all criminal justice agencies suffer from them to one extent or another. A few of these problem areas are identified in the following paragraphs.

Failure to Identify or Understand Problems

How we as individuals see another person's (or group's) problems may be quite different from how *they* view those same problems. If our solutions to other people's problems are based solely upon our own perceptions, they may not wind up being very effective solutions because the other "side" may not accept our solutions as being realistically related to their problem. Remember, we are talking about *perceptions*, not about who is actually right or wrong. Related to this is the situation in which someone else sees what they think is a problem, but which we do not believe is a problem at all; we might be tempted to regard the other person as simply stupid, ill-informed, or wanting to waste our time. Worse yet, we might view the world from the perspective of our own problems and completely ignore those of others, assuming their concerns are identical to ours.

Each element of the criminal justice system has a set of rules and procedures for dealing with the problems which come to its attention. These rules and procedures are usually legalistic and bureaucratic in nature. Viewed another way, the criminal justice system has a set of answers and solutions which they are willing to apply to those problems that seem to fit. This is not as callous or insensitive as it might seem at first; the criminal justice system cannot be all things to all people, and there is a limit to the range of problems it can or should deal with. You cannot reasonably expect to go into a hardware store for a haircut just because they sell clippers and want to make money. Neither can you take many social problems to the police or courts just because they are dispensers of "justice."

The criminal justice system can try to understand the problems of its clients and make referrals where possible. In some cases the system can do a great deal of good by simply helping people or groups clarify their problems so they themselves can seek out the proper solutions.

Unclear Objectives

In spite of the fact that those within the criminal justice system know what their jobs are, many tend to forget the ultimate *objectives* of those jobs. The key to understanding this problem is the realization that *individual* objectives are not the same as *collective* objectives. Presumably the two are related, but in actual practice this is often not the case at all.

If an organization does not have a set of clear and realistic objectives, it is very unlikely that the organization will even accidentally accomplish them! When an organization does not have clear objectives, the individuals within the organization are likely to substitute their own personal objectives and to work toward them by using the institutional framework of their organization. It should be clear that there is a great deal of difference between bureaucratic ideologies (e.g., "To Protect and Serve," or "Justice for All") and the actual objectives an organization pursues. This is a problem for public agencies that must try to reconcile specific operations with abstract concepts like "justice."

Lack of Organizational Framework

As Gray and Starke point out, "Although the environment in which organizations operate changes constantly, large changes tend to occur only over extended periods of time. Needed changes can often be accommodated by making minor modifications in existing structures at a specific point in time."[45] This means that "getting out of tune" can be a subtle process, and we may become aware of it only when a crisis occurs. Although frequent minor changes might prevent an organization from getting out of tune, if the need for such minor changes is not perceived, they are likely not to be made. The result may be that over time the organizational framework of the agency may no longer be well-suited to the problems with which it must deal. The organization may develop a framework which is incapable of accomplishing its long-range objectives.

Problems of Inertia: Overcoming Resistance

People become comfortable in routine tasks. Many dislike having the rules changed and dislike having to adapt to new requirements — especially when they may not necessarily support the purposes behind the changes. This means that many community relations programs will encounter fairly stiff resistance from those who see such programs as either a waste of time or an imposition. Overcoming this kind of inertia can be both time-consuming and difficult; when resistance takes the form of passive aggression the problem can be especially trying. Organizations which are heavily dependent on formal rules and established procedures are especially prone to problems of institutional inertia.

The Negative Impact of Tradition

Closely related to the problem of inertia is that of tradition. Many organizations base their operations around tradition (this is certainly true of criminal justice agencies), and tradition can be sorely out of touch with contemporary realities. Tradition has long dictated both what kinds of tasks will be performed and who within the agency will perform them. In addition, status hierarchies within agencies are a function of tradition. For example, detectives enjoy higher prestige within their department than do patrol officers, and appellate court judges enjoy higher prestige than trial court judges do in the pecking order of courts. People who seek the rewards their organizations have to offer typically do so by following traditional pathways. The new or unusual is often viewed with suspicion unless it represents a technical advancement over a traditional function. Community relations is new to the criminal justice system, and many who work within the system do not believe it should be a part of that system. Traditional excellence in police work, for example, is based on "good" arrests or skilled detective work. Community relations has never played a significant role in police work and has been even less important to the courts or corrections. Altering tradition and overcoming inertia has proven a formidable task. To be realistic, it will take at least another generation before the weight of tradition can be shifted enough to allow room for community relations as a legitimate and viable part of the criminal justice enterprise.

Conflict Management

In general, government tends to look at conflict as being destructive because it has all too often led to disorder. This tendency is quite natural, especially for the criminal justice system, because the system places a high value on order. Conflict and violence are not synonymous and conflict is a perfectly legitimate aspect of change. In fact, it is unlikely that there would be much change if there were no conflict. It is not the role of government to *supress* conflict, but rather to *manage it in a positive way*. There are essentially three kinds of conflict which involve the criminal justice system. The first involves interpersonal conflict and includes such things as family disorders, fights, and various kinds of brawls. The second kind of conflict involves disputes between groups of people and involves such things as management-labor disputes, campus disruptions, and landlord-tenant disputes. The third kind of conflict is between citizens and government, such as protest group activities and public assemblies. Each kind of conflict presents a different challenge to the criminal justice system, and unless criminal justice agencies are trained in techniques of conflict management, they run the risk of aggravating an already bad situation.

Inadequate Means for Citizens to Bring Complaints

When citizens have complaints about what they believe to be important problems, there should be some means by which those complaints can be received, evaluated, and acted upon. Although many police departments are willing to receive and investigate complaints, those complaints must involve either the violation of some law or, in the case of complaints against the police, a violation of some departmental policy. In some cases a police department will accept and act upon complaints that allege insufficient service or the need to engage in some kind of selective enforcement activity. Nevertheless, police departments generally do not act on complaints involving civil matters.

The courts and corrections do not generally receive complaints, unless they come in the form of a lawsuit. Government itself is not organized to deal with citizen complaints and where mechanisms do exist for receiving such complaints, they are often cumbersome and intimidating, especially to the poor or those with language or cultural problems. The important thing to remember about citizen complaints is that they are not merely "complaints," they are a request for some kind of service as well. They ask government to either do something or to quit doing something that citizens find distasteful. The more effective the mechanisms for receiving and acting on complaints, the more responsive government can be to the needs of its citizens. Problems in this area perpetuate citizen dissatisfaction and maintain barriers where none should exist.

The problem areas listed above are each complex, and taken as an interrelated group of problems, it is easy to see the magnitude of the challenge which the criminal justice system faces. It is also easy to see how people and groups with special needs can be overlooked or given inadequate consideration and how this can happen without malice or any kind of overt discriminatory intentions. These problems also point out the importance of *internal* considerations when considering *external* conflicts or controversies, and the difficulty — if not impossibility — of finding quick and easy solutions to the kinds of complex problems faced by the criminal justice system.

Summary

Community relations requires an intelligent and reasoned approach to community problems along with a recognition of the fact that most communities are quite complex. The diversity within a given community produces a wide range of special needs on the part of individuals and groups. Perhaps the most significant group with special needs is the poor. People caught up in poverty are chronically beset with economic, health, occupational, social, and psychological problems and usually depend on government for solutions to those problems. Some of their problems bring them into contact with the criminal justice system, and that contact may even aggravate the problems they already have. Many of the poor are high-risk cases because they have such a small investment in maintaining the normative system; it has pretty well bypassed them. It is only reasonable that they should not have a strong commitment to social values which have not rewarded them in the past and only serve to point out that they are "outsiders."

Closely related to the issue of poverty is the problem of minority status. Not only are minorities over-represented in the ranks of the poor, they also suffer from specific problems, such as discrimination, language problems, cultural difference within the larger society, and serious problems in self-concept. The largest group of minorities in America is composed of Blacks, who are also over-represented in a significant number of crime statistics. The historical legacy of Black Americans has not only left them heavily impoverished as a group, but has acted upon them in other ways as well. Generations of discrimination and hostility have left many Blacks suspicious of and hostile toward the crimal justice system and seriously under-represented in the ranks of criminal justice professions.

Hispanics, including Mexican-Americans, Puerto Ricans, and Cubans have likewise experienced hardship and disappointment in their attempts to find a place in society. Their problem has been heightened by language and culture barriers as well as by basic economic difficulties. Nearly all minorities, especially those distinguishable by skin color, language or culture, have had problems in assimilation. A realistic community relations effort will not attempt to "homogenize" these people by urging them to become just like their majority community neighbors, but rather should attempt to recognize the particular needs and problems each minority group faces and should help them, both as individuals and as groups, to strengthen their ties to the larger society through a sense of reciprocal obligation and trust.

The elderly constitute another group with special needs, and they are a group which is particularly easy to overlook. The aged, as both offenders and victims of crime, present some very difficult problems to the criminal justice system. At the other end of the age spectrum are the young, and they likewise present their own serious problems to the criminal justice system.

Problems in community relations do not always arise from outside of the criminal justice system; many of them are a direct consequence of the bureaucratic nature of criminal justice agencies themselves. Internal problems such as a failure to identify or understand the problems of their clientele, ambiguous operational objectives, shortcomings in organizational framework, problems of inertia, the negative impact of tradition, inadequate techniques of conflict management, and inadequate means by which citizens can voice complaints, all contribute to the mass of problems which surround efforts at community relations by the criminal justice system.

Discussion Questions

1.   How would you distinguish between problems a "city" has from the problems of individuals and groups within the city? To what extent are they related?

2.   Why is it so difficult for citizens with common problems to "get together" on those issues, especially when they need to deal with local government?

3.   Are the actions of single-issue political action groups healthy for the community as a whole?

4.   Should the criminal justice system concern itself with *special* needs of some group? If they do, would this not be showing discriminatory or preferential treatment?

5.   What kinds of things keep a person confined to the "culture of poverty?"

6.   Some people have said that the poor deserve to be poor: they elect not to get an education or not to work and therefore deserve the poverty in which they live. How do you react to this sentiment?

7.   Why are minorities overrepresented in the ranks of the poor?

8.   What are the "residual effects" of discrimination against Blacks which continue to influence both them and the criminal justice system?

9.   Why did the Cubans who fled to Florida after Castro took over do so much better than the Puerto Ricans who have moved to New York City?

10.   Should minorities with their own language and historic culture give them up and try to become "typical" Americans? Why or why not?

11.   How does confusion over the difference between civil and criminal law contribute to the hostility many minorities feel toward the criminal justice system?

12.   Are the problems of the elderly really that serious? Qualify your answer.

13.   If status offenses are eliminated, will this give young people more latitude to get in trouble?

14.   Can you have a bureaucratic form of organization without the problems typically associated with it?

15.   Why "must" criminal justice function as a bureaucracy?

Glossary

BARRIO   The term applied to residential areas populated by people of Hispanic background.

CULTURE OF POVERTY   A term describing the means by which the poor adapt to (and in so doing perpetuate) their impoverishment.

SINGLE ISSUE POLITICS   The attempts by certain special interest groups to use political action in securing some special advantage.

STATUS OFFENSES   Offenses associated with juveniles because of their status *as* juveniles; includes such "offenses" as disobedience, truancy, curfew violations, etc.

Notes

[1] See for example Alvin Toffler, *The Third Wave* (New York: William Morrow and Company, Inc., 1980). Toffler argues that much of what appears to be chaos belies a "startling and potentially hopeful pattern" which he sees as part of the rise of a new civilization.

[2] See for example Hubert T. Klein, *The Police: Damned if They Do, Damned if They Don't* (New York: Crown Publishers, 1968); Seymour Martin Lipset, "Why Cops Hate Liberals and Vice Versa," *The Atlantic*, March 1969, pp. 76-83; Arthur Niederhoffer, *The Ambivalent Force* (Hinsdale, Illinois: The Dryden Press, 1976); Albert Reiss, Jr., *The Police and the Public* (New Haven: Yale University Press, 1971); and Milton Rokeach, Martin G. Miller, and John A. Snyder, "The Value Gap Between Police and Policed," *Journal of Social Issues* 27 (1971): 155-171.

[3] Louis A. Radelet, *The Police and the Community* (Beverly Hills: Glencoe Press, 1973), p. 217.

[4] Oscar Lewis, *Five Families: Mexican Case Studies in the Culture of Poverty* (New York: Basic Books, 1959).

[5] See for example Herbert J. Gans, "The Uses of Poverty: The Poor Pay All," *Social Policy* 2 (July-August 1971): 20-24.

[6] See for example Graham B. Spanier, "The Black Family's Special Plight," in "Outsiders Looking In," *The Wilson Quarterly* (Summer 1980): 130-131.

[7] U.S. Department of Commerce, Bureau of the Census, *Statistical Abstract of the United States, 1981*, 102d ed. (Washington, D.C.: U.S. Government Printing Office, 1982), passim.

[8] Congress of the United States, Congressional Budget Office, Background Paper Number 17 (Revised), *Poverty Status of Families Under Alternative Definitions of Income* (June 1977). The percentage for white families was 24.7%.

[9] *Statistical Abstract of the United States, 1981*, Table 746, "Persons Below Poverty Level, By Race, Residence, and Family Status: 1975 and 1979," p. 446.

[10] U.S. Department of Commerce, Bureau of the Census, *Statistical Abstract of the United Staes*, 100th ed., Table 574, "Aid Families with Dependent Children (AFDC) - Percent Distribution by Recipient Families and Children By Characteristics: 1973-1977," p. 357.

[11] Charles E. Silberman, *Criminal Violence, Criminal Justice* (New York: Vintage Books, 1978), p. 159.

[12] Timothy J. Flanagan, David J. Van Alstyne, and Michael R. Gottfredson, eds., *Sourcebook of Criminal Justice Statistics - 1981* (Washington, D.C.: U.S.

Printing Office, 1982). See Table 6.26, "Prisoners Under Jurisdiction of State and Federal Correctional Authorities, By Race, Religion, and Jurisdiction, on December 31, 1979," p. 477.

[13] Personal observations by the author or incidents related to him by the participants.

[14] J. Davis, "Justification For No Obligation: Views of Black Males Towards Crime and the Criminal Law," *Issues in Criminology* (1974): 69-87.

[15] Michael J. Lillyquist, *Understanding and Changing Criminal Behavior* (Englewood Cliffs, New Jersey: Prentice-Hall, Inc., 1980), pp. 185-186.

[16] See John R. Howard, "Mexican Americans: The Road to Huelga," in *Awakening Minorities* (Chicago: Aldine Publishing Co., 1970), pp. 89-104.

[17] Manuel P. Servin, *An Awakening Minority: The Mexican Americans*, 2d ed. (Beverly Hills: Glencoe Press, 1974), p. 45.

[18] Bernard A. Weisberger, *The American People* (New York: American Heritage Publishing Co., Inc., 1971), p. 351.

[19] Howard, "Mexican Americans," p. 94.

[20] Cited in Weisberger, *The American People*, p. 353.

[21] Joseph R. Fitzpatrick, *Puerto Rican Americans: The Meaning of Migration to the Mainland* (Englewood Cliffs, New Jersey: Prentice-Hall, Inc., 1972), p. 2.

[22] Weisberger, *The American People*, p. 364.

[23] Silberman, *Criminal Violence, Criminal Justice*, pp. 161-167.

[24] See for example Rob Wilson, "Chinatown: No Longer A Cozy Assignment," *Police Magazine*, July 1978, pp. 18-32.

[25] Lillyquist, *Understanding and Changing Criminal Behavior*, p. 186.

[26] Weisberger, *The American People*, p. 360.

[27] *Statistical Abstract of the United States, 1981*, Table 29, "Resident Population By Age, Sex, and Race: 1960-1980," p. 26.

[28] T. Bernocchi, "La Senilita del Punto di Vista Criminologico," *Quaderni di Criminologia Clinica* 16 (1974): 321-342.

[29] D. Shichor and S. Korbin, "Criminal Behavior Among the Elderly: A Survey of the Arrest Statistics." Paper presented at the 28th Annual Meeting of the American Society of Criminology, Tucson, Arizona, November 4-7, 1976.

[30] James D. Page, *Psychopathology: The Science of Understanding Deviance* (Chicago/New York: Aldine-Atherton, 1971), p. 396.

[31] See for example S.K. Steinmetz, "Battered Parents," *Society* 1978: 55-56.

[32] See for example Nova Institute, *Reducing the Impact of Crime Against the Elderly* (New York: Nova Institute, 1977).

[33] Fay L. Cook and Thomas D. Cook, "Evaluating the Rhetoric of Crisis: A Case Study of Criminal Victimization of the Elderly," *Social Service Review* (December 1976): 632-646.

[34] Nova Institute, *Reducing the Impact of Crime Against the Elderly.*

[35] See for example Frank Clemente and Michael B. Kleiman, "Fear Among the Aged," *Gerontologist* 16 (1976): 329-334.

[36] Victoria H. Jaycox, "The Elderly's Fear of Crime: Rational or Irrational?" *Victimology* 3 (1978): 329-334.

[37] See especially Marlene A. Young Refai, *Older Americans' Crime Prevention Project: Final Report* (Multnomah County, Oregon: Public Safety Division, Community Affairs/Crime Prevention Unit, 1976).

[38] David G. Peck, "Criminal Victimization of the Elderly: Some Implications for Care," *Journal of Humanics* 6 (1978): 53-56.

[39] Harry G. Fox, Murray J. Latzen, and Frank H. Vaquez, "Senior Citizens," *Law and Order* 26 (1978): 20-33, 60-65, and 85-86. See also: "The Blue and the Gray: Should Police Set Up Special Units to Protect the Elderly?" *Police Magazine*, September 1982, pp. 57-64.

[40] See for example Dan Bernstein, "Police vs. Child Abuse: Protecting the Victim Comes First," *Police Magazine*, November 1978, pp. 58-63.

[41] United States Department of Justice, Federal Bureau of Investigation, *Uniform Crime Reports - 1981* (Washington, D.C.: U.S. Government Printing Office, 1982), Adapted from Table 25, "Total Arrest Trends, 1972-1981," p. 165.

[42] Gresham M. Sykes, *Criminology* (New York: Harcourt Brace Jovanovich, Inc., 1978), p. 609.

[43] See for example *In Re Gault*, 387 US 1 (1967) and *Kent v United States*, 383 US 451 (1966).

[44] See for example Michael S. Serrill, "Police Write a New Law on Juvenile Crime," *Police Magazine*, September 1979, pp. 47-52.

[45] Jerry L. Gray and Frederick A. Starke, *Organizational Behavior: Concepts and Applications* (Columbus, Ohio: Charles E. Merrill Publishing Co., 1977), p. 102.

EMERGING ROLES
OF THE POLICE

6

The police as an institution is a contradiction: it is uniquely modern, yet it is also ancient. American police are distinctive; they are unlike those of any other nation, yet the roots of American policing extend far beyond our own national borders into other nations such as England, Italy, and Greece.[1]

The word "police" comes from the Greek *polis*, which refers to both the city per se and to the concept of state. The city, of course, is the physical place; the *state* is the "government" of that place. The principal responsibilities of government have always been to provide for public safety, to safeguard health, and to protect morality (however *that* has been defined). Thus, in its most basic sense, *to police* means *to provide civil government*. The providing of civil government, however, involves a great deal more than simply passing and enforcing laws. To fully understand this, we need to look again at the concepts of private and public control.

Until recent times, private and public control were very nearly the same thing. Prior to the Industrial Revolution, communities were smaller and were bound together more by common sentiment, shared religious belief, and mysticism than they are today. Government was in reality more of a device for maintaining the social class system, defending the faith, and dealing with foreign affairs. The private control system regulated the behavior of the community members more often than did the "government." Why was this the case?

The two major intellectual domains up until the age of Enlightenment (roughly the 18th century) were astrology and religion; indeed, the two were often difficult to fully separate. Astrologers studied the movements and positions of the heavenly bodies and interpreted what they saw in terms of their significance to events on earth. The ability to predict such events as eclipses and floods gave astrologers great power and they were widely respected not only in Europe, but in Asia as well. Astrologers divided the heavens into twelve sections corresponding to the twelve constellations along the path the sun appeared to follow. These twelve sections (or "houses") became the zodiac, and each of the houses was seen as having power over some aspect of life.

Astrology had a major influence on man's intellectual development and is the mother of both astronomy and medicine (the astrological sign of Jupiter ♃ , is *still* placed at the beginning of a physician's prescriptions). Because they did not have the scientific knowledge which is taken for granted today, people thought their lives were controlled by external forces. Astrology helped to provide the means for understanding those forces.

Astrology complemented religion, which expresses concern over things beyond the visible world. Religion generally embodies the idea of a supreme being who not only created the world and all of the other heavenly bodies, but who also controls their destinies. Religion is distinguishable from philosophy in that it is based on *faith*, whereas philosophy is based on reason. The practice of faith is normally regulated by creeds and rituals which also define man's role with respect to all other things. Religion, therefore, defines *morality*, or what is right and wrong in God's scheme of things. The *individual's* role in a theologically-oriented society is not to decide right or wrong, but rather to accept the church's teachings and to live according to what he is *taught* is right or wrong. Things not understood are not to be questioned, but rather to be taken on faith.

The interplay between astology and religion can be seen in the explanations given for the plague which swept Europe in the late 1340's. The medical faculty at the University of Paris offered the explanation that the plague was caused by a triple conjunction of Saturn, Jupiter, and Mars in the 40th degree of Aquarius; this was believed to have happened on March 20, 1345.[2] The common man saw only one explanation: the wrath of God. As the historian Barbara Tuchman noted, "Planets might satisfy the learned doctors, but God was closer to the average man." She further noted that some people genuinely thought the plague "might even be God's terminal disappointment with his creature" because of his sins.[3] It took another 500 years before man the sinner learned that the plague was caused by the bacillus *Pasturella pestis* and was conveyed by the flea and the rat.

The Protestant Reformation of the 17th century, the rise of mercantile capitalism, the age of political revolution, and the Industrial Revolution changed all that. Man was freed from the bondages of superstition, ignorance, and feudalism, and he moved into new and challenging forms of social organization. The *polis* — the city — changed in size, scope, and function as well as in complexity. The government of the polis shifted to secular leadership as religion, medicine, science, and astrology began to go their separate ways. The basis for the authority by which the polis was governed increasingly became that of *law* rather than custom, superstition, or dogma. This application of law to the regulation of human affairs required three major aspects or domains of government. The first was to be composed of those who *made* the laws, the parliaments and legislatures. The second was composed of those who *interpreted* the law, bodies such as the courts and legal tribunals. Finally, the use of law in government required administrators or executives whose job was to discharge the mandates provided for by the laws. It was not until the emergence of secular law that policing in its most rudimentary form could emerge.

The Emergence Of The Police: The Early Steps

The administration of civil affairs and the enforcement of laws were originally pretty much one and the same. That is, they were responsibilities carried out by the same official. Perhaps one of the earliest of these officials was the "Reeve" or "Shire-reeve" — the sheriff. In England the sheriff was the executive authority of his county and as such was a very important official. He had a number of duties, including attending judges at court; executing writs issued by the courts (and prisoners condemned by them); caring for prisoners awaiting trial or execution; and in some instances, collecting taxes. The sheriff thus *administered* justice according to the customs of his time, although he was not a law enforcement officer as we use that term today. Another interesting official was the *coroner*, who, among other things, was a check on the sheriff! If a person died under certain circumstances, his property was forfeit to the crown, and the coroner was supposed to determine the cause of death so the deceased's property could be properly disposed of!

However, the most important forerunner to the police was the *constable*. In medieval England, a number of officers were elected to serve the local lord in the administration of the affairs of the community. These officials included such colorful characters as the ale-taster, the bread-weigher, and the swine-ringer; however, the most important of all was the constable.[4] By the end of the 13th century the constable was recognized by the crown as having special responsibility for keeping the peace; actually, the constable was more of what we would consider a district attorney than a policeman because his basic job was to bring complaints before the courts. Critchley sums up early "policing" in England after passage of the Statute of Winchester (1285) in terms of the following basic principles:

> First, it was the duty of everyone to maintain the King's peace, and it was open to any citizen to arrest an offender. Second, the unpaid, part-time constable had a special duty to do so, and in the towns he was assisted in this duty by an inferior officer, the watchman. Third, if the offender was not caught red-handed, hue and cry was to be raised. Fourth, everyone was obliged to keep arms with which to follow the cry when required. Finally, the constable had a duty to present the offender at ... court ...[5]

Thus, the community was actually "policed" by all of its citizens, with the constable playing more or less of an organizing and officiating role. The constable was, however, supposed to see to it that if violations did take place, they would be brought before the court for proper adjudication.

As can well be imagined, this job was not a popular one and many sought to avoid having to serve as constable. Over time the office fell into disrepute, being considered fit only for the inept, incompetent, or the old. Indeed, much of the control was imposed on the individual through the private control system, which included significant participation by the church. This system of parish constables is known in England as the "old police" and is widely regarded as having been very inefficient. It was allowed to persist for the next five hundred years until the growth of crime and social disorder finally reached proportions that could no longer be tolerated. Even such "police" as did exist were quite different in their approach to crime from police of today. Policemen were not public servants in the way we now think of policemen: "They were members of a liberal profession who operated on the principle of fee for service. If a man had been robbed, he could go to a magistrate's court like that at Bow Street and hire a police officer to try to get his property back."[6] These police officers worked independently of one another and worked essentially for fees from clients and for rewards from the government. The situation in 1821 had reached the following state, as described by a Magistrate of the times:

> The manner in which hordes of thieves are suffered to prowl about the Metropolis and its neighborhood and rob and maltreat passengers when a crowd is assembled, is a disgrace to our police system. Yet while these things are going on, officers in abundance are loitering about the police offices, in

waiting for hire. Protection is reserved for individuals who will individually pay for it.[7]

The lack of an effective civil police combined with increasingly frequent riots which often required military supression alarmed many informed thinkers of the time. People such as Patrick Colquhoun, Jeremy Bentham and the brothers Henry and John Fielding argued in favor of the creation of a civil police. Their recommendations were repeatedly rejected, based on the fear that such a police force would violate English liberty. Ultimately, the fear of riots and recognition of a need for moral reform created a climate which allowed passage of the Metropolitan Police Act on July 19, 1829, through the efforts of the Home Secretary, Sir Robert Peel. This act created a metropolitan police for London, which was to be divided into seventeen police divisions, each under the command of a police superintendent. Each police division had four inspectors and sixteen sergeants, and each sergeant was to supervise nine police constables. Each constable was to be armed with a rattle with which he could summon aid, and a short "truncheon" which was to be carried concealed beneath the constable's coat. The police were unarmed because their founders wanted them to earn support through respect rather than through force (indeed, the English police are for the most part still unarmed — although that may change in coming years).

The men recruited for the job had to be under thirty-five years of age and in good physical condition. They were required to be at least five feet seven and had to be literate. Each applicant had to produce two letters of reference from previous employers, and former watchmen were not accepted into the new police. The pay was low: nineteen shillings a week, and almost total control was imposed over the lives of the new policemen. Significantly, it was a deliberate policy not to hire men who had "the rank, habits, or station of gentlemen" — thus excluding former military officers or members of the aristocracy.*[8] Finally, at 6 p.m. on Tuesday evening, September 29, 1829, the first "new police" marched out of their stations for the first time and into the streets of London. On that evening, the police — as we know them — were born.**

*The founders of the Metropolitan Police, Richard Mayne and Charles Rowan, who also served as its first commissioners, sought to avoid political corruption of the police by keeping its members restricted to the "working class." Although this tactic worked, it had the simultaneous effect of locking police work into the status of a blue-collar (or even "low class") occupation — a pattern that is only now being altered in both England and the United States.

**The new police were not, however, well received at first. They were widely denounced throughout London as an 'outrage and an insult' to the people. Police constables who tried to control traffic were run down and lashed with whips; many others were subjected to unremitting hostility in the form of jeers, insults and taunts. In August of 1830 the first London Police officer to be killed in the line of duty (John Long) was stabbed to death. In 1833, in a clash between the police and a mob, an

The American colonies had already declared their independence some fifty years earlier. Although Americans and Englishmen share a common legal and social heritage, the two countries went their separate ways in the development of their respective police systems. One can only wonder what the American police would be like today had the Peelian reform taken place *before* American independence!

Early American Police

Those who settled in America brought the trappings of their European culture with them, and the influence of Europe was to be felt for many generations, even after the colonies separated from England. The new nation was composed primarily of small agricultural communities and a few large cities. What little policing there was occurred in the cities and copied the English constable-watchman system. As in England, it was at best only marginally effective. Circumstances in the two countries were *not* the same, and as the English moved toward their appointment with the Metropolitan Police Act, Americans moved in a different direction.

Unlike England, America was an "open" country. People could move about as they wished and the new nation was blessed with a rich and constantly expanding frontier which offered both land and opportunity. Social conventions were also different and the United States rejected the use of a class system based on aristocracy.

Along with this enormous opportunity, there was also violence and disorder. The new frontier was not handed over freely by its previous tenants. The new cities quickly became places of diversity which reflected the whole panorama of immigration; there were "divisions not only between classes, but also between whites and Blacks, Irish and native born, Protestant and Catholic, and beer drinkers and prohibitionists," and as Richardson noted, "These political and social cleavages profoundly affected the development of urban police in the United States."[9]

The population of the cities grew rapidly and "political and social cleavages" were aggravated by inadequate housing, crowding, poverty, discrimination and other social ills which resulted in sprawling slums. During the middle decades of the 19th century it became apparent that police departments were essential if the cities were to cope with the

---

officer was killed in a charge against rioters and the officer's death was ruled a 'justifiable homicide' (later overturned). The London police persevered; in the words of one historian, "Such were the intolerable conditions in which the Metropolitan Police forged the reputation which, within a few years, was to make the force world-famous. Their impertubability, courage, good humour, and sense of fair-play won first the admiration of Londoners and then their affection." (Critchley, *A History of Police in England and Wales*, p. 55).

increasing disorder. The old watch-and-ward systems were obviously inadequate. State legislatures met the problem by authorizing the creation of municipal police departments.* The first municipal police department (ie. unified 24-hour police department) was created in New York City in 1845 when that city merged its separate day and night watches into a single police department. Philadelphia followed in 1848, as did Boston in 1854; within a few years police departments appeared in most major cities.

These early police departments were quite different from those of today. At first American police did not wear uniforms, although uniforms became the rule rather than the exception by the 1860's. In order to identify themselves, New York City police officers were supposed to wear a small badge in the shape of a star, and for this reason they were sometimes called "star police."[10] The creation of American police was the product of a political process; it should therefore come as no surprise that politics very quickly entered into all aspects of police departments, from getting hired in the first place to type of assignment or eligibility for promotion. Fogelson pointed this out clearly when he wrote that

> ...what set the American police apart from the French, German, and British police was not so much their commitment to local control, a civilian orientation, and a responsive style *as their relationship with the political machine.* The machine was urban America's outstanding contribution to the art of municipal government. Exemplified by Tammany Hall, it emerged in New York, Philadelphia, and other eastern cities in the early and middle nineteenth century and in Chicago, Kansas City, San Francisco, and other western cities not long after. (emphasis added)[11]

Although American policemen were armed and had ranks, they were organized with a distinctively civilian orientation. Few would have mistaken them for military personnel. At first, the police had only a fuzzy idea of what it was they were supposed to do. The maintenance of order was probably the most important task of the policeman, and he did it by physically walking his beat and keeping a watchful eye. They were not used in fire suppression or in the administration of prisons nor were they given any judicial duties (all of these things are common roles in police agencies in other countries). The police were, however, used for a wide range of public duties:

---

*During the 19th century cities were considered to be instrumentalities of state legislatures; the idea of home rule charters was not yet popular. This allowed the state legislatures to impose very tight controls over cities.

> In the absence of other specialized public bureaucracies, the authorities found the temptation almost irresistible to transform the police departments into catchall health, welfare, and law enforcement agencies. Hence the police cleaned streets and inspected boilers in New York, distributed supplies to the poor in Baltimore, accommodated the homeless in Philadelphia, investigated vegetable markets in St. Louis, operated emergency ambulances in Boston, and attempted to curb crime in all these cities. By the end of the century most departments engaged in a wide range of activities other than keeping the peace.[12]

The police were in very close contact with the people in the city — and so were the politicians. Today most of us only see politicians on television or hear from them at election time. In the 19th century, politicians were in much closer contact with their constituents. Ward leaders made it their business to know who needed what and to help them get it; this was, after all, how one got elected! A policeman's job was very desirable and local politicians played a major role in helping a would-be policeman land his job. Once appointed, the policeman was expected to remember his benefactor — especially at election time: "Empowered to preserve order at the polls, the patrolmen decided whether or not to eject repeaters from the lines, protect voters from the thugs, and respond to complaints by poll watchers and ballot clerks. If the officers abused their authority, the citizens had little or no recourse...."[13] Naturally, the police became closely entwined with politicians, sowing seeds of difficulty that would take decades to change.

Another problem soon developed. Legislation was introduced which sought to control morality, particularly in the regulation of alcohol, gambling and vice. The police were charged with the responsibility of enforcing these laws, and the establishments most likely to suffer from strict enforcement were often owned or controlled by individuals who were also active in politics — or who were connected with politicians. The problem of corruption emerged and has remained firmly entrenched to this very day.

Gradually the police became shaped by the nature of their cities and their work. Politicians fought for control of the police, and officers learned that political connections were needed not only to get the job in the first place, but to advance in it as well. They learned that the highly moralistic laws expected more of them than they could give. They also realized that they were people *of* the community but also people *apart* from it at the same time. By the end of the 19th century "...police departments became highly inbred. Customarily new blood entered only at the lowest level, and men usually spent a number of years in the ranks before attaining command positions."[14] Police departments started to become *instruments* for their members, providing them with security, acceptance, and a place in life. At the same time, their departments became *institutions*, developing a number of characteristics which would persist over time and become part of the legacy of the police well into the 20th century.

American Police In The Twentieth Century

It is very difficult to separate one's self from the *present* when looking at the *past*. It is easy to look at the police of eighty years ago in the light of what we know and expect of the police today; however, we are really talking about two very different worlds. Many of the officers of eighty years ago walked foot beats in cities still lit by gas. They knew virtually nothing about fingerprinting, ballistics, toxicology, physical anthropology, two-way radios or squad cars. The law itself was much less restrictive. The officers were ill-educated, poorly led, tough, practical men. Some had fought in the Civil War; others had seen action in the Indian Wars or in Cuba or the Philippines. They were street-wise men of action who seldom concerned themselves with the theory of criminal justice. In cities such as New York or Boston, many were either first generation Americans or immigrants (especially Irish).

Communications at the turn of the century were primitive at best. Some cities had Gamewell boxes — call boxes with either telephones or telegraph keys in them — with which a patrolman could contact his headquarters to see if he was needed. This was also a way for headquarters to check up on the officers, because they had to call in at set intervals. While some officers walked foot beats, others were horse-mounted. Some cities even had patrol wagons which were drawn by horses and which were used to go to the various beats to collect people arrested by the "beat cop." Perhaps we can develop a better sense of appreciation for how the police have emerged if we look at the evolution of the police practices over this span of seven decades.

Law Enforcement

In its most basic application, law enforcement means the arresting of an offender who is suspected of having committed a crime. For an arrest to be worthwhile, it must support a conviction. The best situation is one in which an officer sees the crime in progress and apprehends the perpetrator. The next best situation is one in which the officer does not see the crimes take place, but does identify a suspect and is able to get evidence which would support a conviction. A weaker situation is that in

171

which the officer knows a crime has been committed and has a suspect, but lacks evidence. The worst situation is one in which the police know a crime has been committed, but have neither suspects nor evidence.

Since most serious crimes known to the police are *reported to* them by citizens, their task becomes that of developing a suspect and obtaining evidence. Developing suspects in *most* cases has never been difficult.* Evidence, however, is a different matter. In the first half of the twentieth century the best source of evidence was the suspect: if he would only be kind enough to confess to his crime, then securing a conviction was easy. In the early years of the century, evidence per se was limited. Forensic science was in its earliest stages, and its application was seldom seen on the streets; indeed, police photography was at that time an innovative and exciting advancement! Police did not collect blood stains, tool marks or trace materials for comparison in a laboratory. Evidence in those days was much less sophisticated: a gun, a knife, or perhaps an article of clothing which had been left at the scene of the crime. The best means of obtaining evidence was to interview suspects, and some of these interviews were severe tasks indeed! Consider the following statement, made in 1910 by the Chief of the Memphis Police Department at a meeting of police chiefs, concerning an incident which had taken place several years earlier:

> ...he began questioning the man, who refused to divulge his name, where he was from, where he roomed, or who his confederate was .... He was very abusive to Captain O'Haver, so I was informed the next day, and that officer finally concluded that the Police Station proper was too public a place for him to further question the thief, and took him downstairs into the cellar.
>
> What followed I don't know, but Captain O'Haver reported the next day that he succeeded in getting from him where he roomed, the description of his partner .... They were convicted and each sentenced to ten years in the Tennessee Penitentiary.
>
> Now I don't know what Captain O'Haver did to secure the information he desired. ...as I said to Captain O'Haver the next morning; whatever you did was right.
>
> You may call it whatever you please, the 'Third Degree' or any other kind of degree, but it had the desired effect. No innocent man suffered and the guilty parties were punished.[15]

It is impossible to ascertain the number of cases of torture, third degree, and illegal arrest perpetrated by the police in the first decades of the

---

This of course varies by type of crime; larcencies and other property crimes tend to produce fewer suspects than crimes against the person.

twentieth century. It is not even possible to speculate on what proportion of successful convictions involved tactics of this type, although it was probably much more common than most people would suspect. Rampant abuses in the use of police authority in order to secure evidence led to a series of court rulings which limited the methods which the police could employ. Indeed, one of the most significant aspects of the development of the law enforcement function of the police has been written into constitutional law.

One early case was that of *Weeks* v. *United States*, a 1914 case which dealt with searches, seizures, and arrest.[16] In this particular case, the defendant was arrested without a warrant at his place of employment by a police officer. It seems that other police officers had gone to the defendant's house, suspecting that he had been involved in an illegal use of the mails for gambling purposes. Upon arriving at Weeks' residence, they were told where a key was kept and after retrieving the key, entered the house, searched Weeks' room, and took possession of various items of evidence which they later turned over to the federal authorities. Later in the day, the police returned to the house with a U.S. marshal, thinking additional evidence could be found. They were admitted by a boarder and again searched Weeks' room, this time taking some letters and other items. Weeks alleged that his rights under the Fourth and Fifth Amendments to the United States Constitution had been violated, and he appealed his conviction on those grounds. The Supreme Court agreed and the case was reversed. At that time the limitations of the Fourth amendment were not regarded as applying to *state* officials; Constitutional safeguards were seen as limitations on the *federal* government. This meant that although evidence obtained by federal officers in violation of the Fourth Amendment would be barred from *federal* prosecution, state and local police officers were permitted to secure evidence in accordance with the state rules of evidence. If local police officers obtained evidence against an accused and then turned the evidence over to federal officers, those officers could use that evidence in a federal prosecution. This came to be known as the "Silver Platter Doctrine" because state officers could use procedures forbidden to federal officers, handing the evidence over on "a silver platter." The "Silver Platter Doctrine" continued until it was barred in the case of *Elkins* v. *United States* in 1960.[17] That case held that evidence seized by local officers by means of an unreasonable search could not be admitted into evidence in a federal prosecution. Finally, in the landmark case of *Mapp* v. *Ohio*, the Supreme Court ruled that all evidence obtained by searches and seizures in violation of the Constitution is inadmissible in even state courts.[18]

One of the most significant legal shifts affecting law enforcement has been the "absorption" of the Bill of Rights. What this means is that the United States Supreme Court has declared that rights provided for in the Bill of Rights of the U.S. Constitution apply to the actions of state and local governments as well as to officials of the federal government. In other words, the rights set forth in the federal Bill of Rights are "absorbed" into the actions of local police and accordingly limit their actions. Continuing legal scrutiny of the police by both federal and state courts has limited what they can do. Some have claimed that this has "handcuffed" the police; yet others say that it has reduced many serious abuses of police authority. It certainly has made law enforcement — from a legal perspective — a much more demanding job and has placed a much greater burden on individual police officers. Many of these court decisions have resulted in the release of persons convicted or accused of very serious crimes, and this has appalled and disgusted many private citizens. These court decisions have also forced the police to be more circumspect in their tactics and to place a much greater emphasis on training. Although it may be more difficult to arrest suspects or to obtain evidence, "sweat boxes," the third degree, unlawful searches and seizures, and other gross violations of police behavior have gone the way of the gas light. Suspects are now advised of their rights, legal counsel is made available, and strong basic safeguards of individual liberties protect *all* citizens. When police absues *do* occur, they tend to be very much the exception rather than the rule and they generate considerable publicity.[19]

Another aspect of the law enforcement role that has changed over the years is what could be termed the police willingness to apply direct, corrective action. In the years prior to World War II the police were much more likely to "deal with a problem at its source." This amounted to a well-placed rap with a night stick; a swift kick in the pants; or a "talking-to" out behind the house. It also included driving drunks or bums to the city limits and tossing them out with a stern warning to stay away. These were seen both as ways of maintaining order and of avoiding unnecessary official intervention into the affairs of others. Although this sort of treatment still exists, it is much less prevalent than in the past, and one suspects that it is more likely to take place in smaller or rural communities than in cities. Because most police officers now work out of patrol cars, and because many of them no longer have the close, intimate contact with citizens which the police once had, most city officers tend to dichotomize events: they either require official action, or they require no action. Personal, "unofficial" involvement is generally not encouraged, and in some cases it is not tolerated.

"D.C. POLICE OFFICER IS REPRIMANDED
FOR SPANKING YOUTH, 13"*

The above headline accompanied a brief article about a Washington, D.C. police officer who was officially reprimanded for spanking a 13-year old youth who was caught stealing potato chips and cookies from a supermarket. The boy was spanked on February 17, 1982, after the store manager turned him over to the police officer. The officer said later that he decided the 13-year old needed discipline, and, with the permission of the boy's guardian, "I put him across my knee and whomped him four times." Washington, D.C. police regulations forbid officers from striking children, even if parents or guardians give permission.

The officer, a 12-year veteran, was taken off his regular beat and assigned to stationhouse duties for five months while the incident was investigated by the U.S. Attorney's office. The police department issued the officer a reprimand.

If changes in the interpretation of the law have had a far-reaching impact on law enforcement, it pales into insignificance when compared to the effects of changes in technology. Technology has truly altered our world, and its influence on the police has been profound.

Technology and the Police

Although the whole spectrum of scientific and industrial technology has had a major impact on the police, it has perhaps been most evident in the areas of transportation, communications, and forensics. In the case of transportation, at the beginning of the century there were only about 4,000 passenger cars produced per year in the United States. Today there are over 115 million automobiles in use, and the automobile is probably one of the most basic pieces of equipment used by the police. The automobile has given the police a relatively new and unpopular task: traffic law enforcement. Of course, transportation has also expanded the scope and mobility of crime; changes in the technology of transportation have been both a boon and a bane to the police. It has enabled them to do their job much more effectively, but as is so often the case, it has also had its price. Advances in transportation have also contributed to the isolation and alienation of American police.

Communications is another area of technology which has had a major impact on the police. The police originally "took to the streets" because there was no effective means of communicating citizen needs to their

---

* "D.C. Police Officer is Reprimanded for Spanking Youth, 13,"
The Washington Post (September 16, 1982), p. B11.

175

stations. The police by and large had to go out and find their work, and they accomplished this by mingling with their clientele. The telephone provided the first critical link, and in 1929 the two-way radio provided the second. The combination of the two enabled citizens to call the police for help and allowed the police headquarters to relay those calls to officers in their cars. Police communications are now highly sophisticated and extend well beyond car radios and frequencies with limited ranges. In spite of some occasional problems, the police are now — for the first time in their history — in close, quick, and effective communication with the public and are able to provide almost instant response to reported crimes or emergencies.

Finally, scientific technologies have made major contributions to police work. This is seen most dramatically in the field of forensics.

FORENSICS: THE RECOGNIZED SPECIALTIES*

Criminalistics - This involves the collection and examination of bloodstains, fibers, hair, glass, bullets, trace items and other physical objects of which the correct identification might be important to a criminal case.

Toxicology - The analysis of poisons or other toxic substances which are suspected of playing a role in a criminal event.

Pathology - The examination of dead bodies to determine the cause of death; includes autopsies which are conducted by medical examiners.

Psychiatry - The application of psychiatry or clinical psychology to crime, as in the use of clinical hypnosis or the construction of psychological autopsies and psychological profiles of suspected offenders.

Physical Anthropology - The examination of the skeletal remains in cases of questioned or suspicious deaths where only skeletal remains or their parts are recovered.

Odentology - The examination of teeth and/or their impressions in the identification of individuals.

The application of science to crime has enabled law enforcement agencies to discover clues, reconstruct events, develop suspects, and tie specific people to crime scenes in ways that had hitherto been impossible.

---

* Michael S. Serrill, "Forensic Sciences: Overburdened, Underutilized," *Police Magazine* (January 1979), pp. 22-24; See also, Joseph P. Bond, "The Forensic Scientist in the Judicial System," *Journal of Police Science and Administration* 9 (June 1981), pp. 160-166.

Although forensics is still under-utilized, it does enjoy a growing popularity and respect by law enforcement agencies and its application seems to be on the rise. Many of the forensic techniques developed by scientists are in widespread use: polygraph examinations, fingerprint examination, the use of comparison microscopes, gas chromatographs, and mass spectrometers. New techniques are being developed which should help make criminal investigation in the twenty-first century a highly technical and scientifically oriented undertaking. All of this will, of course, be magnified by the use of computers, scientific devices which will probably have a greater impact on western man than any other single technological innovation.

Crime Prevention

When the Metropolitan Police was established in London in 1829, the objective behind its institution was the concept of a "preventive police." This idea was clearly articulated by Patrick Colquhoun who, when describing the power of the police, stated that is was to be "upon the broad scale of general prevention — Mild in its operations, — Effective in its results; having justice and humanity for its basis, and the general security of the State and Individuals for its ultimate object."[20] In fact, the first of the *Nine Principles of the British Police* was (and still is) "To prevent crime and disorder, as an alternative to their repression by military force and severity of legal punishment."[21] This is an important point, for a police based on *prevention* is a police quite different from one based on *repression*.[22]

One of the problems with police history is that very little is known about it — in spite of all of the commentary to the contrary.[23] There is precious little literature which documents the means by which American police have sought to prevent crime. Shortly after the turn of the century, American police put a major effort into "crime prevention" — however, the emphasis was on the *crime* part.[24] Crime prevention was seen as the rigorous and effective application of law *enforcement*. More realistically, the Wickersham Commission noted in 1931:

> Police departments in the United States have not been long familiar with crime prevention as a distinct function of the police organization. Some of the largest cities have only recently made provision for separate units, with official recognition, to care for this important work. Much of the reluctance of departments to assign separate standing to this activity has possibly been due to the absence of any clearly defined field in which such a unit should operate, as well as to the habit of preserving the status quo. In the hard school of experience the police have learned that it is usually safest to 'let well enough alone.'[25]

The Commission went on to explain that "crime prevention" for most police departments meant "property protection" — checking doors and advising merchants on security measures; it noted however, that a new emphasis was needed. That new emphasis stressed the "recruitment of criminals" and was based on a belief in the need to understand and change the *causes* of crime. The Commission was especially interested in attacking crime by working with youth. The situation has not changed drastically in the intervening 50 years, although a great deal of money has been spent by the police on "crime prevention."

At this point it is important to draw a distinction between *primary* and *secondary* crime prevention. Primary crime prevention, which is a function of the private control system, is basically the socialization process which instills in the individual a sense of personal and social responsibility. This sense of responsibility translates into lawful conduct. Obviously, there are many family and child-rearing situations which do not produce this outcome. A family may suffer financial or emotional poverty, instability, or even overt hostility. These and many other factors can produce a person who is deviant. The failure of the private control system to achieve primary crime prevention throws the problem into the lap of the public control system. The public control system can attempt to prevent crime by either deterring crime or by dealing with actual or would-be offenders. For this reason it plays a *secondary* crime prevention role. This role is shared in part by the police.

Police efforts at secondary prevention are usually directed at *things* rather than people. For example, the most popular crime-prevention techniques used by police today tend to fall into four classes. The first is composed of the various Operation ID Schemes whereby people mark their property with either a driver's license number or their social security number so the property can be identified if it is stolen. Second, police departments may conduct security surveys or "target hardening" programs to reduce the possibility of theft by reducing the entry. This is usually done by suggesting better locks and lighting systems and installing burglar alarms. Third, some departments engage in Neighborhood Watch programs in which the police encourage citizens to keep an eye on one another's homes and to develop a stronger sense of community. Fourth, there are some programs which deal with environmental design as it relates to criminal opportunity.[26]

The problem, however, is not *things* — it is *people*. The people who are most likely to be involved in crime are also likely to be young, poor, alienated, poorly educated and lacking in job skills. The police are simply not trained or equipped to deal with these root problems; they must therefore deal with crime prevention at a rather superficial level. As a result, much of their efforts in crime prevention are targeted at either high risk locations or at getting citizens to assume more responsibility themselves. The police simply cannot make other people "be good."[27] A major part of the problem of crime prevention and the police is that crime prevention is not rewarded within the police value hierarchy and second, police generally do not care for crime prevention. An officer earns a reputation for good arrests or for excellent work in detecting crime — not for keeping it from happening in the first place. Even where police officers do work in crime prevention programs, those programs are often silly: conducting tours of the police station, passing out stickers to children, or making speeches to bored luncheon groups. It has yet to be shown how these efforts prevent crime.

Why do police departments give crime prevention so much emphasis and so little action? The answer lies in the role of *bureaucratic ideologies*.[28] These ideologies, which are statements of how an organization can help society achieve its ideal state, are developed by top-level officials as an efficient means of communicating with certain groups, both inside and outside the organization. Most people are both unaware of and uninterested in the details of police work, so administrators must come up with a short but effective method of conveying to the public messages which it is willing to accept. Of course, these ideologies should be tied to ultimate policy objectives, and it is more palatable to give a positive ideology (e.g., prevent crime) than a negative one (e.g., catch crooks after they have committed crimes). These ideologies can serve several important functions.

First, they can be used to generate external support. In the case of police, the bureaucratic ideology of preventing crime has the virtue of being just exactly that: a virtue. What reasonable person would argue *against* preventing crime? Second, the ideology can provide a means for developing stronger goal consensus among members of the department. Interestingly enough, this is done by calling for the prevention of crime with the tacit understanding that operationally that actually means more emphasis on traditional *enforcement* operations. Downs notes that bureaucratic ideologies all have seven common characteristics:

1. They emphasize the positive benefits that can accrue from actions of the agency (while de-emphasizing the *cost* of achieving them).

2. Changes in the bureaucratic ideology almost always require either maintaining the agency's operations or expanding them; they never call for a curtailment.

3. The precision with which the department or agency defines its ideology will depend on whether or not it has any competition. The less the competition from other agencies, the more likely the ideology will be very broad.

4. The ideology will emphasize the benefits it provides to society as a whole (that is, they do not address either self-interests or special interests).

5. Each bureau or agency's ideology emphasizes both the desirability and the high present state of its efficiency and centralized coordination; the police, as they say, are ready and willing to do their duty 24-hours a day!

6. Bureaucratic ideologies by their very nature are general in scope.

7. The ideology emphasizes the achievements of the agency and stresses its capabilities for dealing with future problems; ideologies do not discuss either failures or inabilities.

Thus by maintaining crime prevention as a bureaucratic ideology the police can emphasize a positive service to the public and can justify their routine operations. Indeed, many — if not most — police officers *do* feel that their primary task is crime prevention, but they also feel that crime prevention is primarily the consequence of enforcement action and to a lesser extent, it is the consequence of order maintenance. Crime prevention via social case work or psychological intervention is not generally accepted by the police as part of their responsibility, although the youth division in the larger police departments may have officers who involve themselves in such activities. Many officers are quite good at referring citizens to community mental health and social services organizations where they can receive services which might enable them to avoid crime as a response to their problems.

Maintenance of Order and Public Service

We have become accustomed to having the police provide a wide range of services, ranging from locating missing persons to settling marital disputes; however, few people realize just how recent a phenomenon this is. One only has to look back at the beginning of this century to see a very different picture. Fogelson points out that virtually all aspects of American policing (at least in the cities) was dominated by machine politics: "To control the police, or at any rate to influence departmental policy, was therefore among the principal objectives of the ward bosses."[29] There was a tremendous disparity between *rank* and *power*, and this created an aura, if not the reality, of corruption and incompetence. It also meant that the *reality* of urban policing was in conflict with its *theory*.

The theory held that the police enforced the law, maintained order, and served the public. This theory was based on two assumptions; first, that the typical policeman did his job, and second, that society was composed of two classes: the dangerous criminal class and the respectable non-criminal class. The police were supposed to enforce the law against the former and protect the latter. These two assumptions, unfortunately, did not correspond with reality: many if not most, did *not* do their jobs.

There were exceptions to this gloomy picture, of course, but they *were* exceptions. Most of the service citizens received came through politicians who were exquisitely sensitive to the needs of their constituents. They depended on these constituents to keep them in public office so they could pursue the profitable activity of looting the public coffers. The police probably responded more readily to requests made by politicians than to those made by needy citizens.

The first third of the twentieth century was a period of great reform in the cities. Machine politics and the role of the political boss declined dramatically, and cities saw the introduction of professional city management. Major efforts were undertaken to break the stranglehold politicians had over police departments, and this produced the professional model of police in which political intervention in operations (but not administration) was eliminated or at least drastically reduced.

This professionalization of the police was a major factor in the emergence of the service role of the police. Other factors included technological developments, and public assistance and welfare programs established by local government in the 1930's. In the area of transportation the police assumed responsibility for investigating traffic accidents (which is primarily an insurance company problem) and providing traffic control. Perhaps the key factor in the emergence of the service role is the 24-hour availability of police to virtually anyone who calls for them.

What happens is simply this: a complainant calls the police about a non-criminal matter and an officer is sent to talk to him. After learning that the individual's complaint is outside the scope of his authority or ability, the officer tells the complainant that there is nothing he can do. However, there are two things a police officer does *not* want to happen: he does not want the person to complain to his sergeant or others in the department about the treatment he received, and he does not want to be called back to the same place later. The answer is obvious: the officer can offer advice; he can make a referral to another agency; he can transport the complainant to a hospital or welfare or mental health office; he can explain the complainant's options to him. Sometimes all he needs to do is just listen to the person's tale of woe and offer sympathy. Although many officers consider such assistance a waste of police time, it might represent a welcome and valued service to those on the receiving end. Sometimes police officers are confronted with impossible, unusual, exasperating, or bizarre situations and they may "make up" solutions.

PUBLIC SERVICE CALLS*

A distraught Bahamian, now living in Florida, called the police. When the officer arrived she claimed that an enemy had put a curse on her, and her health — indeed her *life* was in danger: what could the police officer do? The officer, a man with experience in such matters, knew what had to be done. He went back to his car and returned with a mojo bag filled with proper things. He uttered magical phrases, cast the special powders around the house, and made certain gestures. He then told the woman the spell had been broken and she was now safe. He left with her being relieved because she was now safe — and very grateful to the police department.

An officer in a Texas city went to a "meet the complainant" call. It was the address of a person who frequently complained to all who would listen that "they" were trying to "get him" by pumping electric rays into his house which were building up in his body and which would ultimately kill him. The officer took a handfull of paperclips and connected them together; he then attached one end of the chain to the man's pants-leg and told him it was a "ray-discharger." He said it would drain all of bad electricity out of his body — but that it would only work for a week, after that he would have to disassemble it, boil the paper clips for a half-hour, and then reassemble them. The crazy man was delighted.

An Arkansas officer had been repeatedly called to the home of a couple who were living together without benefit of matrimony. They had frequent and bitter fights which usually resulted in one or the other calling the police. The officer gravely told the couple that they had called the police too many times, and based on Official Police Regulation, he was going to administer a divorce to them. He instructed the couple to hold hands, with the woman raising her right hand and the man putting his left hand on the officer's badge. He then said, "By the power vested in me by the State of Arkansas and the Official Police Regulations, I now pronounce you divorced."

*These tales — and many more — have been either related to the author or witnessed by him and represent part of the rich lore of the police seldom discussed with outsiders.

> He then asked whose house it was, and upon learning that the
> woman held the lease, he told the man he was trespassing and
> instructed him to leave. He left, and the story was told later at
> the station to the amusement of the officers going off duty.

Although some of these solutions may not be "correct," they are often what seems best at the time. Over time, people have come to expect the police to provide this kind of service and the police have themselves become accustomed to doing so.

Another approach to justifying the use of police officers in a service role is that it is hard to tell just what does or does not involve a criminal matter. It is sometimes difficult to determine what is or is not a potential crime. The failure to respond to a private problem, such as a domestic quarrel, can ultimately result in an assault or a homicide.

Police Officers: The People Who Must Deliver The Services

The actual job of "policing" is carried out by the officer on the street. The majority of these officers are generalists assigned to radio patrol. These are the uniformed officers in the marked cars who routinely patrol a given area and who respond to calls for police assistance within those areas. Other police officers tend to perform more specialized functions, including investigative or traffic work. Most officers work alone or with a partner, and they have an enormous degree of latitude in how they approach their work. The police are vested with tremendous powers of discretion, and this means that the individual officer must assess most situations and then make up his mind as to how he will deal with the problem he has encountered. The decision to arrest, in addition to being controlled by rigid legal requirements, is but one possible action an officer may take in any given situation. Indeed, in *many* situations the option of arrest is not even present!

It is vital to remember that a police officer is not just a symbol of state authority; he is also a human being, and he is subject to all of the strengths and frailties that any other person is likely to have. Police officers have good days and bad days; they have feelings and opinions, likes and dislikes. They represent all religious, ethnic, and educational backgrounds. Thus, when we talk about the "police" it is important to remember that we are talking about both an organization and the individuals within that organization.

It is also important to remember that policing is a job with a great deal of emotional content. Many people feel very strongly about the police (although not necessarily about individual police officers), and police officers themselves work in an emotion-laden environment. They constantly deal with people who are frightened, angry, confused, bewildered, hostile, and lonely. This type of contact certainly has an influence on the perceptions that police officers hold.

Police Officers: A Typology

Generalizations can be misleading; yet sometimes they help us to organize and analyze. With this in mind, Broderick has developed the following typology of police officers in which he described four types of police personalities.[30]

A POLICE TYPOLOGY*

THE ENFORCER — Crime control advocate who has little use for liberal politicians, Supreme Court decisions, or deviant subgroups. Views the solution to crime as arresting offenders and putting them away. Strongly committed to rigid, military organizational styles in police work.

THE IDEALIST — Supports the due process model and has an unrealistically high expectation of society. Tends to be well educated and is the most likely of all types to become cynical and alienated because they believe social reality makes "ideal" police work a pipe dream. Expects the best and is disappointed when it does not occur.

THE REALIST — Falls midway between advocates of control and due process. They know there is not a lot they can do about pressing social problems, but they try to do the best they can under the circumstances. Seldom bite off more than they can chew and tend to be loyal officers who like their jobs.

THE OPTIMIST — More "people oriented" than "crime oriented." They are less concerned about crime fighting and keeping a macho image. Many are college educated and feel that the future holds a great deal of opportunity and that they can have an impact on the future. Optimists are at ease with themselves and can realistically accept the hardships of police work without becoming overly cynical or withdrawn.

Each of these categories is an *ideal* type, and there obviously are many officers who would not fit neatly into one of his categories; yet he sees the typology as a convenient and helpful way of looking at police officers, especially in terms of how they perceive themselves and their roles. In constructing his typology, Broderick has made two assumptions about policing in a democracy and these assumptions contain a built-in conflict.

For a discussion of these types, see John J. Broderick, *Police in a Time of Change.* Morristown, New Jersey: General Learning Press, 1977.

They are that law enforcement has the dual responsibilties of protecting the constitutional rights of all citizens and at the same time it has the task of enforcing all of the laws. He notes that police officers vary in the degrees to which they emphasize these two objectives, and this accounts at least in part for the differences among police officers.

This conflict is not new; Herbert L. Packer discussed it in his analysis of the conflict between the "due process" model of law and the "crime control" model.[31] If the objective of controlling crime is the most important aspect of police work, it would be easy to accomplish. Most chronic offenders are well known to the police. If there were no constitutional limitations on police authority, crime could be greatly reduced. Extracting confessions by force, obtaining evidence through unrestricted searches and seizures, compelling people to offer testimony against themselves, or simply locking up known offenders would do the trick. These are of course *extreme* tactics, but there is no doubt that they would work. At one time or another all of these tactics *have* been employed by the police — and certainly would be applied by many officers if they were still allowed. However, would such tactics, although they might work, be consistent with the values we expect in a free society? The courts have ruled that they are not.

The due process model maintains that a person is innocent until he is proven guilty, and that there are many limitations on the means by which the State can establish the guilt of the accused. This model holds that if the state cannot make its case without resorting to unacceptable methods, then the state *has no case* and the accused must go free. Police officers see this happen to many people whom they know to be predators on fellow citizens and often feel a sense of genuine frustration and even anger at not being able to do anything about it. Some of these officers become cynical and claim that by handcuffing the police, society gets what it deserves; others are patient and know that sooner or later they will get their chance. Some officers simply do not care, as long as they get paid on time.

A police department is likely to be composed of officers with a wide range of perspectives and attitudes. How they perform their jobs, what they think of themselves, their roles, and their clientele will be determined by many factors. There are extremely liberal police officers just as there are extremely conservative policemen; although no one description of the police would be accurate, the typology constructed by Broderick does give us a way of examining broad categories of officers.

A New Generation of Police:
The Young Turks and Higher Education

For years policing was a white, male, blue-collar occupation which attracted men who were interested in a secure job which allowed them some degree of personal freedom. Although the requirements for employment varied widely from one area to another, becoming a policeman in the past required relatively little:

— A high school education or less;
— Minimum height, weight, and age requirements;
— A "clean" background; and in *some* cities,
— A civil service test.

According to the President's Crime Commission (report on the *Police*) in 1967, although about 70 percent of the nation's police departments required a high school diploma at that time, approximately one fourth of the departments required no more than some degree of elementary education.[32] For the most part, physical requirements were much more rigorous than mental requirements. The Crime Commission went on to note that "The quality of police service will not significantly improve until higher educational requirements are established for its personnel."[33] The President's Crime Commission strongly endorsed college education for police officers, and in 1969 the newly created Law Enforcement Assistant Administration started its Law Enforcement Education Program (LEEP), which provided federal funding for both pre-service and in-service individuals. LEEP's scholarships and loans started at a total of $6.9 million in its first year of operation and went to $40 million by 1973. By the end of 1976 LEEP had awarded more than $234 million to over a quarter of a million students who had enrolled in about 1,800 colleges. From 1960 to 1974 the number of police officers who had completed at least one year of college had jumped from 54,000 to 205,000 — or about 46 percent of the nation's police officers.[34]

This has had a major impact on the police service. As the *National Manpower Survey of the Criminal Justice System* indicated in 1978, "The proportion of sworn personnel with less than a high school education was 37 percent in 1960, 19 percent in 1970, and only 10 percent in 1974."[35] It also appears that the emergence of criminal justice programs on college campuses has brought police careers to the attention of large numbers of middle-class young people who before had only seen the police on television. Many of these courses have also been taken by non-police students as electives, and it is impossible to measure the long-range attitudinal impact generated by those courses.

This rapid growth of educational programs for criminal justice personnel has not been without its problems. As one commentator noted, "In a period when many colleges were falling on hard times, enough federal money had come along to arouse the financial wheeler-dealer that lurks in the heart of many college deans."[36] Many of these programs were thrown together with little serious thought, leading one respected educator to conclude that there were "an awful lot of hustlers, and some college presidents serving as pimps, all looking for this LEAA dollar. In fact, I think that what is going on now in criminal justice higher education is perhaps the most scandalous thing in the history of our education..."[37] The rapid growth of these programs has generated enormous controversy, especially concerning their quality.[38] This has produced yet another contradiction — we now have more educated police officers than ever before, but the value of their education is debatable.

In any event, many police departments, especially those in urban areas, have seen a major influx of young, well-educated and enthusiastic middle-class applicants. More and more minorities and females are being recruited into the police service, and this is also changing the make-up of the police labor force. In addition, since police jobs pay relatively attractive salaries (which are often much better than a humanities or social science degree can otherwise command), the competition for police positions is keen. This in turn has led police departments to select from among the best candidates, thus assuring even more well-educated officers coming into the service.

Many of these new police officers are coming into police work because they are genuinely interested in the nature of the work, not because they simply desire security. They are proving to be substantially different from incoming police officers of past generations. They are much less likely to blindly obey orders or to tolerate autocratic supervision. They are very demanding of their departments and many of them are eager to use their education in the development of their careers — and this has produced some serious problems, as will be noted below.

Veteran Police Officers: The Old Guard

As the National Manpower Survey noted, "...the more tenure an officer has, the less likely he or she is to have graduated from high school."[39] This is often the case among many of the nation's senior-ranking police officials. Only 34 percent of all police chiefs of departments having 75 or more employees have bachelor's degrees; only 43 percent of the police executives in agencies with 400 or more employees graduated from a four year college.[40] As the National Manpower Survey notes, "Police chiefs as an occupational group are on the low end of the educational generation gap..."[41] The reason for this is fairly clear; these people entered the police service an average of 22 years ago, when educational requirements were low and advancement in the ranks did not require any additional education.

To make matters even worse, many of the senior officers who do have degrees may have an education of questionable value. As noted above, many of the criminal justice degree programs now in existence were quickly thrown together; they were often staffed with part-time faculty composed of police officers with weak academic credentials and consisted of curricula that were either highly operations-oriented or which were shallow in their approach. Many senior officers attended off-duty degree programs and were given "life experience" credit or majored in amorphous "general studies" degree programs. Many senior officers have been granted academic credit for participation in the FBI National Academy program or for other training programs. It is certainly worth noting that not all degrees represent a good education, and higher education in criminal justice is still a relatively new concept.

In many departments a conflict has developed between the newer, more educated officers and the older, more traditionally-oriented senior officers: a classic case of the Old Guard and the Young Turks. Many younger officers are scornful of their department's ranking officers and view them as out of touch with reality and as inept managers — and there is a great deal of evidence to support those contentions. Unfortunately, many of their chiefs (and their higher-ranking subordinates) see themselves as high ranking *police officers* whose job it is to *command* the members of their departments; their primary emphasis is on *police operations* and their decision-making is based on often-repeated bureaucratic ideologies. They claim that their failures are the product of the courts, an unsupporting public, and the unwillingness of municipal budget officials to give them enough money to hire the men they need to do the job. The Young Turks claim that what they need are police executives who are *managers of a complex organization.* They see their duties as being management-oriented rather than command-oriented and believe that the *command* of field operations should be delegated as far down the hierarchy as possible. Of course, a clear distinction must be made between large and small departments. The smaller the department, the more the chief *must* involve himself in operations; however, in the larger departments of 100 or more officers, this is not usually the case.

The senior officers in many of the larger departments entered the police service long before the current emphasis on education and managerial skill. Many of them advanced in their departments through adroit politics and careful attention to assignment. Many of these officers lack formal training or effective experience in the basic management skills needed to run an organization: planning, organizing, coordinating, and controlling. Many chiefs have become isolated within their departments, often fulfilling little more than a figurehead role. In April of 1976, Robert di Grazia, then Commissioner of the Boston Police Department, delivered a speech before the Police Foundation's "Executive Forum on Upgrading the Police," entitled "Is Your Police Chief a Pet Rock?" The speech unleashed a storm of criticism and controversy — but raised some very important questions on the quality of police leadership. In his speech, di Grazia said (among other things):

> Mere survival — that's the goal of most of us and that's one major thing wrong with police leadership. For the most part, we police chiefs have no vision of ourselves beyond that of being survivors with gold braid.
>
> As police chiefs, most of us have allowed ourselves to be the underlings of American municipal government, somewhat as pet rocks unable to move, grow, change, or innovate.[42]

The environment in which police chiefs must function has become very complex and difficult. Problems associated with productivity, equal opportunity/affirmative action, community relations and fiscal authority call for increasingly high levels of skill — levels which many police chief executives simply do not possess.*[43]

It would certainly be unfair not to mention that there are a large number of police executives who are excellent managers. Although they appear to be a distinct minority, they do exist. As the new officers move up through the ranks, they will become more and more common. Until then (probably for the next ten to fifteen years), there will be tension within police departments between the Young Turks and the Old Guard. This tension will ultimately give way, because the Young Turks will win — as indeed they always do. Time is on their side, and the urgent requirement of increased police productivity and declining revenue bases will accelerate the process. What we are seeing is an emerging professionalism which is accompanied by substantial growing pains.

Summary

The police are a uniquely modern institution, although their origins reach back into antiquity. The idea of police has grown out of the need for governing the *polis* (city). American police have their foundations in

---

*One chief told the author, "Trouble is, we can't expect anyone to respect us since no one is afraid of the police anymore. We need more *fear*; then we can get the job done."

English history, particularly that of the old parish constable. The "New Police" in England date from the Metropolitan Police Act of 1829; however, by that time the American colonies had separated from England and American police therefore developed in a different set of social, political, and cultural contexts than did the modern English police.

Since American police were the product of the political system which created them, politics and policing were closely entwined until recent times (indeed, they are still closely connected in some places). American police practices emerged during the present century according to the dictates of two major forces. The first was the development of *constitutional law*, especially as it affected police practices in such areas as arrest, search, and seizure. The second major force has been *technology*, especially in transportation, communications, and forensic science, the last of which is still in the process of developing and influencing police practices.

American police at first were probably more service oriented than anything else, at least in the watch-and-ward days; in the latter part of the 19th century they developed a primary thrust in the area of law enforcemen. Starting in the 1930's an emphasis on crime prevention emerged, but that particular emphasis was really just another way of approaching enforcement tactics; it has, however, developed into a major bureaucratic ideology today. The police do provide a considerable amount of public service; they probably assumed this role inadvertently, rather than having conscientiously developed it for themselves. Perhaps this was a consequence of developments in technology, primarily transportation and communications.

Police officers themselves are a diverse group. Although they have all of the strengths and weaknesses of any other occupational group, the particular nature of their work does seem to have had an impact in attracting people to the job and in shaping attitudes once on the job. It may be convenient (although arbitrary) to view police officers as *enforcers, idealists, realists,* and *optimists.* Although these distinctions are artificial and arbitrary, they do give some means of examining police work from the attitudinal perspective of the officer himself.

The emergence of higher education for police officers has wrought a significant change in American policing. Although many of the degree programs created for police are of dubious quality, this should not obscure the fact that many police officers have returned to school and have improved their levels of education. They have also attracted large numbers of middle-class people into police work, a circumstance which has had the effect of changing the social ecology of the police service. This has created a serious conflict between new police and their older, more senior-ranked and less-educated superiors. Indeed, the very quality of police leadership is now being questioned.

Discussion Questions

1. What factors made policing a blue-collar occupation in the United States, and how has that contributed to problems of police-community relations?

2. How did politics come to play such an important role in developing police departments in the late 19th century?

3. What does the text mean when it says, "The police became shaped by the nature of their cities and their work?" Is this still the case — or do the police shape the cities and their work"?

4. How have changes in procedural law altered the police function in the past six decades and how have those changes contributed to police-community relations?

5. Has police involvement in traffic law enforcement helped or hurt the relationship between the police and the public?

6. In what ways do you think forensics can improve the relationship between the police and the public?

7. Just how realistic is it to expect the police to prevent crime? How do the police interpret this role?

8. Are the bureaucratic ideologies of the police realistic, or do they actually contribute to citizen dissatisfaction?

9. How has higher education for police officers contributed to tension within the police service?

10. Do you think the concept of police-community relations would have been viable twenty years ago? Why or why not?

Glossary

BUREAUCRATIC IDEOLOGIES   Statements of how an organization can help society achieve its ideal state (e.g., "To Save Lives and Protect Property," "Justice for All," "Progress is our Most Important Product ").

FORENSICS   The application of scientific principles to the detection and investigation of crimes. Forensics consists of six recognized specialties: ballistics; forensic toxicology; forensic pathology; forensic psychiatry; forensic physical anthropology; and forensic odentology.

PRIMARY CRIME PREVENTION   A function of the private control system, it is essentially the socialization process which imparts to the individual a sense of social responsibility that results in behavior which is consistent with law.

REEVE   Formerly an English officer appointed to execute processes, make arrests, and keep the peace. The Shire-reeve is the predecessor to the contemporary sheriff.

SECONDARY CRIME PREVENTION   Efforts by the public control system to prevent criminal misconduct. It has typically been associated with aggressive law enforcement.

WICKERSHAM COMMISSION   The National Commission on Law Observance and Enforcement, chaired by George W. Wickersham. Formed in 1929 by President Herbert Hoover, the Wickersham Commission was created in response to widespread public concern with problems of crime and immorality and was the first of a series of high-level government crime commissions formed to examine problems of crime and criminal justice.

Notes

[1] For overview, see Philip John Stead, ed., *Pioneers in Policing* (Montclair, New Jersey: Patterson Smith, 1977).

[2] Barbara W. Tuchman, *A Distant Mirror: The Calamitous 14th Century* (New York: Alfred A. Knopf, 1978), p. 107.

[3] Tuchman, *A Distant Mirror*, pp. 107-108.

[4] T.A. Critchley, *A History of Police in England and Wales*, 2d ed. (Montclair, New Jersey: Patterson Smith, 1967), p. 5.

[5] Critchley, *A History of Police in England and Wales*, p. 7.

[6] James F. Richardson, *Urban Police in the United States* (Port Washington, New York: Kennikat Press, 1974), p. 7.

[7] Leon Radzinowics, *A History of English Criminal Law From 1750, Volume II, The Clash Between Private Initiative and Public Interest in the Enforcement of the Law* (London: Stevens and Sons, 1956), p. 262, cited in Richardson, *Urban Police in the United States*, p. 7.

[8] Critchley, *A History of Police in England and Wales*, p. 52.

[9] Richardson, *Urban Police in the United States*, p. 20.

[10] Richardson, *Urban Police in the United States*, p. 24.

[11] Robert M. Fogelson, *Big-City Police* (Cambridge, Massachusetts: Harvard University Press, 1977), p. 17.

[12] Fogelson, *Big-City Police*, pp. 16-17.

[13] Fogelson, *Big-City Police*, p. 20.

[14] Richardson, *Urban Police in the United States*, p. 49.

[15] "A Dissenting Opinion on 'Third Degree' by Chief Davis, Memphis, Tennessee, 1910," in Donald C. Dilworth, ed., *The Blue and the Brass: American Policing: 1890-1910* (Gaithersburg, Maryland: International Association of Chiefs of Police, 1976), pp. 78-81.

[16] *Weeks v. United States*, 232 U.S. 383, 34 S. Ct. 341, 58 L. Ed. 652 (1914).

[17] *Elkins v. United States*, 364 U.S. 206 80 S. Ct. 1437, 4 L. Ed. 2d 1669 (1960).

[18] *Mapp v. Ohio*, 367 U.S. 643, 81 S. Ct. 1684, 6 L. Ed. 2d. 1081 (1961).

[19] See for example Bruce Cory, "Police on Trial in Houston: 'They Were Wrong, but ...' " *Police Magazine*, July 1978, pp. 33-40.

[20] Patrick Colquhoun, *A Treatise on the Commerce and Police of the River Thames* (1800; reprinted in Montclair, New Jersey: Patterson Smith, 1969), p. 38.

[21] Cited in William H. Hewitt, *British Police Administration* (Springfield, Illinois: Charles C. Thomas, Publisher, 1965), p. 130.

[22] To appreciate the difference between the two, see for example Aleksandr I. Solzhenitsyn, *The Gulag Archipelago, 1918-1956* (New York: Harper and Row, 1973); George C. Browder, "The SD: The Significance of Organization and Image," in George L. Mossee, *Police Forces in History* (Beverly Hills, California: Sage Publications, 1975), pp. 205-229.

[23] See for example Samuel Walker, "The Urban Police in American History: A Review of the Literature," *Journal of Police Science and Administration* 4 (September 1976): 250-260.

[24] Fogelson, *Big-City Police*, pp. 60-61.

[25] National Commission on Law Observance and Enforcement, p. 111.

[26] Kevin Krajick, "Preventing Crime," *Police Magazine*, November 1979, pp. 7-16.

[27] Charles P. McDowell, "The Police as Victims of their Own Misconceptions," *Journal of Criminal Law, Criminology and Police Science* 62 (September 1971): 430-436.

[28] This discussion of bureaucratic ideologies is adapted from Anthony Downs, *Inside Bureaucracy* (Boston: Little, Brown and Co., 1967), pp. 237-246.

[29] Fogelson, *Big-City Police*, p. 21.

[30] This typology is based on the police types presented in John J. Broderick, *Police in a Time of Change* (Morristown, New Jersey: General Learning Press, 1977); see also Ellen Hochstedler, "Dimensions of Police Types: A Study of Perspective and Passion," *Criminal Justice and Behavior* 8 (September 1981): 303-323.

[31] Herbert L. Packer, *The Limits of Criminal Sanction* (Stanford, California: Stanford University Press, 1968).

[32] President's Commission on Law Enforcement and the Administration of Justice (President's Crime Commission), Nicholas de B. Katzenbach, Chairman, *Task Force Report: The Police* (Washington, D.C.: U.S. Government Printing Office, 1967), p. 10.

[33] President's Crime Commission, *The Police*, p. 126.

[34] David C. Anderson, "The Off-Duty Degree," *Police Magazine*, May 1978, p. 30.

[35] National Institute of Law Enforcement and Criminal Justice, *The National Manpower Survey of the Criminal Justice System*, Vol. 2, *Law Enforcement* (Washington, D.C.: U.S. Government Printing Office, September 1978), p. 3.

[36] Anderson, "The Off-Duty Degree," p. 30.

[37] Anderson, "The Off-Duty Degree," p. 30.

[38] See for example Lawrence W. Sherman, *The Quality of Police Education* (San Francisco: Jossey-Bass, Publishers, 1978); see also Lee W. Potts, "Higher Education, Ethics and the Police," *Journal of Police Science and Administration* 9 (June 1981): 131-134.

[39] *National Manpower Survey of the Criminal Justice System*, Vol. 2, p. 17.

[40] *National Manpower Survey of the Criminal Justice System*, Vol. 2, p. 19.

[41] *National Manpower Survey of the Criminal Justice System*, Vol. 2, p. 19.

[42] Cited in *Target*, July 1976, pp. 6-7.

[43] David M. Kleinman, "Zinging it to the Chief," *Police Magazine*, May 1979, pp. 39-44.

POLICING AS A PUBLIC ENTERPRISE

7

> *"The punishment suffered by the wise who refuse to take part in the government, is to live under the government of bad men."* Plato

The criminal justice system is essentially a public enterprise; its work is carried out for the most part by public employees whose job is to fulfill legislative mandates and whose salaries are paid out of public funds. What makes the criminal justice system particularly complex is that its operations cut across all three branches of government and are carried out at multiple levels of government. The legislative branch, for example, makes the laws which must be enforced by the executive branch, but those laws and the means by which they are enforced are subject to review by the judicial branch. The police are part of city government, but the courts are not.* Corrections can take place at all levels of government; the State normally takes the major role in the case of serious crimes and the county usually assumes responsibility for minor crimes. If we want to understand the police and their relationship to the rest of the community, we must see how they fit into the organizational structure at the city government level.

First, it is important to remember that the cities are "creatures" of the state. Cities have charters granted by state legislatures which give them the authority to act as municipal governments. This means that city

---

*There are exceptions to this. In some jurisdictions one can find a *county* or *metropolitan area* police force; and, of course, sheriff's departments are law enforcement agencies and many of them actively carry out police duties. Most states also have state police agencies, although their role is normally of a specialized nature. For the most part, however, when we talk about the *police*, we are talking about a *municipal* or *city* agency. Although some courts are city courts, most are either state courts or serve a judicial district. The courts, of course, can and do extend from those of limited jurisdiction at the local level all the way up through the various types of federal appellate courts.

governments carry out the mandates of the state, but they do it at the *local* level, on behalf of and for their own residents. In order to do this, the state grants the city the right to raise taxes and to provide services; these rights are of a limited nature. Cities are also authorized to pass laws in the form of local ordinances. Just exactly what is it that cities do? As Richardson and Baldwin note, "Historically, municipal governments have exercised predominant responsibility in urban areas for enforcement of what constitutions call the 'police power': law enforcement, nuisance abatement, fire protection, street maintenance, parking and traffic control, sewage treatment and refuse collection, and similar public functions."[1] City government probably touches us more directly than any other level of government because it provides the regulatory and service aspects of the environment in which we live. Clearly, police departments are a very important part of city government; however, to understand how police departments function, we need to know first how city government is organized and then where and how the police fit into that organization.

Forms Of City Government

There are basically three forms of local government. It should be noted, however, that the models discussed below are *ideal constructs* and that a given city will most likely be a *variation* of one of the three basic types. The three differ for the most part in the extent to which they separate *policy making* from *administration*.

The Mayor-Council   This is one of the most popular forms of city government, and it consists of a popularly-elected city council (sometimes called board of aldermen) and an independent, popularly-elected mayor, who is the chief executive of the city. In the *strong mayor-council* form, only the mayor and the members of the city council are elected, and the mayor has the power to appoint and remove city officials and also exercises considerable power over the budget. In the *weak mayor-council* form, other local officials are also elected and the mayor does not have as much authority over either them or the budget.

This form of municipal government is more popular in the larger cities and is especially sensitive to local politics. In fact, critics of the mayor-council form of government argue that it allows political favoritism, encourages inefficiency, introduces partisan spoils (patronage), and protects political bosses.

The Council-Manager   This form of city government emerged early in the present century as a reform measure in local government. The council-manager government has a city council which is elected from a slate of non-partisan candidates and a city manager, who is appointed by (and is responsible to) the city council. The city manager is a professional municipal administrator whose job is to provide executive management for all of the city's operations. He appoints department heads, prepares and administers the budget, and acts as an intermediary between the policy makers (the city council) and the operating departments. Most city managers are specifically educated for the job (the Master of Public Administration degree is the proper academic credential). The council - manager form of government is especially prevalent in small or medium-sized cities, and its primary emphasis is on professional management.

Although a city manager is a generalist because of his wide range of responsibilties, many are in fact specialists in public works, public finance, or public personnel administration. Very few city managers are specialists in public safety. One way of looking at the city manager/city department head relationship is to view the department head (eg., fire chief, public works director, city librarian, etc.) as *functional specialists* with the city manager providing the executive controls needed by all departments. Obviously, the problem with this is that in large city departments the "chief" or department head is *not* just a functional specialist; he himself is a manager with a wide range of executive functions, including planning, budgeting, and personnel. In this sense, the city manager becomes a senior coordinator of all these functions, providing consistency and stability.

The Commission   This form of government grew out of the devastation wrought by the hurricane which ravaged Galveston, Texas in 1900. Local government was unable to cope with the problems; in fact, Galveston's local government simply broke down. The governor appointed a commission composed of five businessmen to administer the city. As it finally emerged, the commission form of local government was composed of a commission of elected officials much like a city council, but each of those elected officials in addition to being a policy-maker for the city as a whole was also in charge of the administration of one of the city's departments. This became a very popular form of city government in the early decades of this century; however, its popularity has diminished and it is now the least common of the three major forms of city government. Part of the problem is that cities cannot be run if they were just profit businesses, and the commission form of government provides weak leadership and plenty of opportunity for conflict.

In local government, the final authority still rests with the people. Members of city councils or boards of aldermen are popularly elected either at-large or from wards or districts, depending on the particular city. These councils make public policy for the city, and because they are popularly elected, they *can* represent public sentiment. One problem with city councilmen, however, is that many of them are not sufficiently familiar with specific municipal functions (such as fire and police) to be able to make narrow decisions concerning those departments, yet many are tempted to go beyond broad policy-making and to actively involve themselves in the operations of those departments. City councils are not always representative of the communities they serve; they are frequently over-representative of business and commercial interests such as real estate brokers, land developers, and funeral home directors.

In the council - manager form of government, city council members select the city manager, and theoretically he selects the department heads (although if he is smart, he will clear his appointments with the city council). In the case of selecting a police chief, many city managers are confronted with what will probably be the single most important personnel action they can make, and their frequent failure to understand or appreciate the complexity of the police role in the community may lead them to select a chief on the basis of criteria which are far too narrow. Ideally, the police chief and the city manager share a mutual and overlapping set of responsibilities, both to the residents of the city itself and to the members of the police department. In reality, many police chiefs and their respective city managers tend to go their own way, to the detriment of both the city and the police department.

Public Policy

As Richardson and Baldwin note, "Governments are not great slot machines in which you insert your money, pull the handles, and await the outcomes ... there is generally universal and highly complex process through which ideas are translated into action."[2] What government does and how it does it is no accident; it is a function of *public policy*. Public policy is not narrow decision-making; it does not represent the decision to buy Fords instead of Plymouths for the motor pool, although a decision to shift the motor pool over to much more cost-efficient automobiles would be a policy decision. In the broadest sense, public policy decisions determine matters affecting the quality of life, style of administration, and performance levels of government. A public policy is normally made in response to a problem or requirement. The policy makers evaluate the problem, explore the resources which are available, establish criteria for acceptable treatment of the problem, and then create a system to deal with the problem.

Public policy, however, is made by *people* and is based on their perceptions of both the seriousness of the problem and the adequacy of the resources which are available. Just exactly *who* these policy makers are is extremely important, as different groups of people are apt to view the same situation in a different light. What might be a serious problem to one person or group could be of no real interest to another.

Ideally, the making of public policy should include inputs from many sources — public officials at all levels, community leaders, specialists, political leaders, and those whom the policies will affect. In this sense it should be clear that *public* policy can also derive from *private* initiative; indeed, much of the public policy supporting the women's movement is a case in point. It should also be remembered that public policy is not always the result of identifying a problem, formulating a solution, and then attempting implementation of that solution. Some areas of public policy "... often result not from conscious mapping out of a rational course of action but from smaller and cumulative choices resulting from drift and inertia."[3]

Public Policy and the Police Department: What Shall It Be?

Perhaps the basic public policy question with respect to a police department is simply, "What are our goals?" That is, how is the police department to contribute to the quality of life in the community?

James Q. Wilson, a political scientist, studied the police departments in eight communities and although he acknowledged the fact that those cities were not necessarily "typical" of all American cities, he did discover three "styles" of policing which serve as models for studying the police in other communities. These styles of policing are valuable because they permit us to look at not only political culture but the relationship between it and public policy with respect to policing.[4]

The Watchman Style   Wilson says that, "In some communities, the police in dealing with situations that do not involve 'serious' crime act as if order maintenance rather than law enforcement were their principal function." This kind of police style, which Wilson calls the "watchman style," reflects a public policy which affirms the status quo.[5] This kind of police department deals with problems according to the status of the parties involved and the perceptions of the police officers. Wilson notes that,

> The police are watchman-like not simply in emphasizing order over law enforcement but also in judging the seriousness of infractions less by what the law says about them than by their immediate and personal consequences, which will differ in importance depending on the standards of the relevant group — teenagers, Negroes, prostitutes, motorists, families, and so forth. In all cases, circumstances of persons and condition are taken seriously into account ....[6]

POLICE-COMMUNITY RELATIONS:
THE ROLE OF POLICY*

The structure and operations of a police department must be responsive to carefully constructed policy if they are to be effective. The principles listed below have been applied in a number of communities and have been found to be very helpful.

* * * * * *

ALL POLICIES SHOULD EMBODY A COMMITMENT TO DEMOCRATIC VALUES, TO THE LEGITIMACY AND APPROPRIATENESS OF CONSTITUTIONAL LIMITATIONS, AND TO THE FUNDAMENTAL GOALS OF COMMUNITY SERVICE AND RESPONSIVENESS.

Policy-making can be a tool to improve the police/community relationship only if these principles are kept in mind.

THE DEPARTMENT SHOULD USE THE POLICY-MAKING PROCESS AS A FRAMEWORK IN WHICH TO EXAMINE OR ESTABLISH ITS BASIC GOALS AND PRIORITIES.

Meaningful policy — that which is truly relevant to operations — cannot be developed if the department adheres to narrow definitions of police responsibility, such as that which confines the policeman's role to crime-fighting. Effective policy-making must take place in an environment which recognizes the complexity of police work. It must raise questions about priorities, and about the adequacy of its responses to those priorities and to all other obligations inherent in policing a community.

THE DEPARTMENT SHOULD USE THE POLICY-MAKING PROCESS TO EXPLORE NEW ROLES AND AREAS OF SERVICE WHICH TRADITIONALLY HAVE NOT BEEN CONSIDERED THE BUSINESS OF THE POLICE.

Some departments are experimenting with referrals to other social agencies as a routine part of police work; others are providing counseling on the rights of parties involved in civil disputes; still others are intervening in tenant conflicts and consumer-fraud complaints.

---

*Robert Wasserman, Michael P. Gardner, and Alana S. Cohen, "Improving Police/Community Relations," U.S. Department of Justice Prescriptive Package (Law Enforcement Assistance Administration, National Institute of Law Enforcement and Criminal Justice), June, 1973, pp. 18-23.

THE ISSUES TO BE ADDRESSED IN THE POLICY-MAKING PROCESS SHOULD BE CAREFULLY SELECTED, ESPECIALLY DURING EARLY EFFORTS AT ESTABLISHING POLICY IN THE DEPARTMENT.

Policy-making should be recognized as complex, and its development as difficult. Often a good place to begin is with the ambiguities remaining after a Supreme Court decision to limit police power in some particular area; from this starting point, many departments have been successful in outlining concrete policies with respect to eyewitness identification, warrantless searches, search and seizure of automobiles, and dissemination of arrest records.

THE DEPARTMENT SHOULD DEVELOP AND ENFORCE STRICT POLICY GOVERNING THE USE OF DEADLY FORCE.

THE DEPARTMENT SHOULD INVOLVE BEAT OFFICERS IN POLICY DEVELOPMENT.

Although traditionally considered a responsibility of command, policy-making most intimately affects the operating personnel. By involving patrolmen in the formulation of policy, the department greatly increases the prospect of having that policy accepted and obeyed. Moreover, the patrolmen have the most recent experience on the streets and can contribute current, first-hand observations. Finally, patrolmen involved in policy-making are exposed to views and perspectives not previously considered, thus deepening their understanding of the job.

THE DEPARTMENT SHOULD EXPERIMENT WITH COMMUNITY PARTICIPATION IN POLICY-MAKING.

An initial step might be the widespread circulation of proposed policies, together with an opportunity for community comment. Such a step does not mean the department is surrendering its responsibility for making decisions. It does mean, however, command officers will have the benefit of a process in which police representatives and their constituents work together to forge mutually acceptable policy.

THE DEPARTMENT MUST CIRCULATE POLICY TO ITS MEMBERS IN A FORM WHICH MAKES IT USEFUL, COMPREHENSIBLE, AND CREDIBLE.

Police policy, no matter how skillfully developed, is of no value unless understood by the members of the department. Police officers receive great amounts of paper; the new policy will not be effective unless they understand that it is operational instruction, that both supervisors and officers will be held accountable for its implementation, and that it is built into the system for evaluating performance.

THE DEPARTMENT SHOULD USE THE POLICY-MAKING PROCESS TO ELIMINATE PETTY RULES.

Many current manuals contain obsolete rules concerning dress, hair, or other matters of professional appearance that can be used to harass police officers. Policy should be confined instead to important issues in the operation of the department and the exercise of police authority. By eliminating trivial detail, much of it resented by patrolmen, the department will encourage rank-and-file acceptance of policy.

THE DEPARTMENT SHOULD TAKE ADVANTAGE OF THE POLICY-MAKING EXPERIENCE OF OTHER CITIES.

This does not imply that policy manuals should be adopted in their entirety. Police requirements differ among cities just as they do among neighborhoods. But neither is it necessary for a department to begin anew.

THE DEPARTMENT SHOULD ADOPT A PROCESS OF REGULAR, AUTOMATIC POLICY REVIEW SO THAT OUTDATED, INAPPROPRIATE POLICY IS ELIMINATED OR REPLACED.

One method of achieving this goal is the formation of a standing committee of patrolmen who meet regularly — perhaps monthly — to review policy and to receive policy-related complaints from the community and the department itself.

Thus, the quality of law enforcement in communities with a watchman style of policing "depends not simply on how the police make judgements, but also on the socioeconomic composition of the community, the law enforcement standards set, implicitly or explicitly, by the political systems, and the special interests and concerns of the police chief."[7] Communities with this type of police system tend to offer relatively low levels of public service and tend to be characterized by influence based on personal relationships (e.g., "having pull"). This style of policing is more likely in a community with a mayor-council form of government and strong partisan political divisions. The police are poorly paid and typically receive the minimum required training. The chief tends to be virtually autonomous in his rule of the department and the administration of his department is likely to be characterized by rigidity, conservatism, and emphasis, at least verbally, on "law and order" bureaucratic ideologies.[8]

The Legalistic Style A police department which emphasizes a legalistic style of policing stresses the *law enforcement* role of the police. As Wilson notes, "The police will act, on the whole, as if there were a single standard of community conduct — that which the law prescribes — rather than different standards for juveniles, drunks, and the like."[9] If legalistic police *do* intervene in a situation, they are more likely to act *formally* than *informally*; that is, they will not seek to privatize situations. Obviously, arrest rates in such a department will be high.

Wilson points out that in a legalistic police department, the police themselves obey the law! He also notes that such departments were invariably once corrupt or favor-granting departments. Scandal has often forced the chief of such a department to retire or resign. His replacement was often given a mandate to clean up the department (a public policy decision). The best way to clean up a department — and to separate it from local politics — it to emphasize "professional" conduct, and this typically means strict law enforcement, avoidance of ambiguous situations, and close accountability within the police department.

A legalistic police department is conscious of its image. It is likely to recruit new members from the middle-class and often places a premium on education. Its officers are likely to be well trained and well paid. Advancement within a legalistic department is a function of high levels of performance, both qualitatively and quantitatively. One's conduct reflects adversely on the image of the department and is likely to be dealt with severely:

> Item: Two police officers in a large, legalistic department were working the third shift (11:00 p.m. to 7:00 a.m.). Early one Sunday morning about 6:00 a.m. they were seen stealing a newspaper out of a yard by an early-rising citizen who noted the vehicle number on their car and reported the theft to the police department. The two officers were called in and promptly fired.

> Item: An officer answering a call at a residence was bitten by a bulldog belonging to the owner. A few weeks later, late at night, the officer drove by the same house, and seeing the dog in the front yard, shot it with his pistol. The dog survived, but the officer did not. After an internal affairs investigation, he was fired.

> Item: In another legalistic department a citizen approached a parked police car to ask the officer directions. When he reached the car he noticed that the officer was asleep. The citizen went to a pay phone and called the police department and the man's sergeant went to the location. The officer subsequently lost his job.

Departments which operate in the legalistic style are also more likely to experience conflict with such groups as minorities and the poor because in their frequent contact with these groups, their strict enforcement of the law is often perceived as discriminatory and harsh. The formal, official manner of officers in such a department is also interpreted by some citizens as a lack of flexibility and disinterest on the part of the officers.

Cities with a manager-council form of government, especially those in which the city manager has a high degree of personal identification, are likely to have a legalistic-style police department. The existence of a legalistic police department almost requires a strong chief executive, as he must act as a buffer between community politics (e.g., the city council) and the police administration. If a strong city manager brings in a legalistically oriented police chief in the aftermath of a departmental scandal, the new chief will probably be well received by community leaders but not by the middle-managers of the police department itself; those officers would probably resent giving up status or losing influence.

The Service Style[10] In some communities the police take their order-maintenance and law enforcement responsibilities very seriously, but prefer to avoid the use of formal sanctions, if possible. As Wilson says, this kind of department is one in which "The police intervene frequently but not formally." He further noted that

> This style is often found in homogeneous middle-class communities in which there is a high level of apparent agreement among citizens on the need for and definition of public order but in which there is no administrative demand for a legalistic style.[11]

Because of their emphasis on providing service to the community, this is labeled the *service style* department. To a large extent, the communities which have service style police departments are self-policing. Community members are less tolerant of the arbitrary manner of police in a watchman style department, and they will likewise resist the formal and quasi-punitive manner of the legalistic style police department. Police officers in the service style department are expected to be competent, courteous, and somewhat deferential. They will usually be well trained, with strong emphasis placed on "community relations." If they encounter a situation which can be better dealt with by some means other than arrest, then those other means will be employed.

In terms of type of government, a service style police department is most likely to be found in a smaller or suburban type of community. It is often part of the council-manager form of government and the chief of police is probably rather independent of the city manager, although the two essentially agree on the department's style of policing. The police department itself is probably more traditional than innovative, and city government is not likely to encourage the expenditure of large sums of money to develop new programs within the department.

These three styles — watchman, legalistic, and service — represent public policy decisions. They determine *what kinds* of police services will be delivered to the community and *how* they will be delivered. To a certain degree, they represent policy decisions which involve many aspects of the community including the police department itself, citizens, community leaders, and other public officials. The extent to which the various elements of the community participate in this decision-making varies from one style to the next and there will certainly be people within each type of community who are not at all happy with the type of police service provided.

Public Policy and the Police Department: Who Shall Make It?

The question of who makes public policy for the police is part of the larger question, "Who governs?" There has been a long-standing debate among sociologists over whether cities are governed by "elites" or whether there is a *pluralistic* goverance (which is, to a large extent, nothing more than competing elites).[12] In the case of the police, this is an especially interesting question because their development over the past fifty years has stressed a separation of police from politics.[13] It seemed that political influence over police operations was the basis of corruption and favoritism. Much of the reform (i.e., "professionalization") of the police was designed to separate them from political control — and politics is the vehicle by which those who govern obtain and legitimize their authority!

To appreciate the current status of public policy and the delivery of police services, it is important to see today's police administration as the product of several decades of reform. This reform was based on the political control of the police during the late 19th and early 20th centuries, and this political control was part of a broader picture of municipal corruption and racketeering of which the police were only a small part.[14] The massive urban corruption of this era brought with it an increasingly sharp demand for reform at all levels of government, and the police were swept up in this movement.

Actually, the reform of both the cities and the police were simultaneous and overlapping events. As the age of the robber baron and the political boss faded, the administration of cities became more efficient and honest. At the same time, the police began to develop a more professional style of administration and organization. To remove the police from unwanted political influence, departments started emphasizing the centralization of administration and the development of impersonal management techniques. Personnel were upgraded, training was instituted, and special squads were created to deal with certain offenses such as vice, narcotics, and gambling. This was done to narrow the role of the patrolman working an area and to reduce his opportunities for corruption. The police were organized along quasi-military lines, and officers were placed under a rigid military discipline which emphasized accountability through the ranks and obedience to authority. Police departments were placed under civil service in order that officers could be promoted on the basis of merit and be removed only for just cause. In some areas the police function was narrowed, salaries were improved, and conditions of employment were related more to the police function than to political considerations. Thus, police departments began to consider themselves as formal municipal law enforcement agencies rather than sources of patronage employment or as adjuncts to the political machine. Each of these major steps — all designed to professionalize the police — also had long-term policy consequences concerning the delivery of police services.

The type of organization into which the police evolved has played a major, perhaps a controlling, role in the kinds and quality of services which the departments now provide. Each of the major reform measures was an *instrument* in the professionalization of the police, and each played a role in the creation of the kind of *institution* the police have become. This brings us back to our original question: Who makes public policy for the police? It is this author's contention that for the most part, *nobody does!* The police deliver their services according to two major imperatives: tradition and structure. That is, the department does what it is *organized* to do and it does what it has been doing in the past. Major changes in the delivery of police services do not result as much from a conscious policy decision on the part of the police chief, mayor, or city manager as they do from improvements in technology and modifications in either substantive or procedural law. This has been tolerated for several reasons, two of which are especially important. First of all, politicians are now extremely reluctant to involve themselves in police matters for fear their intervention will be labelled political interference. Second, police departments are managed by chiefs who are usually highly conservative individuals who lack sufficient background in management theory to bring about any significant organizational revitalization. The average chief of police is nearing the end of his career and has relatively few incentives to bring about any major changes within the department. It should be noted in passing, however, that in recent years the police profession has seen the emergence of a new breed of well-educated and dynamic police chief; this trend will eventually have a dramatic impact upon police organization.

Another major reason why public policy developed by police departments is relatively undynamic is because of the peculiar nature of public agencies in the first place. It is almost impossible to measure the quality of police outputs when the objective of those outputs is an indivisible benefit. We can certainly observe and even measure specific things the police do, but relating those things in the long run to ultimate policy objectives is nearly impossible (although it is rather easy to show how a department *fails*). Because of the difficulty in measuring outputs, it has become routine for departments to look for other measures of their performance.

Public Policy And The Police: Measuring Outputs Versus Inputs Deciding public policy requires two basic elements: knowing what needs to be done in the first place (identifying problem areas) and then knowing what to do about it. In the case of the fire department, we see this relationship very clearly* — fires need to be put out, and fire engines do it by pumping water which enables the firemen to extinguish the fire. Firemen have different solutions for different kinds of fires: some can be dealt with by using CO^2 or dry powder extinguishers; others require 1000 gallon-per-minute pumpers tied in tandem to deliver a massive cascade of water. Although fire departments *do* concern themselves with fire prevention, the thrust of their organization and operations is directed toward putting them out. Firemen also perform certain service functions, such as washing down gasoline at accident sites, rendering first aid and providing rescue service — but in each case, they deal with very specific problems and they produce measurable results.

---

*A word of caution: comparing the fire department with the police department is like adding apples and oranges (in spite of some very superficial similarities). The fire department is an excellent example of an agency which clearly understands the relationship between inputs and outputs, but that by no means indicates that their operations are everything they ought to be. Fire departments are probably the most traditional of all municipal agencies; in spite of their very great courage and dedication, firemen almost universally subscribe to a delivery system which is extraordinarily inefficient in terms of its cost. The kind of equipment used and the manner in which it is deployed is extremely expensive. Alternatives are not actively sought because of the traditionalism of the fire departments and the stranglehold the insurance industry has on cities through its rate-setting mechanisms.

The same is true for most other municipal departments. The water department provides water and can very accurately measure just how much water a subscriber uses. The cemeteries department provides and administers public cemeteries and can easily count the number of bodies buried in them, and so on. The major exception to this is the police department. As has already been noted, the police department deals with an incredible array of problems ranging all the way from serious crimes in progress to giving directions to lost motorists. Police departments do all of this in deference to public demand and tradition, and to accomplish their wide range of tasks, they organize themselves into two major categories: generalists and specialists.

The generalists are the uniformed officers assigned to radio patrol or foot beats. When they go to work, they simply go to the areas to which they are assigned and await calls either from their dispatcher or directly from citizens, or actively look for something to do which is appropriate. In the case of the latter, that can be to observe traffic and look for violators, or it can be a systematic scan of the environment to detect signs of trouble, crime, or disorder. When a patrol officer is mobilized, he then uses his wide powers of discretion to determine the most appropriate solution to the problem. Some cases may involve an arrest, whereas others might call for a warning or advice. Police officers in this generalist role will make their interpretations in the light of the style of policing encouraged within the community. In a legalistic department, the officer called to deal with a given problem may disregard the problem if it does not call for enforcement action, whereas an officer in a service-style department may take a completely different approach.

The *specialists* in the police department fall into a number of categories. The most important for our analysis are (1) operational specialists and (2) administrative specialists. The operational specialists are the detectives and other investigators who deal with selected aspects of police work, such as youth crimes, homicide investigations, hit-and-run investigations, crimes against property and other special areas. These specialists do not provide any of the broader general services which patrol officers may give. They do not normally wear uniforms, and they typically concentrate on a relatively narrow area of police work. Administrative specialists run the department. They are usually sworn police officers of higher rank whose job is to insure that the other members of the department do their jobs.

Where do these specialists come from? Nearly all police officers start their careers as generalists. This is where they gain the broad-based experience that constitutes their essential background in police work. It is also a socializing experience which teaches the individual officer what the department expects of him and where he learns how to cope with recurring events related to his career (e.g., how to make arrests, the circumstances under which force may be employed, how to deal with disturbed or violent people, etc.). Some of these generalists advance into specialist slots either through promotion or as a result of reassignment into an investigator's position. In this new capacity they learn the specialized requirements of the new job. Other generalists are promoted in rank but remain assigned to the patrol division as supervisors, gradually working their way up in rank until their duties keep them in the office more than on the street. Police sergeants are operations specialists who remain on the street for the most part. Lieutenants and captains and their superiors tend to be administrative specialists, even though that which they administer is itself a generalist function. At this level they must become more concerned with manpower availability, resource deployment, shift scheduling and so on. What is interesting is that as an officer moves into either operational or administrative specialist positions, he finds his work role already established. There is relatively little question about what the job *ought to be*; rather, the emphasis is on how it will be accomplished.

This means that most police outputs are not measured in terms of their *effectiveness* or how *well* they serve the community, but rather in terms of their *efficiency* or whether the job was done with a minimum of time, people, or effort being expended. This means that it is entirely possible to have a police department which is highly efficient but which is at the same time only marginally effective. Efficiency in police departments is often measured in terms of such variables as:

— Number of arrests made;
— Number of traffic citations issued;
— Number of calls responded to;
— Number of radio transmissions sent; and,
— Average response time to calls received.

Such statistics, by themselves, are meaningless. The number of arrests made may bear no relationship to their *quality* as measured by convictions or some other criteria. The number of traffic citations issued may not deal at all with traffic safety. The number of calls to which the police have responded may include large numbers of calls which were unfounded or may even be recalls by the same complainant. The number of radio transmissions sent is likewise meaningless, as is the average time it takes to respond to a call. More useful output measures would include such things as a shift in the rate per 100,000 of selected crimes, or an

211

increase in the number of arrests resulting in convictions, and the identification of high accident locations with the corresponding development of effective traffic countermeasures to reduce the hazards at those locatidns.

The Police Department Budget : Perhaps the most important policy document issued by a city is its budget. The budget tells whether or not the city is going to put its money where its mouth is: if something is *not* budgeted for, it most likely will not be done. The city budget has two basic parts: revenues and expenditures. Revenues tell where the city gets its money (e.g., taxes, inter-governmental transfers, etc.) and expenditures tell how that money will be spent. There are several types of budgets, although they all do basically the same thing — manage the city's cash flow and fund its operations.

Most budgets require the various city departments to explain their operations, relate those activities to some performance measure, and then to detail the cost of providing those services. The cost of government operations, especially personnel and energy costs, have increased in recent years, but revenues have declined. This has put the cities in a financial quandry and as a result, objects of expenditure must be carefully justified before being included in a forthcoming budget. This is particularly the case with manpower. Departments are less likely to be granted new positions unless those positions can be clearly justified. The catch to all of this is that existing programs are seldom seriously questioned. Thus a police department does not have to justify *what it has*; it needs to justify *what it wants*.

To further complicate the matter, substantial sums of money were funneled into local law enforcement through the now defunct Law Enforcement Assistance Administration (LEAA). The idea was that if the federal government would at least partially fund a new program, perhaps when the federal funding ended, the cities would pick it up. The philosophy behind this program was admirable; it was intended to provide money which would enable law enforcement agencies to upgrade their personnel and operations. Technically, the official recipient of the federal money was the State Planning Agency (SPA), which then provided the money to local governments to fund "action projects." The overall program has had both notable failures and successes. One important aspect of the program, however, was to alter local public policy by making the availability of these federal funds contingent upon accepting certain federal guidelines, especially those having to do with civil rights requirements.

Federal involvement in local law enforcement through funding programs has had several important consequences. First, it has brought local public policy into closer harmony with federal objectives. Second, it *has* upgraded the quality of law enforcement in a variety of ways. Third, it has drawn attention to the basic nature of police work in the cities through research and action programs ranging from highly technical topics such as the use of X-Ray systems for bomb disarmament to practical basic research, such as the Kansas City Preventive Patrol Experiment.[15]

The basic point is, however, that what a police department does and how it will do it is determined for the most part at the local level, and the city's budget is the key to change within the department, for that is the document which prioritizes and funds specific police operations. Most departments are content to accept an "incremental" budget, one which basically asks for what was approved the previous year with slight increases to cover inflation. This type of budgeting process does not call for a careful review of both what is done and why it is done as does zero-based budgeting in which the entire budget must be justified each year. Thus the administration of a police department can be very mechanical in its approach to budgeting and will be assured of at least "business as usual."

Perhaps the most significant point of intervention available to any interested citizen is the budget process. The budget is a public document and it is available for inspection prior to being passed by the city council. In fact, citizens may attend city council meetings and make comments or recommendations on the budget. The amazing thing is that *very few ever do so*. If the executives within the police department do not use energy and imagination in developing their budgets, and if the citizens decline to participate in the process, the public policy within police departments will continue to be a function of tradition and technology, applied in , incremental increases year in and year out.

Finally, in order to formulate a thorough and responsive public policy for the police (which the department at least implicitly recommends each year via the proposed budget), the department needs well-trained budget experts. Very few departments have that kind of expertise. What frequently happens is that a sergeant or a lieutenant is given the task of working up the budget; he coordinates his efforts with the finance department to make sure the form is correct and that he has accounted for all of the required elements. Police chiefs very seldom see the budget as the remarkable management tool it is or as a device for shaping police services for the community; most simply look upon it as an unpleasant experience which has to be dealt with each year.

The Police As A Formal Organization

Police departments are not just agencies of city government, nor are they merely aggregates of police officers who are either generalists or specialists. Police departments are also *formal organizations* and are subject to many of the same functions which control all other formal organizations. According to Parsons, organizations are social units deliberately constructed and reconstructed to seek specific goals.[16] Etzioni states that formal organizations share the following characteristics:

> —Divisions of labor, power, and communication responsibilities which are deliberately planned to increase the likelihood that the organization will achieve certain goals;
>
> —The presence of one or more power centers which control the concerted efforts of the organization and direct them toward its goals;
>
> —The ability to substitute persons; that is, people whose performance is unsatisfactory can be removed and replaced with others.[17]

Formal organizations have *goals*; in fact, the reason for their existence is to accomplish some set of goals. However as we have already noted, once an organization is formed, it may develop its own needs and these sometimes take over the direction of the organization. When this happens, the organization reduces the degree to which it services its original goals in order to service its new (internal) goals. In some cases, the organization will quit serving its original goals altogether in order to pursue a new or more suitable set of goals.

We have already seen how the police as a public agency shifted and emerged over the years. Notwithstanding the bureaucratic ideologies, the police as a formal organization experienced considerable difficulty in establishing precise goals. In many departments there is a significant difference between what the department *says* it does and what it *actually* does. How does this come about?

> There are at least two reasons why the head of an organization is seeking certain goals which in fact differ from the ones it actually pursues. In some instances the head may be unaware of the discrepancy; the true situation is hidden from him. ... More commonly, organizational leaders quite consciously express goals which differ from those actually pursued because such masking will serve the goals the organization actually pursues.[18]

This book argues that the majority of police departments pursue two sets of goals most of the time. Its *stated goals* are bureaucratic ideologies and may be neatly summarized as follows: "the goal of the police department is to save lives and to protect property." Or, as some departments paint on their cars, "To Protect and Serve." The *real goals* are to satisfy the *Institutional Imperative** and to maximize self-interest. Both the stated and the real goals of the police as a formal organization are approached through a series of secondary goals which actually makes the police department a multi-purpose organization and thereby assures internal conflict because the various secondary goals will often make incompatible demands on the organization as a whole.

The real goals of a police department — its institutional imperative — are primarily to maintain its current organizational style and administrative structure in order to preserve current operational functions, processes, and purposes. Doing this in turn theoretically accomplishes the objective of having the department achieve its stated goals and it also maximizes the self-interests of its members. It should be noted, however, that the goals of an *organization* are not the same as the goals of the *people within the organization.* Specific individuals may achieve some or all of their personal goals through the organizations of which they are a part. If the individual's and organization's goals are in harmony, that is all the better for all parties concerned. This point has some very important implications for the police service and they will be discussed later in the chapter.

The Real Goals Of The Police Department: The Institutional

Imperative In its most basic sense, the institutional imperative simply says that the goal of an institution is to do what the institutions does. That does not address the reason why it does what it does or the reasons why people join the organization — or even how they really feel about what they do. One's job is what he does, not why he does it, although sometimes it is impossible to realistically separate the two. Earlier we mentioned the fact that police officers enter their departments as novice generalists and over time they may move into specialist positions. We also noted that those specialist positions could be either administrative or operational. In any event, as an officer moves into those positions he learns what is expected of him (i.e., what his *work* is). As he moves up in

---

*The Institutional Imperative, you will recall, states that "Every action or decision of an institution must be intended to keep the institutional machinery working." Robert N. Kharasch, *The Institutional Imperative: How To Understand the United States Government and Other Bulky Objects* (New York: Charterhouse Books, 1973), p. 24.

the organization or as he gains experience, he will assess the work of his subordinates in terms of what was expected of *him* when he was in the same job. He also looks to his immediate superiors for feedback on how well he is doing his job, and they in turn evaluate him on the basis of what was expected of them. This system resists new ideas. "It was good enough for me, it ought to be good enough for you." "That's not the way we did it in my day." When changes do occur, they are usually the result of technical improvement in an established process or procedure rather than the result of some radical new innovation. Change is also facilitated by the gradual entry of new members into the department and the simultaneous exit of old members, via death, retirement, or resignation.

The Formal Organization: Goals

The traditional goals of the police are two-fold: to save lives and to protect property. These stated goals are theoretically achieved through a pattern of organization which produces *police services* or *police operations*. These services are themselves collectively designated as being crime preventive in purpose, but the actual prevention is presumed to be a result of *law enforcement*. In order to provide these services, the police must formally organize themelves, and they do this by organizing according to *function, place,* and *purpose.*

Organization by *function* separates the generalists from the specialists and further subdivides administrative from enforcement or technical specialists. Thus police departments are frequently formally organized along operational, administrative, and support lines. There is certainly nothing wrong with this; in fact, organization by function is often a very desirable way to structure an organization so that both effectiveness and efficiency can be maximized. It does assume, however, that the functions upon which the organization is structured are valid instruments for achieving the organization's ultimate purpose.

Organization by *place* is another valid way of structuring a formal organization — especially one which has responsibilities spread out over a geographic area. The police are an excellent case in point. They deliver their services "on the street"; they go where the problems are. They generally do this on the basis of public demand; they are called by citizens more than they themselves initiate activity. It is only reasonable for the police to concentrate their resources in the areas where they will be needed the most. Departments do this by dividing the city up into districts, zones, response areas, or beats. The size of a particular zone and the number and kind of officers assigned to it will be a function of the work load within the zone. Very "active" parts of town are usually cut up into smaller zones and are provided with more concentrated manpower.

Finally, organization by *purpose* further refines organization by place and function. This permits the grouping of people according to what they do. Thus patrol officers (the generalists) work out of their cars in the zones to which they have been assigned. Traffic officers are not normally assigned to the same zones as patrol officers; their areas are usually much larger, if not city-wide. Detectives usually work out of a central office and are grouped according to specialized function (e.g., homicide, robbery, sex crimes). Other specialists within the department likewise tend to be grouped together: administrators, lab technicians, training staff, property control officers, communications personnel and so on.

By means of this type of formal organization, the police department provides its services to the public. However, because the *effectiveness* of those services cannot be (or are not) accurately measured and related to specific public policies, the *services themselves* become the goals of the department, and ultimately the police department's public policies are determined by the department's organization. Many police executives do not realize this and would probably take rather strong exception to it; they not only offer bureaucratic ideologies as operational goals — they believe them. This raises the whole issue of police administration.

The Formal Organization: Administration

Decisions must be made even in very simple organizations. In larger organizations the number and complexity of the decisions can be staggering. One of the primary purposes of *administration* is to make decisions. Another purpose is to create an environment in which quality decisions can be made on a timely basis. One reason why most large organizations have formal rules is that these rules not only coordinate complex activities, they also facilitate decision-making — at least in the case of routine events. The use of formal rules also assists an administrator because it allows him to deal with *exceptions* to the rules or unusual events not covered by the rules. The use of formal rules also assumes a minimal amount of consensus on the rules: everyone in the organization must either agree with them or agree to abide by them. Thus, in many complex organizations administration really means the creation and management of rules and the making of decisions for events not covered by rules.

In the case of police work, law enforcement quite obviously involves the enforcement of *laws*, and laws are very specific as are the procedures which may or may not be used in their enforcement. If a major emphasis within a police department is on law enforcement, then the administration of that department must develop a rather rigorous set of rules so that the law enforcement process can be carried out properly. Thus, a legalistic department would be expected to have a very extensive set of rules, whereas a watchman type of department might have relatively few.

Administration is not just a question of the number and complexity of rules an organization has. It also deals with how leaders employ those rules and make their decisions, but even more important is the philosophy which administrators have regarding the motivation of their subordinates (or looked at another way, the extent to which bosses see their subordinates as being willing to either work in the first place or follow the rules at all). For purposes of analysis, it is instructive to look at two opposing theories developed by Douglas McGregor.[19]

Theory X vs Theory Y McGregor argued that traditional systems of management were based on a series of assumptions about people. He labelled these "Theory X" assumptions and said they included the following:

1. Employees are inherently lazy and will avoid work unless forced to do it.

2. Employees have no ambition or desire for responsibility; instead, they prefer to be directed and controlled.

3. Employees have no motivation to achieve organizational objectives.

4. Employees are motivated only by physiological and safety needs.

Based on these assumptions, many organizations (especially police departments) are structured in a manner which permits maximum control over all employees. In the case of police departments, this type of organization and administration actually arose from the need to professionalize the police and to remove them from political influence. It could be argued, however, that the result has been more of a self-fulfilling prophecy. By administering a department in a Theory X manner, many of its members develop the traits noted above, and administrative competence is judged to be the extent to which ranking officers can successfully impose rigid controls on their officers.

McGregor felt that the assumptions which underlie Theory X are inaccurate and he formulated a second set of assumptions which he called "Theory Y." These are:

1. Employees find work as natural as play if organizational conditions are appropriate. People appear adverse to work

only because their past work experiences have been unsatisfactory.

2. Employees can be motivated by higher-order needs such as ego, autonomy, and self-actualization.

3. Employees seek responsibility, since it allows them to realize the needs in number two above.

The difference between the two theories is the difference between *autocratic* and *democratic* administration. Although there are some notable exceptions, most police departments tend to be Theory X agencies and are ruled by autocratic chiefs. There are reasons for this other than the use of rigid administration to combat corruption. Perhaps the most significant reason is that because police administrators do not really concern themselves with the public policy process and since many of them have relatively little collateral contact with other community leaders, they concentrate their efforts on imposing and maintaining control within their own organizations. In other words, many of them surround themselves with all of the accoutrements and trappings of *command* and administer by being the senior police officer in the department. To fully understand this, one must be aware that there are several kinds of bureaucrats, and these types determine administrative style.

Although police departments are formal organizations, and although they do have the responsibility for enforcing the law, they are still *human* organizations and the bulk of their work is done on a people-to-people basis. The men and women who work for the police department are no less human than those whom they must counsel, warn, arrest or even in some cases kill. One of the great dangers of any formal organization is that it loses sight of this fact. It is clear that there is a need for change in formal police organizations, but the likelihood of that change occurring in the near future is less than promising.

A study sponsored by the Police Foundation in 1971 surveyed eight demonstration projects. This survey concluded that unless action programs were an integral part of a long-term plan for improvement, they would be "like ornaments on a Christmas tree and create a facade of progressiveness" that would raise expectations, but would neither improve the quality of police service nor advance their knowledge of how to do so. Yet another survey of three police departments found a negative relationship between the *need* for change and an *openness* for change to be made.[21] Walker offers an interesting postscript on this subject:

...The history of police reform seems to suggest two lessons. First, reformers should take care to consider the full consequences of new techniques of police administration. The history of police reform illustrates the pitfalls of unanticipated consequences. But the second lesson suggests very real possibilities of change. The myth of the unchanging police, as well as a pervasive pessimism about 'the bureaucracy problem,' discourages creative thinking about change. The history of police reform suggests that significant, even radical changes are indeed possible. Both the opportunities and the perils of police reform confront a new generation of reformers.[22]

The Police As A Public Bureaucracy: The Informal Organization

Although the formal organization is a major component of the police as a public bureaucracy, there is another and equally important dimension — the *informal* organization. This might even be called the "other organization" because it is such a real part of any organization and because it is so important to the total functioning of institution.[23] In a nutshell, the informal organization "refers to the patterns of behavior and influence that arise out of the human interaction occurring within the formal structure."[24]

The formal organization is the *official* structure and includes the formal lines of authority and communication. It also establishes the official patterns of work which are expected of each specific employee; that is, the *"work"* of the organization is formally established, as are the *formal goals* of the organization. Whether or not those goals actually make any sense is another matter. The formal organization also monitors the performance of its employees. When a person applies for a job in an organization, he is actually asking the *formal* organization to assign him a task for which he will be compensated.

People, however, are far more than just labor machines. Each person has his own complex array of motivations, attitudes, expectations, beliefs and dislikes which he takes to work with him! In fact, the personal individual-oriented attitudes, beliefs, motives, and feelings of all the employees make up the basis of the *informal* organization. As Gray and Starke point out, "informal organizations represent the human side of organizations and are thus dependent on the nature of individuals in the organization...."[25] One of the reasons most people are apprehensive when they first start to work in a new job is not because they are worried about their ability to perform their task, but rather because they wonder about the people with whom they will be dealing. In other words, they are apprehensive because they do not know what kind of *informal organization* they will encounter.

One of the primary tasks confronting any new employee, therefore, is to learn what is *really* expected of him in the way of work output; who *really* has influence within the organization; whom he can trust and those whom he should avoid; and finally, he needs to learn just who knows what is going on — who can provide reliable "inside" information on matters of importance to employees. People are not comfortable in a job until they learn such things. The process starts immediately. On the first day on the job, *someone* will come to the new employee and pass on some informal but necessary bit of information (e.g., "don't worry about being back from lunch right on time — the boss never comes back until 2:00"). That same person will also *ask* some questions (e.g., "Where do you live?" "Where did you go to school?"), so that he can see generally how the new person will fit into the informal organization.

Just exactly *why* is there an informal organization? The reason is because the formal organization is essentially *product* oriented, not *people* oriented. Most businesses, including government, tacitly assume that people are willing to do the work they have applied for and that they can use their salaries during their private time to pursue other, more personal interests. Of course, most jobs *do* satisfy the most basic needs of their employees — what Maslow would call their physiological and safety/security needs. Some organizations even try to satisfy higher order needs, such as status/ego needs or social needs. However, this is often done at a superficial level and is likely to be tied in with the formal organization's objectives. This is often only partially successful and can sometimes even backfire. For example, when the author was a young investigator with a federal agency in New York City he worked in a division that had a high (and usually overdue) case load. The chief of the division announced one day that he was instituting an "agent of the month" award, and the agent who closed the most cases on a timely basis each month would be the winner. His reward was to be taken to lunch by the chief. The problem was that the chief did not appreciate the fact that not all cases were equally easy to close; he had made the contest unfair. None of the agents liked him because he had such an obnoxious personality — no one wanted to go to lunch with him! It doesn't take much imagination to figure out what happened!

Job satisfaction and job performance are closely related and both arise out of the interplay between the formal and informal organizations. If the formal organization allows the individual to meet his own needs and goals, then that person is more likely to be satisfied with his work and will probably be more productive than a person who is unhappy. Of course, the most ideal situation is one in which the person's job is

221

something he loves to do and which does not give him any grief (doesn't every stamp collector want to own or at least work in a stamp shop *after he retires?*). Unfortunately, most people apply for jobs, not because they enjoy the nature of the work, but rather because they are sure they can do the work and they need the money. Thus for many people their work is not what they *really* want to do, and through the informal organization they seek to compensate by making the work environment as satisfying as possible. For some workers that may mean doing as little work as possible or it may mean making the work environment as pleasant as circumstances allow.

For a long time researchers thought that job *satisfaction* and job *dissatisfaction* were polar extremes, opposite ends along a continuum. Given that perspective, if something were found to produce *dissatisfaction*, its removal would automatically result in *satisfaction*. All management would have to do would be to remove those things which dissatisfied employees and they would then be happy. Frederick Herzberg disputed this concept as being far too simplistic; he suggested that different groups of factors cause satisfaction and dissatisfaction.[26] He labeled those factors which caused satisfaction *motivators* and those factors which cause dissatisfaction *hygiene*. He theorized that *motivators* appear to be closely related to *job content* and include such things as achievement, recognition, advancement, personally satisfying work tasks, and responsibility. The *hygiene* factors, on the other hand, derive from the *context* of one's work and include such things as fringe benefits, salary, job security, supervision, and style of administration. Obviously, both sets of factors can and normally do operate at the same time.

Herzberg's theory can be used to explain much of what takes place within police departments. Individual officers may enjoy the nature of police work (especially at the street level) and they may like the enormous personal responsbility it gives them as well as the recognition they receive from certain of their peers and the public. At the same time, they may intensely dislike the manner in which they are supervised, the administrative rules and the means by which they are applied, and specific aspects of their work such as appearing in court or changing shifts. They may love being police officers, but hate the police department!

Police administrators (senior police officers) are inclined to like their work even more than patrolmen because they have both motivation and hygiene needs being met (their personal set of motivations may not be the same as those of patrol officers; they may have a very different set of ego needs). Police administrators who are happy with their work might ask "why then are so many street men so unhappy?" To many administrators it is because "These *new* cops are different" or because "All they do is bitch." What many administrators in all types of organizations fail to realize is that people at different levels within the same organization are probably motivated by a different set of needs, and what is good for people at one level is not necessarily what those at another level need. For this reason many police departments are fragmented organizations and personnel in one section do not really understand those in other sections. This is, of course, aggravated by a rigid reliance on rules when what is really needed is a little understanding and even some common sense.

But instead of looking at just administrators, what about those at the bottom of the hierarchy? They enter the department as recruits and are promptly sent to the academy.[27] During their stay in the police academy the rookies are socialized into the *formal* organization; they are taught its rules and roles. Their informal organization is composed of other rookies, which is unrealistic when viewed against the backdrop of the larger organization. When they graduate from the academy, however, their introduction to the real informal group begins — usually with the blunt instruction from a new and experienced partner to "forget all that crap they taught you in the academy. Out here you will learn how it *really* works." Perhaps the most articulate popular writer on the police is Joseph Wambaugh, a former Los Angeles police sergeant who left the police service after writing a best seller on the police. His books clearly illustrate the conflicts between the formal and informal organizations and tell how street cops learn to survive the pressures of the job — and why they sometimes do not survive.[28]

The point of all of this is that police departments are incredibly complex organizations. They are composed of both formal and informal groups and the members of those groups can differ considerably. Any effort to change the police must keep this in mind because no significant change can occur by either altering or re-emphasizing bureaucratic ideologies or by trying to bring about change in one part of the organization without considering its impact on the rest.

The police are not a unitary phenomenon and the superficial treatment they are given by many writers is both inaccurate and misleading.

The Informal Organization In A Time Of Change   The police as an institution are clearly in a period of change. Not only are more middle-class people entering police work, but equal opportunity and affirmative action mandates are bringing more minorities and women into police departments. As different kinds of people enter police work, it can be expected that they will change the nature of the informal organization. Women may very well bring a slightly different set of motivations and expectation with them into police work. Blacks, who have had a very different set of experiences with the police, might likewise have a somewhat different perspective on what policing is all about than more traditional officers.

Young people coming to the police service with two year degrees, bachelors' degrees, or even masters' degrees may also have a different perspective on what they should or should not do as police officers. All of these groups may have overlapping yet conflicting expectations of one another and of the administration of the department. The long-term result of this is likely to be an alteration of the police culture. It is still far too early to tell what kinds of changes we might expect, but there *will* be changes! These changes will also have an effect on the nature and style of delivery of police services and will ultimately influence the way in which police departments are organized and administered. In the meantime, these differences will probably generate a certain amount of conflict within the department, although it is hard to predict precisely what effects this will have.

The Police And Bureaucratic Pathology   As Berkley points out, "organizations, like individuals, often act in strange, irrational, and even, at times, self-destructive ways. But, as with individuals, such organizational behavior usually has a logic of its own, albeit one that is frequently perverse and sometimes pathological."[29] The pathologies found in organizations tend to be similar from one kind of organization to the next, although public bureaucracies do have certain pathologies related to their inability to measure outputs in terms of the cost of their corresponding inputs. Levine et al. have noted some of these pathologies and have termed them *bureaucratic games*.[30] These include:

> —**The Diversion of Resources Game.** In this game, the money meant for one goal is used for something else.

> —**The Easy Life Game.** In this game the goal is to tailor the work environment to suit the interests of the bureaucrats rather than the needs of their clients, or for that matter, even their subordinates.

> —**The Deflection of Goals Game.** In this bureaucratic game stated goals become added to, distorted, or changed outright. For example, many cities use federal funds designed to impact on high crime areas simply as a means of providing police officers with over-time pay for questionable enforcement tactics.

—**The Reputation Game.** In this game the bureaucrat attempts to aggrandize his own reputation. When crime rates drop because of demographic changes, police administrators often disregard the real reason for the drop and claim it came about because of their superb administration!

—**The Territorial Imperative Game.** This is a favorite of many administrators and consists of trying to expand their functions to include activities which they consider advantagous to them (or to get rid of functions they don't like or which give them headaches).

A certain amount of pathology is normal in any organization, especially those which are large and complex. One of the reasons these "games" or pathologies don't completely paralyze large bureaucracies is because the organizations themselves are so complex that many of these games are self-cancelling. There are a large number of pressures and cross-pressures, and the activities of one person are apt to offset the activities of others within the organization. For example, if a high ranking officer is a conserver, the climbers beneath him may use his own weaknesses against him, and they may do it by playing some of the bureaucratic games noted above — but they themselves are vunerable to other climbers (or even other types) within the organization. If one walks down the hallways of a large police department, it might appear that everything is neat, orderly, and well organized. Yet beneath that calm exterior there may be much activity that never shows: an informal organization that is in constant motion, some of it productive and some of it counter-productive. It is all part of the bureaucracy.

Summary

The criminal justice system is a public enterprise and functions at multiple levels; however, "policing" is essentially a municipal function. Even though cities are creatures of state government, there is considerable variety in just how they are organized to provide police services because this is a function of the structure of local government. In the United States there are three principal forms of city government: the mayor-council, council-manager, and commission forms. Each of these forms of local government has a different emphasis on the administrative and policy-making processes of local government and therefore plays a major role in defining the quantity and quality of services to be delivered.

Exactly how a given city delivers its police services will reflect the public policy of that city. This is typically seen in the "styles" of police service, as described by Wilson. These styles range from the "watchman" to the "legalistic" to the "service" style of policing. Each style contains a different set of community expectations (public policy) which governs police practices and also defines what the individual officer may expect of himself. This is a reciprocal relationship between the police and the community.

The history of American police forces during the twentieth century has focused on the issue of public policy and the police: specifically who was to make the policy which governs police organization, administration, and operations. Because of efforts to separate them from political interference and corruption, the police have been increasingly isolated from the public policy process. Although this has strengthened the autonomy of the police, it has also made them somewhat less responsive to community needs — to the detriment of both the communities and the police officers themselves. For example, the police have not proven themselves to be particularly adept at formulating effective budgets, although the public budget is the key policy document in any city. On the other hand, the police have been the recipients of massive external (federal) funding which has not only upgraded the quality of police services, in many ways, but has also brought them considerable public attention.

Discussion Questions

1. Is is true that city government touches the lives of citizens more directly than does government at any other level? If so, why?

2. How can the make-up of a city council influence the kind or quality of community relations in a given community?

3. What kinds of problems can arise as a result of a city hiring a new city manager who is basically unfamiliar with the nature of police work?

4. How can the style of policing in a community affect the quality of law enforcement?

5. What does the text mean when it says the police deliver their services according to "tradition and structure"?

6. Do you think police chiefs should (at least in the larger cities) also be drawn from the executive ranks of business and industry? Why or why not?

7. Why is citizen apathy in the annual budget process a problem for police community relations?

8. How can conflicts between the *formal* and *informal* organizations of a police department influence its community relations?

9. What are the implications for police community relations in McGregor's Theory X and Theory Y types of organizations?

10. Why does virtually every organization have a corresponding *informal* organization?

11. Could a person realistically hope to become a police chief if he were not a "climber?"

12. How should a police department go about reviewing or examining its "public policy?"

13. If it is true that there are very few "statesmen" in the police service, why is this the case?

14. Many people believe that the absence of a formal effort at communications is an intentional situation. Can anything else account for it?

15. Why are so many chiefs of police unfamiliar with (or unaware of) the informal organization of their own departments?

Glossary

ADVOCATES Public officials who are loyal to a broader set of functions than are zealots. They also seek power because they want to have significant influence on their organizations.

COMMISSION FORM OF CITY GOVERNMENT A form of municipal government in which a council composed of elected members also uses those members as heads of city departments.

COUNCIL-MANAGER FORM OF GOVERNMENT A form of city government in which the city council is elected and in which the council appoints the city manager, who is a professional management specialist.

FORMAL ORGANIZATION The organization as it is described in organizational charts and in its formal rules; the formal, structured aspect of an organization. Formal organizations emphasize authority hierarchies, internal regulations, and the formal purpose of the organization.

INFORMAL ORGANIZATION The network of informal associations, expectations, and processes through which employees personalize their formal duties and relationships at work.

MAYOR-COUNCIL FORM OF GOVERNMENT A form of municipal government in which only the mayor and city council are elected to office, and in which the mayor is the chief executive officer of the city.

PUBLIC POLICY The decisions (and decision-making process) whereby government identifies and addresses those problems which they consider worthy of attention.

Notes

[1] Ivan L. Richardson and Sidney Baldwin, *Public Administration: Government in Action* (Columbus, Ohio: Charles S. Merrill Publishing Co., 1976), p. 69.

[2] Richardson and Baldwin, *Public Administration*, p. 121.

[3] Jerome B. McKinney and Lawrence C. Howard, *Public Administration: Balancing Power and Accountability* (Oak Park, Illinois: Moore Publishing Company, Inc., 1979), p. 67. See also James E. Anderson, *Public Policy-Making* (New York: Praeger Publishers, 1975).

[4] James Q. Wilson, *Varieties of Police Behavior* (New York: Atheneum, 1972).

[5] Wilson, *Varieties of Police Behavior*, pp. 140-171.

[6] Wilson, *Varieties of Police Behavior*, p. 141.

[7] Wilson, *Varieties of Police Behavior*, p. 143.

[8] Wilson, *Varieties of Police Behavior*, pp. 172-199.

[9] Wilson, *Varieties of Police Behavior*, p. 172.

[10] Wilson, *Varieties of Police Behavior*, pp. 200-226.

[11] Wilson, *Varieties of Police Behavior*, p. 200.

[12] See for example C. Wright Mills, *The Power Elite* (New York: Oxford University Press, 1956); Floyd Hunter, *Community Power Structure* (Chapel Hill: University of North Carolina Press, 1952); Robert Dahl, *Who Governs?* (New Haven: Yale University Press, 1961).

[13] Robert M. Fogelson, *Big-City Police* (Cambridge, Massachusetts: Harvard University Press, 1977; see also Samuel Walker, *A Critical History of Police Reform* (Lexington, Massachusetts: D.C. Heath Books, 1977).

[14] Walker, *A Critical History of Police Reform*, p. 3.

[15] For a good overview see *A Comprehensive Bibliography: Publications of the National Institute of Law Enforcement and Criminal Justice* (Washington, D.C.: U.S. Government Printing Office, 1978).

[16] Talcott Parsons, *Structure and Process in Modern Societies* (Glencoe, Illinois: The Free Press, 1969), p. 17.

[17] Amitai Etzioni, *Modern Organizations* (Englewood Cliffs, New Jersey: Prentice-Hall, Inc., 1964), p. 3.

[18] Etzioni, *Modern Organizations*, p. 7.

[19] Douglas McGregor, *The Human Side of Enterprise* (New York: McGraw-Hill Book Company, 1960).

[20] C.H. Milton, "Demonstration Projects as a Strategy for Change," in *Innovation in Law Enforcement* (Washington, D.C.: U.S. Government Printing Office, June 1973), p. 132.

[21] R.B. Duncan, "The Climate for Change in Three Police Departments: Some Implications for Action," in *Innovation in Law Enforcement*, pp. 31-47.

[22] Walker, *A Critical History of Police Reform*, pp. 31-47.

[23] George F. Berkley, *The Craft of Public Administration* (Boston: Allyn and Bacon, Inc., 1975), pp. 92-94.

[24] Jerry L. Gray and Frederick A. Starke, *Organizational Behavior: Concepts and Applications* (Columbus, Ohio: Charles E. Merrill Publishing Co., 1977), p. 131.

[25] Gray and Starke, *Organizational Behavior*, p. 135.

[26] Frederick Herzberg et. al., *The Motivation to Work* (New York: John Wiley and Sons, 1959).

[27] For an interesting perspective on this aspect of police culture, see R.N. Harris, *The Police Academy: An Insider's View* (New York: John Wiley and Sons, 1973).

[28] See especially his novels, *The New Centurions; The Blue Knight; The Onion Field; The Choir Boys.*

[29] Berkley, *The Craft of Public Administration*, pp. 101-126.

[30] James P. Levine, Michael C. Musheno, and Dennis J. Palumbo, *Criminal Justice: A Public Policy Approach* (New York: Harcourt Brace Jovanovich, Inc., 1980), pp. 142-144.

THE POLICE
AND THE PUBLIC

8

*I guess what our job really boils down to is not letting the
assholes take over the city. Now I'm not talking about your
regular crooks ... they're bound to wind up in the joint anyway.
What I'm talking about are those shitheads out to prove they
can push everybody around. Those are the assholes we gotta
deal with and take care of on patrol ... They're the ones that
make it tough on the decent people out there. You take the
majority of what we do and it's nothing more than asshole
control.*[1]

Police Response To Deviance

The comment cited above was made by a veteran patrolman and sums
up the outlook of many police officers. Regardless of whether one
classifies police work as law enforcement, order-maintenance, or service,
it still amounts to dealing with people who

—are doing something they shouldn't be doing; or
—are complaining about someone else who is doing
something they shouldn't be doing; or
—are *not* doing something they *ought* to be doing; or
—are complaining about someone else who is not doing
something they ought to be doing; or
—are complaining about some situation that ought not to be
happening, such as an accident, a loss, or a sick person.

Each of these categories represents some kind of deviance. It can be a
deviance from a legal norm (a crime); a behavioral norm (misconduct);
or it can simply be a deviance from a normal standard (e.g., a car accident
or a person in a store having a heart attack). In this sense, a deviant act is
something that is *wrong* according to someone's standards. It may or may
not involve a crime, but if those who witness the deviant episode feel
unable to deal with it themselves, they will probably call the police.

The work of the police, therefore, consists of responding to situations which they must assess, diagnose, sort out and deal with. In some cases they may refer the situation to a more competent authority such as a hospital, or they may correct it on the scene by giving advice. In other cases they may elect to invoke the criminal justice process by arresting an individual.

What choices the police make and what actions they take obviously depend on the circumstances; however, it is clear that the police encounter a great deal of deviance. They not only encounter people at their worst, but they also encounter the worst kind of people. They constantly see society where it "cracks" — at that thin line between what "ought to be" and "what actually is." Because standards of social deviance vary so much from one group to another and from one setting to another, and because they are exposed to such an array of deviance, the police sometimes have difficulty in coping with all that they encounter. When this happens the officers can strike back at the perceived source of the deviance, or they can insulate themselves emotionally from what they encounter. They sometimes become victims themselves, both physically and psychologically.

Police and Deviance : The Problem of Assessment

Some of the calls police receive are quite specific and the officers have a good idea of what to expect. For example, traffic accidents, fire calls, robberies in progress, and certain other types of calls are very specific. Of course, the officers may not know the extent of the accident or the degree of involvement of the fire, but they have a fairly good idea of the range of probabilities they might encounter. However, the majority of the calls they receive are ambiguous: "meet the complainant"; "fight in progress;" "domestic trouble"; "report of a prowler"; and so on. These calls can turn out to be just about anything:*

> Item: Two patrol officers received a burglary in progress call. Upon arriving at the scene they discovered a tree branch had been brushing against a window, and the elderly lady who lived in the house was terrified that someone "was coming to get her."

> Item: Two officers were dispatched one Saturday evening to a reported disturbance in a parking lot and upon arriving discovered a man who had been stabbed in the stomach. Although the man was conscious (but seriously injured), he refused to say who had done it. He said it was "strictly a personal matter."

*From the author's field notes.

When the police arrive at the scene of a call the first thing they must do is to assess the situation. This assessment is a quick evaluation of the situation to determine what broad category it might fall within; these categories include the following:

1. **Crimes** These can be either serious or minor; crimes of violence or non-violence; personal or property crimes. They all share the common fact that they violate some law or ordinance.

2. **Disturbances** These can also technically be crimes, but that is not how they would be viewed initially. This would include such things as loud music and barking dogs.

3. **Domestic or Neighborhood Disputes** These are inter- or intra-family squabbles. They include a limitless variety of complaints, ranging from husband-wife arguments to fights between neighbors over who has the right to fruit from a tree which hangs over a property line.

4. **Non-Criminal, Serious Incidents** These include such things as car accidents, fires, broken gas mains or natural disasters.

5. **Civil Matters** These are complaints which the police receive, but about which they can do nothing, and include such things as landlord-tenant disputes and bad debts.

6. **Unfounded** These are calls which are simply not what they were reported as being. They can be pranks on others or malicious false alarms.

The central problem in the assessment phase of an incident is that of determining whether or not the situation calls for *real* police work; that is, work in which the police can "...act out the symbolic rites of search, chase and capture...," work in which the officer's self-image as a *police officer* can be affirmed and through which his morale can be enhanced.[2] *Real* police work can involve crimes or it can involve a serious disruption of public order which requires the police to respond in an emergency mode. The following incidents illustrate *real* police work:

A patrol officer saw a car run a stop sign. He pulled behind him, turning on his roof lights. The car accelerated away in an attempt to elude the police car. The officer notified the dispatcher that he was involved in a chase and requested assistance from other units. After a hair-raising high-speed chase through town — sometimes at speeds well in excess of 100 miles per hour — the car being pursued lost control while attempting to make a turn and struck a phone pole. The driver (who was the sole occupant of the car) was killed in the accident. He was later found to have a small quantity of marijuana in his shirt pocket.

Two officers were summoned to a parking lot about 6:30 p.m. on a report of a loud disturbance. Upon their arrival, they found a man and a woman "engaged in an altercation." As they attempted to disengage the pair, the woman hit one of the officers in the head and kicked him in the groin. The other officer, seeing his partner being assailed, radioed for help (putting out an emergency "assist officer" call) and rushed to the aid of his comrade. Meanwhile, the man had managed to get the first officer's nightstick and used it to strike the second officer on the head. The crowd which had gathered egged the man and woman on, and while the officers were trying to subdue the woman, a member of the crowd struck one of the officers and ripped his badge off his shirt. Within minutes the area was swarming with police officers responding to the assist officer call, and a number of arrests were made.

Early one Monday morning a small private airplane taking off from a municipal airport developed engine trouble and lost power. It attempted to make an emergency landing on a street; however, it missed the street and struck a house. In the ensuing explosion the two occupants of the plane were killed, as was one person in the house. The police went into an emergency response to the event, setting up a special command post from which a large number of officers could be deployed for traffic control and other activities.

In the first case, the initial "crime" was trivial — running a stop sign. Stopping a violator for running a stop sign is not *real* police work (it is routine), but the chase was *real* police work.[3] By the same token, answering the disturbance call in the second case was not *real* police work, but responding to the "assist officer" call was. In the case of the plane crash, setting up an emergency command post and processing a highly non-standard event was also *real* police work. If a call requires *real* police work, it will be attended to very quickly and with a great deal of seriousness. These events allow very little discretion on the part of the individual officer and are handled with efficiency and formality. Other situations are normally less demanding and allow officers to use their own discretion to a greater extent. Perhaps the best way to look at the police response to deviance is to start by breaking deviance down into two broad situation categories: crime and misconduct.

The Police and Deviance: The Case of Crime

There are a number of sociological typologies of crime. One well-known typology developed by Clinard and Quinney breaks crime down into "behavior systems."[4] Other sociologists have likewise constructed typologies of criminal behavior based on similar perspectives.[5] The police, however, make no effort to classify crime and criminals according to such sophisticated variables. Their appraisal of crime and criminals is highly phenomenological; it is based on what they see and deal with. Thus members of organized crime, white collar criminals, and certain specific crime categories (e.g., counterfeiting and kidnapping for ransom) are of little concern to *street cops* because they seldom encounter them, and when they do it is not within their purview to deal with such offenses.*

Police officers view deviance and deviant people in terms of three factors and the way in which these three factors interact; indeed, the task facing the novice police officer is to learn to read and interpret these factors. The three factors are (1) visibility, (2) impact, and (3) degree of legitimacy of the offender.

Visibility   The bulk of police work is carried out by patrol officers, who are generalists. They work the streets and are especially alert to what they can *see*. Some crimes are simply not visible when committed, nor do they produce visible results. Patrol officers do not see white collar crime or violations of trust (as in many fraud cases). Crimes which they *do* see are vandalism, assaults, certain types of thefts, fights, disorderly conduct, reckless driving, and indecent exposure. Although they may not actually see these crimes being committed, *others* are likely to see them and the police see their immediate results. They encounter the victims and quite often they even encounter the offenders because some offenders are themselves highly visible. In discussing *visibility*, it might be best to consider three perspectives: (1) crimes and criminals which are highly visible; (2) those visible only to those who know what to look for; and (3) those that are invisible.

Highly visible crimes are those committed by people or which occur under circumstances when secrecy is unimportant. One such case involved a young man, apparently under the influence of drugs, who was walking down the sidewalk in a downtown area cursing loudly, challenging motorists to fight, and punching out store windows. Another case involved two men who had begun an argument in a tavern and who went out onto the sidewalk to fight. Some offenders are highly visible, such as prostitutes who work the street, and some of their pimps who wear flashy clothes and drive conspicuous automobiles. Many of these highly visible crimes and criminals are minor in importance, although they can have serious outcomes (for example, fights can produce serious

---

*Such crimes are dealt with by specialists in either headquarters departments or by federal agencies such as the Secret Service or the Federal Bureau of Investigation.

injuries or even deaths, although such outcomes are not normally intended).

The crimes and criminals which are visible only to those who know what to look for tend to be somewhat more subtle and may involve offenses which are more serious. Examples of crimes in this category would include vice and narcotics transactions, the disposition of stolen property, and some types of frauds. Experienced police officers, especially those who have worked a specific area for any length of time, generally know which semi-visible crimes commonly occur in the area, and they also have a pretty good idea of who is committing them. Their problem is one of being able to make a case. In many departments crimes that fall into this category are not a *patrolman's* business — they are usually handled by detectives.

Finally, there are crimes which are not visible — at least not normally. These include crimes of stealth, such as burglary and many thefts or crimes which are committed with premeditation and at least some degree of planning, such as armed robberies. Examples of other crimes which are not visible — at least when they take place — include child abuse, wife-beating, and rape. Many of the people who commit these crimes do not come to the immediate or direct attention of the police because the crimes often go unreported or the victims refuse to assist the police in their investigations.

Impact Not all crimes are equal in their impact, and the police must distribute their time and resources according to a scale of priorities which makes the best use of those resources. Whether or not the police will take an active interest in a given crime is determined at least in part by the kind and extent of impact that crime has. For purposes of analysis we can distinguish among four categories of impact: (1) Heavy; (2) Intermediate; (3) Minor; and (4) Disgusting. *Heavy* crimes are those which are major felonies and are serious because they represent either large dollar losses or because they hurt people. They are the traditional *malum in se* crimes. Some crimes, such as armed robbery, are included in this category because they have a potential for either major monetary loss or serious personal injury. The heavy crimes include such offenses as murder, robbery, grand larceny, arson, maiming, rape, and aggravated assault (where there is serious injury). Heavy crimes get speedy and formal responses from the police and generally constitute *real* police work.

Intermediate crimes are those which have the *potential* for serious impact but which do not normally achieve that potential. Included in this category are such offenses as breaking and entering, assaults, driving while under the influence, and persons reported with firearms. These crimes also receive close attention, but the outcome is determined more by the officer's discretion and the actual nature of the circumstances than is the case with heavy crimes. The police view these kinds of crimes seriously because they do have the potential for serious impact.

Minor crimes are routine and do not generally result in a serious impact in and of themselves. They include such offenses as disorderly conduct, shoplifting, traffic offenses, and status violations. These are really violations of good order than crimes which are *mal in se*. The person most likely to suffer as a result of them is the offender himself, and the police do not usually place a high priority on strict enforcement of such crimes.

Disgusting crimes may be heavy or they may be minor; their distinguishing characteristic is that they offend the sensibilities of both the community and the police. Examples of this kind of crime include the torturing of animals, cases of child abuse and neglect, and crimes committed with wanton disregard for the life, safety, or the well-being of others. The following actual cases are examples of disgusting crimes:

> Item: Two teenage boys were arrested in a midwestern city after they were caught killing cats by attaching large firecrackers to their necks and blowing their heads off.

> Item: A husband and wife were arrested after public health officials learned that they had kept their retarded daughter locked in a hot water heater closet for several years. She had been fed like a dog — out of a bowl on the floor into which they placed scraps and leftovers. She was significantly below the average size for a girl her age and could not talk.

> Item: A young woman who was an informant for federal drug authorities was found in a wooded area. She had been killed by persons unknown, but before being killed her eyes and tongue had been cut out.

Disgusting crimes are handled — at least initially — in the same manner as heavy crimes. In fact, the police tend to be very careful in handling such crimes so as not to allow their feelings to interfere with their judgment. Such crimes are relatively rare, but when they do come to the attention of the public, they tend to attract considerable notoriety.

Degree Of Legitimacy Of The Offender Not only are *crimes* assessed, so are those who commit them. Anyone can commit a crime; given the right set of circumstances, nearly anyone might commit a fairly serious crime. In assessing a crime the police therefore look at the *legitimacy* of the offender. Legitimacy actually involves three criteria: (1) *work*; (2) *competence*; and (3) *justification*. In the case of *work*, the police like to know what an offender does for a living. If the person is employed full-time in a legitimate occupation, he will be viewed in a different light than a person who either does not work or who works in a tainted or illegal occupation. Prior time in prison is almost a "master status" and can even override current full-time legitimate employment. Even if a person works full-time, the quality of that employment may be a factor in the officer's assessment of his legitimacy. People with low status jobs or jobs which pay very little money are apt to be regarded in a different and more negative light than people who work in high status or well-paying jobs. Much of this also has to do with deference hierarchies: the police are deferential to some classes of people and expect others to be deferential to them. Able-bodied men who either do not work or who claim to be on public assistance do not rate very highly with the police, and obviously people whom the police know to be involved in criminal enterprise are not respected or accorded legitimacy (even though their criminal enterprise may net them a high income).

Competence is a major factor in the determination of legitimacy. People who appear to be demented, retarded, or senile are not seen as legitimate offenders; their diminished capacity clearly segregates them from those whose crimes are the product of normal ability. Special circumstances can also confer legitimacy:

> Item: A German citizen who was visiting the United States on official business for his government decided to take a couple of days to visit an American acquaintance in a nearby state. The German (who held a doctorate in physics and spoke fluent English) was stopped by a highway patrolman for speeding. The German spoke to the officer only in German, claiming he could not speak English. He produced an international driver's license and a German passport — all the time smiling and acting very friendly. The police officer tried to tell the German through gestures and what was probably G.I. - German to slow down. No citation was issued.

People who are seen as being incompetent are likewise seen as not being fit subjects for police action, although the police may refer them to mental health facilities or take them to a hospital or to some other kind of treatment center. The police are very reluctant to act against a person who is not viewed as a legitimate offender, even though he may very well have committed a crime.

Justification Finally, the police accept the fact that some crimes may be violations, but they still see them as being justified. If the crime is not very serious, the police will usually either decline to act against the offender or may even assist him. For example, people with a sick or injured passenger in the car may run traffic lights and stop signs and speed while en route to the hospital. If their driving attracts the attention of the police, they will be stopped. Upon verifying a medical emergency, the police will probably provide an emergency escort to the hospital and will not cite the driver for the violations they witnessed. Other situations may be seen as justifying outcomes:

> Item: A man and his attractive wife went into an all-night restuarant for a late snack as they were coming home from visiting some friends. While sitting in a booth, another customer began to annoy them with suggestive remarks. The man asked the customer to please leave them alone, and the abusive customer directed an obscene statement to the woman and pushed the man's water glass into his lap. The man got up, grabbed the abusive customer and pulled him outside the restaurant. He then told him to "shove off," and when the customer told him "make me" he did: he punched him in the nose (which he broke). A police car passing by saw the assault and after learning what had happened, arrested the man with the broken nose and took no action against his assailant.

Many calls which come to the police as assaults, kidnappings, thefts and the like are the products of conflicts involving people known to one another or who may even be married to one another. In many of these cases the police elect not to act, based either on their feeling that the "crime" was justified under the circumstances, or because they feel one party just wants to use the police against the other.

As a general rule, it is the product of the *interrelationship* of these assessment factors which guides the officer's attitude and actions towards a given criminal or crime. Most high impact crimes are dealt with full seriousness and formality because they are the ones which are the most likely to wind up in court. Lack of competence, however, diminishes the seriousness of even high impact crimes. For example, a person who is mentally ill may receive the serious attention of the police without his behavior being regarded as a crime.

> Item: Police were summoned to the home of a woman who was creating a loud disturbance. When they arrived they found her on her front porch holding a small infant, with a knife poised at its throat. She said she would kill the infant if anyone came close. During the standoff which ensued the police learned that the woman had a history of mental problems going back many years. She was eventually subdued and turned over to mental health authorities. No charges were filed against her.

In some cases, the police will file an official report with the prosecuting attorney's office with the informal recommendation that the case not be pursued. In some such instances the prosecutor will routinely refer the case to the grand jury, and if they return an indictment he will then decline to prosecute. Of course the law itself provides for legal justification in some cases (e.g., mistake of fact; self-defense; diminished responsibility, etc.), but in other cases the police do not formally pursue the matter to the point where a defendant has to formally raise such a defense.

In general, the less the impact of the crime, the less likely the police are to *formally* intervene. Exceptions to this include low impact crimes committed by "illegitimate" offenders, or disgusting low-impact crimes (especially if they are highly visible). Legitimate people who commit low impact crimes are typically dealt with informally. For example, neighbors sometimes complain to the police about loud parties. The police will almost always respond by simply asking the host to either lower the volume or to invite the complaining neighbors to the party. On the other hand, "illegitimate" offenders may receive much more formal treatment. Illegitimate offenders include known criminals, nasty people*, and legitimate citizens who wish to test the limits of a police officer's authority.

> Item: Late one night a police officer saw a car run a red light. The officer assumed that the driver was being lax because it was late and there was no traffic, so he decided to pull him over and give him a verbal warning. When the officer asked for the man's drivers' license (a routine procedure), the driver told the policeman he didn't need it: his word was good enough. After the officer finally got the man's license he asked him if there were any reason why he ran the light. The driver then cast aspersions on the officer's parentage and suggested that he might enjoy attempting certain physical impossibilities and ended by advising the officer that his mother was more closely related to other members of the animal kingdom than to *homo sapiens*. The officer calmly wrote the driver a citation, and when the driver (who turned out to be a prominent architect) refused to sign the ticket, the officer placed him under arrest and put him in jail.

The police also recognize the fact that socioeconomic differences *do* make a difference in how people act and how they perceive themselves. Behavior which would deserve attention in some areas does not deserve the same kind of attention in other parts of town. The police know, for example, that in poor neighborhoods the front steps are used in the same way more affluent suburbanites use their patios; a local tavern is the poor man's den, and in warm weather many people do private things in public

---

*"Nasty" people are the "assholes" and "shitheads" referred to in the quote with which this chapter opened. They come in all sizes, sexes, colors and ages.

places. They also recognize the fact that the poor are beset with many problems and few coping resources, and their fights, arguments, petty thefts, and other disruptions do not necessarily merit being treated as *crimes*. Unless one of the assessment factors indicate that a situation should be treated with serious formality, the police will usually try to negotiate with them.

Thus, the "crime" itself is only a *basis* for a police intervention. The particular form of intervention will be determined by the other assessment factors as well as by the crime itself. Indeed, in many low-impact crimes the reason the police are called in the first place is simply to try to make someone "be good" or to leave. Many of the people who call the police under these circumstances are really much more interested in having the police perform an order maintenance rather than a law enforcement function. This is one reason why family fights pose such a problem to the police. Even though someone in the family may have called the police, if officers try to arrest one of the parties they often find themselves in a hostile confrontation with the others!

The Police and Deviance: The Case of Misconduct

A great deal of the deviance encountered by the police more properly falls under the heading of *misconduct*. Although technically misconduct may involve low-impact crimes, the problem which it presents to the police is not viewed as *criminal* in nature. These events are often characterized by high levels of aggressiveness on the part of some people, or high levels of excitement, anxiety, confusion, depression, agitation or fear. These situations can present a serious threat to the physical safety of the police officers who respond because many of these people may not be in a totally rational frame of mind. The first step in dealing with such people is often simply that of getting them to calm down.

The police routinely become involved in the misconduct of others and this misconduct is usually part of a larger crisis. The police are much less interested in the actual misconduct (as long as it is not serious in its own right) than they are in the crisis which produces the misconduct. If they can successfully resolve the crisis, then the misconduct will take care of itself in most cases. Certain crisis situations are more common than others, and we will look at several of them as good examples of police response to noncriminal deviance.

Domestic Disturbances   Police officers do not like responding to domestic disturbances; a significant proportion of police officer fatalities and injuries occur on these kinds of calls.[6] Police officers have few options in these cases; for example, the police cannot compel a person to leave his own home nor can they insist that the people who live there behave in a certain manner. If people wish to get drunk in their own homes or if they wish to raise alligators in their bathtubs — that's their business. If a police officer does decide to make an arrest, it may not solve the problem at all. Other members of the family may become hostile, a wife who insists on an arrest may withdraw her complaint the next day or an arrest may result in retaliation later on.

Many domestic disturbances result from long-standing situations and often arise from stressful events within the family. In some instances, the police are powerless to control pathological aspects which exist within the family. The police frequently encounter people living together in an intimate setting which is characterized by some degree of disorder or misconduct. The police may be called by family members or summoned by neighbors. Their task is to sort out the situation they encounter and to ascertain if they can do anything constructive about it. They are often greeted by angry people, disarray, frightened children, and adults who make violent threats. Indeed, "killing talk" is very common, and in family quarrels which involve minorities racial epithets and invective are common. Usually, only one party wants the police present; often no one desires the presence of the police. Men may resent what they consider an unwarranted intrusion into their homes; women often want the police to take action which transcends their authority. The police themselves are frequently repelled by what they see because these crises seem to occur most frequently in poor neighborhoods and officers see firsthand the evidence of poverty and disorganization.

Most domestic disturbances are non-criminal events, and other than trying to calm the participants, there is not a great deal that the police can do. The police *do* try to calm the participants, both for their own safety and to keep the situation from escalating into a more serious problem. In some cases the police can help the family members to deal with their problem; more often, they can only offer advice or make referrals to other community agencies. The police sometimes contact mental health or social services, especially if they feel that the needs of young children are not being met or that children may be in danger.[7]

One problem with domestic disturbances is that many police officers regard them as *normative behavior* in some areas; they simply take them for granted. When this happens, many of the police who respond to domestic disturbance calls look to see if an arrest is indicated and if not, they extricate themselves from the situation as quickly as possible. Often the officers warn the persons involved that a second visit will result in an arrest. Although that threat may ameliorate the situation somewhat, it does not deal with the basic problem. The police frequently resent the fact that they have to deal with such problems because they do not perceive them as being *real* police problems. Officers are well aware of the fact that they are not very well trained or equipped to deal with the issues involved in many of these disputes.

Mental Health Problems The police also come into frequent contact with people who suffer from various types of mental problems. The police are expected to deal with mentally disturbed people because those people not only violate routine order, but they may also constitute a serious threat to their own safety or that of others.

> You see them almost everywhere. In the bus terminal, a woman wanders aimlessly, her head craned skyward as she talks to God through the fluorescent lights. In a flophouse down the street, a man leans out of a third-story window, pleading for protection from the 'space rays' invading his filthy hovel. In the poshest section of town, a half-naked man on the corner shivers in the night wind, refusing offers of help and hissing at passers-by. And, of course, you see them trudging along the sidewalks, often in the filthy bare feet swollen with malnutrition, carrying shopping bags with all their worldly possessions, mumbling to themselves or screaming at some imaginary adversary.[8]

The public is frightened of these people, and the police are the first to be called when the mentally ill exhibit their symptoms in public places. Many officers do not regard dealing with the mentally ill as *real* police work, even though the police in most states do have legal authority to take such people into protective custody. Much of the current problem stems from the trend away from the warehousing of mental patients which began in the 1960's. The federal government has encouraged the development of community mental health resources, and the use of improved drugs in the control of mental disorders has made thousands of patients excellent prospects for outpatient treatment. This has resulted in fewer mental patients being retained as long-term residents of hospitals. As a result, more of those who experience problems come to the attention of the police. This liberal discharge policy toward mental patients has not been without its tragedies:

> In St. Louis, a patient who had just signed himself out of a mental hospital ripped a shotgun off the rack in a patrol car and gunned down two officers, killing one. In Chicago, a 19-year old former mental patient raped and robbed two elderly women. And in New York, a man took a power saw to his right arm, slicing it off 'to show Jesus I didn't need it.'[9]

Most mental cases are not so violent, however. Their typical problems are associated with family rights, public drunkenness, and minor infractions. If a police officer encounters a person he believes to be a mental case, his best course of action is to refer that person to the proper mental health resources — if there are any available. This is often a time-consuming and unpleasant process. Few departments have specialists who deal in psychiatric cases and relatively few police officers are trained to recognize the major kinds of mental illness; many officers simply do not know what to do with such cases. The police themselves are justifiably frightened of screaming ax-wielders, wild-eyed men who claim to be God, people who think everyone is trying to "get" them, and others whose behavior seems both threatening and unpredictable. About the best that most officers can do is to assess the extent to which a person is mentally disturbed and then see to it that he is referred to a mental health agency for proper treatment.

The police do not view mental patients as criminals, regardless of the impact of their crimes. When mentally ill people commit crimes of violence, those crimes tend to reflect their disorder: they do not merely stab — they mangle; when they destroy property, they do it with gusto, often with unnatural strength. The police usually recognize serious mental cases as such and deal with them as best as they can.

Life-Threatening Behavior   Many people engage in behaviors which threaten their mental, physical, and social well-being and, in some cases which threaten their very lives. Perhaps the forms of life-threatening behavior most often encountered are those which are associated with drug and alcohol abuse. These are both highly complex problem areas and, as is so often the case, police officers are called upon to deal with them, but are provided with little in the way of either training or resources. The police do not deal with these problems at an abstract level as do sociologists, or in a controlled clinical setting as do physicians or mental health professionals. Police deal with them where they occur: on the streets. The decisions which the police make concerning drug and alcohol abusers reflect not only their own perceptions, but are also controlled by the *immediacy* of the presenting problem. Some of the techniques used by the police have generated considerable criticism and controversy because of the conflict between the individual's perception of his right to use his body as he sees fit and society's desire to control the use of dangerous substances.

Drug Abuse   Throughout history man has used pharmacological substances — to heal, for recreation, to reduce pain, and to bring about desired changes in body and spirit. Seers and spiritualists have used drugs to induce trances during which they claimed it was possible to enter into closer communion with the Gods or to understand the mysteries of life. Drugs have eased the burden of pain and the use of anaesthetics has made possible surgical techniques otherwise inconceivable. Unfortunately, drugs also have their negative side. The abuse of drugs is a serious problem in both its consequences to the individual and in its loss to human productivity; like most other social problems, the *enforcement* of "legal" remedies has fallen directly on the police.

The police *have* attempted to deal with the drug addiction problem, and they have done so with the best means available to them: arrest. The police as individuals have grown up in the same society as the rest of us, and many of them — especially the older officers, those who are more likely to be administrators — grew up in the era of the dope-fiend myth. Because of the hidden nature of drug abuse, specialized police resources and strict enforcement of the law have been employed in the drug war. Unfortunately, the easiest people to catch are also the least important: low-level consumers. As a result, more emphasis has traditionally been placed on *consumers* of drugs than on those who manufacture, import, or distribute them.* Because of the severe penalties in many states, this has meant that young people arrested and charged with possession of marijuana received stiff sentences or fines, which many consider to be inconsistent with the crime. Although the severity of the punishment in minor possession cases is lessening, public sentiment at both extremes remains high.

One result has been a widening dislike and distrust of law enforcement personnel on the part of large numbers of young people. Many youths see themselves in an adversary position with the police rather than as citizens whose rights the police protect. The fault is not entirely that of the police; the affluence of American youth, together with a hedonistic outlook, has produced a contempt for society's norms that has been aptly termed the *generation gap*. Yet the problem persists. There *is* a drug problem in most communities, and parents are unwilling to accept the fact that drug abuse by children and teenagers is as much a statement of their repudiation of parental norms as it is a deviant act in its own right.

---

*In recent years the Drug Enforcement Agency has changed its policy, and they now concentrate their efforts on clandestine laboratories, major importers and distributors and high-level dealers who market drugs in large quantities. Local police, however, lack the funds, personnel, resources or *jurisdictional authority* to do the same thing, so most of them continue to concentrate their efforts on low-level consumers.

Ours is a society which demands achievement and the possession of status symbols. There are relatively few strong, positive reinforcements for families in our contemporary economically-demanding society. The problem of drug addiction may well be part of a larger problem of loneliness, unhappiness, frustration, and rage; drugs may provide an alternative reality as well as a means of striking back at one's self, parents, or society. If this is a valid assessment of the situation, then the police face an almost hopeless task.

Alcohol Abuse   Alcohol is also a drug; it is a depressant. Unlike many other drugs, alcohol *may* have long term debilitating effects such as toxic psychosis, addiction, and neurological damage. It definitely plays a major role in traffic fatalities. The consumption of alcohol in American society is not only condoned, but in many ways it is encouraged. It is easily available and is an essential ingredient in many social gatherings. Alcohol is consumed as a social drug and it is used for religious purposes as well. It is the *abuse*, rather than the *use* of alcohol which produces problems.

Alcoholism is not only a personal tragedy, it also represents a significant social cost as well: The annual economic cost of alcohol-related problems has been estimated at 25 billion dollars.[10] The loss of productivity of people who are chronic alcoholics cannot be measured, and the effect they have on the quality of life in their communities can only be speculated upon. Alcohol has also been closely related to crime, although in ways that some people might find surprising. Although there does seem to be a relationship between alcohol consumption and such crimes as assault, murder, and rape, the nature of that relationship seems to be somewhat exaggerated.[11] As a depressant, alcohol may actually *lessen* the possibility that a person will engage in assaultive behavior.[12] The same factors that lead a person to commit a crime may also lead him to drink; thus both alcohol consumption and crime may be related to a cluster of factors to which the use of alcohol is only incidental. Although alcohol and crime are frequently *associated* with one another, it might be presumptuous to assume that alcohol *causes* crime. There is, however, one major area in which crime and alcohol are directly and causally related — traffic.

All states have laws which make it illegal to operate a motor vehicle while under the influence of alcohol. A blood alcohol content of .10 is the norm for legal intoxication. The reason for these laws is obvious; a person who has a blood alcohol content in excess of .10 will probably demonstrate a noticeable impairment of fine coordination and some clumsiness and distortion of mental faculties. This results in an inability to safely operate an automobile.[13] The United States experiences approximately 50,000 traffic fatalities per year, and alcohol is involved in approximately half of those accidents. Again, the relationship is very complex, and the exact relationship among all of the variables is not yet clearly understood — but there *does* seem to be a clear causal relationship between drinking, driving, and accidents.

Alcohol abuse presents many problems for the police. There is nothing the police can do about the problem of *alcoholism*. In the recent past, they did arrest alcoholics and other drunks on the charge of public drunkenness; however, most jurisdictions have eliminated that particular charge. They can still be arrested for disorderly conduct when they become boisterous, abusive, or try to panhandle the public. Some merchants want public drunks arrested for cosmetic reasons. Such arrests do not deal with the problem of alcoholism and simply use police resources unproductively. Some communities have developed detoxification centers where drunks can be taken for treatment of sorts; others have simply quit dealing with public drunks unless circumstances demand some kind of action. Police tend to attach low legitimacy to chronic drinkers, especially if they are unemployed or if they are nasty in either appearance or attitude.

The police also have alcohol-related problems with other members of the community, including teenagers with liquor and intoxicated drivers. In the case of teenagers, it is a common police practice to privatize the incident so as to make it a learning experience:

> Item: Two patrol officers stopped a car which had eased through a stop sign, and in the car they found five teenage boys and a fresh case of beer. Each of the boys had an opened can of beer (which each was trying — without success — to conceal). The police asked the boys to get out of the car and to produce identification. They then told the boys that it would be against the law for them to have beer with them, but if they didn't have any beer, then all they (the police) could do would be to tell them to go home. The boys looked puzzled until one of the officers said "Now, you boys wouldn't have any beer if you poured it all out, would you?" With looks of both disgust and relief on their faces, the boys poured all the beer down a sewer drain and the police departed without taking any further action.

The police do not see young males who are drinking beer as being deviant; perhaps they remember their own teenage years. What they *do* see as deviant, however, is teenage boys who have consumed liquor and who fail to show proper deference to the police. Deviants often learn the hard way: they go to jail.

247

The police do not like DWIs — those who drive under the influence of alcohol. The police view driving under the influence as deviant and are likely to arrest the offender and charge him with DWI. In the watchman-style department the decision to arrest will be influenced by who the driver is or what his status is within the community. In a legalistic department, no such distinction is usually made. In a service-type department a drunk driver is likely to be warned or even taken home, but if encountered again, he will probably be arrested.* The major exception to this is that as shift-changing time approaches, police are less likely to actively look for drunk drivers. It takes a long time to process DWIs, and by the time their tour is up, most police officers are more interested in getting off duty than in spending an extra hour or two with a drunk. This does not mean, however, that they will overlook such cases! Perhaps the police place such a heavy emphasis on pursuing drunk drivers because they see first-hand the outcome of drunk driving. They are, after all, the ones who must work the accidents, render first aid to the victims, and notify the next-of-kin of fatalities.

Communities are seldom consistent in how they view drunk drivers. Although most people consider drunk driving a serious offense, it seldom receives serious treatment in the courts, even when the case involves a fatality. Many citizens resent police traffic law enforcement tactics yet become very unhappy when they see careless or reckless driving (giving rise to the famous quip about the police, "There's never one around when you need him!"). It is particularly repugnant to many police officers when middle-class members of society charged with DWI show up in court accompanied by attorneys who tell the judge what responsible members of society their clients are.

Problems in the Enforcement of Morality

Many forms of misconduct are primarily matters of morality. The use of drugs or alcohol, gambling, sexual behavior, and similar offenses are regarded by many as personal matters which should be outside the reach of the law, at least as long as no one is hurt. For this reason these are sometimes called "victimless crimes." Such crimes have been defined by one noted authority as "the willing exchange, among adults, of strongly demanded legally proscribed goods or services."[14] Low visibility, low impact, and no complainant characterize these crimes. The key problem arises because the state has an interest in preserving the morals of its people, but in a heterogeneous society, there is considerable conflict as to

---

*A major factor, obviously, is the degree of intoxication.

what those morals should be. Some argue that the law should affirm its stand against immoral conduct for symbolic purposes, if for no other reason. This creates the problem of laws which cannot be enforced — a serious contradiction within itself. If these laws are on the books, *they will be enforced*, at least to a degree. In other words, they will be enforced *selectively*, often at the convenience of the police and for purposes other than those originally intended. Attempts to enforce such laws can have a number of negative consequences:

1. They can produce "status-degradation." By publicly exposing people who practice such offenses they are humiliated and embarassed needlessly.

2. Enforcement of laws against morality can result in the development of deviant subcultures in order for participants to reassure themselves and to facilitate their behavior.

3. The enforcement of legislation dealing with morality can breed disrespect for both the law and law enforcement agencies. Since these offenses do not normally have complainants, the police must seek offenders out, often through the use of undercover and other covert means which many citizens find both wasteful and repugnant.

4. The enforcement of morality creates illegal industries which derive enormous profit from the provision of such goods and services; furthermore, by being outside of the law, those who provide such goods and services do not pay taxes and cost the government an enormous loss in revenue. They are not subject to sanitation and health standards, thus placing the consumer in jeopardy.[15]

The central issue seems to be the definition of *harm*. There is some debate that the enforcement of laws against victimless crimes may generate more harm than the victimless crimes themselves. The issue is not clear because the results of these crimes often harm society indirectly. The simple presence of pornography shops and public drunks may be harmful because they detract from the pleasant ambiance of a place; many consider the public soliciting of prostitutes an unseemly activity. Many citizens strongly feel that they have a right to not be subjected to the presence of such activities.

The police, however, see these activities in a somewhat broader perspective. They know many of the people involved in the so-called victimless crimes are often marginal people who are also involved in other more serious criminal activities. They can use victimless crime charges as a means of harassing some of these people, or they can avoid arresting them as a basis for obtaining their cooperation on other matters. Regardless of the reason for the arrests, victimless crimes still account for an extremely large number of arrests each year; in fact, more people are arrested for drunkenness than any other single offense in spite of the fact that the number of persons arrested on that charge has diminished by approximately 50 percent.[16] It is clear that the police are involved in these matters basically because they are defined as crimes, yet they are crimes which the police simply cannot prevent or eliminate.[17]

The Police and Deviance: The Problem of Race

One of the most persistent themes in the issue of policing is that of race, especially as it concerns prejudice against Blacks. Accusations, charges, and counter-charges abound on both sides and passions run high. However, the troubled relationship between the police and Blacks is only the tip of a larger iceberg. As Silberman noted, "At its core, the urban problem is a problem of race; so is the welfare problem, the migrant and farm labor problem, the school busing problem — and, to a degree that few people have been willing to acknowledge openly, the crime problem."[18] To examine the relationship between Blacks and crime only by analyzing statistics gives a curiously incomplete picture.*

Blacks were brought to this country as slaves, and that fact alone distinguishes them from any other group. There are other groups which have experienced dislocation and poverty, but no other group has had the experience of slavery. The status of *slave* is not just an economic relationship; it is a status which has a profound effect on the individual as well as the group. When a race is subjected to slavery, it is not only condemned to do the work others will not do, but it must also repress the richness of personality inherent in all human groups. Slavery denies the freedom of expression. Slavery cannot, however, completely suppress self-expression; it occurs in culturally acceptable forms. Among southern Blacks of the last century, it emerged in the form of "folk songs" — those melancholy spirituals which allowed Blacks to share their grief, express their feelings, and affirm hope in the future. These spirituals, by the way, later gave way to the blues — songs which conveyed much of the same feeling, but with less emphasis on the spiritual. Few white middle-class Americans fully appreciate how much of our musical heritage we owe to Black musicians, including the "perfessers", who composed and played in New Orleans whore-houses to entertain waiting customers; their music

---

*Although the factor of poverty can account for a great deal of crimes committed by Blacks (and Blacks are indeed over-represented among the poor and the lower class), the element of poverty is only one factor. The peculiar historical, sociological, psychological, and economic status of Blacks in America has made them particularly vunerable to crime. This is not to suggest that *being Black* causes crime per se, but rather because they are Black, their subculture within American society has been shaped in ways that have "overproduced" criminal outcomes.

became known as jazz.

As slaves, Blacks could not strike out against injustices; to do so was to invite harsh punishment or death. In fact, Blacks were expected to show servility, deference and an exaggerated politeness. They were expected to know and remain in their "place" and to avoid "uppity" behavior. Their continued frustration *did* produce aggression, but that aggression had to be channeled into either passive or symbolic forms, and even that was done with great caution. A side of Black culture developed which still remains largely unknown to most whites — a fact which many Blacks find thoroughly amazing. As Silberman noted,

> The overwhelming majority of Black Americans have had to stay in the dark without power and influence, and without contact with powerful and influential people. Hence they have had to find their own sources of dignity and pride — their own ways of investing their lives with meaning and significance, and their own outlets for their anger. One way has been through an elaborate fantasy life of heroism and triumph over the rich and powerful. Nowhere is this fantasy life revealed or celebrated more clearly than in Black folklore and narrative poetry....[19]

The best known stories of Black folklore are the Uncle Remus stories. Although "Uncle Remus"was the literary creation of a white journalist, Joel Chandler Harris, the stories came straight from Black folklore. At first glance they seem to be amusing fairy tales about animals which find themselves in various kinds of predicaments. In a very real sense they *are* like fairy tales, for they mask a much harsher and malevolent theme: "....a biting parody of white society, as well as an outlet for Black fantasies about the day when the weak would triumph over the strong."[20]

After the Civil War the lot of American Blacks worsened considerably, although they had been legally emancipated. At the beginning of the Reconstruction period, the Black family was a relatively stable institution; during the last three decades of the nineteenth century this began to change and the social and economic condition of Blacks worsened. Up until this time they had worked in many skilled areas (construction trades, railroad firemen, brickmasons, etc.) but they were quickly forced out of these occupations. Jim Crow legislation regulated the lives of Blacks as strictly as had slavery. Black frustration began to manifest itself in a new form, a type of narrative poetry known as "toasts." The toasts are part of an oral tradition which is quickly fading but which gave structure to Blacks' feelings as well as an opportunity to express those feelings. They consist for the most part of an exchange of tall tales, jokes, and insults.[21] Closely related to them are "the dozens," which are highly structured, rapid exchanges of obscene, rhymed insults typically directed at the participants' mothers or other female relatives. These are games of verbal skill in which frustration, hostility, and aggression are sublimated and used in a physically nonthreatening way and can bring peer approval and respect to skilled practitioners. Not only do they provide practical training in the use of wit and self-discipline, they allow for the discharge of hostility without recourse to actual violence.

Around the time of the First World War, large numbers of Blacks began to move from the rural areas to the cities and from the South to the Northeast. Since World War II this movement has been massive and has had serious economic consequences. During the later years of this massive migration, unskilled and semi-skilled factory jobs have declined in number and availability, and many of the jobs are located outside of the central cities to which the majority of the Blacks have migrated.[22] This and other factors have resulted in a serious unemployment problem among inner city Blacks. Upon reaching the cities, the Blacks found Jim Crow in the form of institutionalized racism, a dearth of opportunity, and inadequate schools. They found their very culture in grave jeopardy: the much-discussed disintegration of the Black family is a relatively *recent* phenomenon and may be seen as an outcome of the urbanization of American Blacks.

One of the most popular toasts dealt with Stacker Lee, a "badman" whose violent and wild nature gets him into trouble with everyone and eventually leads to his undoing. In fact, his attributes are extensions of stereotypes about Blacks:

> Because Black Americans, and especially Black men, have been imprisioned by white stereotypes of them — because they have found it so difficult, if not impossible, to escape those stereotypes — they have fought back, in part, by accepting the stereotypes and turning them upside down. Through the medium of folklore, Black men have converted their supposed exaggerated sexuality, physical prowess, and animal-like or (child-like) inability to control their impulses from negative to positive attributes.[23]

Thus Stacker Lee became the badman who stood up to authority in a suicidal gesture of defiance. The *badman* of the toasts merged into and finally became embodied in the *Bad Nigger*. In slave folklore, he was "the docile fieldhand who suddenly goes berserk" and posed a threat to both Blacks and whites.[24] Because the *bad nigger* is not afraid of death or anything else, he cannot be threatned: he is completely free. Silberman points out that the *bad nigger* image was cultivated by Malcolm X:

Until the last year or two of his life, when he was struggling to develop a more goal-oriented approach, Malcolm X deliberately cultivated a 'bad nigger' image, and Black Americans in every walk of life loved him for it. 'That Malcolm ain't afraid to tell Mr. Charlie, the FBI or the cops or nobody where to get off,' a New York cabdriver observed. 'You don't see him pussyfootin' 'round the whites like he's scared of them.' 'Malcolm says things you or I would not say, 'a civil-rights leader remarked. 'When he says those things, when he talks about the white man, even those of us who are repelled by his philosophy secretly cheer a little inside ourselves, because Malcolm X really does tell 'em, and we know he frightens the white man. We clap.'[25]

The *bad nigger* image is reinforced in song and movie and the ethos it represents is a stand from which many young Blacks will not retreat. One result is that the long-standing fabric of servility, exaggerated politeness, and a willingness to accept abuse is giving way to a fearsome violence. The blues, toasts, the dozens and other devices for converting rage into play have ceased to function and the *bad nigger* is moving from myth to reality; "from toasting, signifying, and playing the dozens to committing robbery, murder, rape, and assault"; this is one of the major factors which "underlies the explosive increase in criminal violence on the part of Black offenders."[26]

Equally important, Black men have new and more effective ways of deadening the pain; as narcotics, toasts and the dozens cannot compete with heroin, cocaine, or the increasingly popular (and potent) combination of methadone and wine. Drugs not only kill the pain, they provide a euphoric high as well. Nor can toasts or the dozens provide as much (or as satisfying) 'action' as a mugging, robbery, or burglary, or as much evidence of an indivdual's manhood.[27]

It is not possible to do justice to so complex and difficult a subject as the relationship between race and crime in just a few paragraphs; there are obviously other factors involved. Blacks, however, have a unique history which cannot be ignored when looking at Black crime. The involvement of Blacks in crime is heavy indeed: in 1981 they accounted for 45.7 percent of all arrests for violent crime, and for more than 50 percent of all arrests for robbery and gambling; and 49.3 percent of all arrests for prostitution and commercialized vice.[28] Over half of those Blacks who were arrested were under 18 years of age![29]

Police officers are not historians or sociologists. They do not generally know a great deal about the cultural heritage of Blacks, nor do they know the psychological mechanisms Blacks have employed to deal with their problems. They *do* know that Blacks constitute the bulk of their work (at least in most areas where there are large concentrations of Blacks). Most police officers do not have much contact with responsible, middle-class Blacks, and therefore, have little opportunity to see the warmth and richness of Black society. Worse yet, many police officers do not know how to distinguish between low-class and middle-class Blacks and therefore tend to treat them all alike — something which is deeply resented by Blacks. Perhaps because they witness so much violence and brutality among Blacks, police officers insulate themselves.

Over time many officers come to associate the violence and brutality not with *individuals*, but with *race*, and come to view Blacks as violent and distasteful people. This is reinforced by their frequent contact with young males who are playing the *bad nigger* role. The police generally do not know anything about the sociology of that particular role, but they *do* know when their authority has been challenged and the police as a group do not take such challenges lightly. What makes these situations difficult is that they are normally played out before a bystander audience which knows the *bad nigger* is playing a manipulative game. The police officer normally does not know that it is a game and does not know the rules — so he plays by *police* rules and arrests the *bad niggers*. This often infuriates the crowd, and creates a volatile situation. Indeed, much of the problem between Blacks and the police is not a matter of natural emnity or even mutual hostility — it is the product of mistaken perceptions and lack of communications on both sides.

Hispanics

As the fastest growing ethnic minority in the United States, Hispanics also merit special attention. The term "Hispanic" refers to persons who identify themselves as Mexican, Mexican-American, Chicano, Puerto Rican, Cuban, Central or South American, or of other Spanish culture origin regardless of race. Obviously the Hispanic community is diverse and complex.[30]

Hispanics are distinguished by both their culture and language, and because in many cities Hispanics form close ethnic enclaves, they have often been viewed as outsiders by their Anglo neighbors. This has also isolated them from the mainstream of the criminal justice system itself, resulting in community relations problems. Although these barriers are diminishing, their effect over the years remains highly visible, especially in the Southwest.

As victims of crime, Hispanics experience personal and household crimes at about the same rate and in the same distribution as non-Hispanics. Indeed, there are few noteworthy trends which distinguish

Hispanic from non-Hispanic crime victims. In terms of arrests, Hispanics accounted for eight percent of the 1981 crime index (11.7 percent for violent crime and 7.2 percent for property crime). Thus Hispanics do not seem to suffer more from crime or to contribute more to it than their numbers within the overall population would indicate.[31]

The principle problem of Hispanics within the criminal justice system is one of basic community relations. There have been persistent complaints of police misconduct against them, especially in the Southwest. These complaints have included allegations of inadequate police protection, discourtesy, and discrimination in the enforcement of the law. Although there can be little doubt that these complaints have merit, perhaps a more serious problem has been the under-representation of Hispanics on juries and in criminal justice employment; this lack of participation has isolated them psychologically and socially from the larger society of which they are a part.

The lack of participation in criminal justice processes (such as jury duty) has been based on both language problems and a strong distrust of the criminal justice system itself on the part of many Hispanics. This has been compounded by economic considerations. For example, jury members are often called from tax roles, which assumes property ownership. Such a measure will nearly always exclude the poor and many Hispanics fall in that category. A lack of educational opportunity (complicated by the lack of bilingual education in most areas) has limited educational achievement and opportunity. Finally, many Hispanics who have recently entered the United States are not American citizens, thus limiting employment opportunities in the criminal justice system. A substantial proportion of the Hispanic community has had to fight the traditional problems associated with poverty: lack of job mobility, inadequate education, misinformation, and prejudice. The result has been expensive to both Hispanics and to the larger community.

The Police and Deviance: Its Cost to the Police

The police deal with deviance constantly. They see it in virtually every form in which it can possibly manifest itself. They must try to solve problems for which there are no solutions and they must make decisions under the most trying of circumstances. They often make mistakes — mistakes which are made in good faith as a result of *trying* to do what seems best at the time. They encounter experiences which frighten them, disgust them, and amuse them. Although many departments govern their conduct with exhaustive sets of rules, street cops are essentially on their own when they are at work, and must live with the decisions they make. Is there a cumulative effect from all of this? Is there a cost?

Apparently there is, and it produces both physical and psychological factors which in turn serve to influence police behavior. One of the factors which must be considered is violence which is directed *against* police officers.

Violence Against The Police   Police work is potentially dangerous work; officers are often the object of violent actions. According to the figures published by the FBI, the rate of assaults against police officers, nation-wide, was 17 per 100 officers (1981).[32] On the basis of 20,000 reported cases, police officers sustained injuries in these assaults at a rate of 6 per 100.[33] During a ten year period (1972 through 1981) a total of 1,110 police officers were feloniously killed, producing an average of 111 per year.[34] Although the rate of violence against police officers is not high when compared to injuries and deaths sustained by members of other occupations, it is a different *kind* of violence: it is *intentionally* inflicted upon them. Although relatively few officers sustain serious injuries during the course of a year, the potential is always there and an officer never knows when or under what circumstances he will be victimized. It is very difficult to develop effective protective measures to combat this type of violence.

> Item: A Port Authority Police Officer arrested a person who was creating a disturbance in a bus terminal, and as he was leading him through the terminal a struggle took place. The offender managed to grab the policeman's pistol and fired all six shots, killing the officer and wounding three bystanders. He then beat the mortally wounded officer on the head with his pistol and threatened another police officer who had arrived on the scene. After ignoring orders to drop the gun, he was shot and killed.

Behind a lot of police bravado is a very real concern for personal safety. In many areas it is common for police officers to not ticket nurses and physicians because one day they might be looking up at these people from a treatment table in the hospital! This concern for personal safety carries over into work practices and becomes a part of the officer's "working personality."[35] This working personality consists of perceptual sets, dispositions to act in certain characteristic ways, and devices for assessing the probable danger of both persons and situations. Skolnick says that one aspect of the working personality of the police involves the use of "....a perceptual shorthand to identify certain kinds of people as symbolic assailants, that is, as persons who use gesture, language, and attire that the policeman has come to recognize as a prelude to violence."[36] The symbolic assailant is an artificial composite consisting of all of the traits which the police know to be consistent with what violent people do, wear, say or project.

Through actual encounters with hostile and violent people, they learn to spot signs which alert them to the probability of violence. These include the presence of "time markers", a type of tattoo many convicts put on themselves, or certain kinds of scars. Young Black males especially those who play the *bad nigger* role, people who indicate by their style of dress, their language, or attitude that they might fight, and other uncooperative people, all evoke protective responses from experienced policemen. This defensive action may take a formal or even an *offensive* format.

The irony of this is that danger is seen, at least implicitly, as being part of *real* police work, and many officers find themselves drawn to dangerous situations — perhaps, so they can affirm their own status as *real* police officers. Skolnick drew attention to this in a footnote where he noted that a journalist who had ridden with the police in the community where Skolnick did his research commented that juvenile police appeared to him to be curiously drawn to seek out dangerous situations, as if juvenile work without danger was degrading.[37]

Although the police do experience physical violence directed against them, they probably encounter a great deal more psychological violence. They regularly receive taunts, insults, slights, and reminders that they are second-class citizens.

Such incidents reinforce the solidarity which is so characteristic of the police profession, but even that solidarity is not enough to completely shelter a person's feelings. In addition to the insults and slights, there are other forms of psychological violence. Dr. John Stratton, a police psychologist, lists four types of police stressors:

1. Stressors external to the police department, such as verbal abuse from the public, leniency officers perceive in the courts and the inability of the criminal justice system to stem crime;

2. Stressors originating in the police organization, such as low pay, excessive paper work, arbitrary rules and few opportunities for advancement;

3. Stressors connected with the performance of police duties, such as rotating shifts, work overload, boredom, fear, and danger;

4. Stressors particular to the individual officer, such as being a member of a minority group, marital difficulties, or inability to get along with peers.[38]

Some of the psychological violence (stress) is direct: having to deal with terrible situations such as grisly automobile accidents, suicides, murders, cases of child abuse, maiming, rapes, and other traumatic events or having to deliver death messages and trying to calm or console people whose lives have just been shattered by some tragedy. Other stressful events may seem comical at first, but over time even they can begin to exact their toll. Harvey Schlossberg, a former New York City police officer who has a Ph.D. in clinical psychology, gives an example of the kind of situation that can puzzle and disturb an officer. He and his partner had just stopped a female motorist at night who had only one headlight. His partner went to give the driver a ticket, but she refused to roll the window down. Schlossberg dediced to try his luck:

> I asked again, "May I see your license and registration?"
> She said, "Certainly not." Then: "How do I know you're a policeman? You might be a rapist. Or Jack the Ripper."
> "Madam, I'm wearing a uniform. I'm driving a police patrol car. See, it has a red light that spins around. And I have a partner who is also in uniform."
> "That means nothing. You might have stolen the car. And the uniforms. After murdering two policemen. And now you want to murder me."
> I had never encountered such a bizarre fantasy on the road. I said patiently, "If you don't give us your license and registration, we'll have to place you under arrest." A summons stands in lieu of arrest, but I had been unable to give her a summons.
> With that, things happened fantastically fast. She threw open the door of her car and dashed out on the highway as though her life were at stake. It was a dark stretch of Flatbush Avenue, where there were no signal lights and the streetlights were covered by tall trees. Traffic was spinning past, and she ran directly into the middle of it, screaming, "Help! Police! They're trying to kill me!" She really believed we were murderers. I gave chase to try to save her life, for brakes screeched as cars swerved to avoid striking her.
> Suddenly another patrol car came along the highway. It stopped by her side. She threw herself into the arms of the patrolman who stepped out of it.
> "He's trying to kill me!" she shrieked, pointing at me.
> The patrolman knew me. "Hi Harvey," he said. "What's up?"[39]

Over time the parade of the crazy, the banal, the frightening, and the disgusting becomes too much for some officers and they may begin to develop protective psychological mechanisms which often show up as a type of gallows humor and a pervasive cynicism. Sometimes the protective mechanisms break down and the officer becomes deviant himself.[40] That, however, is relatively rare. What is more likely is that an officer will experience *burnout* — "a syndrome of emotional exhaustion and cynicism that frequently occurs among individuals who do 'people work' — who spend considerable time in close encounters with others under conditions of chronic tension and stress."[41] Burnout shows up in several ways: officers become callous and indifferent in their work and begin to dislike the people they police. They may begin to develop negative feelings about themselves and show signs of physical exhaustion. Their morale may plummet and they may even develop such physical symptoms as headaches, muscle tension, and ulcers. Adding to the problem is the fact that many police officers who need counseling for stress refuse to seek it out; although many departments now recognize the problem and are dealing with it, most still ignore it.[42]

Is the problem of stress among police officers really all that serious? One study which examined 2,300 officers in 29 departments around the country discovered that 37 percent of the officers studied had serious marital problems, 36 percent had serious health problems, 23 percent had serious alcohol problems, 20 percent had serious problems with their children, and 10 percent had problems with drugs.[43]

Perhaps the community expects too much from the police. It is clear that they lack adequate resources for the wide range of problems which they routinely encounter. Social workers, psychologists, clergymen, and academicians may be quick to criticize the police for errors and inadequacies, but when all of these other professionals are home from work and enjoying their families, the police are still on the streets.

Misconduct By Police

Police misconduct is a reality that cannot be ignored; in fact, it has proven itself to be a persistent problem in many police departments throughout the country. Police misconduct can take many forms and ranges from inconsequential acts to serious criminal behavior. Police misconduct can usually be classified into three categories: malfeasance, misfeasance, and nonfeasance.

Malfeasance

Malfeasance is the performance by a public official of an act that is not legally justified or is harmful or contrary to law. Police officers who commit acts of malfeasance typically do so in connection with their work. For example, a Seattle police officer was assigned to investigate a traffic accident. The officer arrested a man involved in the accident, and upon discovering that he was the officer's ex-wife's new husband, he knocked him to the ground, and then hit him again while transporting him to the police station.*[44]

An even more dramatic case occured in Houston, Texas on May 5, 1977. Joe Torres, a 23-year old ex-paratrooper was arrested by Houston officers after Torres had been involved in a barroom brawl. Torres resisted arrest and had to be subdued by the officers. After his arrest Torres was taken to a bayou where he was beaten by the arresting officers — while still handcuffed. Afterwards, Torres was taken to police headquarters. A duty sergeant saw Torres' bruises and bloody nose and instructed the officers to take him to a hospital for a checkup. Instead, the officers returned to the bayou where (according to subsequent testimony) they shoved him down a 17-foot embankment and into the water. The officers then departed. Three days later Torres' body was found floating in the bayou.**[45]

There are, unfortunately, many well-documented cases of police malfeasance. Some involve individual officers such as a Florida Highway Patrolman who enticed an eleven year old girl into his patrol car and then sexually molested her. Others, like the Torres case, involve groups of officers and yet other instances appear to involve a substantial proportion of the department such as the corruption scandals which seem to hit the New York City Police Department about every twenty years.

Misfeasance

Misfeasance is the wrongful and injurious exercise of lawful authority. One of the most widely reported examples of this was the so-called "police riot" which took place in Chicago during the 1968 Democratic National Convention. In this case members of the Chicago Police Department were accused of "unrestrained and indiscriminant police violence" in dealing with highly provocative counterculture demonstrators and bystanders.[46] Another view of misfeasance by the law enforcement community emerged as details of the Federal Bureau of

---

*The incident was witnessed by several people who reported it to the department. The officer involved was subsequently fired. It is worth noting that this same officer, several years earlier, had been convicted of third-degree assault and fined $50 for pistol-whipping an army sergeant he was attempting to arrest. No action was taken against the officer in that case.

** A state court gave two of the officers involved a $1000 fine each and a one year sentence. Both the fine and the sentence were probated; thus, even though the officers were convicted of criminally · negligent homicide they effectively evaded punishment by the State of Texas. The Chief of Police, who was disappointed with the lightness of the sentence, said the outcome represented "a gross miscarriage of justice." The same two officers (plus a third) were subsequently tried in Federal court for violating Torres' civil rights and each received a one year term in Federal prison and five years on probation. The Hispanic community was outraged.

Investigation's COINTELPRO (Counterintelligence Program) became known.[47] This top-secret program represented an attempt by the FBI to disrupt the lives and activities of their targets through the use of covert activities designed to harm their reputations and interfere with their activities.

Misfeasance takes place in police departments in many ways. For example, when people are arrested on "cover charges" misfeasance is likely to be involved. In this kind of situation victims are arrested for "resisting arrest" or "interfering with a law enforcement officer" because the arresting officer either wants to harrass the victim or wants to "cover" himself after having assaulted the person to be arrested.

Another example can be illustrated through one of the favorite tactics of a certain highway patrolman. This officer liked to approach other motorists from the rear on a four lane highway late at night with his bright lights on. When he began to tailgate his victim, the car he was following naturally began to speed up. The highway patrolman then closed the gap again, and continued to do so until he had nudged his victim up to 15-20 miles over the speed limit. He then pulled him over and wrote him a ticket for speeding.

Some officers practice a form of misfeasance by using their authority to insult or humble citizens. Calling minorities by racial epithets or nicknames or using a condescending tone of voice and demeanor are examples. In other cases, police may speak to citizens in ways designed to anger them or at least irritate them, sometimes in the hope the victim will do something for which the officer feels he can justify an actual arrest.

> ITEM: One winter evening the police were diverting traffic from a main thoroughfare onto a side street because of an accident. The accident, however, could not be seen from the point where an officer was diverting traffic. The author (on his way home) was stopped by a patrolman and told to exit on the side street. He said, "O.K. — what have you got up ahead?" The officer walked up to the author's window and said, "What's the matter, asshole, are you deaf? I said MOVE IT!"

Nonfeasance

Nonfeasance is the omission of some act which ought to have been performed. Again, there are many ways in which this can be done. For example, a veteran police officer in one large Texas city was widely regarded by most other members of the department as being both stupid and incompetent. He was assigned to the police garage as a "liaison officer," but in fact only showed up on payday, and then only long enough to collect his paycheck and leave.* In another Texas city a young rookie received an "assignment" which was traditionally passed from one rookie to the next: he was the "late night radio pimp." He was supposed to remain in his car which was parked in a cemetery. Other senior officers were also in the cemetery — asleep on air mattresses which they had brought to work and kept in the trunk of their police cars for this purpose. On the third shift (11:00 p.m. to 7:00 a.m.) after things got quiet, usually around 2:00 a.m., some of the officers would go to the cemetery to sleep. The rookie had a list of the officers and their radio call numbers. If one of the sleeping officers got a radio call, the rookie would acknowledge the dispatcher and then go wake the sleeping officer up, giving him his call.

Many police officers "hide" when things are slow. Some go to the movies, others visit girlfriends, and some go shopping (the use of hand-held radios greatly facilitates this practice). Many of these officers do not give the practice a second thought, saying that if they get a call on the radio, they will respond.

More serious forms of nonfeasance occur when officers simply refuse to act in cases where their action is called for. For years in the South, the police routinely disregarded crimes by Blacks against other Blacks. One of the most difficult forms of nonfeasance is when police officers refuse to act against other officers who are clearly guilty of malfeasance. Again, this can be major or minor. Police officers often extend "professional courtesy" to other police officers whom they catch in off-duty traffic violations. In other cases the police refuse to act against officers who are involved in substantive crimes; the department often prefers to request their resignation unless the crime has come to the attention of the media. Even then, in some departments police officers who are forced to resign because of criminal misconduct are allowed to officially resign because of "personal reasons." It is argued that this is done to avoid damaging the credibility of the department as a whole and the reputations of "good" officers. People outside of the department call it "whitewash" and ask one of the most difficult questions in law enforcement: who is to police the police?[48]

---

*This case raises some interesting questions. Some would argue that the officer is guilty of *malfeasance* because he is stealing his pay (taking a check without working for it). Others would argue that he was actually paid *not* to work (as the lesser of two evils), and thus was doing what he was paid to do. It might also be argued that he can't be accused of not doing his job because the department did not give him a job to do, unless it was literally just to collect his check. If it is any comfort, the officer is now long gone — as is most of the administration which condoned this shabby practice.

Misconduct, the Police, and Community Relations

When the police involve themselves in the activities of others, regardless of whether it concerns crime, misconduct, or disorder, they are likely to make at least *someone* unhappy. Many people do not view their own actions as criminal, disorderly or even as the proper subject of scrutiny by the police, and they resent police intervention of any kind unless they specifically call for it in the first place. Not only do many people resent unsolicited police intervention, many resent *how* the police intervene even when that intervention is consistent with law and departmental regulations. At the same time, when the police respond to complaints made by citizens, many of those who complain are left unhappy because the police did not do what they wanted them to do. These complainants may have even wanted the police to take action that might violate substantive or procedural law or both. Often, *regardless* of what the police do, they will leave some people unhappy. The police are even frequently blamed for not acting in areas in which they have absolutely no authority at all (e.g., civil matters or making people be nice).

To make the problem even more complex, the police have considerable discretion in how they will perform their duties. This discretion is read by some citizens as *discrimination* (which, of course, it can be, depending on the situation). Discretion calls for the making of decisions — many times in situations about which officers have incomplete information or about people whom they do not fully understand. To err under such circumstances is not only possible, it is probable. Often when they make honest mistakes, the police are blamed as if they acted with malicious intent. These are some of the reasons why police officers tend to keep their own company and shelter themselves from the public — a characteristic which many members of the public interpret as evidence of police hostility toward the public.

It is probably not the honest mistake which generates the worst police community relations: that honor is most likely reserved for intentional police misconduct (misfeasance, malfeasance, and nonfeasance). Nothing is more fearsome or depressing than police who abuse their office to hurt others. Fear of the police because they seem dishonest, unfair, or disinterested must surely be one of the worst ills that can befall a community. Unfortunately, the history of American police contains too many examples of communities which had good reason to fear their police.

Although most police misconduct is individual rather than collective, the misconduct of but one officer can seriously damage the reputation of

263

the entire department. When an officer does engage in misconduct and gets away with it, the whole department is viewed as culpable and public confidence quickly erodes. Some police departments are very defensive; indeed, this is part of the legacy of the quasi-military style in which supervisors are expected to "take care of" their men. This is a situation quite different from that in England, where the police do not hesitate to enforce the law against other police officers!

Perhaps we can see by now that the issue of police-community relations is far more complex than it first appears. It is not just a matter of creating a bureaucratic ideology, opening up a storefront, or printing up comic books for children. Police-community relations goes even beyond public policy and involves conflict resolution, the making of difficult operational decisions under ambiguous circumstances, and the very basic question of police integrity at the individual and collective levels. There is no prescription for police-community relations, although certain tactics or programs have been successful at certain places under certain circumstances. Police-community relations is at its core a matter of people (both inside and outside of the police department) being willing to deal with mutual problems. It is not a question of developing tactics to appease minorities; it is not a means of wooing young people; it is not a technique for simply improving the public image of the department. It *does* take into consideration the special needs and problems of groups within the community, including the police! It seeks to resolve problems with the least disruption to either individuals or the community. It also seeks to resolve those problems in a context which is fair, open, and productive.

Summary

Police work is *people* work; officers do their work by dealing with people, normally after something has gone wrong or under conditions of stress; thus the police deal simultaneously with *people* and *problems*. What the police do about these situations depends on the nature of the problem and the officer's perception on what the best course of action would be. In dealing with deviance the first task of the police is that of *assessment*. The majority of calls received by the police are ambiguous and the officers must first determine what the actual problem is before they can decide what response would be most appropriate.

One of the first things police try to determine is whether or not a situation involves *real* police work — those kinds of activities that call for emergency or law-enforcement skills. *Real* police work is performed with speed, efficiency, and formality whereas other tasks are dealt with less formally and allow the officer to use a good deal more discretionary latitude in making his judgments.

Most of the deviance encountered by the police involves either criminal behavior or misconduct. In terms of crime, although there are a number of sociological typologies, the police normally assess crimes and criminals according to *visibility, impact,* and the *degree of legitimacy of the offender.* Misconduct, on the other hand, covers a much wider spectrum of events, many of which test the limits of police capabilities. Problems arising from domestic disturbances, mental illness, drug and alcohol abuse and other forms of misconduct often involve much deeper problems which the police are powerless to solve. A good deal of misconduct is embodied in the so-called victimless crimes. In these cases police intervention may not be sought or might be actively resisted by people who believe such matters as sexual conduct, gambling, drug consumption and so on are personal matters which ought to be beyond the reach of the state.

A great deal of crime and deviance encountered by the police takes place among the poor, especially among poor Blacks. To be properly understood, Black crime must be viewed in the developmental context of Black culture — something the police are not usually trained to do and which many of them feel is irrelevant anyway. Although crime among Blacks is extraordinarily high, much of the conflict between the police and Blacks can be attributed to mistaken perceptions, lack of communications, and a lack of knowledge on *both* sides.

The police themselves are the targets of both physical and psychological violence. As a result, they develop operational and psychological techniques for averting or coping with violence and some of these defensive measures are mistakenly interpreted by citizens as being expressions of police hostility — thus generating further estrangement. The stress of police work has its consequences on many officers who either become cynical or who develop *burnout*, which further impairs their ability to deal with their own problems, much less with those of society!

The problem of misconduct by the police is closely related to how the community views its police department. There are three categories of misconduct: *malfeasance* (the performance by a public official of an act that is not legally justified or is harmful or contrary to law); *misfeasance* (the wrongful and injurious exercise of lawful authority); and *nonfeasance* (the ommission of some act which ought to have been performed). Police misconduct can be individual or collective, and it can be condoned or rejected by the department. Citizen perception of police misconduct may be based on actual misconduct, or it may represent a value judgment based on what citizens believe the police *ought* to be doing, and a great deal of citizen perception (or lack of perception) of police misconduct arises from the tremendous discretionary latitude the police have in how they perform their work.

Discussion Questions

1. How does the problem of police officers having to personally "assess" a situation give rise to problems with those who report the problems in the first place?

2. Why do you think police officers dislike many of the routine tasks they are called upon to perform, and how can this interfere with good police-community relations?

3. What is meant by the "legitimacy" of an offender, at least as far as the police are concerned?

4. Do you think the wide discretionary latitude the police have helps or hinders police-community relations?

5. Why are domestic disturbances typically "no-win" situations for the police?

6. What *can* the police do about drug abuse, and what *should* they do?

7. What are the principle problems which arise from public expectations that the police should enforce morality?

8. In what ways is alcohol related to crime? What role should the police play?

9. Do you think the police are overly sensitive to the possibility of being physically harmed by those with whom they deal?

10. Can a "street cop" avoid developing a "working personality?" If not, why not?

11. How can the problem of "burnout" in a police department seriously threaten the relationship between the police and the community?

12. In looking at police misconduct, to what extent should individual acts of misconduct be "blamed" on the department or on the individual officer?

13. How are police officers routinely enticed into nonfeasance?

14. Who should "police" the police?

15. How much of the difficulty in police-community relations arises from the way police departments are *organized*, and how much arises from what they actually do?

Glossary

BURNOUT   A psychological response to stress in human services occupations which is characterized by exhaustion, depression, disengagement and hostility.

DOMESTIC DISTURBANCE   Any of a variety of conflicts arising within intimate living situations. Family fights.

HARRISON ACT   A 1914 legislative enactment designed to make the distribution of certain drugs a matter of public record; it marks the beginning of law enforcement efforts to control drug abuse.

MALFEASANCE   The performance by a public official of an act that is not legally justified, or is harmful, or contrary to law.

MISFEASANCE   The wrongful and injurious exercise of lawful authority.

NARCOTIC   Opium, its derivatives, or its synthetic substances.

NONFEASANCE   The omission of some act which ought to have been performed.

NORMATIVE BEHAVIOR   The behavior expected of a person (or group) under a given set of circumstances.

SYMBOLIC ASSAILANT   A form of perceptual shorthand through which police officers tentatively identify people who are likely to pose a threat to them. It is a concept based on the interpretation of demeanor, gestures, language, dress, etc., especially as seen in the light of past negative experiences.

NOTES

[1] John Van Maanen, "The Asshole," in Peter K. Manning and John Van Maanen, eds., *Policing: A View From the Street* (Santa Monica, California: Goodyear Publishing Company, Inc., 1978), pp. 221-238.

[2] Jerome Skolnick and J.R. Woodworth, "Bureaucracy, Information and Social Control," in David Bordua, ed., *The Police: Six Sociological Essays* (New York: John Wiley and Sons, 1967), p. 129.

[3] Kim Chapin, "If A Guy Goes Flying By, the Decision is to *Get Him* ...", *Police Magazine*, November 1978, p. 38.

[4] Marshall B. Clinard and Richard Quinney, *Criminal Behavior Systems: A Typology* (New York: Holt, Rinehart and Winston, Inc., 1973).

[5] See for example Julian B. Roebuck, *Criminal Typology: The Legalistic, Physical - Constitutional - Hereditary, Psychological - Psychiatric and Sociological Approaches* (Springfield, Illinois: Charles C. Thomas, Publishers, 1967); Alfred R. Lindesmith and H. Warren Dunham, "Some Principles of Criminal Typology," *Social Forces* 19 (March 1941): 307-314; Don C. Gibbons, *Society, Crime, and Criminal Careers* (Englewood Cliffs, New Jersey: Prentice-Hall, 1968), pp. 193-433; Edwin D. Driver, "A Critique of Typologies in Criminology," *The Sociological Quarterly* 9 (Summer 1968): 356-373.

[6] Federal Bureau of Investigation, U.S. Department of Justice, *Uniform Crime Reports, 1981* (Washington, D.C.: U.S. Government Printing Office, annual), Table 80. "Law Enforcement Officers Assaulted, Police Activity and Type of Weapon, 1981," p. 305.

[7] Morton Bard, "The Family Crisis Unit," in Robert Shellow and Morton Bard, *Issues in Law Enforcement: Essays and Case Studies* (Reston, Virginia: Reston Publishing Co., Inc., 1976), pp. 107-131.

[8] Philip H. Taft, Jr., "Dealing with Mental Patients," *Police Magazine*, January 1980, pp. 21-27.

[9] Philip H. Taft, Jr., "Dealing with Mental Patients," p. 23.

[10] *Alcohol and Health: New Knowledge*, Second Special Report to the United States Congress from the Secretary of Health, Education and Welfare (Washington, D.C.: U.S. Government Printing Office, 1974), pp. 49-57. See also Harrison M. Trice and Paul M. Roman, *Spirits and Demons at Work: Alcohol and Other Drugs on the Job* (Ithaca, Industrial and Labor Relations Paperback, 1972).

[11] See for example Kai Pernanen, "Alcohol and Crimes of Violence," in Benjamin Kissin and Henri Begleiter, eds., *Social Aspects of Alcoholism* (New York: Plenum Press, 1976), pp. 351-444.

[12] Morton Bard and Joseph Zacker, "Assaultiveness and Alcohol Use in Family Disputes: Police Perceptions," *Criminology* 12 (1972): 281-292.

[13] See Sheldon D. Bacon, "Traffic Accidents Involving Alcohol in the U.S.A.: Second Stage Aspects of a Social Problem," *Quarterly Journal of Studies on Alcohol*, Supplement 4, 1968.

[14] Edwin Schur, *Crimes Without Victims* (Englewood Cliffs, New Jersey: Prentice-Hall, Inc., 1965), pp. 169, 170-171.

[15] See for example Harold Garfinkle, "Conditions of Successful Degradation Ceremonies," *American Journal of Sociology* 61 (March 1956): 421-422.

[16] *Uniform Crime Reports*, 1981. See Table 23, "Total Estimated Arrests, United States, 1981," p. 162.

[17] For an excellent discussion of this issue, see James P. Levine, Michael C. Musheno, and Dennis J. Palumbo, *Criminal Justice: A Public Policy Approach* (New York: Harcourt Brace Jovanovich, Inc., 1980), Chapter 11, "Decriminalization and Legalization: Shrinking the Scope of Criminal Codes," pp. 430-461.

[18] Charles E. Silberman, *Criminal Violence, Criminal Justice* (New York: Vintage Books, 1978), p. 160.

[19] Silberman, *Criminal Violence, Criminal Justice*, p. 189.

[20] Silberman, *Criminal Violence, Criminal Justice*, p. 191.

[21] Silberman, *Criminal Violence, Criminal Justice*, p. 194.

[22] James F. Richardson, *Urban Police in the United States* (Port Washington, New York: Kennikat Press, 1974), pp. 162-163.

[23] Silberman, *Criminal Violence, Criminal Justice*, p. 202.

[24] Silberman, *Criminal Violence, Criminal Justice*, p. 203.

[25] Silberman, *Criminal Violence, Criminal Justice*, p. 204.

[26] Silberman, *Criminal Violence, Criminal Justice*, p. 206.

[27] Silberman, *Criminal Violence, Criminal Justice*, p. 211.

[28] *Uniform Crime Reports, 1981*, Table 36, "Total Arrests, Distribution by Race, 1981," p. 179.

[29] *Uniform Crime Reports, 1981*, Table 36, "Total Arrests, Distribution by Race, 1981," p. 180.

[30] U.S. Department of Justice, Bureau of Justice Statistics, *The Hispanic Victim* (Washington, D.C.: U.S. Government Printing Office, August 1981).

[31] *Uniform Crime Reports, 1981*, p. 231.

[32] *Uniform Crime Reports, 1981*, p. 303.

[33] *Uniform Crime Reports, 1981*, p. 303.

[34] *Uniform Crime Reports, 1981*, p. 309.

[35] Jerome H. Skolnick, *Justice Without Trial: Law Enforcement in a Democratic Society* (New York: John Wiley and Sons, 1966), Chapter 3, "A Sketch of the Policeman's 'Working Personality',", pp. 42-70.

[36] Skolnick, *Justice Without Trial*, p. 45.

[37] Skolnick, *Justice Without Trial*, p. 47.

[38] John Blackmore, "Are Police Allowed to Have Problems of Their Own?" *Police Magazine*, July 1979, p. 49; see also Leonard Territo and Harold J. Vetter, "Stress and Police Personnel," *Journal of Police Science and Administration* 9 (June 1981): 195-208.

[39] Harvey Schlossberg, *Psychologist With a Gun* (New York: Coward, McCann and Geoghegan, Inc., 1974), p. 56.

[40] This is the theme of Joseph Wambaugh's novel *The Choir Boys*. A "choir practice" (a drinking binge) is held after the completion of a tour of duty by police officers when one of them experiences some especially upsetting event. In the novel, the "choir practice" itself ultimately leads to a tragedy.

[41] Christina Maslach and Susan E. Jackson, "Burned-Out Cops and Their Families," *Psychology Today*, May 1979.

[42] Blackmore, "Are Police Allowed to Have Problems of Their Own?" p. 47.

[43] Blackmore, "Are Police Allowed to Have Problems of Their Own? p. 47.

[44] Ed Cray, *The Enemy in the Streets: Police Malpractice in America* (Garden City, New York: Anchor Books, 1972), p. 167.

[45] Bruce Cory, "Police on Trial in Houston: "They Were Wrong, But...' " *Police Magazine,* July 1978, pp. 33-40.

[46] Daniel Walker, *Rights in Conflict* (New York: Signal Books, 1968), p. xix.

[47] Nelson Blackstone, *COINTELPRO: The FBI's Secret War on Political Freedom* (New York: Vintage Books, 1975).

[48] See for example Kevin Krajack, "Police vs Police," *Police Magazine*, May 1980, pp. 6-20.

PROSECUTION: THE HIDDEN POWER 9

Prosecution is an active intervention by the state into the life of an individual offender. The basis for this intervention is the belief that the person has violated the law and intervention by the state is necessary. The reasons for this intervention might include the desire to *protect society* from a person who has indicated that he is a menace to public safety or order. The intervention could be based on a desire to *help the offender*, even though he may not want to be helped. The intervention could be based on a desire to *make an example* of him in an effort to deter others from following in his footsteps. The intervention could also be the result of a desire to *punish* the offender for his crime as a means of affirming the moral position of the state against criminal behavior in general and that offender's behavior in particular.

There are other reasons which are also rational, although somewhat less idealistic. A prosecutor may wish to build an impressive string of convictions so that he can point to "a solid record of achievement" when he runs for higher elective office. Some prosecutions are based on the simple fact that the role of prosecutors is to prosecute, and cases which "look good" will be prosecuted *regardless* of what it means to the offender, the victim, or society!

Prosecution is a process which may involve many people and a number of decisions. The simple fact that a person committed a crime and got caught is by no means a guarantee that he will be prosecuted. In fact, odds are that in the case of many kinds of crimes, the offender will *not* be prosecuted for one reason or another. To understand this process, it is necessary to first take a look at the primary actors, the roles they play, and the means by which these roles are acted out.

The Defendant: born in 1948

The Record: _____

            12 arrests in 2½ years (between January 1973 and July 1975)
             8 cases dropped
             3 convictions
             1 case combined with another and convicted

Date	Charge	Disposition	Sentence
Jan. 19, 1973	Robbery—felony	Rejected at screening (witness problem) January 20, 1973	
March 22, 1973	Bail Reform Act violation—misdemeanor	Rejected at screening (insufficient evidence) March 23, 1973	
June 3, 1973	Robbery—felony	Rejected at screening (witness no show) June 4, 1973	
Aug. 23, 1973	Bail Reform Act violation—misdemeanor	Nolled September 11, 1973	
Sept. 13, 1973	Commercial armed robbery—felony	Convicted at trial January 19, 1974	
Jan. 22, 1974	Armed robbery—felony	Nolled (insufficient evidence) February 1, 1974	
June 22, 1974	Commercial robbery—	Dismissed because complaining witness did not appear in court March 7, 1975	Probation
Dec. 9, 1974	Bail Reform Act—felony	Pled as charged March 7, 1975	Probation
March 20, 1975	Attempted robbery—felony	Ignored by grand jury April 9, 1975	
April 15, 1975	Robbery—felony	Convicted at trial December 11, 1975	3 to 9 years
April 22, 1975	Threats to bodily harm—misdemeanor	Dismissed April 28, 1975	
July 7, 1975	Robbery—felony	Case combined and convicted with the robbery resulting in the April 15 arrest	3 to 9 years concurrent with the other case

Source: *Promis Newsletter,* Vol. 3, No. 2 (October 1978), p. 5 inset (reproduced with permission of INSLAW).

Who Prosecutes?

There are several government agencies which may initiate a criminal prosecution, but there are few which may actually charge an offender with a crime. *Which* agency charges is a function of two primary factors, the type of crime and jurisdiction. The crime could be a minor violation of a city or county ordinance, or it could be the violation of a major state or federal law. In general, the terms *misdemeanor* and *felony* distinguish between the less serious (misdemeanor) and more serious (felony) crimes. The second major fact that controls which agency brings charges is the *jurisdiction* of the court in which the case will be heard. The seriousness of the crime and the place where it was committed determine jurisdiction. Some courts have limited trial jurisdiction in terms of the kinds of cases they may hear, but all courts have limitations on the geography of their cases.

Incorporated cities may have a *city attorney* whose job consists to some extent of initiating prosecutions of violations of city ordinances in the municipal (sometimes called the corporation or police) court. These cases typically involve minor misdemeanors such as the unlawful burning of trash or selling without a license. These municipal courts deal with offenses against the city which, because of its geographic limitation, cannot be tried in other courts. This same arrangement may also operate at the county level, where a *county attorney* may initiate prosecution against residents of the county (or of the cities within it) for violation of county ordinances, although this is more often done by the district attorney.

Most states are divided into *judicial districts* which may vary in size according to population. Some judicial districts serve only a county or a single municipality, whereas others serve a multi-county area. There are usually two types of criminal courts within these judicial districts. The lower court (frequently called the *district court**) hears misdemeanors, such as traffic offenses, simple assaults, and bad check cases. These cases, however, are violations of *state* law, and this level of prosecution represents state rather than city or county action, even though the offense may have been committed and tried within the same city. The second level of court within a judicial district is the court of general jurisdiction (frequently called the *circuit* or *superior court*) which is empowered to try all cases up to and including capital crimes.

---

*The reader should be very wary, as court terminology differs considerably from one state to another.

A judicial district includes the office of the *district attorney*, an elected state officer whose job is to prosecute state cases in the courts which hear cases within his judicial district. The district attorney actually brings cases before the proper court. He may have a large staff and a heavy caseload, or he may be the sole prosecutor within his district and have a private law practice on the side. There are about 3,400 county prosecutors and district attorneys in the United States, and most of them preside over small offices with only one or two assistants and a low volume of actual criminal cases.

At the federal level, the chief prosecutor is the United States Attorney General; however, the country is divided into federal judicial districts, each of which has its own courts and prosecutor. The local federal prosecutor is the United States District Attorney (usually simply called the U.S. Attorney) who may have a staff of several assistant U.S. Attorneys.

Where Do Prosecutors Get Their Cases?

In general, prosecutors get their cases from the police or other criminal investigative agencies which serve them. An individual can contact a prosecutor directly and make a complaint, but in most cases where this happens, the prosecutor will refer the person making the complaint to the proper law enforcement agency. In cases where the prosecutor has reason to suspect that such a referral would not be advisable (as in cases involving dishonesty or corruption on the part of the law enforcement agency itself), he may exercise his own extensive police powers and have the allegation investigated by his own staff. In most cases, however, the primary input to the prosecutor's office is the output of the law enforcement agencies which serve him.

It should be noted, however, that the size of the community can play a major role in how the prosecutor manages complaints. In small communities, individuals may come directly to the prosecutor with complaints concerning borderline issues such as domestic relations matters or bad check cases. These types of cases are not usually the sort of thing a prosecutor actually wants to take to court, and he often uses his office to informally settle the conflict. In smaller communities, the status of the people involved in a conflict may play a major role in how a prosecutor elects to handle a case.

> Item: In a rural community a local citizen went to the county attorney and complained about a member of the city council, a local plumber, who had a number of lucrative contracts with the city — a clear violation of the state's conflict of interest law. The county attorney was reluctant to accept the case, and

at the citizen's insistence referred the case to the grand jury. On the day the grand jury met to consider the matter, the county attorney met with them. Although it is not known what he told them, the grand jury returned a "no bill." Afterwards, the county attorney went to the plumber-councilman and, shaking his hand, congratulated him. He then told the citizen that the matter was closed.

In larger cities the prosecutor plays a more formal and structured role. His primary task is in the management of his office and he usually has little time for taking a personal interest in minor matters. Thus in the larger communities, the prosecutor normally receives his cases from official agencies rather than from private individuals.

For crimes against state law which take place inside incorporated cities, the primary law enforcement agency is the local police department. For crimes against state law which take place in the unincorporated areas of the county, the primary servicing law enforcement agency is usually the sheriff's department or the county police, depending on the part of the country in which one lives. A number of states have state police or investigative agencies, such as a state bureau of investigation. These agencies usually confine their activities to very complex state-wide cases or serious crimes committed in areas in which local law enforcement personnel lack the manpower or training to deal with the particular crime. Offenses against federal laws are investigated by federal agencies such as the Federal Bureau of Invesitgation, United States Secret Service, or the Internal Revenue Service. Thus each jurisdiction (federal, state, and local) has its own law enforcement or investigative agencies, its own prosecutor, and its own courts. Although prosecutors may work very closely with law enforcement agencies, they do *not* usually direct those agencies to investigate certain crimes. Some prosecutors, however, may inform the law enforcement agencies which serve them that they will not prosecute cases unless certain criteria are met, such as minimum dollar values in thefts or minimum drug quantities in narcotics cases.

The prosecutor has numerous tasks which he must perform in carrying out his job. Project STAR has identified 20 tasks as being appropriate for the position of a prosecuting attorney.[1] They are:

1. Advising
2. Collecting and preserving evidence
3. Communicating
4. Conferring about cases
5. Contacting families of suspects and clients
6. Engaging in legal research
7. Engaging in professional development

8. Interacting with other agencies
9. Interviewing
10. Investigating
11. Issuing complaints
12. Participating in community relations and education programs
13. Participating in courtroom proceedings
14. Participating in plea negotiations
15. Participating in trial preparation conferences
16. Preparing reports
17. Preparing search warrant requests
18. Referring
19. Reviewing case materials
20. Training

Out of all these requirements, however, the *basic* task of the prosecutor is to screen criminal accusations and to bring those which have prosecutive merit before the proper court for adjudication. In doing this, the prosecutor has four major objectives:[2]

1. To effectively present the prosecution position, the prosecution evidence, and the need to protect society.

2. To determine if the issuance of a criminal complaint is justified on the basis of adherence to statutes or ordinances and an evaluation of whether the evidence was obtained in accordance with acceptable procedures.

3. To initiate actions necessary for effectively prosecuting a case.

4. To recommend dispositions that are in the best interests of society.

The Process

Prosecution is a sequence of actions and decisions, some of which overlap and others which depend on preceeding ones. The process works somewhat like a sieve; cases are disposed of by the most appropriate means at each step of the process. In general, this process involves four major phases:

1. **Screening.** The prosecutor must determine whether or not he will accept the case for prosecution (or for some other action);

2. **Diversion.** Many cases clearly require *some* action, but not necessarily criminal prosecution. The prosecutor removes these kinds of cases and diverts them into channels which he feels are better suited to deal with the problem.

3. **Charging.** This step involves all of the considerations which go into deciding exactly what a given offender will be officially accused of and why. It is at this point that plea negotiations are entered into and indictments might be sought.

4. **Litigation.** This is the final phase of prosecution. It consists of bringing the accused person to court and holding him accountable for his crime. It may be an uncontested litigation, in which the offender simply pleads guilty, or it may involve the full adversarial process with a trial by jury.

Screening

Although the goals of the police and the prosecutor may be compatible, not all cases which the police present to the prosecutor are accepted. Available evidence indicates a significant rejection rate by prosecutors. For example, in 1974, 21 percent of all arrests brought to the Superior Court Division of the U.S. Attorney's Office in Washington, D.C. were rejected at the initial screening.* The information presented in Table 9.1 summarizes the reasons for these rejections.

Table 9.1

ARREST REJECTIONS AT INITIAL SCREENING: REASONS GIVEN BY PROSECUTOR, BY MAJOR OFFENSE GROUP
(1974)

Rejection reason	robbery	other violent	nonviolent property	victimless	other	crime group
Witness problem	43%	51%	25%	2%	5%	25%
Insufficiency of evidence	35%	18%	37%	40%	41%	34%
Due process problem	0%	0%	2%	20%	3%	5%
No reason given	0%	0%	1%	0%	1%	1%
Other	22%	30%	36%	38%	50%	36%
Total rejections	100%	100%	100%	100%	100%	100%
Number of rejections	242	876	1,257	654	621	3,650
Number of arrests	1,955	3,176	6,562	3,659	2,182	17,534
Rejection rate	12%	28%	19%	18%	29%	21%

Source: Prosecutor's Management Information System (PROMIS).

Many problems which result in rejection by the prosecutor are outside the control of the police and include such things as lack of credibility of a witness or refusal to testify. Other problems, such as the failure to obtain sufficient physical evidence, result from inadequate police work. Part of the issue seems to be the type of case and how the police came to be involved in it in the first place.[3] For example, in those cases where the police are called by a complainant who identifies himself, where the identity of the offender is known, and where physical evidence is legally

---

*Although Washington, D.C. is a city much like other metropolitan areas, it lies exclusively within the federal jurisdiction; hence, its cases must be filed with a federal prosecutor in a federal court.

available, any problems which emerge at a later date will most likely result from matters largely out of the control of the police. On the other hand, if the case is initiated by the police (as in many vice and narcotic cases), there is a greater likelihood of the case later being rejected by the prosecutor because of such errors as a lack of probable cause in making the arrest or because of an illegal search.

Case Dismissals   The prosecutor may initially accept a case from the police but later decide that it should be dropped. The prosecutor has the right to do this; that is, to decline to prosecute a case (technically known as a *nolle prosequi*, or nol pros) at his own discretion. This is a power which Newman calls "one of the broadest, most powerful examples of discretionary authority in the entire criminal justice system."[4] A prosecutor may nol pros a case for a variety of reasons:

> —the case may be weak in terms of either evidence or witnesses and the prosecutor may simply decide against "going with it."

> —The case may be dismissed by the prosecutor at the request of the police as part of an arrangement made by the offender and the police (as in the case of an offender who agrees to act as a police informant).

> —The prosecutor may not deem the case important enough to pursue, given his limitations on manpower and resources.

Diversion

Diversion projects normally take place during the pre-trial period; that is, after an offender has been arrested but before he is actually brought to court and charged with his crime. The prosecutor, by using a diversionary program, in effect "suspends" the offender by placing him in a program which may deal sufficiently with the offender's problem to merit dropping the criminal charges. The philosophy behind diversion is both humane and pragmatic. On the humane side, it uses the arrest for a crime as the means of identifying people who have a greater need for treatment than they do for criminal conviction. It also spares the offender the social and economic hardship of a criminal trial and attempts to deal with the problem which produced the criminal activity in the first place, thus reducing the likelihood of recidivism. On the pragmatic side, it reduces the congestion of the criminal courts, eases the prosecutor's case load, and saves the state money.

In most diversionary projects the offender is placed in some type of program for a period of time ranging from a few months to a year. If he cooperates with the program and avoids re-arrest during this period, the prosecution rewards him by dismissing the charges.* Most diversion projects try to take minimum risk cases off overloaded court dockets and to place them in the hands of *intervention* agencies. This latter point is important, because *diversion* and *intervention* are not one and the same. Although pre-trial "intervention" and "diversion" are often used interchangably, the two may be distinguished as follows:[5]

> **Diversion:** Based on the traditional discretionary authority of the prosecutor or the court, the primary function of diversion is that of case screening. The objective is to conserve official criminal justice resources for those requiring close control and supervision, removing from the sanction of the court defendants who may not require a full criminal disposition.

> **Intervention:** Although diversion occurs, the primary function is rehabilitation. The objective is to identify defendants in need of treatment and to deliver requisite services with the expectation of providing a more effective alternative to normal criminal or juvenile justice system processing.

In practice, most programs provide both services, but the prosecutor *diverts* while the rehabilitation program *intervenes.* One problem with diversion projects is their evaluation. It is hard to say how effective a program really is if it only takes low risk offenders; however, it is clear that a great many people charged with crimes can and should be dealt with by some means other than a criminal prosecution.

Problems With Diversion Diversion programs may be an excellent way to apply community resources to some criminal events through such devices as counseling, conflict resolution, and community-based treatment programs, but diversion can still pose some substantial problems. Diversion programs tend to operate on the implicit assumption of the offender's guilt. This means that people who wish to take advantage of a diversion program are expected to acknowledge their guilt and show cooperation if not contrition. This raises the possibility that some offenders may feel coerced to go along with a diversion program as the lesser of two evils, thus avoiding a criminal prosecution which could result in a harsh sentence. Somewhat related to this problem is the prospect that if a person fails in a diversion program, he might be more vigorously prosecuted for the crime than might have otherwise been the case.

Yet another problem with diversion is that it may be used more in the

---

*Although the offender has a court record, this allows him to state that he has not been *convicted.*

self-interest of the criminal justice system than for the benefit of the offender. Diversion projects allow prosecutors and courts to reduce their work-load and may give them some added flexibility in how they can approach certain cases. Although this is desirable, these considerations should not necessarily be primary *goals* in their own right, especially when such practices could operate to the·detriment of those who are placed in diversion programs.

Another problem is that diversion programs can be unfair if they deny equal treatment to similar offenders. The decision to select a person for a diversion program rather than for criminal prosecution has the potential for being arbitrary unless some safeguards can be established to assure a fundamental fairness in selection procedures.

Because some diversion projects select offenders who are most likely to succeed, they may in fact waste time and resources on people who are the least likely to get into trouble again anyway. This is related to yet another problem with diversion projects: since such programs are operated informally, many of them are never subjected to any kind of systematic evaluation, thus leaving gaps in our knowledge of what *really* works and what does not.

Charging

According to Miller, the decision to file charges against an offender involves three major questions:[6]

> —Is there sufficient evidence to show probable cause that the defendant is guilty of a crime?
>
> —Is the prosecution of this offense in the public interest?
>
> —What is the specific crime with which the suspect is to be charged?

Regarding the first point, the National Advisory Commission on Criminal Justice Standards and Goals stated that "An individual should be screened out of the criminal justice system if there is not a reasonable likelihood that the evidence admissible against him would be sufficient to obtain a conviction and sustain it on appeal."[7] They did not, however, define "reasonable likelihood," but they did go on to say that "where the need is high (e.g., the defendant is clearly dangerous and his preventive detention is essential, or the crime is such that convictions are valuable for deterrent purposes) a prosecutor would be justified in proceeding with formal action even though the probability of a conviction was low."[8] In some instances a case may be technically valid but very difficult to prosecute because the credibility of a witness or the nature of the crime presents serious ambiguities. In one such case, a woman was picked up by a man in a bar and accompanied him to his apartment. They spent the night together, and the following morning the woman went to the police and filed a complaint alleging the man had raped her. The woman had an arrest record for many minor offenses and was a known "barfly". The man admitted having intercourse with the woman, but denied raping her. Because of the woman's prior reputation and the lack of supporting evidence, the prosecutor refused to accept the case.

The second issue — whether or not prosecution is in the public interest — may play a controlling role, even if the crime is serious.

OUTCOMES OF 100 "TYPICAL" ARRESTS BROUGHT TO THE
SUPERIOR COURT OF WASHINGTON, D.C., IN 1974

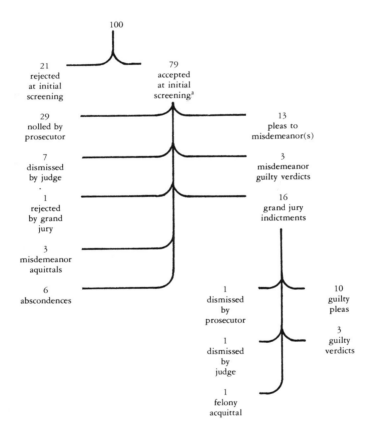

Source: Based on the actual flow of 17,534 arrests recorded in the Prosecutor's Management Information System (PROMIS).
aTotal does not agree due to rounding error.

Sometimes major cases are not prosecuted because to do so would be counter to the public interest. For example, counterespionage cases conducted by the FBI sometimes involve hostile foreign agents who attempt to obtain U.S. defense secrets through people within defense industries or the military. In such cases, where the person passing the secret information to the foreign agents is under U.S. government control, the arrest is usually made as soon as the classified material changes hands. If the person arrested were tried for espionage, the secrets which were passed would become evidence and would have to be admitted in open court where their public disclosure could be very much against the national interest. Rather than do this, government prosecutors normally do not charge the offender with espionage. He may, however, be charged with conspiracy to commit espionage, which does not require disclosure of the secret material. This raises the final issue mentioned by Miller: the specific crime with which the suspect is to be charged.

If the most important decision for a prosecutor is whether or not to charge in the first place, then the second most important decision is to ascertain what charge the offender will face. This decision is based in turn on a whole host of considerations, such as:

—The strength of the case, based on availability of witnesses and evidence;

—The degree of cooperativeness on the part of the offender (that is, his willingness to "bargain");

—The complexity of the case;

—Probable defense tactics;

—The notoriety of the case;

—The dangerousness of the offender;

—The degree of the prosecutor's caseload burden and the congestion of the court's docket;

—Anticipated cost of a trial (in both time and money);

—The likelihood of a conviction; and

—The availability of diversion programs.

In general, the rule of thumb is that an offender will be charged with the "highest" crime for which the prosecutor feels he has a good chance of winning a conviction. In this respect it is important to remember that most serious crimes have included within them *less serious* crimes. For example, burglary "contains" the lesser, included offense of criminal tresspass, and depending on the wording of the state's laws, might also include housebreaking. Murders in the first degree "contain" manslaughter, and rape includes various forms of the crime of assault. A prosecutor, examining all the circumstances of a given case, may believe that it would be easier and more certain to obtain a conviction on one of these lesser included offenses. For example, in one city a baby was brought into the emergency room of the county hospital by its parents. The infant, which was less than a year old, was dead. Examination of the body clearly indicated that although it was malnourished and showed signs of other injuries, the baby had died as the result of a severe scalding. Although the parents claimed the death was an accident, the doctors, the police, and the district attorney were certain the child had been intentionally scalded by its stepfather. However, the prosecutor believed that his best chance for a conviction was to charge the stepfather with negligent manslaughter rather than first degree murder, which he proceeded to do. Perhaps the single-most important consideration in charging decisions is that of plea bargaining, in which the offender "accepts" guilt on a charge in return for some consideration.

Charging Decisions And Plea Bargaining   In jurisdictions with large populations, prosecutors normally have a heavy case load. Even though the prosecutor may reject many cases and may "nol pros" many others, there still remain a substantial number of cases which must be brought before the courts. If each case actually went to litigation, the courts would become bogged down very quickly, and lengthy delays would soon be the rule rather than the exception. Chief Justice Warren Burger pointed this out very clearly:

> The consequences of ... a small percentage change in the rate of guilty pleas can be tremendous. A reduction from 90 percent to 80 percent in guilty pleas requires the assignment of twice the judicial manpower and facilities — judges, court reporters, bailiffs, clerks, jurors and courtrooms. A reduction to 70 percent trebles this demand.[9]

The solution to the problem has been that of "making a deal." If an offender agrees to plead guilty, the courts are then spared the time, cost, and inconvenience of a contested case. Some people might be willing to plead guilty simply because they got caught, the evidence against them is strong, and they have no reasonable defense. In other words, they might be sufficiently certain they will be convicted anyway that they decide to "throw themselves on the mercy of the court."

On the other hand, many offenders realize the prosecutor can be flexible if he wants to, and that the convenience of the prosecutor can be traded for some consideration that would benefit the offender. Sometimes this benefit is a reduced charge, and sometimes it is the prosecutor's promise to recommend leniency in sentencing. Some people may plead guilty as a part of a "negotiated outcome."

A great deal of plea bargaining boils down to each side's perception of its chances of winning. If the prosecutor thinks he has a very good chance of getting a conviction on the highest possible charge in a serious case, he probably will not be inclined to bargain with the defense for a reduction. He might, however, be willing to bargain on the sentence he recommends to the judge. On the other hand, if the prosecutor thinks he had a weak case on the most serious charge, he might well be willing to bargain for a reduction in charge in return for a plea of guilty.

If the offender's lawyer thinks he has an excellent case for the defense, he may not wish to bargain at all with the prosecutor. Sometimes a defense lawyer knows he has a weak case and in spite of it, will demand a jury trial for his client in the hope that the district attorney will bargain for a reduction just to avoid the aggravation of having to go to trial. This is often done in cases which do not involve major property loss or physical injury. A general guide used by many prosecutors is that they will accept a guilty plea in a case if the offender gets a sentence that is close to the most the prosecutor thinks he could have secured anyway. Thus, in the final analysis, an offender is usually charged with the most serious charge for which the prosecutor thinks he can obtain a conviction without actually going to trial. The charge or sentence is usually the least serious that the defense attorney believes he can obtain by bargaining his client's case. In general, the procedure of plea bargaining is not reviewable by higher courts, and the agreement reached by the prosecutor and the defendant is *not* binding on the court before which the plea is entered. A prosecutor can make a deal with a defendant in which the offender agrees to plead guilty if the prosecutor will recommend the minimum sentence, only to have the judge throw the book at him! In such a case (and it does happen, although not often), the offender has no grounds for appeal.

Information and Indictments

In some jurisdictions, after the prosecutor decides the charge he wishes to bring against the offender, he files an "information." This is a formal document accusing the offender of the crime for which he is being charged. This document then becomes the basis for arraignment and trial. In the case of misdemeanors, the information process is used almost exclusively in the form of a summons or complaint. The traffic ticket you receive for running a stop sign is actually an information document accusing you of a minor crime. On the basis of that ticket, you must appear in court, enter your plea (arraign yourself), and answer to the allegation — unless you choose to pay the ticket.

In many jurisdictions (including the Federal jurisdiction) serious crimes must be sent to a grand jury. The grand jury is composed of local citizens, usually between 16 and 23 in number, and sits for a specified period of time (a term) to hear all "presentments" which come before it. The purpose of the grand jury is to decide whether or not there is sufficient cause in a given case to warrant bringing the case back to trial. If the grand jury believes there is, it returns a *true bill* or *indictment*. If it finds insufficient cause, the grand jury returns a *no bill*, and the prosecutor normally drops the case.

An indictment is not evidence of guilt; it only means there is enough reason (probable cause) to suspect guilt and that the accused should be compelled to answer to the state's formal accusation in court. The grand jury is a closed hearing, and the person accused of a crime has no right to either offer evidence before the grand jury or to even be present during its deliberations. If a grand jury returns a no bill, this does not mean the accused has been declared innocent. The prosecutor may quite legally take the same case before a subsequent grand jury and secure an indictment. A prosecutor will seldom do this, however, unless he is able to uncover new evidence in a case which strengthens the original accusation.

Grand juries are not bound to render findings based on purely legalistic grounds, although most do just that. One complaint about grand juries is that they tend to be rubber stamps for the prosecutor. For instance, one Thanksgiving Day in Texas a distraught woman attempted to kill herself by jumping in front of a truck on an interstate highway. The driver swerved the truck aside and missed the woman, but the car following him was unable to avoid her. The car struck and killed the woman, but the driver of the car panicked and fled the scene without stopping. The cause of the woman's death was officially listed as a suicide and the driver of the car was subsequently identified and charged with Failure to Stop and Render Aid — Felony (because it involved an injury or death). The district attorney sent the case to the grand jury, and in spite of the fact that *legally* it was an air-tight case, the grand jury returned a no bill. One member of the grand jury later commented that the driver of the car had been punished enough by the anguish he had suffered over the incident. No further action was ever taken.

Prosecution Management

Although the prosecutor is an attorney for the state, he must also be a manager within his agency. He must insure that the citizens within his jurisdiction get the best service for their tax dollar. This is often easier said than done; in the more active jurisdictions, the prosecutor's office may be flooded with pending cases. This can produce high rates of inefficiency with minor offenders being prosecuted while serious ones get away. Serious delays in getting cases docketted before the courts may result in the loss of witnesses and other elements essential for a successful prosecution.

One answer to this problem has been PROMIS — Prosecutor Management Information System. Pioneered in Washington, D.C., PROMIS uses an automated management information system to select high priority cases for intensive pre-trial preparation by a special team of prosecutors. Using this system, pending cases are ranked daily according to four criteria:

1. Seriousness of the offense
2. The offender's criminal record
3. The strength of the state's evidence
4. The age of the case and the number of continuances it has received

Using this special targeting system during its first 19 months of operation, the conviction rate for cases which received this special preparation was 25 percent higher than the conviction rate of cases which had been processed routinely. The PROMIS program also helped to identify scheduling problems in criminal cases and to maintain fairness in using prosecutorial discretion.

Prosecution As A Public Enterprise

Although "justice" is a collective good, prosecution is a public business and deals with specific individuals. As a business, it has a job to do and that job is simply to dispose of the cases which it receives. As has already been noted, there are a number of ways of disposing of cases — through diversionary programs, plea bargaining, and trials. Each of these techniques should theoretically be carried out in such a way that the "efforts of the prosecutor and the court are directed toward fairness and justice."[10] As a matter of practical reality, however, prosecutors are "part lawyer, part bureaucrat, and part politician."[11] This means that the work of the prosecutor sometimes translates into outcomes which are less interested in fairness and justice than other considerations.

As with the police, a prosecutor's *output* is difficult to measure, especially in light of the fact that criminal convictions are not always the best way to "treat" a crime. How then *is* a prosecutor's effectiveness to be measured? Blumberg argues that "the occupational role of the prosecutor is characterized by five major functions in our system of criminal justice:

(1) collection agent; (2) dispenser of justice; (3) power-broker-fixer; (4) political 'enforcer'; and (5) overseer of the police."[12] This is a valuable perspective, for it clearly illustrates how prosecution — as a public enterprise — serves a number of constituencies, each of which evaluates performance. Blumberg's perspective also recognizes the *complexity* of the prosecutor's role.

Collection Agent   Blumberg points out that "one of the most important services that a prosecutor's office renders, especially in smaller communities, is as an agency to collect and disburse debts which arise in a variety of legal contexts."[13] Most of these situations are clear-cut: bad checks, child support payments which have fallen in arrears, and some cases of fraud or embezzlement.

Dispenser of Justice   Statutes are cold and impersonal, whereas the cases which come before a prosecutor for charging decisions are very real *human* situations as well as legal problems. Moreover, not all "crimes" which stand in violation of a given statute are equal. Silberman has noted, for example, that "by and large prosecutors distinguish between 'real crimes' — crimes committed by strangers — and 'junk (or garbage) cases,' i.e., those which grow out of a dispute between people who know one another."[14] The prosecutor sorts out the real meaning of a given case and looks at it in the light of its own merits and then decides which direction to take with the case. In this respect the prosecutor is acting as a judge; that is, as a dispenser of justice. Hence, he may elect to dismiss charges or he may decide to go forward with a no-holds-barred courtroom battle and seek the maximum punishment the state can inflict.

Power-broker-fixer Blumberg says this role is performed by prosecutors from time to time and involves cases in which "a defendant is being prosecuted for reasons or purposes other than, or extraneous to, underlying factors of guilt in a crime."[15] Probably the most frequent motive for such an action is publicity. As elected officials, prosecutors must maintain a certain amount of visibility, and one of the best ways of doing this is by "cashing in" on certain crimes, especially those which have already captured the public's attention. Prosecutors sometimes engage in what amounts to malicious prosecution — even if there is reason to doubt the guilt of the offender.[16]

Political 'Enforcer'   The district attorney is a part of what is often called "the courthouse gang," which is composed of elected officials such as the sheriff, the district attorney, and judges. These people not only represent specific roles within the criminal justice system, but they also represent a certain amount of political power within the community.

They may use this power in the dispensing of patronage jobs and to keep a tight rein on local politics.

Overseer of the Police When a prosecutor evaluates a criminal case, he also evaluates the work of the police officers who prepared that case. Under the most desirable circumstances, the prosecutor will actively assist the police in the preparation of a case, especially when there is a strong likelihood that it will result in a litigated trial. The relationship between the prosecutor and the police is very close and in a sense the prosecutor does oversee the criminal case preparation of the police through both his charging decisions and his decisions to not prosecute. If the police wish to secure criminal convictions in the cases which they prepare, they must see to it that those cases are prepared in a manner consistent with the expectations of the prosecutor.[17]

The Prosecutor As A Private Entrepreneur Prosecutors, whether elected to office (district attorneys) or appointed (assistant district attorneys), are lawyers who are attempting to build their careers. Assistant prosecutors are usually people who have recently graduated from law school and who are just entering the legal profession. Most of them have neither trial experience nor any real practical experience in their new craft. Because most new lawyers must start at the bottom and good jobs are not easy to find even for lawyers, many decide to get started in the prosecutor's office.

There are a number of reasons why this is a good idea. Although salaries are not high, they are usually adequate. It also gives the young attorney a wide range of experience in dealing with criminal cases and in the general practice of criminal law. He learns the ropes of how prosecution actually works, and he tries cases and thereby gains trial experience. He also learns about the administration of dockets and participates in plea bargaining sessions with defense attorneys. The young lawyer can also maintain high visibility within the legal community. Attorneys defending or otherwise representing clients must deal with him and, thus, have the opportunity to see how well he works. A good assistant prosecutor can develop a favorable reputation among local attorneys; this may eventually result in an offer of a job in a law firm, especially one which needs a good, aggressive attorney with recent experience in criminal cases.*

*Law firms are complex organizations; they are composed of attorneys who share a set of offices and who provide most kinds of legal services (of which criminal defense is only one such service). Many lawyers do not like criminal work and seek to avoid it as much as possible. A good law firm (with a number of lawyers) normally has one or more members who do enjoy criminal work and an attorney with prior experience in the district attorney's office can be a major asset to a law firm.

The elected prosecutor is also interested in managing his personal career; being an elected prosecutor is not usually a career position in its own right. Getting elected in the first place is not always easy. As one text points out, "police chiefs are appointed and judges are too numerous to keep track of, so, by default, the desire of voters to have a voice in criminal justice matters is focused on the district attorney's office."[18] Once elected, however, a district attorney has ample opportunity to develop his image with the public and to become involved with the local political infrastructure. Although some district attorneys do make a career of their office, most do not; the average tenure of office for all elected prosecutors is only one and a half terms.[19] Many prosecutors do go on to seek higher political office — a judgeship, a seat in Congress, or some other public position.

The Prosecutor's Bureaucracy: Some Problems

One of the major tasks of the prosecutor is that of deciding what to do with cases which are sent to him. He must consider those cases in the light of the case itself, community opinion, status of the offender, sufficiency of evidence, connecting evidence (e.g., physical evidence, statements, and witnesses), status of the victim (and victim's relationship with the offender), and other factors. The decisions which the prosecutor makes may be at odds with what others within the community expect.

In a busy prosecutor's officer there is simply not enough time nor enough people to fully prosecute all cases which can technically be brought to trial. This means that the prosecutor must streamline his process and essentially eliminate those cases which he feels either have the least merit or would be the most difficult on which to secure a conviction. To do this, of course, the prosecutor uses his power to dismiss and the whole procedure of plea bargaining. Thus, in many jurisdictions as many as 95 percent of the convictions secured by a prosecutor come through the plea bargaining process. Dismissals are usually limited to situations in which prosecution would not serve the interest of justice or in which the case is so weak that the prosecutor knows he is unlikely to secure a conviction. A case may be weak because evidence is lacking or because of some serious error on the part of the police (such as an illegal search or an improperly obtained confession). Although plea bargaining may help the prosecutor to push his case through, "Few practices in the system of criminal justice create a greater sense of unease and suspicion than the negotiated plea of guilty."[20] As the President's Crime Commission noted back in 1967:

> The correctional needs of the offender and legislative policies reflected in the criminal law appear to be sacrificed to the need for tactical accommodations between the prosecutor and the defense counsel. The offense for which guilt is acknowledged and for which the sentence is imposed often appears almost incidental to keeping the business of the courts moving.[21]

Many people feel that the use of the negotiated plea is much more of a matter of convenience for prosecutors than a tool for securing "fairness and justice." Many of these same people are concerned that negotiations are carried out "in an informal, invisible manner."[22] The President's Crime Commission went on to note that

> The judge, the public, and sometimes the defendant himself cannot know for certain who got what from whom in exchange for what. The process comes to look less rational, more subject to chance factors, to undue pressures, and sometimes to the hind of corruption. Moreover, the defendant may not get the benefit he bargained for.[23]

Charging Decisions And Police Expectations

Although there are certainly exceptions to every generalization, it is probably safe to say that most experienced police officers are basically familiar with the laws they enforce. When they make an arrest, they usually know what they are doing and what the elements of the crime are. In preparing their cases for presentation to the prosecutor, the police are usually pretty sure about what they have, and many of them are equally certain as to what they expect from the prosecutor. The prosecutor, however, does not always meet those expectations. In some cases his charging decisions vary significantly from what the police expect. There is, however, nothing the police can do about it. Police officers also note that prosecutors tend to be critical of the quality of cases sent forward by the police, but that the prosecutor often does not offer any helpful suggestions. Until recently there has simply been a mild degree of animosity between police and prosecutors, with guarded allegations muttered darkly on both sides but no real evidence to support one side or another. The Institute for Law and Social Research (INSLAW) has analyzed data concerning 100,000 street crimes, both felonies and misdemeanors, processed by Washington, D.C. prosecutors over a six year period. In looking at what happens *after* an arrest, INSLAW staff examined performance differences among police officers and discovered that "...over half of the 4,347 Metropolitan Police Department arrests made in 1974 that ended in conviction were made by as few as 368 officers — 15 percent of all the officers who made arrests, and 8 percent of the entire force."[24] An examination of the characteristics of officers with high arrest and conviction rates revealed that the factor most closely associated with this kind of productivity was *experience*: "among the officers who made arrests in 1974, those with more experience performed at significantly higher levels — in terms of both the quality and quantity dimension ... than their less experienced associates."[25] This does support the contention that police officers learn by doing and further suggests that police officers might learn more quickly if they had more active assistance from the prosecutor.

Charging Decisions and Community Expectations   The average citizen is not trained in the complexities of substantive or procedural law; most people do know that the law makes it a crime to do certain things and that the law sets punishments for those who violate the laws. It is only reasonable for people to expect those who commit these crimes to be punished for them. Indeed, there is more than ample evidence which indicates that the general public is *not* tolerant of crime. Many citizens are concerned about the fact that so many criminals appear to be "getting off on technicalities," and they attribute this problem not to the police, but to the courts. Unfortunately, most citizens do not realize that there is a significant difference between *factual* guilt and *legal* guilt. Factual guilt refers to the fact that a suspect committed an illegal act. Legal guilt is the proper, procedural establishment of the person's guilt in a court of law. In some cases factual guilt is not an issue at all — but the state cannot establish legal guilt. If insanity is a defense, legal guilt cannot attach to a crime committed by a person adjudged to be insane. In some cases legal guilt cannot be established because evidence in support of the case is either non-existent or was obtained improperly and must therefore be "supressed." In this situation, the court must either charge the offender with whatever charge it *can* "prove up" or the prosecutor or court must dismiss the case; this has left many citizens disgruntled and unhappy. These same citizens seldom realize, however, that their reluctance to testify as witnesses or to serve on juries does not add to the efficiency and effectiveness of prosecution.

Repeat Offenders and Prosecutors   Some prosecutors have discovered that one way they can please their clients *and* do something practical is through the rigorous prosecution of career offenders. There is mounting evidence that a small number of people account for a large proportion of the serious crimes reported to the police.[26] Through selective prosecution of these habitual felons, prosecutors are able to effectively remove a serious threat from the community and at the same time perform their role in a manner which wins high approval from both the public and the police.

Summary

Although it is the police who investigate crime and arrest offenders, it is the prosecutor who actually *charges* them with some crime. The prosecutor is an elected state official who has responsibility for a specific geographic jurisdiction, and within that jurisdiction he is responsible for disposing of criminal cases which are brought to his attention. Some of these complaints come to him from private individuals, but the bulk of a prosecutor's cases come from police or other law enforcement agencies within his jurisdiction. Once a prosecutor receives a case he must decide what to do with it; this decision involves four major steps or processes. The first is that of *screening*, in which he assesses a case in terms of its prosecutive merits. The prosecutor may wish to refer the case to a *diversionary program* in which some non-prosecutive remedy may be employed. In *charging*, the prosecutor must decide the most appropriate charge to file against an accused, and in *litigation* the offender is actually brought to trial.

In serious cases, the prosecutor will either file an *information* or attempt to secure an indictment through a grand jury. An information is simply a formal step in which the offender is accused by the prosecutor of having committed the crime for which he is being charged. In the case of jurisdictions which use the grand jury system, the prosecutor forwards the case to the grand jury which deliberates to see whether or not the facts of the case appear to justify a formal accusation. If they do, the grand jury may *indict* the offender by returning a *true bill*, if not, the grand jury may return a *no bill*, and the prosecutor will normally drop the case.

After a person has been indicted or after the prosecutor presents his information, both prosecution and defense may enter into a negotiation known as *plea bargaining*. In plea bargaining the accused agrees to plead guilty in return for some consideration, which could be a lesser charge, an agreed-upon sentence, or some other consideration advantageous to the accused. The vast majority of convictions are obtained through such negotiated pleas, even though the practice has come under considerable criticism in recent years. Plea bargains actually do more to serve the convenience of the prosecutor and the courts than they do to insure justice!

A prosecutor's office is a public bureaucracy; like all other public bureaucracies, it suffers from certain problems. It is difficult to accurately measure either the efficiency or the effectiveness of the prosecutor's output. One reason for this is that he plays a number of informal (but important) roles, each of which structures his working environment.

These roles include acting as a *collection agency*; a *dispenser of justice*; a *political enforcer*; a *power broker-fixer*; and as an *overseer of the police*. These may sometimes be conflicting roles, and the prosecutor is constantly in danger of angering one of his many constituents.

Self-interest is also a factor in the role of prosecutor. Most prosecutors are young attorneys who are in the early phase of their careers. Some of them (usually the assistant district attorneys) work for a prosecutor in order to gain experience so they can move into a more lucrative private practice. Elected prosecutors often use their job as a springboard for higher elective office. As a result, both the prosecutor and his assistants perform their duties with thoughts of personal benefit, and may on occasion be less than objective or fair in the official performance of their duties.

Discussion Questions

1. What are the purposes of prosecution? Can those purposes be at odds with one another?

2. Do the police act as a "buffer" between the prosecutor and the public? If so, what are the consequences, if any?

3. Does the prosecutor have too much power in the screening of cases? How can case screening practices contribute to citizen unhappiness with the criminal justice system?

4. How can the use of diversion projects by a prosecutor create community relations problems for the police?

5. What is the difference between *intervention* and *diversion*?

6. Why is the charging decision such an important role for the prosecutor?

7. Is plea bargaining *really* necessary? Why (or why not)?

8. Do you think prosecution produces such an individualized product that the ends of justice are inadequately served?

9. What are the advantages or disadvantages to having the prosecutor elected?

10. Do you think the role of prosecutor is important when considering the overall relationship between the criminal justice system and the community?

Glossary

DISTRICT ATTORNEY   The state official within a given judicial district whose job it is to prosecute crimes which occur within his jurisdiction.

DIVERSION   The shunting of a criminal complaint from a trial track to some other more appropriate form of resolution; may include counseling, an informal community-based correctional program, or some similar kind of effort.

INDICTMENT   A written accusation that a person has committed a crime, presented upon oath, by a grand jury.

INFORMATION   A formal accusation by a prosecutor accusing someone of having committed a crime (similar to *indictment*, except a grand jury is not used).

JURISDICTION   The authority of a court to hear and decide an action or lawsuit; the geographic district over which the power of a court extends; the legal and geographic limits within which a criminal justice agency is empowered to act.

NOLLE PROSEQUI   The decision by a prosecutor not to prosecute a case. It is neither a declaration of guilt nor innocence, but rather a decision not to move forward with a case.

SCREENING   The process by which prosecutors review cases for potential prosecution, eliminating those with a low probability of success and the related process of deciding as to the best charge to levy against an accused.

Notes

[1] Charles P. Smith, Donald E. Pehlke, and Charles D. Weller, *Role Performance and the Criminal Justice System*, Volume I (summary), PROJECT STAR (Cincinnati, Ohio and Santa Cruz, California: Anderson-Davis, 1976), p. 71.

[2] Charles Smith, PROJECT STAR, Module 14: "Advocating for Prosecution," pp. 14-1; 14-2.

[3] See for example Albert J. Reiss, *The Police and the Public* (New Haven, Connecticut: Yale University Press, 1972).

[4] Donald J. Newman, *Introduction to Criminal Justice* (Philadelphia: J.B. Lippincott Co., 1975), p. 192.

[5] Joan Mullen, *The Dilemma of Diversion* (Washington, D.C.: U.S. Government Printing Office, 1975), p. 6.

[6] Frank W. Miller, *Prosecution: The Decision to Charge a Suspect with a Crime* (Boston: Little, Brown and Co., 1969).

[7] National Advisory Commission on Criminal Justice Standards and Goals, Russell W. Peterson, Chairman, *Courts* (Washington, D.C.: U.S. Government Printing Office, 1973), p. 20.

[8] *Courts*, p. 21.

[9] Chief Justice Warren Burger, "Address at the American Bar Association Annual Convention," *New York Times*, 11 August 1970, p. 24.

[10] Harold J. Grilliot, *Introduction to Law and the Legal System*, 2d ed. (Boston: Houghton Mifflin Co., 1979), p. 315.

[11] James P. Levine, Michael C. Musheno, and Dennis J. Palumbo, *Criminal Justice: A Public Policy Approach* (New York: Harcourt Brace Jovanovich, Inc. 1980), p. 202.

[12] Abraham S. Blumberg, *Criminal Justice: Issues and Ironies*, 2d ed. (New York: New Viewpoints, 1979), pp. 133-139.

[13] Blumberg, *Criminal Justice*, p. 133.

[14] Charles E. Silberman, *Criminal Violence, Criminal Justice* (New York: Vintage Books, 1978), pp.358-359.

[15] Blumberg, *Criminal Justice*, p. 136.

[16] See especially the cases of Bruno Hauptmann, who was executed for killing Charles Lindbergh's baby (Anthony Scaduto, "Bruno Hauptmann Was Innocent," *New York Magazine*, 22 November 1976, pp. 59-76); Clay Shaw, the man relentlessly pursued by New Orleans District Attorney James Garrison for

complicity in the assassination of John F. Kennedy (*Shaw* v. *Garrison*, 467 Fed 2nd 113, 1972); and the case of the "Scottsboro Boys," nine Black youths accused of raping two white girls in the absence of any evidence in corroboration (*Powell* v *Alabama* 287 U.S. 45 1932).

[17] For a good example of how this relationship works (both good and bad), see Vincent Bugliosi with Curt Gentry, *Helter Skelter* (New York: Bantam Books, 1975).

[18] Levine, *Criminal Justice*, p. 203.

[19] James Eisenstein, *Politics and the Legal Process* (New York: Harper and Row, 1973), pp. 20-25.

[20] The President's Commission on Law Enforcement and Administration of Justice, Task Force on the Administration of Justice, Nicholas de B. Katzenbach, Chairman, *Task Force Report: The Courts* (Washington, D.C.: U.S. Government Printing Office, 1967), p. 9.

[21] *Task Force Report: The Courts*, p. 9.

[22] *Task Force Report: The Courts*, p. 9.

[23] *Task Force Report: The Courts*, pp. 9-10.

[24] Brian Forst, Judith Lucianovic, and Sarah J. Cox, *What Happens After Arrest? A Court Perspective of Police Operations in the District of Columbia*, Publication Number 4, PROMIS Research Project (Washington, D.C.: Institute for Law and Social Research, 1977), p. 48.

[25] Forst, *What Happens After Arrest?*, p. 49.

[26] See for example Joan Patersilia, Peter W. Greenwood, and Martin Lavin, *Criminal Careers of Habitual Felons*, Rand Report R-2144-DOJ (Santa Monica, California: The Rand Corporation, August 1977).

THE DEFENSE LAWYER: HERO OR VILLAIN?

10

Norman G. Kittel

The average American gets most of his information from the television set — which he watches an average of six hours and eleven minutes a day.[1] Many Americans have become familiar with defense lawyers through television shows which purport to show them at work; the problem is that the hard-working, glamorous and often flamboyant defense lawyer of TV fame is a far cry from the typical defense lawyer of real life.

Development of the American Legal Profession

The legal profession did not get off to a particularly good start in the American colonies.[2] Lawyers were, for the most part, poorly trained and unskilled and were of little benefit to the common man. At the same time, they were often seen as a threat by the landed gentry and the commercial interests. In short, they had little to offer but stood to gain much — usually at someone else's expense. The rapid growth of mercantilism in both Europe and the American colonies soon produced the need for contracts, commercial instruments, deeds, and other legal documents too complex for the layman to prepare on his own, and lawyers began to take over the task. Also, the right of laypeople to practice law (most of whom were clearly incompetent) gradually came to an end; by the close of the seventeenth century, non-lawyers were prohibited from practicing law.[3]

During the eighteenth century the colonial courts became increasingly formal and legalistic in their administration and operations, requiring responsible and trained lawyers to represent the cases which came before them. The need for competent lawyers resulted in the creation of law programs at the leading American universities and the profession began to grow in stature. The Revolution, however, seriously damaged the slowly emerging prestige of the legal profession; colonial lawyers, whether trained in the colonies or in the English Inns of Court, were trained in English Common Law. After the Revolution, lawyers' prestige dropped because their training was associated with the earlier English hegemony over the colonies and because of the nature and circumstances of their work:

> During this period a primary task of lawyers was to collect bills. People resented lawyers not only for this onerous task, but also because lawyers were kept busy litigating and advocating in courts while everyone else was unemployed. Lawyers were also criticized for refusing to work without an advanced retainer (the government's money was practically worthless and therefore few people had good credit).[4]

Not only lawyers, but the courts as well became very unpopular during this period.[5] However, as the nation recovered from the war, and as the effects of the Industrial Revolution became obvious, the fortunes of lawyers began to rise both literally and figuratively. The legal profession started to make inroads into the commercial-mercantile community and the practice of corporate law began to emerge as a prestigious occupation. The legal profession was splintered, however, by the fact that "from 1800 to 1860, lawyers were admitted to the bar irrespective of educational background or professional training (apprenticeships). Throughout this period, legislation sought to open up the practice of law by abolishing educational requirements and by either reducing or eliminating the length and quality of professional training."[6] The subsequent influx of unethical or dishonest practitioners undermined the reputations of honest lawyers and had a negative impact on the profession's overall status.

After the Civil War, the more competent and better trained lawyers gravitated to the expanding industrial and business world. This brought about significant changes in the profession:

> Two complementary trends are discernable during this period: a general movement within the legal profession to advocate less in court while advising legal clients outside of court more often and, at the same time, *independent general practice of three generations earlier was beginning to give way to specialization.*[7]

Lawyers found major opportunities in the corporate setting, and a great deal of legal practice was not advocate-oriented, but was rather in the form of legal consulting to and on behalf of businesses. The practice of criminal law was not an attractive option to an aspiring lawyer, and even a successful criminal practice did not confer either the monetary or status benefits that came with a successful practice. The quality of criminal advocacy therefore remained poor and unevenly distributed, resulting in an emphasis on law over justice. It should be remembered that the period between the Civil War and World War I was an era of great industrial and technological growth. Enormous fortunes were made; indeed, empires were built and the great names of American finance emerged during this era. Corporate lawyers played a major role in this process by guiding businesses through legal thickets and also through the creation of or control over legal enactments which directly affected business. Legal services for the public were minimal at best. Lawyers were motivated more by fat retainers than by ethics, and the legal profession imposed few realistic controls on its members. Thus unsuccessful lawyers — those condemned to criminal work — were often predators on the unwary.

Law firms emerged which employed many specialists to better serve the business and financial communities, and this specialization further divided the legal community. The exploitative reputation of business began to color public opinion of the legal profession, and the solo practitioner who had to scramble to make a living was regarded as marginal within his own field. Although the *status* of lawyers rose with their power, their reputations declined. A license to practice law seemed to many a license to steal.

Gradually standards for admission to the bar and standards of legal education improved. The government began to take more active interest on behalf of the common man, a practice which started with New Deal reforms and has continued to the present. An increasing public awareness of individual rights, a growing sophistication of government regulatory agencies, and a reform movement within the legal profession itself have all combined to produce a legal profession which, although far from ideal, is increasingly responsive to public needs. There are still many differences of opinion within the legal profession, and many attorneys still hold the practice of criminal law in low regard — but the profession as a whole is beginning to develop some measure of respectability!

The Environment of the Defense Lawyer

There are many types of lawyers: tax attorneys, corporation counsel, patent attorneys, and many other kinds of legal specialists. Many of these lawyers would be quite lost acting as a defense counsel in a criminal court, for that is part of the working environment of the lawyer who works in the *criminal* practice. Like many other occupations, a defense lawyer operates in a unique environment.

Defense lawyers are part of a larger community of legal professionals who work within the criminal justice system. This group includes judges, prosecutors, the police, public defenders, and other professionals and para-professionals. To function effectively in this environment, the defense lawyer must maintain close and cooperative relationships with those other officials.[8] It is not at all unusual for the members of this legal community to be on a first-name basis with one another. Their ties may be so close that jailers, police officers, bailiffs, or other officials often recommend certain lawyers to newly arrested defendants.[9] In addition, judges motivated by a desire to develop political allies or to repay political or personal debts may favor some defense lawyers over others, especially when selecting counsel to be paid at public expense for defendants who cannot afford attorneys. Although the defense lawyer is technically an officer of the court, he is also an individual who must function in a highly complex and competitive environment which is often dominated by other people who may have both political power and strong personalities. The defense lawyer's ability to operate effectively within this environment often depends on how well he can deal with these other members of the criminal justice community.

While the defense lawyer is an integral part of the criminal justice bureaucracy, he is also a member of the legal profession and possesses the "work habits" of that profession. Bargaining and compromise are characteristic of the work of the legal profession — especially of defense attorneys. The negotiations that lead to the arrangement of a guilty plea exemplify this process of bargain and compromise. Although many "outsiders" find the process appalling, it is basic to legal practice.

Public perception of the legal profession is an additional factor that helps to form the environment of the defense lawyer. The low status of the legal profession cited at the beginning of the chapter has not been confined to American lawyers: criticism of the legal profession is a sentiment of ancient vintage in other countries as well. We see this in the second part of Shakespeare's *King Henry VI* when Dick the butcher (who advocates turning England over to the commoner) cries out, "The first thing we do, let's kill all the lawyers!" Other critics have included the satirist Jonathan Swift and the novelist Charles Dickens (whose novel *Bleak House* is a bitter, scathing attack on the English courts).[10]

Some defendants in criminal cases are extremely critical of their lawyers, especially when those lawyers are public defenders.[11] Unsuccessful defendants often blame their attorneys for losing their cases; sometimes they are not without justification. In spite of the fact that Americans appear to share a general dislike of lawyers and their seemingly unnecessary litigiousness, unintelligible jargon, dilatoriness, and high fees, Americans also accord lawyers high status and often wish that they or their children could become members of the legal profession! The current explosion of applications for admission to law schools attests to this interest. Strong public criticism of lawyers combined with the contrasting prestige of the profession illustrates what an ambivalent love/hate relationship the public has with the legal profession.

In addition to sharing the public's ambivalence toward lawyers in general, the defense lawyer is considered by many to be at the bottom of the legal profession's "class structure." Despite the fact that some defense lawyers earn excellent incomes and a few (such as F. Lee Bailey and Percy Foreman) are public figures, the defense lawyer's prestige does not match that of the corporate lawyer or most other specialists within the profession. This lack of prestige may well stem from the somewhat unsavory nature of his practice, the flamboyant and highly unique professional style of some defense lawyers, and the lack of social standing of most criminal defendants.

Defender of the Client and Officer of the Court: A Conflicting Role

The American legal system is based upon the duty and obligation of the contending lawyers to represent their clients' cases to the best of their ability.* Lawyers are expected to present every scrap of evidence, to find favorable legal precedents, and — as persuasively as possible — to argue the merits of their clients' cases. If both sides to a lawsuit present their cases as ably and persuasively as possible, the logic of this approach, the *adversary system*, holds that all possible evidence will emerge and the judge or jury will thus be able to discern the truth and render justice.[12] The adversary system places a high duty upon the lawyer who defends individuals accused of a crime. *Only the defendant's lawyer* looks out for the defendant's interests and consequently makes a major contribution to achieving justice within the adversarial system — at least in theory.

In addition to his role as an advocate for his client, the defense lawyer is also an officer of the court.[13] Consequently, it is the defense lawyer's duty to aid and assist the court in seeing that justice is done. This duty entails making only truthful statements and in presenting true and accurate evidence to the court. As a result, the lawyer technically has a dual obligation to both his client and to the court. The problems of compatibility in this situation might best be dealt with by exploring a hypothetical case.

*The "client" in the case of the prosecutor is *the people* — society as a whole, whereas the defense lawyer is obliged to represent only the person who is accused of the crime.

A. Mugger is charged with robbery and has been convicted of several prior crimes, some involving physical violence and others which involved only property offenses. Mugger has admitted his guilt to his lawyer, D. Fender, and strong corroborating evidence exists. In spite of this, Fender knows that he can obtain an acquittal because the police have illegally obtained evidence against Mugger. Barring the unlikely possibility that Mugger does not wish to be acquitted, Fender is obligated by professional ethics and the logic of the adversary system to obtain Mugger's acquittal. If Fender finds such an outcome repugnant to his personal ethics and morals, according to professional ethics he should seek to be relieved as Mugger's counsel. The prevailing view, as mandated by legal ethics, finds no conflict between Fender's duty to Mugger and his obligation to the court.

Some might contend that a lawyer in such a situation has an obligation to the public interest that supersedes his duty to the offender and consequently the lawyer should not seek his client's acquittal.[14] It is probable that a large portion of the public would also accept this view and would consider the action taken by Fender to acquit Mugger to be contrary to the public interest. Such a contention would be, of course, in direct opposition to the logic and ethics of the adversary system — a system which a large portion of the public simply does not understand and which seems to defy common sense.

Another factor may present a much greater conflict of interest or even a dilemma of considerable proportions. The close working relationships that are so necessary for effective representation of a defense lawyer's clients may also be used to the detriment of those whom he represents. Prosecutors and judges might make demands, often subtly expressed, of the defense attorney which can be detrimental to his client. Might not the defense attorney have to consider such demands in order to keep his good relationships with the rest of the judicial establishment? Such demands might take the form of unstated expectations by a judge to plea bargain, question witnesses expeditiously, or otherwise speed up the process. Obviously, a defense lawyer would have to regard these expectations seriously because of his role as an integral part of the judicial bureaucracy. Ample grounds exist for a conflict of interest between judges and the defense attorney. Judges are concerned with the regular movement of the cases which come before them. Once created, a logjam becomes difficult to break. Crucial to most concepts of justice in America is a reasonably quick disposition of a criminal case. The inability to move cases and to keep his docket up to date can be used for negatively evaluating a judge's performance. Thus we see again instruments which become institutions and which develop a logic of their own, separated from the reasons why they were created in the first place.

The trial judge is legitimately concerned with prompt handling of his cases. The most expeditious way to move cases is by encouraging the use of plea bargaining; negotiated cases consume a relatively small amount of time and there is little risk of reversal. Without a preponderance of guilty pleas, many criminal courts would be unable to function and the assembly-line justice which is characteristic of so many American courts would grind to a stop. Consequently, what is more natural than overt or subtle pressure by the trial judge upon defense counsels to encourage their clients to plead guilty? Judges also may communicate to defense attorneys their desire that time-consuming motions and pleadings be curtailed or expedited.

Such dependence upon the system is greater for public defenders who are employed by the state, and is particularly heightened for public defenders or assigned counsel appointed by the judges before whom they practice.[15] To go against the judge's expectations could jeopardize the defender's source of livelihood.

The defense lawyer is presented with a dilemma. Professional ethics and the logic of the adversary system demand that he make the greatest possible effort on behalf of his client. Yet this very effort could harm his relationships with the judge and the prosecutor, relationships crucial to his continued effectiveness in the criminal court. Different attorneys respond to this dilemma in different ways. Complete adherence to the norms of the judicial-prosecutorial establishment is one possibility. A middle ground of occasional adherence and occasional circumspect defiance is another possibility. Outright rejection of these norms is also a possible response.[16] Each defense lawyer must find his own mix of responses and develop his own means of coping with the dilemma. This results in the wide diversity of defense styles encountered in the courts.

Defense Lawyers: How Do They Defend Their Clients?

The tactics and strategies that defense lawyers employ will vary greatly depending on the seriousness of the charge, the resources available for a defense, the laws, customs, and practices of the jurisdiction, the type of client to be defended, the lawyer's relationships with the appropriate criminal justice personnel, and the overall nature of the case. A well-designed strategy for one case could be a very poor strategy for another case. Similar cases in different jurisdictions may require   totally different defensive strategies.

The defense lawyer will try to have the case decided in the most favorable form and area. He will seek to avoid judges who may be unfavorable or prejudiced against his client. He does this by requesting a change of judge, when the law so allows. By the same token, he will attempt to move the trial to a more favorable geographic location if he believes that substantial pre-trial publicity may be prejudicial to his case if it were to be heard in the area. In addition, when selecting jurors in a contested case, he will attempt to pick jurors during voir dire who are likely to be favorable toward his client.

A very cumbersome and sometimes creaking judicial machinery is often vunerable to defense lawyers who utilize these inefficiencies to aid their clients. Numerous postponements (known as *continuances*) may ultimately result in the failure of a key witness to appear and a consequent dismissal of the prosecution for lack of evidence. Jury trials may be requested as a possible delaying tactic. The more ineffective the process in an area, the easier it is for a case to fall between the cracks of the system, and defense attorneys play these inefficiencies with consummate skill. These kinds of procedural attacks will work most effectively for misdemeanors and less serious felonies, and in addition, run-of-the-mill cases can often be disposed of through these tactics. Notorious cases — especially those with considerable public interest — are much less amenable to these kinds of procedural attacks.

The more standard tactics and strategies employed by defense attorneys are similar to those employed by all attorneys both in and out of court. Their clients are portrayed as favorably as possible, sometimes just barely stopping short of a description of a candidate for sainthood. Glowing descriptions of marginal citizens are common, and redeeming characteristics are extolled. However, witnesses testifying against the defendant may be subjected to intensely critical interrogation in court in which every silence, pause, lie, inconsistency, or any conceivable weakness in testimony will be used to attempt to discredit the witness in the eyes of the judge and jury. The prosecution will also employ the same tactics.

The demeanor, appearance, attitude, and criminal record of the defendant may significantly influence a defense lawyer's strategy. An individual who is resentful and contemptuous of authority and who can be provoked easily makes a very poor witness for a lawyer. The prosecution can bait such a witness on cross examination and accentuate his resentment and contempt for authority. Unusual or eccentric dress can also produce an unfavorable reaction. When the defendant is an individual who is likely to give a poor impression, it is usually a better strategy not to place him on the stand. If the defendant is not placed on the stand by his own counsel, he cannot be called to the stand by the prosecutor. A witness who makes a bad impression can substantially weaken a defense lawyer's case, and the same holds true for the defendant.

A witness or defendant who keeps his feelings to himself, who keeps his emotions under control, and who shows respect in the courtroom will generally make a favorable impression on the judge and the jurors; this can strengthen a case. As a result, the characteristics of the defendant and the witnesses are vitally important in developing the defensive strategy in a criminal case.

Alternative Means of Handling Criminal Prosecutions

Recent alternatives to the conventional criminal justice process expand, the number of options open to a defense lawyer. If employed, such alternatives often precede and supplant ordinary defense techniques. While these alternatives have always existed, they have been subjected to increased use and attention in recent years and are now becoming an institutionalized aspect of the criminal justice bureaucracy.

These alternatives are not defenses to a criminal charge. Instead, the defendant admits that he has committed a criminal act and promises to take action which will correct his behavior and either eliminate or control the problem that caused the behavior in the first place. In return for this corrective action, a prosecutor may drop the charge, or a judge may find the defendant guilty and either place him on probation or suspend the sentence pending "good behavior." Such a case could, perhaps, involve an assault and battery charge against a youth who is prone to quarrels and fist-fights being dropped upon his decision to enter the army. An individual predisposed to starting fires could be treated lightly if he successfully pursues psychiatric treatment for his problem. A husband charged with assaulting his wife could have the charges dropped if he agrees to undergo martial counseling.

More formalized programs of this type have developed recently and are collectively referred to as diversion programs.[17] Operating out of the police department, the prosecutor's office, or the court itself, diversion programs are usually employed in the case of first offenders, those charged with nonviolent crimes, and those whose problems clearly require some help other than legal intervention. The services range from job training and placement to marriage counseling or psychological treatment. In return for a stay of prosecution, conviction, or sentencing, the accused promises to complete the specified treatment or other agreement and promises not to commit any additional crimes for a specified period of time (usually one year). If the accused successfully meets his part of the agreement, the prosecution is dropped and the charge is dismissed. From the defendant's standpoint, such a resolution is very advantageous because he thereby escapes active punishment. It is also advantageous to the state because it saves time and money and perhaps even discourages crime.

The Defense Lawyer's Greatest Strategic Dilemma: To Bargain or Fight?

The most common practice in the manipulation of criminal justice is a deal between the defense lawyer and the prosecutor. In return for a guilty plea from the defendant, the prosecutor may request a lighter sentence from the judge, agree to a plea to an offense carrying a lesser punishment, or agree not to prosecute other crimes the accused may have committed. Usually the defendant receives a lighter punishment than would have been the case had he pled not guilty, been tried and convicted. However, in the process, the defendant gives up all of his legal rights, including the right to a trial. The defendant who pleads guilty to a felony receives the opprobrium of being convicted of a crime, the resultant legal disabilities, the lessened punishment, and the chance of being regarded as an habitual offender if he is convicted of additional felonies.

First and foremost among the incentives to plea bargain is the practice followed by many judges of meting out more severe punishments to those defendants who stand trial and are convicted than if the same person agreed to a guilty plea.[18] This practice is strengthened by prosecutors who willingly bargain in most cases, defense lawyers who dispose of large numbers of cases by means of bargains, and a mass production system of justice which could not function without the use of plea bargains.

Additional incentives to plea bargain include the tremendous expense of a trial for defendants who must pay their own legal expenses. If a defendant is unable to post a bail bond and is awaiting trial in the county jail, a bargained plea would mean an end to an often unpleasant incarceration in jail with either a probated sentence or commitment to a more tolerable state prison. A plea bargain also means a very quick resolution of a prosecution and an end to uncertainty; the accused need no longer wonder what will happen to him.

An illustration of the strong pressure to plea bargain is found in the United States Supreme Court case of *Bordenkircher* v *Hayes*.[19] The defendant, Paul Lewis Hayes, was charged with uttering a false instrument in the amount of $88.30. In Kentucky, where the offense took place, the sentence for this crime was two-ten years in prison. During a session for the purpose of negotiating a plea bargain, the prosecutor agreed to recommend a five year sentence in prison if Hayes would agree to plead guilty to the charge. In addition, the prosecutor said that if Hayes refused to plead guilty and did not save the court the inconvenience and necessity of conducting a trial, he would ask the grand jury to indict Hayes under the Kentucky Habitual Criminal Act. Hayes did not plead guilty, and true to his word, the prosecutor obtained an indictment charging him with violating the Habitual Criminal Act. At the subsequent trial Hayes was found guilty on the charge of uttering a forged instrument. In a separate hearing, based on two prior felonies, he was also found guilty of violating the Habitual Criminal Act. Consequently, Hayes was sentenced to a life term in a Kentucky penitentiary.

The United States Supreme Court upheld the conviction, stating that this was a valid exercise of prosecutorial discretion. In explaining its decision the court stated that

> ... in the 'give and take' of plea bargaining, there is no such element of punishment or retaliation so long as the accused is free to accept or reject the prosecutor's offer. Plea bargaining flows from 'the mutuality of advantage' to defendants and prosecutors, each with his own reasons for wanting to avoid trial.

> Defendants advised by competent counsel and protected by other procedural safeguards are presumptively capable of intelligent choice in response to prosecutorial persuasion, and unlikely to be driven to false self-condemnation ...

> While confronting a defendant with the risk of more severe punishment clearly may have a 'discouraging effect on the defendant's assertion of his trial rights, the imposition of these difficult choices (is) an inevitable' — and permissible — attribute of any legitimate system which tolerates and encourages the negotiation of pleas ...

> It follows that, by tolerating and encouraging the negotiation of pleas, this Court has necessarily accepted as constitutionally legitimate the simple reality that the prosecutor's interest at the bargaining table is to persuade the defendant to forego his right to plead not guilty.[20]

As a consequence of the emphasis that the criminal justice system places upon plea bargaining, most defendants face strong pressures compelling them to make such bargains. The pressures favoring plea bargaining are so strong that the decision of whether or not to plea bargain is a major decision for the defense lawyer and his client. The majority of all defendants find the pressure too strong and go ahead with the plea bargain.[21]

Defense of the Poor

A very cursory visit to a municipal court, a felony court, or a county jail will soon convince the observer that the majority of criminal defendants are very poor. Many defendants are certainly too poor to retain their own lawyer. While today such defendants accused of serious crimes are represented by counsel, the quality of such representation is often inferior to that received by defendants able to afford their own attorneys. Consequently, the poor often receive an inferior brand of justice.[22] Poverty is thus a central problem for the criminal justice system and is a major impediment to the realization of equal justice for all who are accused of committing crimes.

The stark realization of the great gap between the ideal of equal justice and the reality of unequal justice, and the greater concern with human rights of the last forty years have combined to produce a line of United States Supreme Court cases demanding that all criminal defendants be represented by counsel. The first of these cases, *Powell* v. *Alabama* held that in capital cases, defendants who were poor, illiterate, and young, were entitled to a lawyer supplied by the state.[23] This very confined and limited decision grew out of the controversial case in which nine young Black men were charged in the Alabama courts with raping two white women (this case was mentioned in Chapter 8). Throughout the proceedings there was a hostile mob, which at one point threatened to lynch the young men. The men were indicted on March 31, 1931, and trial was set for six days later on April 6, 1931. After confusion over the appointment of the defense counsel, an inebriated Tennessee lawyer, Steven Roddy, represented the defendants although he had not had any preparation time and only a half-hour interview with the youths prior to commencement of the trial. Consequently, Roddy was able to construct only a flimsy defense, the defendants were convicted, and the greatly accelerated trials were concluded. The Supreme Court later overturned the decision and held that the Due Process Clause of the Fourteenth Amendment required that the right to counsel be offered, in capital cases, to defendants in the state courts who were poor, young, and illiterate.

A significant broadening of the narrow *Powell* rule took place in *Gideon* v. *Wainwright* (1963). Gideon was charged with breaking into and entering a pool hall. Upon arraignment Gideon stated that he was not able to pay for a lawyer and asked that a lawyer be appointed for him. He was told by the Florida District Judge that the Fourteenth

Amendment Due Process Clause only required that defendants in state courts be supplied counsel in capital cases when the defendants were poor, illiterate, and young (*Powell* rule). Gideon represented himself and was convicted. Gideon's handwritten appeal to the United States Supreme Court was accepted. In its opinion the Court susbtantially broadened the right to counsel by applying it to all defendants accused of a felony who are too poor to afford their own lawyer.

The *Gideon* case was further expanded by *Argersinger* v. *Hamlin* (1972).[25] Hamlin was convicted of a misdemeanor and was sentenced to sixty days in jail. As in the *Gideon* case, Hamlin was not offered the right to counsel because the requirements of the Fourteenth Amendment did not extend to cases such as his. The U.S. Supreme Court extended the right to counsel to all those accused of a crime which carried the possibility of even a one day sentence in jail. This decision completes the long process by which the right to counsel is provided for all defendants too poor to afford their own lawyers.

These U.S. Supreme Court cases have forced state and county judicial systems to set up mechanisms for providing attorneys for the poor. Under one method, the assigned counsel system, the judge appoints lawyers from a pool of interested attorneys to represent the poor on a case by case basis. This method probably is most effective when the lawyers are compensated at a scale approximating a private attorney's fee schedule and the lawyers who are selected have already handled substantial numbers of criminal cases. Public defender systems are the second basic means of providing counsel for the poor. A public defender is a public official who is charged with the task of defending the poor. Often a full-time public servant, the public defender may head an office of several lawyers, paraprofessionals, investigators, clerks and secretaries. Offices for populous urban counties may have more than fifty attorneys.

These systems are most effective when adequately financed, when their case loads are reasonable and when political influence is low. They function well when defense counsel is independent of the trial judge, and support services such as investigators are available. Naturally, the system needs to be effectively administered.[26] When systems lack one or more of these criteria, or possess some other fault, they frequently provide less than adequate representation for their clients. When case loads are high the amount of time that can be spent per case is very limited. Consequently, the lawyers may not prepare adequately, cut corners, and consequently fear that they are not performing at professional standards. Too many cases, too much work, and the constant "parade" of new defendants can lead to disillusioned, cynical and "burned-out" public defenders.[27] The consequent "burn-out" is an almost universal problem of lawyers for the poor.

Lawyers and Non-Lawyers: A Conflict of Expectations

There is more to the adversary nature of criminal justice than the demeanor of lawyers in the courtroom. The police, the official initiators of action against an accused, tend to have a very low opinion of defense lawyers, whom they see as trying to undo their work. The reason is simple: the police see the consequences of crimes in the most direct way possible. They must deal with victims who have been beaten, murdered, robbed, or raped. They see the agony and loss. They also see offenders in their "natural environment" and therefore know from firsthand experience the tragic, disgusting, and banal nature of crime and criminals. Many police officers see that a wrong has been committed and feel that many of these wrongs genuinely deserve to be redressed. They also see the tactics of defense lawyers and feel that these efforts are actually used to thwart the ends of justice rather than to serve them. They often conclude that justice is in fact an immoral game played in courtrooms according to lawyers' rules for lawyers' benefit. Unfortunately, this perception is not entirely inaccurate. As a result of plea bargaining and the peculiarities of the trial process, many police officers become embittered toward lawyers and cynical toward the courts.

> ITEM: Before the laws were changed in one Southwestern state, a first offender in a marijuana possession case received a minimum sentence of five years upon conviction. If it were a first offense, the sentence was almost always probated. The police in one college community made numerous marijuana arrests of students only to see lawyers tell the students that a first offense carried a heavy *maximum* sentence (which was true); but for $1,500 the lawyer would defend them if they would agree to plead guilty. The lawyer would tell the students that he would get them a five-year probated sentence, which was the very minimum allowed under the law. Most students accepted and got what they would have gotten anyway and then dropped out of school to earn the money to pay the lawyer, who had in reality done nothing but take their money.

> ITEM: The police routinely see lawyers tell courts how wonderful their clients are. In a North Carolina court a defense lawyer argued a drunk driving case on behalf of his client, whom the police knew to be an alcoholic. The lawyer spoke at great length on his client's standing in the community as a businessman, church member, and so on. Although the

defendant was convicted, his lawyer was successful in keeping his driver's license from being revoked. Several months later, in a drunken stupor, the client crossed the traffic median and struck another car, critically injuring the driver and killing a teenage girl who was a passenger.

Perhaps the most disturbing thing about criminal justice is that in so many cases justice *is* for sale, and it is lawyers who get the money. Yet criminal law is only one area of law practice. This raises the interesting question of just *what* do lawyers *practice?* Unlike most workers, lawyers do not increase the value of a natural resource through their labors, nor do they produce a "thing of value," like a pair of shoes, a clipboard, or an automobile, which can be sold in an open competitive marketplace. Lawyers do not have a tangible product, unless you are willing to accept legal forms and other pieces of paper as tangible products. What lawyers do is enable clients to avail themselves of legal rights: to form corporations, dissolve marriages, transfer property, obtain patents, raise defenses in criminal proceedings, and so on.

This perspective on lawyers is certainly not a new concept, nor is it without its critics. Adam Smith, the founder of modern economics, in his classic *Wealth of Nations*, distinguished between *productive* and *unproductive* labor. The former produces a "value" (as in the manufacture of a product); the latter, although useful, adds nothing to value per se. In this latter group Smith included "menial servants, ... the sovereign, ... with all the officers both of justice and war, ... the whole army and navy," and also "churchmen, lawyers, physicians, men of letters of all kinds; players, buffoons, musicians, opera singers, ... etc."[28]

Since the rights enjoyed by all citizens are set forth in and are described by laws, and since the procedures for obtaining them are essentially *legal* procedures, lawyers sell their services as guides, expediters, facilitators, and advocates. Through their services clients are able to obtain the benefits and rights to which they are entitled. All of this is done, of course, for a fee. Lawyers also gravitate toward those places where laws are made and administered. Legislatures include lawyers, as do many administrative and political positions in all branches of government. In a very real sense, lawyers make laws, administer them, and act as paid gatekeepers to the law, admitting outsiders "in consideration of fee simple or for some other consideration" — that is, upon payment.

It is obvious that this is to the advantage of lawyers. In all probability the general public would grant its approval if it felt that the lawyers also met the social obligations which lawyers themselves clearly set forth in their own canons of ethics. All too often this does not appear to be the case. The public is painfully aware that most of the highly paid principals in the Watergate scandal were lawyers. The public saw how Vice President Spiro Agnew bargained his way through his legal problems and how neither money nor influence was spared on behalf of heiress Patty Hearst. It has become painfully clear that there are many standards of justice, and the key independent variable is money.

Those who use lawyers, regardless of which side they are on, expect the same thing: they expect their lawyer to do a good job. The criminal defendant expects and deserves to be adequately represented. His lawyer *should* ascertain that the police or other officials acted properly in apprehending him and in preparing their case. The defense lawyer *should* follow every proper legal procedure available to him in the defense of his client. But is it "fair" for a lawyer to argue that a chronic drunk driver should not lose his license on the grounds that he is a merchant and a church member? Does that not place the life of the client and the lives of others in danger? It seems reasonable to argue that the defense lawyer has an obligation to see to it that his client's rights are protected, but he has no obligation to seek the acquittal of a person who is both obviously guilty and dangerous to himself and others. This last point is the subject of heated discussion among legal theorists.

The victim is represented by the state through the prosecutor in criminal cases, and ought to have the right to expect the state to seek redress for the harm he has suffered. This is not quite true, for the injured party is *not* the victim — society as a whole is the victim, and the prosecutor represents the entire community, not just an individual victim. Many victims do not understand this and feel the system does not care about them, an indifference they attribute to either malice or incompetence. Nothing could be further from the truth; prosecutors are neither malicious nor are they incompetent. They don't normally care about the victim because they are not supposed to! Fortunately, there appear to be some recent changes which may make the roles of both victims and witnesses much less traumatic and unpleasant.

These changes are long overdue in light of the central role played by victims and witnesses in the administration of justice. These changes also have the potential for greatly enhancing the quality of the relationship between the community and the criminal justice system, and they can provide for expanded opportunities for the community to involve itself directly into the criminal justice process.

A number of jurisdictions have established programs to help those who have been victimized by serious crime.[29] These efforts may be undertaken by actual agencies of government such as the prosecutor's office or by the courts themselves. These programs make compensation to the victims of certain types of crimes. Private or quasi-public agencies likewise have begun to provide valuable services to victims, including such things as rape counseling and legal referral. Such agencies sometimes provide temporary housing, and other services for women who need to flee from abusive environments but lack to resources to do so.

Witness assistance programs, usually operated by the prosecutor's office, seek to ease the burden of a witness by educating the witness as to what will be expected of him and how the trial process itself works. In some cases the prosecutor is able to reduce the number of appearances a witness has to make or to shorten the waiting time prior to testimony. Some jurisdictions have experimented with providing transportation for witnesses who would otherwise have difficulty getting to and from court. These basic considerations contribute to a more positive feeling on the part of those who must participate in the criminal justice process itself.

The use of community resources to assist both witnesses and victims is very much in the best interest of all parties concerned for a variety of reasons. From the perspective of the prosecutor, it enhances the likelihood that witnesses will appear and provide the testimony vital for the completion of a case. For the victim, it is a means of restoring the equilibrium that was lost when the crime was committed and for reducing the sense of shock, loss, and self-destruction. For the community, it is a means of providing support and care which in turn fosters a sense of community and feelings of positive regard toward government.

Even if government agencies such as the police or prosecutor are limited in what they can do for victims, they can still play a valuable role by encouraging groups within the community to operate victim and witness assistance programs. In fact, it is a responsibility of government to educate the public regarding the means by which it can secure its own best advantage through such programs. By bringing data before interested groups on both needs and opportunities, the criminal justice system not only serves its own purposes but brings the community into closer involvement with its own problems.

Victims and witnesses who walk away from the courts either disappointed or disgusted may have been handled with a lack of sensitivity and care. Moreover, they may not know that what they expect of lawyers is simply not what lawyers expect of themselves. Lawyers realize that conflicts are rather like mazes, and the correct path through

CRIMINAL JUSTICE: A COMMUNITY RELATIONS APPROACH

the maze is defined by law and procedure, not by how people feel or by an abstract concept of justice. They follow these paths and essentially assume that the outcome represents justice. If, in an adversary system, a defense lawyer does not advocate his client's cause, then who will? One does not act as an advocate by taking the position of the other side. The defense also realizes that the prosecution has some powerful tools at its disposal, including the police and other investigative resources, and that the defense's strength lies in its understanding of the law and the means by which it is administered. This is a healthy process, and it is corrupted only when either side fails to meet its obligations: that is, when prosecutors fail to prosecute or defenders fail to defend. This, of course, is the problem with the negotiated plea. It waters down the adversary process and reduces counsel on both sides to legal clerks. The negotiated plea denies both the offender and society as a whole the fruits of justice under the rule of law. It also encourages the careless and haphazard treatment of those who have been victimized and those who must come forward to testify.

Summary

The practice of law in the United States has taken shape over the past three hundred years and has gradually evolved from what could best be described as humble beginnings. Originally, the practice of law was unsystematic and largely unregulated. As a result of mercantile capitalism and the Industrial Revolution, lawyers began to operate in a more receptive climate. The increasing regulation of business and industry by law and government created whole new fields for lawyers; not only did numerous schools of law emerge, but the actual practice of law came under close regulation by the states. As the legal profession grew, it became highly specialized, and out of this division of labor the practice of criminal law became a specialty, although one which has been held in relatively low esteem within the legal profession.

Defense lawyers operate in an environment which is unique to the legal profession, and although a defense lawyer represents a person accused by the state of having committed a crime, the defense lawyer is himself an officer of the court and must maintain a close and cooperative relationship with the rest of the criminal justice system if he is to be able to work effectively within the system. This sometimes represents a conflict of interest which typically operates to the defendant's disadvantage.

When defending their clients, defense lawyers develop tactics which are suited to the merits and circumstances of the case and to the lawyer's own personal style. This produces considerable variation in defensive styles which may range from a minimal defense (urging the defendant to plead guilty) to a spirited and vigorous defense. Since most defendants know little or nothing about procedural law, they must place considerable faith in lawyers, and if the lawyer's efforts are based on the lawyer's self-interests rather than those of the client, the client will be the loser.

Perhaps those who have realized the least benefit from defense advocacy have been the poor and those otherwise unable to afford good legal counsel. Although a succession of Supreme Court cases has established the right of persons accused of crimes to be represented by defense counsel, that right does not necessarily guarantee that appointed lawyers or public defenders will provide the same kind and quality of defense that would be forthcoming from a well-paid private defense counsel.

There are many mistaken ideas concerning the proper roles of defense lawyers. Many — including police and some prosecutors — are disdainful of defense lawyers because they feel that the defense's attempt to get the defendant acquitted runs counter to the interests of justice. Defense lawyers argue that it *is* their job to seek acquittals for their clients, and to do so by every legal and proper means available. Members of the public become irate when serious offenders "get off on a technicality," but defense lawyers argue that these "technicalities" are not minor, inconsequential issues; they are major points in the administration of justice.

Perhaps the greatest threat to the integrity of the courts, however, is the negotiated plea. This tactic provides convenience for the courts and for the lawyers, but at the same time it waters down both prosecution and defense and in the process attacks the adversary system upon which the administration of justice is based.

Discussion Questions

1.   Does the defense's close contact with the rest of the criminal justice system help or hinder him in his services to his clients?

2.   Does the "bargaining and compromising" which is so typical of the legal profession dilute justice and work essentially to the convenience of lawyers — or is it really necessary?

3.   Does the public's ambivalent love-hate relationship with the legal profession influence its attitude toward the whole criminal justice system?

4.   Is there a conflict in a defense lawyer being an "officer of the court" and an advocate for his client?

5.   What accounts for the wide diversity of defensive styles one sees in the criminal courts?

6.   Why do so many defense lawyers eventually opt for the "middleman" role?

7.   Should victims of crimes be compensated for the harms which they suffer?

8.   How can private organizations within the community play a more effective role in criminal justice, especially with respect to both witnesses and victims?

9.   Do you think we are correct in considering society as a whole to be the victim of a crime, or do you think more emphasis should be placed on victims who actually suffer as a result of crimes? How would you deal with crimes in which the victim played a role in his or her own victimization?

10.   Do you think an ombudsman system would be of benefit to the criminal justice system?

Glossary

ADVERSARY SYSTEM   A legal system in which contested claims are argued by legal counsel in a court of law according to established principles of legal procedure. In a criminal case the prosecutor represents the victim (the public) and defense counsel represents the offender.

BAR   The whole body of the legal profession. A person is admitted to the bar when he is authorized to practice before a court.

DISCOVERY   A method by which the opposing parties in a lawsuit (or criminal case) may obtain full and exact factual information concerning the area of controversy.

PUBLIC DEFENDER   Publicly paid legal counsel for an accused; they are employees of the state and it is their job to defend those who cannot afford private counsel.

VOIR DIRE   The preliminary examination of a prospective juror in order to determine his or her suitability for serving on a trial jury.

Notes

[1] "TV Notes: Who Watches Even More TV Than Americans?" *The New York Times*, 29 June 1975, p. 27.

[2] Greg Barak, *In Defense of Whom? A Critique of Criminal Justice Reform* (Cincinnati: Anderson Publishing Co., 1980), pp. 27-51.

[3] Roscoe Pound, *The Lawyer from Antiquity to Modern Times* (St. Paul: West Publishing Co., 1953), p. 136.

[4] Barak, *In Defense of Whom?*, p. 33.

[5] Esther L. Brown, *Lawyers and the Promotion of Justice* (New York: Russel Sage Foundation, 1938), pp. 11-12.

[6] Barak, *In Defense of Whom?*, p. 37.

[7] Barak, *In Defense of Whom?*, p. 37 (emphasis added).

[8] Abraham S. Blumberg, "The Practice of Law as a Confidence Game: Organizational Cooptation of a Profession," *Law and Society Review* (June 1967): 20.

[9] Samuel Dash, "Cracks in the Foundation of Criminal Justice," in John A. Robertson, ed., *Rough Justice* (Boston: Little, Brown and Co., 1974), pp. 249-250.

[10] Jonathon Swift, *Gulliver's Travels* in Walter F. Murphy and C. Herman Pritchett, *Courts, Judges and Politics* (New York: Random House, 1961), pp. 129-131.

[11] Jonathan D. Casper, *American Criminal Justice: The Defendant's Perspective* (Englewood Cliffs, New Jersey: Prentice-Hall, Inc., 1971), pp. 109-110.

[12] Jerome Frank, *Courts on Trial* (NewYork: Atheneum, 1971), pp. 80-81.

[13] American Bar Association, *Legal Ethics* (Chicago: American Bar Association).

[14] Howard James, *Crisis in the Courts* (New York: David McKay Co., Inc., 1971), p. 95.

[15] Norman G. Kittel, "Trial Judges Should Not Appoint Counsel for the Indigent," *The Legal Aid Briefcase* (June 1967): 171-181. See for example the role played by the defense counsel in Joseph Wambaugh's *The Onion Field* (New York: Delacourte Press, 1973).

[16] See for example the role played by the defense counsel in Joseph Wambaugh's *The Onion Field* (New York: Delacourte Press, 1973).

[17] Raymond J. Nimmer, *Diversion: The Search for Alternative Forms of Prosecution* (Chicago: American Bar Foundation, 1974).

[18] Raymond J. Nimmer, "The Influence of the Defendant's Plea on Judicial Determination of Sentence," *Yale Law Journal* (December 1956): 207-208.

[19] *Bordenkircher* v *Hayes*, 98 S. Ct. 663 (1978).

[20] *Bordenkircher* v *Hayes*.

[21] Lee Silverstein, *Defense of the Poor in Criminal Cases in American State Courts* (Chicago: American Bar Foundation, 1965), Vol. I, pp. 92-93.

[22] Norman G. Kittel, "Defense of the Poor: A Study in Public Parsimony and Private Property," *Indiana Law Journal* (Fall 1969): 110-112; National Legal Aid and Defender Association, *The Other Side of Justice* (Chicago: National Legal Aid and Defender Association, 1973), pp. 36, 77, 78.

[23] *Powell* v *Alabama*, 1932, 287 U.S. 45, 53 S. Ct. 55, 77 L. Ed. 158.

[24] *Gideon* v *Wainwright*, 1963, 372 U.S. 335, 83 S. Ct. 792, 9 L. Ed. 2d 799.

[25] *Argersinger* v *Hamlin*, 1972, 407 U.S. 25, 92 S. Ct. 2006, 32 L. Ed. 2d 530.

[26] Norman Kittel, "Defense of the Poor: A Study in Public Parsimony and Private Property."

[27] Peter Goldman and Don Holt, "How Justice Works: The People v Donald Payne," *Newsweek*, 8 March 1971, pp. 28-32.

[28] Adam Smith, *An Inquiry Into the Nature and Causes of the Wealth of Nations*, cited in John Fred Bell, *A History of Economic Thought* (New York: The Ronald Press Co., 1953), p. 179.

[29] See for example Joseph Garofalo and L. Paul Sutton, *Compensating Victims of Violent Crime: Potential Costs and Coverage of a National Program*, Applications of the National Crime Survey Victimization and Attitude Data, Analytic Report SD-VAD-5: National Criminal Justice Information and Statistics Service, Law Enforcement Assistance Administration (Washington, D.C.: Government Printing Office, 1977); see also "Restitution Programs are Likely Candidates For Expansion," *Crime Control Digest*, 15:28.

THE COURTS

11

Norman G. Kittel

Because people have different needs, values, and perceptions, it is inevitable that conflict will arise; indeed, one of the functions of social organization is to provide mechanisms for the resolution of conflict. Most conflicts employ formal techniques for resolution. The parties involved agree to a solution which both are willing to accept. Our socialization process provides many rules and procedures which facilitate the resolution of conflict, and those rules vary according to one's social position and the values of particular subcultures. As long as the nature of the conflict is fairly simple and involves parties who know one another, the resolution is usually a simple matter of negotiation among those directly concerned.

When the conflict involves a major issue or is highly complex or involves people who are unable or unwilling to negotiate, then the problem may require a *formal* means of resolution. In our society the formal institution for the resolution of conflict is the courts. There are many types of courts, and they deal with many kinds of conflicts. It is important to remember that the courts do not simply listen to a conflict and then render a decision; in fact, the courts are not actually interested in the conflicts per se which come before them. They hear disputes and render judgments in the light of existing *legal concepts*. A conflict is resolved not just on the "merits" of the case, but also in the light of existing legal norms which deal with that category of conflict. In this sense the court actually measures the facts and issues of a conflict according to existing standards and renders a judgment which affirms those standards. Legal concepts generally arise from established *rights* and *duties*. A right is "a legal capacity to act or to demand action or forebearance on the part of another."[1]

If a right is a legal capacity to act — what is an act? Used in this sense, an act is a voluntary physical movement of a human being. But a right can also be the ability to demand action or forbearance on the part of another. A forbearance is a consciously willed absence of physical movement. And a forbearance can be a very valuable thing. If you have the ability — the right — to prevent someone from doing a certain thing, say for instance, from selling a piece of land to anyone else but you, it can be worth a great deal of money to you.[2]

A duty, on the other hand, is a legal obligation to either act or to refrain from acting. When a *right* is vested in one person or group, there is always a corresponding duty on the part of some other person or group.[3] The conflicts which come before the courts invariably deal with some failure concerning rights or duties. These rights and duties are not just abstract ideas, but fall into specific areas or categories and constitute the major facets of the practice of law. An individual conflict will fall into one or more of these legal areas or categories, which are known by their generic titles. They include, but are not limited to:

—Crimes	—International law
—Environmental law	—Equity
—Consumer protection	—Administrative agency
—Torts and damages	—Gas and petroleum
—Antitrust	—Maritime
—Labor law	—Probate
—Bankruptcy	—Taxation
	—Commercial law

Within each of these areas there is a large body of decided cases, rules, legal norms and concepts, and remedies. If an individual becomes involved in a serious conflict, he may use the proper court (ie., the court which hears cases dealing with his particular kind of problem) to ascertain just what rights and duties should operate in the case in point according to established legal principles. He can also determine just what remedies are available. Before a court may hear a case, it must first have *jurisdiction*, which is "the power or authority of a court to determine the merits of a dispute and to grant relief."[4] A court has jurisdiction only when it has this power over both the subject matter of a case *and* the people who are the parties to the case. A given court may have jurisdiction which permits it to hear a wide variety of cases; others have very limited jurisdictions and hear cases of only one kind (e.g., traffic courts or domestic relations courts).

This text will focus on courts which have jurisdiction in criminal and juvenile cases. Although many of these courts also have "civil" jurisdiction, civil matters will not be discussed.

The Criminal Courts

Crimes are conflicts between the state and the offender. The state is regarded as the victim, even though it may have been a single individual who actually "suffered" as a result of the crime. Basically, the criminal law sets forth certain rights and duties; for example, all citizens have the right to be safe and secure in their homes and persons, and all citizens have the duty to respect that right. To break into another person's home for purposes of committing some other unlawful act violates both rights and duties and results in a conflict between the offender and the state. The criminal courts accept an accusation from a prosecutor and then hear the facts of the case so that the law pertaining to that particular offense may be reviewed and the appropriate remedy can be issued.

There are fifty-one court systems in the United States. Each state has its own court system, as does the federal government. The courts within a given system are created either by constitutional provision or by legislative enactment. Within a given system there are essentially two kinds of courts: *trial* and *appellate*. Trial courts hear cases, determine facts by applying the appropriate legal rules, and grant remedies in those disputes. A trial court *cannot* initiate a case on its own simply because it wishes to consider some legal issue, nor may it decide purely theoretical controversies. The cases which come before the courts must be actual cases involving real disputes and the parties to those cases must have "standing" before the court. This means that only the people who are harmed have the right to bring a case before a court. The prosecutor has standing in all criminal cases because he represents the state, and the state is always regarded as the victim of any crime.

Trial courts resolve the conflicts which come before them by having the opposing parties present their respective arguments through their attorneys. They may argue on points of law as it applies to their case and they may present evidence in the form of physical objects and the testimony of various witnesses. These arguments may be presented to a jury, or the case may be heard by a judge who then makes the final decision. The procedure to be followed is very formal and the participants are guided by a comprehensive set of legal procedures which defines just how trials are governed.

Appellate courts do *not* try cases; they review cases which have already been tried to see if there were any errors in the way the trial court handled the case. Appellate courts determine whether or not the trial court acted in accordance with the legal rules which govern trial courts. No new arguments or proofs may be introduced, and appellate courts do not concern themselves with the specific facts of the case (i.e., the crime which was actually committed). If an appellate court finds that the state erred, then it may vacate the remedy granted by the trial court. If upon appeal, it is determined that an accused was convicted on the strength of a confession which was illegally obtained, the appellate court would rule that the trial court erred in permitting the confession to be entered as evidence and would reverse the findings of the trial court. Notice that the appellate court did not say that the defendant did not commit the crime; it only said that the trial court made a serious error by admitting inadmissable evidence, and that because of that error, a conviction cannot be sustained.

State Trial Courts Having Criminal Jurisdiction   As has been noted, each state has the right to create its own system of courts, and although all of the states' courts have some characteristics in common, there are also many differences. The description of the court system of one specific state does not apply to the court systems of all states. Trial courts typically exist at two levels. The courts at the lower level are courts of limited jurisdiction; they have *original* jurisdiction over misdemeanors and are limited in the remedies which they can apply. This means that these courts are limited in the maximum fines and terms of imprisonment which they can set. They are not courts of record. A transcript of the proceedings which come before them is not usually kept, although the disposition of the case is recorded.

In some states the judges who preside over these courts are not required to be lawyers or to have legal training. These are very busy courts, for the majority of cases which do come before the criminal courts are heard in courts of limited jurisdiction. Although these courts do not try felony cases, they may accept "first appearances" of persons arrested for serious crimes. People who are arrested for such crimes have the right to be brought before a magistrate where they are informed of the charges being brought against them and their legal rights. These first appearances are also where bail is usually set.

The higher level trial courts are courts of general jurisdiction and have original jurisdiction over serious crimes (felonies). They usually also have appellate jurisdiction over the lower trial courts; thus if a person is convicted by a lower court for some misdemeanor, he can appeal his case to the higher trial court for a hearing *de novo* (literally, a new hearing). This is not an appeal in the sense that the actions of the lower court are reviewed; it is simply a new trial. These superior courts are courts of record, and a transcript is kept of the proceedings. The judges who preside over these courts are lawyers and their judgeship is a full-time occupation. Since these courts have jurisdiction over the serious crimes, they also have the power to impose the maximum sentences allowed by the state, including the death sentence. The majority of the litigated cases heard in these courts are heard before juries and the procedures which are followed are very formal and highly structured.

State Courts of Appeal   Each state has at least one appellate court, and in most states the highest appellate court is termed the supreme court of that state. Some states have an intermediate appellate court, usually called the Court of Criminal Appeals. These tribunals differ from trial courts because they have more than one judge (usually called "justices"). Depending on the particular state, appellate courts have between three and nine justices. These courts review the actions of the trial to see if any errors of law were made. These errors can involve:

—Depriving a defendant of his Constitutional rights;
—Violating the rules of evidence which govern trial procedures;
—Accepting guilty pleas that were not properly given;
—Admitting into evidence an illegally obtained confession;
—Charging a jury improperly;
—Allowing a racially biased jury to be impaneled;
—Failing to make clear the possible consequences of a guilty plea, despite any sentencing promises made by the prosecutor to the defendant; and
—Passing an unlawful sentence.[5]

The appellate courts serve as a powerful check on both the trial courts and the police, for there are many possible grounds upon which a convicted offender may appeal. As Robin notes,

Almost anything that could have reasonably prevented the defendant from receiving a fair hearing and sentence may become the basis of an appeal: police entrapment; unfavorable pretrial publicity; holding the trial where the entire community is openly hostile to the defendant; racial composition of the jury; failure to give indigents state-supported counsel; sentencing the defendant without a presentence report; not permitting the trial to be held in a different county from where the crime occurred (failure to order a change of *venue*); unethical or illegal conduct by the prosecutor; having a defendant appear in court for trial while still wearing jail clothing, and so on.[6]

329

Thus, it can be seen that the roles of the trial court and the appellate court are quite different. Trial courts spend most of their time considering issues of *fact* whereas appellate courts spend their time considering issues of *law*. These issues of law arise "because a litigant has asked the trial judge to do something. In response, the judge either acts or declines to act in accordance with the request. If the aggrieved party believes that the judge has acted wrongly, he may appeal."[7] Through these appellate decisions the body of "rules" which govern judges' decisions and trial procedures are constantly modified and shaped to fit the times. When a court of appeals finds that the trial court did commit an error, it remands the case back to the trial court for a retrial or some other action, but a court of appeals does *not* acquit a defendant. In many cases the defendant may *not* be retried because if certain items of evidence are supressed, for example, the state may feel it does not have a strong enough case to support a retrial. In such a case the defendant goes free — even though he has *not* been found innocent: it simply means the trial court did not successfully *convict* him, and this highlights the difference between factual guilt and legal guilt.

Judges

Perhaps the central figure in the courtroom is the judge; as the President's Crime Commission noted in 1967, "The quality of justice depends in large measure on the quality of judges."[8] The fact of the matter is that judges have vast amounts of authority which they can exercise in many ways at different points in the legal process. Although he plays many roles, perhaps the most visible and direct role of the judge is as the supervisor of criminal trials. He is continuously faced with issues and conflicts during the course of a trial: questions of the admissibility of evidence; the relevance of testimony offered by witnesses; questions about the techniques used by lawyers in questioning witnesses. The judge is the gatekeeper of information in a criminal trial because of the way he handles these and other issues; he is more than a referee for opposing counsel — he makes the rules!

A judge sets the tone of the trial and even of the courtroom by the way he rules on issues raised during a trial. A judge can also convey non-verbal messages through demeanor, gestures, and general body language. The flavor of a given courtroom is set very quickly by the presiding judge, and all other actors must accommodate themselves to the kind of court "created" by the judge who presides. The judge can also influence a direct control over the verdicts: in about half of the cases which go to trial, the defendant waives a jury and is tried by the judge alone.[9]

Finally, judges exercise tremendous power in the sentencing of those who are convicted. They may impose fines, send people to jail or prison, suspend sentences and otherwise control the future lives of defendants (this will be dealt with in greater detail later in the chapter).

Most Americans respect the judiciary, and judges are generally granted considerable prestige — especially those judges who serve on appellate or supreme courts.[10] There are of course many judges who fully deserve this respect; some of our great jurists such as Oliver Wendell Holmes, Learned Hand, and Benjamin Cardozo have left an indelible imprint on the quality of justice in the United States. Unfortunately, there are other kinds of judges, and they are the ones who have produced such a volume of community concern:

> There are bigots on the bench and arrogant martinets.
> There are the dull-witted, the narrow-minded, the harsh, and
> the lazy. There are those who are merely weak, mediocre, the
> 'gray mice' of the judiciary. And there are the callous and
> insensitive, judges whose exposure to human pride and folly
> has encrusted their own humanity.[11]

It is important to remember that judges are not interchangeable; in fact, there are different "levels" of judges and each level tends to represent a different set of backgrounds and a different outlook toward the judicial function. Judges at the lowest levels, those who sit in the state trial courts, include those who are not lawyers (in the states where this is permitted) and those who attended the least prestigious law schools. Many of these people went to the so-called "proprietary" law schools — law schools which are private institutions and which are not part of a larger college or university system. Many went to law school part-time or at night while holding down jobs so they could support families. At this level we find many of the municipal court judges, magistrates, justices of the peace and other judges in courts of limited jurisdiction.[12] Most of the cases which come before the courts are heard at this level. Although some of these judges may move up to higher levels within the judiciary, most do not.

Judges at the "middle" level typically sit on the courts of general jurisdiction and the intermediate level appellate courts. A judgeship at this level is often considered both a reward and a promotion for loyalty, service, and efficiency; many of those judges are selected by the governor of their state and approved by the legislature or some other body.[13] These judges probably attended somewhat better law schools, frequently as full-time students at a law school which is part of the main university in the state. As Blumberg notes, "recruitment at this level is likely to be from among lower level judges who not only have served the party well but have shown astuteness and imagination."[14]

The "upper level" judges are apt to come from prominent families and are more likely to have attended "national" law schools, such as Harvard, Columbia, Cornell, Stanford, Duke or Chicago. They are also likely to have been partners in major law firms and may have even held some political office. As Blumberg points out, however, "Although many upper level judges have distinguished themselves as legal scholars, having published in the legal journals and in other scholarly journals, for the most part they are politically well-connected and sophisticated in the vagaries of political life. Often they are simply possessed of great personal wealth and political influence and are otherwise prosaic and pedestrian."[15] The strong role of political influence is not hard to discern and was seen in the nomination of both Clement Haynsworth and G. Harold Carswell to the United States Supreme Court (neither was appointed). Another case involved a person close to Senator Edward Kennedy. This individual attended a law school in Georgia which had a dubious reputation and even at that flunked four courses — and failed his state bar exam twice. In spite of this, the Judiciary Committee recommended his confirmation to a federal judgeship by a 6 to 3 vote. He did not become a federal judge, however — he withdrew.[16] This brings us to an important issue: the selection of judges.

The Selection of Judges   It has often been said that a judge is a member of the bar who once knew a governor; a federal judge is one who knew a senator; and a U.S. Supreme Court Justice is one who knew a President. Another commentator simply noted that "judges are politicians in robes."[17] Jackson tells of a judge who

> is a bluff, good-natured man in his early fifties with an
> unpretentious manner and thinning, caramel-colored hair. He
> drives to work in a pickup truck and wears black cowboy boots
> and a large, silverplated belt buckle. He refers to most women
> as either 'sweetie' or 'babe' and men as 'sport.' He keeps a
> cartoon on his desk blotter which shows a judge glaring at a
> long-haired witness and saying, 'You had better show me the
> proper respect, sonny. I kissed a lot of ass to get this job.'[18]

That may well sum up the basic, essential ingredient of getting the job in a large number of cases. In theory, there are four ways a person obtains a judgeship. The first is by appointment. The person is appointed by the governor or by the legislature, and the appointment is then confirmed by the legislature or an executive council. In some states, judges are elected on a non-partisan ballot. Although the candidate may not be identified by party on the ballot, he is usually nominated by his party. A third method is for judges to be elected on a partisan ballot. Where this is done, the primary election is usually the real contest as many of these states are dominated by one of the major parties. The fourth and final method is one which is gaining favor; it involves the merit selection of judges and is sometimes called the "Missouri Plan" because it was first adopted in that state in 1940. In states using this system the governor selects a person from a list of names submitted to him by a merit selection committee, and after the appointment, the judge runs without opposition on a retention ballot, thus actually placing his confirmation in the hands of the voters.

It is obvious that the process of becoming a judge involves many factors; the three most important are the individual's legal education, his work background, and his politics. Most judges are lawyers and they are socialized into their profession by law schools, law practice, and politics. It would be absurd to believe that these variables do not effect their values, perceptions, and judicial orientations. Citizens generally respect judges because they assume judges are value-neutral and objective. These citizens then become perplexed at the ways in which judges manage their courts and handle their cases. Few citizens realize that judges, like the police, have a degree of autonomy which for all practical purposes places them above accountability.

DEFENDANT 5 MINUTES LATE JAILED*

An 18 year old girl in a southeastern city received a traffic ticket for running a red light. She was convicted of the offense in district court and appealed her case to the superior court, where she was scheduled for a trial *de novo*. She was scheduled for a 9:30 a.m. appearance in superior court on a Tuesday morning last March.

She arrived at the parking lot used by people having business in the civic center with time to spare; however, the parking lot was full so she had to drive to a parking garage about four blocks away, where she had to park on the top floor. By the time she made it to the court where her hearing was scheduled, it was 9:35. In a few minutes a bailiff came to her and asked for her name. When she identified herself the bailiff said, "Honey, we have orders to put you in jail." He explained that her case had been called at the start of court and when she did not appear, the presiding judge ordered her to be taken into custody. The startled young lady was removed from the courtroom and placed in a holding cell. Later, she was handcuffed and led to the county jail where she was placed in another cell, this time with two other women.

Greensboro Record, March 25, 1980, B1, 2.

"I have never been in a place that smelled so bad," she later declared. "The toilet looked like it hadn't been cleaned in three years. There was toilet paper on the floor and the dirt on the floor must have been an inch thick." The men in a nearby holding cell used vulgar and abusive language, much of it directed at the three women in the women's holding cell. After about 45 minutes she was taken to the main cell block where she was placed in a cell by herself. Four hours later she was removed from her cell and handcuffed to a man and both of them were taken to the courthouse (the man had been charged with shooting a police officer).

Back in the courtroom, she claims, an official advised her that if she accepted the lower court's guilty verdict in her case, there would be no record of her having been incarcerated for failure to appear. She reluctantly agreed, and after paying her fine was released.

The district attorney later said, "What happened may have been a little unusual, but the judge has a right to do it. It just happened that on this day the judge came into the courtroom at 9:30 and only about half the docket was there and he was peeved. On this particular day there were just too many who didn't show up on time and he ordered them arrested." The judge was later contacted in Florida where he was vacationing, but he could not recall the case.

Most citizens also do not realize that in criminal cases (as in any other legal contest) the courts simply apply legal rules and remedies to the cases which come before them; justice, as an abstract ideal or as a concrete reality, really has nothing to do with the matter. Judges and courts concern themselves for the most part with the *law* — not with people and their personal problems. This is a startling perspective to many people who think the courts exist and function to insure *justice*. Alas, the courts — like so many other social creations — may have started out as instruments for justice, but they have become *institutions* which come closer to serving the needs of lawyers than those who hire them. A victim or a defendant may or may not get justice in the courts — one never knows in advance!

Another point needs to be discussed. It has been said that you can't judge another person until you have walked a mile in his shoes. This obviously does not apply to judges. Few judges have been police officers and even fewer have been street criminals. Very few judges come from the backgrounds of the people whom they judge and very seldom do judges actually see the incidents which bring defendants into the courtroom. Even legal education does little to acquaint them with such issues as poverty, ignorance, alienation or deviance. Judges do not have to make their decisions on the spur of the moment as police officers do, nor must they make the searches or take the confessions which are so hotly debated in criminal courts. Judges can and do command respect under penalty of law. They simply do not operate in the same context as the people who come to them for judgment. Jackson captured this in the following anecdote:

> In Washington Family Court, a black mother tries to explain to the white judge that her delinquent thirteen-year-old son is not a bad child. 'He just resents somethin' y'know? He wants to be recognized.' The judge looks up from the forms he is filling out, asks two or three questions, and orders the boy to a detention center. The mother collapses in sobs, hugging her son. 'I love you, I'm so sorry,' she cries. 'You're breaking my heart. I don't want nothin' to happen to you, I don't want you to go nowhere. Oh, I'm so sorry.' He son begins to cry too, and the sound of their heavy sobs fills the small courtroom. The lawyers and social workers stare at the wall, while the judge continues to fill out forms. 'What's the date of that report?' he asks a social worker. Finally he can no longer ignore the weeping mother and son. 'I want to tell you a story, James,' he says. 'I had a young security guard come up to me the other day when I was parking my car. He said I had put him in the detention center once for delinquency. He said he learned a lot, got a good education, and now he was a guard. You've got a lot of good in you, James. You'll do okay if you cooperate...'[19]

The situation described simply lends credibility to the assertion that the courts are run for the convenience of judges and lawyers, not of victims, witnesses, or defendants.[20] Perhaps this is easiest to see in the area of court administration.

Court Administration

Few people realize that courts are very complex institutions which do far more than conduct trials.[21] Perhaps the primary focus on the trial aspect of courts diverts attention away from less dramatic aspects such as their routine administration. Courts are also bureaucratic government agencies. They keep records, have support personnel, require budgets and perform all the administrative tasks necessary to schedule, process, and dispose of their business. The inability to effectively manage the courts ultimately produces a major outcome of inestimable importance: delay. Delay in the courts translates into a simple formula: justice delayed is justice denied. Delay can produce a number of problems: witnesses disappear; memories fade; accused persons face continuing hardships; the clearing of dockets becomes an end in its own right, often leading to dispositions by dismissal or through plea negotiations; the deterrent effect of trials is diminished; and public confidence in the courts diminishes. Howard James has cited eight reasons for delay in the courts: (1) An acute shortage of judges; (2) too few courtrooms; (3) lazy judges; (4) procrastinating lawyers; (5) the use of "expert witnesses" who confuse jurors and cause delays; (6) lax legislatures; (7) inefficient methods of administrative management; and (8) "cat and dog" cases — minor cases which consume more time than they are worth.[22]

If there is a significant degree of delay in a court system, these and other reasons are the cause. Although delays in trials have focused attention on the need for better court administration and management, there has been a growing reform movement in the courts for many years. This movement actually started in 1906 when Roscoe Pound recommended that the states consolidate their courts into one unified system having two branches — trial and appellate. This concept, known as *court unification*, is a major thrust in court reform designed to establish both uniformity in court operations and efficiency in administration. One of the themes of court unification is the establishment of a centralized supervision of both judicial and non-judicial personnel. Ideally, this would allow courts in one part of the state to use judges from another part in the case of illness or some other absence and it would regularize procedures across the system, assuring uniform treatment of citizens and effectiveness of operations.

There are, of course, other facets to the reform of court management. Personnel problems are important because there must be judges to hear cases; court stenographers (in courts of record) to transcribe proceedings; administrators to manage dockets, purchase supplies, administer other support personnel and handle finances; bailiffs to provide security; and probation officers to prepare investigations and reports and to supervise probationers. Adequate facilities must be maintained, and these include not just the courtrooms, but the judge's chambers, law libraries and record storage facilities as well. Court administrators must carefully monitor the flow of cases and assist in the management of jurors. All of this is part of court administration.

In recent years there has been a strong movement in the direction of hiring professionally trained court administrators to handle these tasks, thus freeing judges to concentrate more on matters of law. The introduction of electronic data processing has facilitated this process and shows even greater promise for the future. Professional administrators have taken on a great deal of the burden of court management and it appears that they will become increasingly important figures in the whole area of courts. Some judges, however, have resisted these improvements for the sake of tradition, but their resistance is being overcome.

Bail or Jail

The awesome power of the courts and of judges starts well before a person actually comes to trial. After a person is arrested (especially in the case of felonies), he is brought before a judge who formally explains to him what he has been arrested for and what his rights are. At this time, the judge may do one of the following things:

—He may release the accused on his own recognizance based on his promise to appear in court when his presence is required;

—He may release the accused to the custody of another person, usually a relative, who is then responsible for seeing to it that the accused appears in court;

—He may require the accused to post a cash bond, which is forfeited if he fails to appear (this is often done in traffic and other misdemeanor cases);

—He may require a surety bond in a certain amount of money, which is usually purchased from a bail bondsman at ten percent of the face value;

—He may require the accused to post a cash bond, which amounts to a percentage of the full bail; if he appears in court when required, most of the cash bond is returned to him, but if he fails to appear, the cash bond is forfeited and he becomes liable for the remainder of the bail originally set; or,

—He can deny bail altogether and order the accused to be placed in jail under preventive detention. This is usually only done in capital crimes or when the offender is likely to flee.

The right to bail is written into the Eighth Amendment to the Constitution, which specifies that "excessive bail shall not be required." However, the issue of whether there is an absolute right to bail has never been fully resolved by the courts; the most common interpretation is that the Constitution does not grant an absolute right to bail, but rather that it does provide protection against *excessive* bail. This does not necessarily apply to state courts though. In a 1964 case the Supreme Court specifically ruled that "Neither the Eighth Amendment nor the Fourteenth Amendment required that everyone charged with a State offense must be given his liberty on bail pending trial."[23] Bail, simply put, "is a procedure for releasing arrested persons on financial or other condition to ensure their return for trial."[24] It is a form of judicial ransom which gives the state a financial hold over the accused to assure his cooperation with the courts.[25] Bail deals with a very real problem: people accused of serious crimes often wish to run away rather than face the consequences of their actions in court. One of the major problems of the bail system has been that it places a disproportionate burden on the poor. If a person cannot afford bail or if a bail bondsman refuses to "go his bail" for him, then he goes to jail and awaits his trial — often at great expense to both the accused and the state.

> ITEM: A man was jailed on a serious charge on Christmas Eve. He could not afford bail and spent 101 days in jail until a hearing. Then the complainant admitted the charge was false.

> ITEM: A man could not raise $300 bail. He spent 54 days in jail waiting trial for a traffic offense, for which he could have been sentenced to no more than five days.

> ITEM: A man spent two months in jail before being acquitted. In that period, he lost his job and his car, and his family was split up. He did not find another job for four months.[26]

Not only can bail abuse bring misery and hardship to the defendant in a criminal case, it can cost the state a great deal of money as well. Persons held in custody represent a very real cost to the state: they must be fed and housed; their loss of income while not working also results in a loss of tax revenues to the state; and in some cases the defendant's family may be forced to go on welfare. There have also been cases of unsavory relationships between bail bondsmen and judges (or other officials) in which judges set high bail so the bondsman can get a fatter fee. As Jackson notes,

> Bail procedures, often scandalous in themselves, present yet another opportunity for covert lining of the judicial pocket. Judge Louis W. Kizas of Chicago attracted more attention than he wanted when he released two men charged with armed robbery on their own recognizance. The subsequent investigation turned up evidence that Kizas had repeatedly granted low bail for a price. Suddenly afflicted with poor health, Judge Kizas resigned before a scheduled hearing by the Illinois Courts Commission in 1967. Two years later he pleaded guilty to criminal charges of official misconduct and was fined $15,000.
>   In 1972 a Los Angeles grand jury accused three judges of signing blank prisoner-release orders and dispensing them to favored bail bondsmen. The bondsmen, who bought and sold the orders among themselves, were then free to set bail at whatever figure they chose — or negotiated. A prosecutor said that one presigned release order was used to bail a suspected Mafia member out of jail for $1000 when arresting officers recommended bail of $100,000.[27]

In some cases bail is intentionally set so high that the defendant cannot make the bond. One reason for doing this is to avoid the negative publicity which the media sometimes generates when a serious offender is turned loose pending his trial. Another reason for setting bail so high that the accused remains in custody is to give the prosecution a bargaining chip in plea negotiations. In this case, if an accused is willing to plead guilty to a lesser charge, the prosecutor may be willing to recommend a reduction in the defendant's bail, thus allowing him to get out of jail. In fact, the amount of the bail is usually more closely related to the seriousness of the charge than to any evidence that the defendant might flee. Of course, it is hard to separate the two factors, because the more serious the charge, the stiffer the penalty and the more incentive an accused has to flee.

In 1961 Louis Schweitzer became concerned over the fact that a man could sit in jail for a year or more in New York, although he was technically innocent, simply because he lacked the money to pay a bail bondsman. He created the Vera Foundation (named after his wife — now called the Vera Institute of Justice) which subsequently developed a project aimed at screening defendants to see how many of them were sufficiently good risks to warrant a release on their own recognizance. Staff members used four key factors in making their assessment: (1) residential stability; (2) employment history; (3) presence of family contacts in the area; and (4) the defendant's prior record. Each of these factors was scored according to a system of points, and if the accused got a score of five or higher, the staff would recommend that he be granted an ROR (release on his own recognizance). Project members felt that if a defendant had sufficient "roots in the community," he would be a good risk. This program (known as the Manhattan Bail Project) proved successful. Between October 16, 1961, and April 8, 1964, staff members screened 10,000 eligible offenders and recommended that 4,000 be released on their own recognizance. The courts accepted 2,195 of these recommendations and of that number, only 15 defendants failed to appear in court.[28]

The Vera project was so successful and saved the city so much money that it has been widely copied. Yet in most jurisdictions the bail system continues to operate much as it has in the past, and scandals continue to appear in the papers from time to time — and bail continues to be used for purposes other than that for which it was originally intended. As Levine notes:

> If the purpose of bail is to ensure appearance in court, ransoming' defendants makes little sense because it usually is

unnecessary and is no guarantee anyway when the stakes of the trial are greater than the loss of bail money. But other purposes like crime prevention, public reassurance, and pretrial punishment of the guilty as well as the innocent prevail. Justice and due process come out the losers.[29]

An interesting dimension of this problem is that the "man on the street" *expects* criminals to be put in jail, and the distinctions between pretrial confinement and confinement as part of a sentence are often lost. People become quite indignant when a person accused of a serious crime is let out of jail to await his trial; indeed, a large proportion of the general public believe that the courts are too lenient in dealing with criminals.[30] The complexity of law and criminal procedure is not clear to many people, and they become disturbed at the thought of a criminal *not* being in jail. The conventional wisdom learned in early childhood is that the *police* put criminals in jail and in recent years people are beginning to voice concern that the *courts* are letting them out! This contradiction between public expectation and legal obligations of the courts has produced a growing mistrust on the part of many people. Of course, some of what the general public expects of the courts is in error; most courts make no effort to educate the public or to speak to their concerns. The reason for this is that the courts are — in their narrowest interpretation — answerable to the *law*, not to the *people*. If the people do not like the way the law works, they must address their concerns to the legislators, not to the courts, but one can speculate that most people either do not know this or feel that the legislatures themselves are unresponsive to public wishes. Americans have a long history of distrust of authority, and this tends to manifest itself more in complaining about government processes, including legal processes, than in actually trying to change them. This is yet another contradiction that is built into our system of criminal justice, and it is unlikely to be resolved in the near future.

Trial Juries

Silberman wisely reminds us that "Criminal courts are multipurpose institutions, charged with protecting society against criminals and with protecting the innocent individual against the coercive power of the state."[31] At the very heart of this process is the jury trial. The function of a jury trial is to determine the guilt or innocence of the accused by analyzing the facts presented through the testimony of the witnesses and by applying the law of the case as it is explained by the trial judge. The jury system has been both widely praised and roundly criticized; yet it remains one of the most fundamental elements of our adversary system.

Although the case may be argued by lawyers and presided over by a judge, it is a jury of common people which gives the ultimate answer.

In spite of its importance, a jury trial is a vanishing species. Most people who are convicted of a crime plead guilty, usually in consideration for some benefit, and most of the remainder are tried by a judge and do not have a jury trial.* In all probability, not more than about two percent of all criminal cases actually come before a jury. The mere existence of the right to a trial by jury serves as the final legitimization of the due-process model of justice.[32] Even though they are seldom used, jury trials underscore the highest ideals of American judicial practice. The irony, however, is that juries are not always rational in either their composition or their decisions.

Jurors and Jury Selection   There are about 3,000 courts which use juries in the United States. Those courts require about 20 million juror days per year, demanding the services of approximately two million jurors.[33] Of course, the principal aim of a jury trial is to provide the accused with a fair and impartial hearing. In order to do this, jurors are theoretically sought who will objectively and fairly weigh the evidence presented before them. The jurors must not be prejudiced either for or against the defendant, nor may the circumstances of their selection contain any built-in bias which could affect the outcome of the trial. This is an *ideal* which often falls short of the reality.

Jurors are picked from pools of prospective jurors. These pools are known as "venires," and the persons on them are "veniremen." The venire consists of people whose names have been selected from such sources as voter registration lists, driver registration lists, local census information, or even city directories. One of the basic tasks in creating a venire is to get a good cross-sample of the community as a whole. This is not always easy to do, for there are a great many "hidden" people in any community — those who do not register to vote (or who cannot because of alien status), and those whose names do not appear on driver registration lists. The use of voter registration lists from which names are randomly selected has been accepted as the best means of getting a cross section of the community, provided there has not been a systematic exclusion of Blacks or other groups from voter registration.[34] Even at that, venires *do* manage to *avoid* being a cross section of the community; they tend to over-represent whites, males, middle-aged people, those from the middle-class, and those with moderate education. At the same

*In *Duncan* v *Louisiana*, 391 U.S. 145 (1968), the Supreme Court ruled that the Constitutional right to a trial only applies to crimes which carry a possible penalty of more than six months; this eliminates quite a few minor misdemeanors from qualifying for jury trials.

time, they tend to under-represent both the young and the old, minorities, and women.[35] These are not necessarily intentional biases, but rather are the outcome of using voter registration lists, and this is why many jurisdictions are now starting to use multiple-source lists.

The next step in the jury selection is probably one of the most important of all: the selection of prospective jurors for a specific case. This is done through a process known as voir dire — literally, to tell the truth — a phase in which jurors are questioned to determine their suitability for serving on a given case. Voir dire is important (many lawyers believe that a case is won or lost on voir dire). The prospective jurors are called from the jury pool and proceed to the court, where they are questioned by either the judge or the lawyers or both. Voir dire might start with the judge asking all of the prospective jurors if they have an interest in the case, if they know any of the parties involved, and other questions which would reveal a possible conflict of interest. The important questioning, however, commences on *individual* voir dire, where jurors are examined by first the prosecutor and then by the defense counsel.

JURY SELECTION IN A CRIMINAL CASE*

In one of the ten largest cities in the United States, the District Attorney has prepared a series of manuals for his assistants. One such manual is entitled "Jury Selection in a Criminal Case," and presents some information seldom seen outside a prosecutor's office. Some of the points he makes:

It is often said that most cases are won or lost on Voir Dire — I agree. It is the first opportunity you have to impress the panel with your sincerity, integrity and ability. I believe in the importance of first impressions; if you can show the panel that you wear the 'white hat,' and if you don't destroy that illusion during the trial, then the jury will *want* to convict. Who you select for the jury is, at best, a calculated risk. Instincts about veniremen may be developed by experience, but even the young prosecutor may improve the odds by the use of certain guidelines — if he knows what to look for.

WHAT TO LOOK FOR IN A JUROR

You are not looking for a fair juror, but rather a strong, biased and sometimes hypocritical individual who believes that defendants are different from them in kind, rather than degree. You are not looking for any member of a minority

*Obviously, the authorship of this manual and the district in which it is used must remain confidential. Please remember that the quotes given are excerpts: the whole manual is 19 pages long!

group which may subject him to oppression; they almost always empathize with the accused. You are not looking for free-thinkers or flower children. Women make the best jurors in cases involving crimes against children. Young women too often sympathize with the defendant; old women wearing too much make-up are usually unstable, and therefore are bad State's jurors. People over forty are more settled and more ready to believe that criminals should be punished.

PUNISHMENT

This is the most important qualifying issue. In many cases, the only issue is that of punishment. A case is never won unless a jury returns more time than you offer on a plea of guilty. A person weak on maximum punishment will usually be weak on guilt. Always stress the maximum in the range of punishment, but advise and qualify the panel on the minimum; otherwise, you may lose your aura of extreme fairness. Always tell the jury that the State is opposed to probation in this particular case.

QUESTIONING THE VENIREMEN INDIVIDUALLY

Ask the length of residence in the county. People who move around very much are often unstable. People from small towns and rural areas generally make good State's jurors. People from the east or west coasts often make bad jurors. People with a family are generally more responsible and therefore better jurors. Men who are self-made successes, or who work with their hands, or work in a managerial capacity are usually good. Engineers, accountants, and scientists: they might pick your case apart; therefore they are bad — but they are not inclined to 'chase rabbits' thrown out by defense attorneys, therefore they are good. Intellectuals such as teachers, etc., generally are too liberal and contemplative to make good State's jurors. Working women are often preferable to other women because they have had a glimpse of the cruel, hard world. Women working in retail stores often make good State's jurors.

Ask if the veniremen have any hobbies or interests that occupy their spare time. Active, outdoors type hobbies indicate the best state's jurors. Hunters always make good State's jurors. Ask men if they have ever served in the military; if so, when, what branch of service, their rank upon discharge and if they saw combat. Marines, master sergeants and those that have seen combat generally make good State's jurors.

Ask veniremen their religious preference. Jewish veniremen generally make poor State's jurors. Jews have a history of oppression and generally empathize with the accused. Lutherans and Church of Christ veniremen usually make good

State's jurors. Those that indicate they have no religious preferences are often non-conformists and are bad state's jurors.

THE DEFENDANT'S VOIR DIRE

If your timing is good, the veniremen will not get tired of Voir Dire examination until a minute or so after defense counsel begins his questioning. Make as few objections as possible, and make sure you are right when you do object.

Lawyers on both sides try to learn as much as they can about the prospective jurors, including their attitudes, prejudices, and backgrounds. In subtle ways, each lawyer also begins building his case through his examination of the prospective jurors. The lawyers are *not* looking for a fair and unbiased juror; rather, they are looking for a person who will be biased in their favor and who will "see things" as they would like for them to be seen. In recent years this has produced some interesting approaches to jury selection.

One case which received widespread publicity involved a 20 year old black female by the name of Joan Little. Little had been in jail in Beaufort County, North Carolina awaiting appeal on a conviction for burglary. She and her brother had been arrested for stealing $850 from two mobile homes; her brother received a suspended sentence through a plea bargain, but she was sentenced to prison. She was unable to post her $15,000 bond and remained in the Beaufort County jail awaiting her appeal. Little had been sexually active since she was 14 and had contracted syphilis at 15. There were widespread rumors that she had worked as a prostitute. According to fellow prisoners of both sexes, she spent much of her time in confinement nude from the waist up.[36] On Augsut 27, 1974, she killed a 62-year old white night jail guard by stabbing him to death with an ice pick; she then fled from the jail. Little later surrendered and claimed the guard had forced her to have oral sex with him by threatening her with the ice pick. She claimed that when he dropped the ice pick, she grabbed it and stabbed him, and then fled. There was some evidence to support her claim. The guard's shoes were found outside the cell; he was nude from the waist down and had semen on his leg. Joan Little was indicted for first degree murder. The case was seized upon by the Southern Poverty Law Center and women's groups, who raised some $350,000 for her defense. Her attorney, Jerry Paul, put the money to good use. Part of the money was used to conduct a survey in the Beaufort County area, which revealed a high degree of racial prejudice and a widespread belief that Little had used sex to lure the jailer into her cell so she could make her escape. They also found Blacks, women, and the young under-represented on venire lists. Based on all of this information they secured a change of venue, moving the trial to Raleigh, the state capital. More money was spent in Raleigh (Wake County) to ascertain if the jury pool was representative of the entire community and to construct psychological profiles of jurors who would be sympathetic to Little. On voir dire, prospective jurors were questioned about such things as their occupation, income, political views, and their attitudes toward Blacks, law enforcement officers, capital punishment, and rape. Paul used a team of five lawyers to comb the evidence and hired three social psychologists and a "body language" expert as well as three statisticians. During voir dire the prospective jurors were intensively questioned in an effort to find jurors who would be sympathetic with the defense case.* There have been other cases in which similar techniques have been used to assist defense lawyers in jury selection and all the evidence indicates that such techniques can be highly successful.

The basic tools used by the attorneys in voir dire are *challenges*. There are two kinds of challenges: *challenges for cause* and *preemptory challenges*. The challenge for cause may be used to remove an unacceptable juror where there is reason to believe that juror would not be impartial (as in prejudice against Blacks, having prejudged the case, being unwilling to impose capital punishment). If an attorney thinks that a prospective juror should be challenged for cause he makes that recommendation to the court, and the judge must act on it. Generally, judges will sustain a challenge for cause unless there is simply no legal basis for the challenge. One reason judges are so lenient on challenges for cause is that those which are overruled can be used as the basis for appealing a subsequent conviction. If an attorney does not "like" a prospective juror (feels that juror is apt to go with the other side), then he normally tries to find some cause upon which he can challenge the juror. Preemptory challenges, on the other hand, do not require any basis — but they are limited in number. They are automatically granted. Defense usually has more preemptory challenges than the prosecution. Lawyers on both sides are very careful in using their preemptory challenges and often save them for jurors about whom they have strong hunches or on whom they were overruled on challenges for cause.

---

*This "scientifically selected" jury deliberated for one hour and eighteen minutes and acquitted Little (in spite of the fact that she hinted that she had previously had sexual contact with the deceased jailer). Jerry Paul confidently stated after the trial "given enough money, I can buy justice. I can win any case in the country, given enough money."[37]

A juror who has been successfully challenged then goes back to the jury room to await being called for voir dire in another case. After the careful and rigorous screening of prospective jurors the trial is ready to begin. In many jurisdictions jeopardy attaches when the jury is sworn: it is at that point that the trial per se actually begins.

Problems Associated With Jury Trials   Numerous commentators have pointed out the flaws of the jury system. For one thing, jury trials produce congestion of the court's calendar and result in delay. This is a valid cricitism, for jury trials *do* take longer than trials heard by a judge. In a major case, jury selection alone can be a lengthy and difficult process. For example, a well-publicized murder case or a "political" case can have a jury selection process that takes weeks or even months. In cases which use expert witnesses, such as psychiatrists or other specialists who can vary in their interpretation of events, the trial may stretch out as each side pits its experts against one another.

Another problem is cost. Jury trials can be very expensive. The average juror pay is $10 per day, or about $200,000,000 per year, although the cost to society based on the average pay is estimated to be about three times this amount, or $600,000,000 per year.[38] Additional cost is incurred by specific jurisdictions in providing meals for jurors and in actually prosecuting the case. Obviously, the longer a trial, the more expensive it is and the more resources it consumes. In some states where there is no public defender system, private attorneys may be appointed by the court, at public expense, to defend the accused and the fees paid to these attorneys often add up to a considerable amount of money.

Another problem is juror ignorance. Herbert Spencer described a jury as a group of twelve people of average ignorance; yet some of the cases heard by juries involve highly sophisticated and subtle points of evidence and law. Jurors are not allowed to take notes during a trial, nor are they permitted to ask questions, slow testimony down, or compel additional evidence to be presented. Some people believe that it stretches the limits of credibility to expect twelve common people to grasp the complexities involved in a difficult case and that jurors therefore tend to make their decisions on the basis of their own subjective feelings. It is difficult to come to a conclusion on this point; in a famous study done at the University of Chicago Law School, judges who presided over 3,591 jury trials across the country indicated they would have convicted in 19 percent of the cases where the jury acquitted and would have acquitted in three percent of the cases where the jury convicted.[39] Jury verdicts are not that far off track from what legal experts would have done, so it might be a bit unfair to criticize juries because of the presumed low intelligence of their members.

A common problem with jury trials is that many people are reluctant to serve on juries. For some of them, it would be a financial hardship. For others, such as doctors and dentists, it would create considerable inconvenience for many other people. Many people who would make good jurors are exempted (lawyers, police officers, medical personnel, pharmacists, legislators, clergymen, firemen and educators). Between the people who can't serve and those who do not wish to, a great deal of good talent is lost. Even when well qualified jurors *wish* to serve, one side or the other may remove them with a preemptory challenge. Scientists, engineers, college professors, and others with strong analytic capabilities are especially likely to be rejected. Of course, the opposite can happen as it did

> ... during the deliberations of the jury that decided the case of John Mitchell and Maurice Stans, two Cabinet members in the Nixon Administration who were charged with conspiracy to impede a Securities and Exchange Commission investigation of a contributor to Nixon's reelection campaign fund. The jury was made up of poorly educated and rather uninformed people, with the exception of Andrew Choa, a vice-president of the First National City Bank. After a ten-week trial the jurors initially voted 8 to 4 for conviction. However, Choa's status, self-assurance, and greater sophistication enabled him to sway the other jurors, who had been quite befuddled by the mass of complex evidence involved in the case. Choa, whose political ideology was described by bank colleagues as 'to the right of Ivan the Terrible' was able to wield inordinate influence to vindicate two conservative politicians. Thus, the goal of public accountability presumably served by jury trials can be undercut when elites are able to wield extraordinary influence.[40]

To be sure, juries *are* unpredictable — but perhaps that only increases their value. If they err, it is no doubt in the direction of leniency. Perhaps juries see the actions of the professionals — the lawyers — and counterbalance on behalf of the defendant. In fact, one noted prosecutor told the author that the thing he dreaded most in a trial was the defendant who wanted to act as his own counsel. He said that it was his impression that juries compensated in these cases — in favor of the defendant. The same prosecutor also said that juries tended to be more lenient with defendants who had lawyers who appeared weak.

Finally, the use of twelve-person juries has been criticized as being unnecessary. Actually, a twelve member jury is as much an accident of history as anything else. The case of *Williams* v *Florida* (1970) has laid the groundwork for significant change in the use of less than twelve jurors in a criminal case.[41] In this case Williams had been convicted of robbery by a six-person jury and was sentenced to life in prison. He appealed the case on the grounds that he had been denied his Sixth and Fourteenth Amendments rights to a trial by jury. The Supreme Court, however, ruled that his rights were not violated and said that the touchstone should be whether the group is large enough to promote group deliberation, free from outside attempts at intimidation, and to provide a fair possibility for obtaining a representative cross section of the community. The National Advisory Commission on Criminal Justice Standards and Goals agrees with the use of smaller juries and has stated that it believes that juries of less than 12 can provide group deliberation on the issue of guilt, resist outside influences, and provide a fair possibility for obtaining a representative cross section of the community. However, fewer than six persons on a jury would be unsound.[42]

The use of six person juries should make jury selection easier and should save time as well as money. Smaller juries should also result in fewer hung juries because the smaller size of the jury is apt to produce a greater degree of consensus. It has been argued that smaller juries reduce the opportunity for minority group participation; however, this is more speculative than factual, and only time will tell whether or not smaller juries will differ in their performance from twelve member juries.

Another important decision concerning juries was handed down in the case of *Johnson* v. *Louisiana*, in which the Supreme Court ruled that a person could be convicted on the basis of a non-unanimous jury verdict. The Supreme Court stated that "In our view, disagreement of three jurors does not alone establish reasonable doubt, particularly with such a heavy majority of the jury, after having considered the dissenters' views, remains convicted of guilt. That rational men disagree is not itself equivalent to a failure by the State, nor does it indicate infidelity to the reasonable doubt standard."[43] This can have a significant impact on trial outcomes. Hung juries which cannot reach a unanimous vote because a single juror holds out and refuses to alter his position would no longer result in a mistrial. Also, a corrupt juror could no longer determine the outcome of a trial by holding for an acquittal. It might also be possible to shorten trial time by reducing the amount of effort which goes into the voir dire examination, because each and every juror as an individual member of the jury would no longer be as important. On the other side of the argument, juries could simply bypass the one or two jurors who hold out and who *ought* to be heard. However, as with the six-person jury, speculation is not enough. Time will tell whether many states will use the nonunamimous verdict and the ultimate impact it will have on jury trials.

The Courts and Sentencing

Upon being convicted, either through a guilty plea or a trial, the defendant is usually sentenced; the court pronounces its judgment and awards a punishment. Although it is usually the judge who imposes the sentence, there may be a number of limitations placed on the sentences judges can give. For one thing, the sentences for crimes are determined by the legislature. When the state makes an act a crime it also sets the limits of punishment which may be inflicted, and judges must sentence within the limits authorized by law. In some states the law is very open-ended and permits *indeterminate sentencing* for felonies. In its most basic form, this is a sentence which simply sends a person to prison. How long he remains there is not determined by the judge but rather by the state's parole board. Thus, a person may be sentenced to prison for an indeterminate period ranging from one year to life and when he actually gets out is determined by the parole board on the basis of the progress he makes toward rehabilitation. This type of sentencing was developed for just that purpose — to be able to confine an offender for as long as it takes to straighten him out. Most states which use indeterminate sentencing, however, use a modified form. A person may be sentenced for a term of imprisonment of not less than four years nor more than eight years. He must serve the minimum, but if his behavior merits release at the end of four years, he may be paroled. If not, he may be kept for the full eight years. This modified indeterminate sentence still gives the state leverage over the offender, but it also protects him from the possibility of being kept in prison for an excessive period.

The opposite of the indeterminate sentence is the *determinate sentence* (flat sentence), in which the offender is sentenced to a specific term. There is no minimum and maximum. Where flat sentencing is used, parole is typically eliminated; however, inmates can reduce their sentences through *good time*, which is time off a sentence for good behavior and is calculated according to fixed formulas. A concept similar to this is that of *mandatory minimum sentences* which provide that in the case of certain crimes a person convicted must spend a fixed minimum amount of time in confinement. It is a hardline approach and is used as a punitive means of dealing with certain kinds of crimes (e.g., those committed through the use of firearms or the sale of drugs).

One of the most widely used sentencing techniques involves the *probated sentence*. In this case the convicted person is sentenced to a term of imprisonment, but the actual execution of the sentence is suspended as long as the accused abides by the conditions set by the court.

If he violates those conditions he may be sent to prison for the full term of the sentence. This is frequently used in the case of first offenders and those who can demonstrate a likelihood for community-based rehabilitation. Probation is not "getting off the hook," as many people think; it is a sentence in its own right and can be very effectively used to the benefit of both the offender and the community.

There are many variations on the basic sentencing schemes, and each is grounded in some set of correctional objectives.[44] However, sentencing as it is practiced in this country has focused a great deal of public disapproval on the courts in general and on judges in particular. One frequently hears reference made to "getting away with murder" and descriptions of "our disastrous court system." People hear about cases like that of Joseph Morse and they worry as much about the courts as they do about Morse:

> When he was eighteen, Joseph Bernard Morse picked up a large rock and bashed in his mother's head. Then he beat his invalid sister to death with a baseball bat. All this happened in San Diego, in 1962. In 1964, while he was serving a life sentence for killing his mother, Morse murdered a fellow inmate by strangling him with a garrote improvised from twine. For this murder, Morse was given a life sentence. Last year (1977) after many sessions with Morse, a psychological tester concluded that the prisoner's potential for violence was low, *provided everything was going his way*. More recently, a psychiatrist reported that Morse is 'antisocial' but that he should nevertheless be paroled and watched to see what happens. As things stand, Morse will be paroled next year.*[45]

There are a number of problems associated with sentencing. One is that there is a tremendous amount of inconsistency in the sentences which are given, especially for what appears to be the same or similar crimes. Perhaps the key element in sentencing is not the *crime* but the *judge*, at least in some of these cases.[46] Judges, after all, have their own biases and personal feelings and it may be difficult for them to shed those feelings when they sentence offenders. In fact, some judges worry quite a bit about the sentences they give and often feel both pressured and isolated. As one judge said, "Who can a judge talk to about these things? There's nobody. Other judges don't help — they can give you advice, but then they're wounded if you don't take it. No one can help you."[47]

---

*The perceptive reader will note that Morse did receive significant sentences for his crimes and that it is *not* the courts which are releasing him. The public however, still holds the courts responsible for such outcomes — even though the defendant may have received the stiffest sentence the court could impose.

Some judges are tough on everyone; some are only tough in certain kinds of cases; others are consistently lenient. There are judges who do not seem to care one way or another and base their sentences on how they feel at the moment or on the recommendations of the prosecutor or the defender. The result is a high degree of inconsistency, referred to as *sentencing disparity*. The decisions made by judges are not the sole reason for sentencing disparity, however. A major role is played by the process of plea bargaining itself. Since most sentences are based on negotiated pleas of guilty, the role of the judge in sentence disparities may well be somewhat over-emphasized. It should be remembered that in plea bargaining a charge may be reduced or the sentence may be set in advance in return for the guilty plea. In this light the disparity in sentences may be more apparent than real, as different defendants are not being given different sentences for the same crime; in reality, the actual crimes may be quite different and there may be other reasons for the sentences which are imposed.

Another problem in sentencing is that many judges have no real concept of what they are doing when they send people to prison; others are very much aware of what they are doing. Howard James pointedly noted, "As I toured the country, I was told that when judges pass sentence, they often do not realize what a prison sentence means to the man convicted."[48] Instead, "decisions are sometimes ... based on the judge's reaction to the way a man is dressed, his age, the length of his hair, the color of his skin, his nationality, or even his religion."[49] Very few judges ever visit the prisons to which they send the people whom they sentence and many spend an entire career on the bench without ever seeing the inside of a prison.

The most serious problem of sentencing, at least as it is perceived by the public, is *leniency*. Virtually all available survey data indicate that the public would like to see more stringent sentencing practices — and in some cases, this attitude seems to be justified. A Wisconsin judge, for example, sentenced a 15 year old defendant to one year on probation for raping a woman, noting that the boy's behavior was a normal reaction in a era of see-through blouses and permissive sexuality. In a subsequent recall election, based on this case, he was removed from the bench. Indeed, may people are appalled at the seriousness of many crimes which result in either light or probated sentences or which even allow offenders to get out of prison:

> In 1966, Charles Yukl strangled Susan Reynolds and mutilated her body. Pleading guilty to manslaughter, he was sentenced to from seven and a half to fifteen years in jail. In June 1973, he

was released on parole. During the following summer, he lured Karin Schlegel to his Greenwich Village apartment and strangled her. Jailed for this crime, Yukl will be eligible in fifteen years for parole consideration.[50]

Repeat offenders, such as Yukl frighten the public, for they symbolize the violent stranger who is at the core of the public's fear of crime. Interestingly enough, many of these same people are much less draconian when the offender is a friend or relative. When that is the case, they are more likely to feel that a probated sentence which requires psychological or other help would probably be best. Public opinion concerning sentencing seems based in part on a general fear of crime, especially violent crime committed by strangers. Many feel that if the "strangers" who commit the violent crimes are given lengthy sentences, the threat of crime will be reduced somewhat.

The public's perception of the leniency of sentences may itself be somewhat flawed; most criminals are in fact caught and punished at some time or another, and many of the "light" sentences are actually much heavier than the public realizes.[51] In all likelihood public indignation over light sentencing is more presumptive than real and is reinforced by sensational cases that may not be representative. Charles Peters, in considering the problem of public safety and criminal sentences, offered the following interesting comment:

> To me the justification for prison is not deterrence or rehabilitation. It is the punishment of the guilty and the protection of society. If you've ever visited a prison, you know that six months is adequate for just about any crime. The only justification for longer sentences — all of which qualify as cruel and unusual — should be to protect the rest of us. This means locking up the violent, sane or insane, until they have ceased to be violent, but for all nonviolent crime six months should be the standard sentence.[52]

The sentiment expressed by Peters seems to reflect a basic concern of many people: the wish to be safe from violent crime and to punish those who commit them. It is not likely, however, that many people would go along with his concept of six month sentences, even though the proposal may have merit. Perhaps the public would be more responsive to a more consistent pattern of sentencing in criminal cases, and this may account for the growing popularity of flat sentences. It remains unclear though, as to exactly how a uniform flat sentencing policy would affect the plea bargaining process; it might result in more litigated trials and possibly even more acquittals.

One method of dealing with sentencing problems is through the use of presentence investigations and reports. These reports are usually prepared by a probation officer. They are detailed case histories of the offender and his social, criminal, and educational background. They also contain recommendations concerning the type of punishment which would produce the greatest benefit. These reports are provided to the court so that the best sentencing decision can be made, one which is consistent with the prisoner's needs as well as those of society. The use of presentence investigations is mandatory in some jurisdictions and discretionary in others.

The Court and Community Relations

One of the key problems of courts is that in spite of the fact that they are public institutions, they continue to be isolated from the public. The position that the courts are answerable to the *law* may be technically correct, but it would be foolhardy to deny the fact that ultimately the courts must also be responsive to the people. They must serve not only those who actually use them, but they must serve the entire community as well — and they must do so in more than a vague, abstract way. To attain this goal, the National Advisory Commission on Criminal Justice Standards and Goals has recommended that court administrators establish a forum that would combine the efforts of members of the community who are interested in judicial administration.[53] This idea certainly has merit, for there are many people within the community who are interested in judicial administration; however, the proposal has little to do with the "average" person in the community. It would probably be better to introduce some form of law-focused education into the curricula of elementary and secondary schools. This would hopefully give citizens a better and more basic understanding of what the courts are and what they can and cannot do.

The problem of the courts also requires some more immediate and direct attention in order to build a better relationship within the community. Public dissatisfaction with the courts can foster a disrespect for the entire criminal justice system and its processes; therefore, efforts must be undertaken to reduce public dissatisfaction. There are a number of specific areas in which substantial efforts are needed. Facilities are inadequate; much of the physical space occupied by courts is either inadequate or deteriorated. This is basically a funding problem which must be dealt with by the state and local governments, yet in a period of increasing fiscal austerity, it seems unlikely that many major improvements will be forthcoming in this area.

The court's treatment of witnesses is another area which continues to contribute to strained court-community relations. Witnesses are seldom adequately compensated for their time, much less the actual expenses they must incur. In addition, many court systems treat witnesses in an off-hand and disinterested way. They are simply told to show up and wait until they are called, without knowing when or even *if* they will be called upon to testify. Most courthouses do not have facilities for witnesses. It would help to inform them of what is going on, when they are likely to be called, and to provide them with a reasonably pleasant setting (in which prosecution and defense witnesses are kept separate) where they can wait. This kind of basic courtesy could go a long way towards easing the unpleasantness of serving as a witness. Pretty much the same thing can be said of jurors. They should also be provided with at least adequate waiting rooms while they are held in the jury pool awaiting call for voir dire.

Another major deficiency in court-community relations is the lack of information services in the courthouse itself.[54] The Standards and Goals report on the courts points out that,

> Participating in the criminal justice process, whether by witness, juror, or defendant, often is a confusing and traumatic experience that leaves the participants with an unfavorable impression of the system. Defendants and witnesses may experience difficulty locating the site of trials at which they are to appear. No provision generally is made for answering basic questions concerning rights and responsibilities of participants, or the meaning of various parts of the process. Consequently, jurors, witnesses, and defendants may fail to exercise rights they otherwise would, or may come away from contact with a criminal case with an erroneous impression of the system.[55]

These deficiencies reflect a general insensitivity on the part of the courts toward virtually *all* who come before them, regardless of why they are there. No government institution can be uncivil without rightfully earning the enmity of those whom it serves, and the courts are an excellent case in point. Like so many other government agencies, the courts have evolved from *instruments* into *institutions* and have come to serve the needs of lawyers and judges more than the interests of justice.

Summary

One of the functions of social organization is to provide means of conflict resolution, both formal and informal. The courts are formal means of resolving conflicts in our society, and crimes are conflicts between an individual and the state. The courts deal with crimes in an effort to restore social harmony. These conflicts are resolved according to established legal rules which regulate rights and duties. In any conflict which comes before the courts, the respective rights and duties of the opposing parties are examined in the light of existing legal principles and the courts provide the remedies allowed by law. All courts have jurisdictions which define the nature of the conflicts which may come before them. The criminal courts operate at two levels; there are trial courts and appellate courts. Trial courts hear disputes of fact and apply appropriate remedies, whereas appellate courts review the actions of the trial courts.

The central figure in a court is the judge, who has wide powers in the conducting of the court's business. Although many judges are competent and hardworking, some are not — and they cause a great deal of the criticism which is levied against the courts. Judges may be inadequate for a variety of reasons, but once they are on the bench it is very difficult to either remove them or to nullify their effects on the quality of justice in their courts. One reason for the large number of inadequate judges is the means by which many of them are selected. In many states judges are selected as a result of political connections rather than pure merit.

Another problem area of the courts is in the area of administration. Courts are also bureaucratic government agencies, and may suffer from basic problems in organization and administration, all of which contribute to the problem of "delayed justice." Recent efforts in court reform, especially in court unification and the hiring of professional administrators, has helped to correct some of these problems, although ingrained tradition has proven very difficult to overcome.

A serious problem of justice which arises from the courts is the whole issue of bail. Bail is the posting of money or sureties in support of a defendant's promise to appear at his trial. The poor often cannot afford bail and must remain in jail until their trial. This is frequently not accidental, as courts often set bail so high a defendant *cannot* get out, even though this is not the purpose of bail. Again, this is a problem which has been addressed through bail reform, but more effort is required before the problem can be resolved.

Trial juries have also been the subject of considerable controversy in spite of the fact that relatively few cases ever result in a jury trial. Jury trials tend to be expensive and time-consuming, and some of them are unpredictable in their outcome. However, in spite of its shortcomings, the jury trial still remains the hallmark of our legal system. Two recent Supreme Court decisions have created a potential for the significant modification of the use of juries. One was the decision to allow six-member juries in felony cases, and the other was the decision to allow courts to accept non-unanimous verdicts; however, the impact of these two factors remains to be seen as it is still too early to predict just what influence they will have.

An area of considerable controversy has been that of sentencing, especially the disparity of sentences awarded for the same or similar crimes. Much of this problem may be more in the nature of plea bargaining than in actual decision-making, however. The public is also concerned over what it perceives as judicial lenience in sentencing. This perceived lenience may be more speculative than real (in spite of some notable examples of leniency) and may be based on the public's fear of violent, stranger-to-stranger crimes. The truth is that most criminals are caught and most of them do receive active sentences, yet the idea of lenient sentencing remains a focal point of public dissatisfaction with the courts.

Finally, there is a major need for courts and their administrators to concern themselves with the whole area of court-community relations, especially in the treatment of jurors, witnesses, and defendants. Better facilities, information services, and basic consideration would go a long way towards improving the relationship between the courts and the public. In addition, law-focused education in the schools would give more citizens a better understanding of the courts and citizen responsibilities toward the courts.

Discussion Questions

1.   How are the roles of trial and appellate courts different?

2.   Do judges have too much power and too little accountability?

3.   Do you think class and status differences between judges and lawyers on the one hand, and most criminal defendants on the other make a difference in how people are treated by the courts?

4.   How can differences in a judge's legal education and work background make a difference in his performance on the bench?

5.   What effects can delay in the courts have on public opinion toward the criminal justice system?

6.   Do you think it is fair for bail bondsmen to have the powers they do possess? How can their actions harm the reputation of the criminal justice system?

7.   Does the use of psychological profiles in jury selection defeat the interests of justice — or is it an effective way for a defense lawyer to secure justice for his client?

8.   The public seems to think criminal sentences are too lenient — what would happen, in your judgment, if criminal sentences were *increased*? Is public sentiment the best guide to follow?

9.   People who receive probated sentences are often regarded as having "gotten off" with their crime. Is this a realistic assessment? Should the victim have a say-so in whether or not an offender gets a probated sentence?

10.   Does sentencing disparity bring into question the credibility of sentencing, or does it merely reflect the diversity of our court systems?

Glossary

MISSOURI PLAN   A means of selecting judges in which a judge is picked by the governor from a list of qualified candidates and must then stand for election on an uncontested retention ballot.

TRIAL DE NOVO   A trial held for a second time, as if there had been no former decision. A trial de novo is usually held when a minor case is appealed after conviction in a court of limited jurisdiction.

BAIL   To set at liberty a person arrested against some security that he will appear when required. The security is usually a sum of money or a bail bond.

TRIAL COURT   Courts which hear controversies and make determinations of guilt or innocence.

JURY   A body of citizens sworn to deliver a true verdict upon evidence submitted to them in a judicial setting.

Notes

[1] William T. Schantz, *The American Legal Environment: Individuals, Their Business, and Their Government* (St. Paul, Minnesota: West Publishing Co., 1976), p. 122.

[2] Schantz, *The American Legal Environment*, p. 122.

[3] Schantz, *The American Legal Environment*, p. 122.

[4] Harold J. Grilliot, *Introduction to Law and the Legal System*, 2d ed. (Boston: Houghton Mifflin Company, 1979), p. 49.

[5] Gerald D. Robin, *Introduction to the Criminal Justice System: Principles, Procedures, Practice* (New York: Harper and Row, Publishers, 1980), p. 174.

[6] Robin, *Introduction to the Criminal Justice System*, p. 174.

[7] William J. Chambliss and Robert B. Seidman, *Law, Order and Power* (Reading, Massachusetts: Addison-Wesley Publishing Co., Inc., 1971), p. 76.

[8] President's Commission on Law Enforcement and the Administration of Justice, Nicholas de B. Katzenbach, Chairman, *Task Force Report: The Courts* (Washington, D.C.: U.S.Government Printing Office, 1967), p. 65.

[9] James P. Levine, Michael C. Musheno, and Dennis J. Palumbo, *Criminal Justice: A Public Policy Approach* (New York: Harcourt Brace Jovanovich, Inc., 1980), p. 263.

[10] Abraham S. Blumberg, *Criminal Justice: Issues and Ironies*, 2d ed. (New York: New Viewpoints, 1979), pp. 247-267.

[11] Donald Dale Jackson, *Judges: An Inside View of the Agonies and Excesses of An American Elite* (New York: Atheneum, 1974), p. 10.

[12] Blumberg, *Criminal Justice*, p. 250.

[13] Blumberg, *Criminal Justice*, p. 258.

[14] Blumberg, *Criminal Justice*, p. 258.

[15] Blumberg, *Criminal Justice*, p. 251.

[16] Levine, et al., *Criminal Justice: A Public Policy Approach*, pp. 269-270. For an interesting insight into this issue, see also Bob Woodward and Scott Armstrong, *The Brethren* (New York: Simon and Schuster, 1979).

[17] Levine, et al., *Criminal Justice: A Public Policy Approach*, p. 267.

[18] Jackson, *Judges*, p. 89.

[19] Jackson, *Judges*, pp. 4-5.

[20] Charles E. Silberman, *Criminal Violence, Criminal Justice* (New York: Vintage Books, 1978), p. 375.

[21] See Larry C. Berkson, Steven W. Hays, and Susan J. Carbon, *Managing the State Courts* (St. Paul, Minnesota: West Publishing Co., 1977).

[22] Howard James, *Crisis in the Courts* (New York: David McKay Company, Inc., 1971), pp. 23-32.

[23] *Mastrian* v *Hedman*.

[24] President's Crime Commission, *The Courts*, p. 37.

[25] Ronald Goldfarb, *Ransom: A Critique of the American Bail System* (New York: Harper and Row, Publishers, 1965).

[26] President's Crime Commission, *The Courts*, p. 38.

[27] Jackson, *Judges*, pp. 144-145. For a further discussion of the bail problem, see James, *Crisis in the Courts*, especially Chapter VII, "Jail or Bail," pp. 112-125; John E. Conklin and Dermot Meagher, "The Percentage Deposit Bail System: An Alternative to the Professional Bondsman," *Journal of Criminal Justice* (Winter 1973).

[28] Robin, *Introduction to the Criminal Justice System*, p. 204.

[29] Levine et al., *Criminal Justice: A Public Policy Approach*, p. 281.

[30] National Criminal Justice Information and Statistics Service, *Sourcebook of Criminal Justice Statistics - 1978* (Washington, D.C.: U.S. Government Printing Office, 1979), Table 2.57, p. 322.

[31] Silberman, *Criminal Violence, Criminal Justice*, p. 402.

[32] Chambliss and Seidman, *Law, Order and Power*, p. 443.

[33] National Institute for Law Enforcement and Criminal Justice, *A Guide to Jury System Management* (Washington, D.C.: U.S. Government Printing Office, 1975), pp. 1-3.

[34] *Swain* v *Alabama*, 380 U.S. 202 (1965).

[35] Haywood Alker, Carl Hosticha, and Michael Mitchell, "Jury Selection as a Biased Social Process," *Law and Society Review* (Fall 1976): 9-41.

[36] James Reston, Jr., *The Innocence of Joan Little: A Southern Mystery* (New York: Time Books, 1977).

[37] Wayne King, "Joan Little's Lawyer Scorns Legal System and Says He 'Bought' Her Acquittal," *New York Times*, 20 October 1975, p. 23.

[38] National Institute, *A Guide to Jury System Management*, pp. 1-3.

[39] Harry Kalven and Hans Zeisel, *The American Jury* (Boston: Little, Brown, 1966), p. 58.

[40] Levine et al., *Criminal Justice: A Public Policy Approach*, p. 281.

[41] *Williams* v *Florida* 399 U.S. 78, 100 (1970).

[42] National Advisory Commission on Criminal Justice Standards and Goals, Russell W. Peterson, Chairman, *Courts* (Washington, D.C.: U.S. Government Printing Office, 1973), p. 101.

[43] *Johnson* v *Louisiana*, 406 U.S. 356 (1972).

[44] Michael Serrill, "Determinate Sentencing: History, Theory, Debate," *Corrections Magazine*, September 1977.

[45] Nicholas Scoppetta, "Getting Away With Murder: Our Disastrous Court System," *Saturday Review*, 10 June 1978, p. 11.

[46] See Marvin E. Frankel, *Criminal Sentences: Law Without Order* (New York: Hill and Wang, 1973).

[47] Jackson, *Judges*, p. 201.

[48] James, *Crisis in the Courts*, p. 148.

[49] James, *Crisis in the Courts*, p. 147.

[50] Scoppetta, "Getting Away With Murder," p. 10.

[51] Silberman, *Criminal Violence, Criminal Justice*, passim.

[52] Charles Peters, "Tilting at Windmills," *The Washington Post*, 1 June 1980, D2.

[53] National Advisory Commission, *Courts*, p. 191.

[54] National Advisory Commission, *Courts*, p. 194.

[55] National Advisory Committee, *Courts*, p. 194.

JUVENILE JUSTICE $\qquad$ 12

The Child is the Father of Man . . .
—William Wordsworth

Historically the English legal system concluded that children under the age of seven could not formulate the intent necessary to commit a crime and consequently could not be charged with the commission of a crime.[1] Children from seven to thirteen were also presumed to be incapable of formulating the intent required to commit a crime; this presumption could, however, be rebutted upon proof that the youth *could* distinguish between right and wrong. At age fourteen a youth was considered an adult and was accordingly believed to be mature enough to determine right from wrong. Consequently, youths aged fourteen and older, and those from seven to thirteen who were proven to be able to distinguish right from wrong, were tried as adults and received the same punishments as adults.

Because of its derivation from the English legal system, American law contained the same presumptions concerning children accused of committing crimes, and American children received essentially the same treatment as those in England. There is evidence, however, that due to the severity of the usual punishments, judges and juries were often reluctant to convict children and many were accordingly acquitted.[2] Youths who were convicted and imprisoned were intermingled with adult felons and were often influenced by adult recidivists, thus starting a life-long career in crime.

These conditions produced a movement during the nineteenth century to humanize the treatment of children by the criminal courts. It was also during this time period that industrialization, immigration, and rapid urban growth combined to create cities characterized by disrupted families, overcrowding, poverty, slums, alcoholism, and spiraling levels of vice and crime. These conditions spurred social reformers who were concerned with improving the overall quality of urban life. Many of these reformers had great faith in the ability of the developing social sciences to help children and at the same time eradicate the social blight which was producing so many problems in the cities.[3]

The first step toward the development of a system of juvenile justice which was separate from the criminal justice system took place when juveniles were segregated from adults in correctional institutions. Separate correctional insitutions for juveniles were established in New York City in 1825 and in Massachusetts in 1847.[4] Separate trials, dockets, and records for juveniles were created in Massachusetts in 1872; in New York in 1892, and, in Rhode Island in 1898. Reform enthusiasm peaked when the Illinois legislature created the first juvenile court in Chicago in 1899. From Illinois, juvenile courts then spread to every state in the Union.

The purposes and objectives of the juvenile court differed substantially from those of the criminal court. Rather than placing blame, finding guilt, and punishing offenders, juvenile court was intended to be nonjudgmental. Instead, the emphasis was to be on helping youths overcome parental neglect and unwholesome environments through extensive help from the social sciences. The analogy frequently made in describing the juvenile court was that of a kindly father (the judge) expressing concern for his wayward child ("parens patriae"); the juvenile court process *did* differ substantially from the processes of the criminal courts.[5] Hearings were informal, records confidential, and statutes generally allowed juvenile court judges to exclude the public. Instead of sitting behind a bench, the judge often sat behind a table or desk, and the processes were usually informal in nature. Since the main objective was to diagnose and treat, the process was deemed to be nonadversarial, and the use of lawyers was discouraged. Probation officers were assigned to the court to investigate alleged delinquent acts or conditions of dependency or neglect, as well as the child's background, and to report to the judge. Psychologists, psychiatrists, social workers and other social scientists began to be attracted to juvenile court in professional, consultant, or volunteer capacities. These objectives, procedures, and characteristics — although somewhat altered over the years — are still descriptive of most modern juvenile courts.

The Juvenile Court Process

Juvenile court jurisdiction generally includes cases of dependency, neglect, and delinquency. Neglected children are those who have been abandoned or mistreated by their parents or caretakers, and also include cases in which parents fail to provide an adequate home environment for their children. The terms "neglect" and "dependency" are often used synonymously. Dependent youths are sent to the juvenile court because there is no other place to send them. The juvenile courts also deal with allegations of delinquency — acts which would be crimes if committed by adults. Delinquency also includes the violation of rules and regulations which apply specifically to children and include such things as curfew violations, truancy, the use of alcohol, drugs, and tobacco, and children deemed by parents or other authorities to be uncontrollable, incorrigible, runaway or in need of supervision. The terminology and extent of special legislation which defines misconduct as it applies to juveniles varies from state to state and is often referred to as *status offenses.* Juvenile courts have jurisdiction over children up to a specified maximum age, usually seventeen.[6] If the offender is over the maximum juvenile age, the criminal courts have jurisdiction over him, and if he is brought before those courts, he will be treated as an adult. A number of adult courts, however, have a "youthful offender" provision which allows them to extend special consideration to some offenders up to the age of twenty-one.

A youth first comes into contact with the juvenile justice process as a result of a referral to the court, and the majority of these referrals come from the police.[7] Police officers apprehend youths under a variety of circumstances: committing a "criminal" act; violating curfew; runaways; under the influence of drugs or alcohol, and under other circumstances. The police exercise a great deal of discretion and have a wide variety of actions available to them. They may admonish or otherwise warn the youth and then let him go. Or the officer may warn him, release him, and then make an official report. An additional method of handling youths, sometimes called a *station adjustment,* is to take the juvenile to the police station, record the incident, warn the youth, and then release him to his parent's custody. If departmental policy permits, the officer may place the youth under a kind of informal "probation" by the police department. Another set of alternatives is to warn the youth, release him, and refer him to a mental health clinic, drug or alcohol abuse agency, youth service bureau, Big Brothers, the Y.M.C.A., a local youth center or some other social services agency. By exercising his discretion in this manner, the police officer effectively elects to divert the youth from juvenile court process in favor of some social service alternative. A final possibility is to take the youth to the police station, release him to his parent's custody, and then direct both the youth and his parents to appear in court on a given day. Rather than releasing the youth, the officer may refer him to juvenile court and place him in a juvenile detention facility, or in the local jail if no juvenile detention center exists.

Most police-juvenile encounters take place on the street and are settled by a warning, a direct order, or by some other informal means. Only a relatively small number of encounters will be referred to the juvenile court. If a police officer believes that the danger to society is serious, that the youth needs guidance or treatment, that his family seems unable to provide the needed help, or that other resources do not seem adequate, then he will probably refer the case to the juvenile court. In some police departments there is a youth division, and all cases involving juveniles are routinely turned over to youth officers who then decide on the best course of action. The decision to go ahead and refer a youth to the juvenile court is based on a number of factors, including the seriousness of the offense, the attitude of the child, community sentiment, the offender's prior record, his age, and departmental policies. In general, most law enforcement agencies prefer to avoid the extreme measure of referring a case to juvenile court if there seems to be any other reasonable alternative.

School administrators, welfare case workers, or citizens who have complaints may also refer a case to the juvenile court. Every once in a while parents or other members of the family may ask the court to discipline a child or to even assume complete responsibility for him. Parents who do this often plead that they can no longer control the child or that they no longer wish to exercise their responsibilities as parents. Children thus judged to be "persons in need of supervision" may become wards of the juvenile court and in some cases may actually be taken out of their family setting and placed under the direct control of the state.

Intake After a youth is referred to juvenile court, a preliminary screening known as *intake* is performed by the probation department of the juvenile court. In larger courts, intake may be carried out by a special section of the probation department. At the intake proceeding the intake officer determines whether or not the matter should be referred to the juvenile court.[8] The inquiry may be a very limited and abbreviated processs, or it may involve an extensive study of the alleged act and the youth's social history. Depending upon his judgment, the strength of the case, and the seriousness of the offense, the intake officer may dismiss the matter, refer the youth to another agency, or place the child on an informal probation. When the latter course is chosen, the proceeding may involve an informal hearing before the judge at which time the act is inquired into and the child warned to change his behavior. Many juvenile cases are handled in this manner. As a final course of action, the intake officer may suggest that formal juvenile court action be taken. If a court referral is decided upon, the intake officer must make a decision concerning detention pending the judicial hearing. In most states, law provides for the release of the child to his parents or some other suitable caretaker unless the juvenile is deemed to be such a severe threat to the community that he must be detained. In a minority of states and the federal system, youths now have the right to bail.[9]

Waiver   At the time the juvenile court officially assumes jurisdiction, a decision concerning *waiver to criminal court* must be made. Waiver means that the child's case is to be transferred to criminal court and he is to be tried as an adult. In other words, the juvenile court waives its jurisdiction and turns the youth over to the criminal courts. If the youth loses the protection of the juvenile court through such a waiver, he will be tried as an adult and may receive the same punishment as an adult. Waiver can only take place when the grounds for delinquency are an act, that if committed by an adult, would be a crime. In addition the child must be at or above the minimum age (for that state) at which a child can be convicted of a crime. The U.S. Supreme Court has held that the juvenile judge must provide a hearing on waiver and state the reasons sufficient to prove that a full inquiry has taken place.[10] Generally, those waived are youths accused of very serious crimes of violence such as murder, rape, or robbery. Juveniles who are not amenable to juvenile court protection or treatment, usually evidenced by repeated prior adjudications of delinquency, are also often waived. Waiver is usually a discretionary act of the juvenile court judge except for those crimes such as first degree murder which in some states must be transferred to the criminal courts. Thus the prison population in some states does include some fourteen to seventeen year old inmates who received waivers to criminal court and were subsequently convicted.

Notice   The U.S. Supreme Court has held that after a petition alleging delinquency is filed, but prior to the initial hearing, the youth is entitled to notice of the specific allegations which are being made against him.[11] At the initial hearing, the youth is warned that he has the privilege of remaining silent and that he also has the right to confront and cross-examine the witnesses who will testify against him. In addition, the youth and his parents are apprised of the fact that they have the right to be represented by legal counsel and that if they cannot afford a lawyer, the court will appoint one. If the juvenile or his parents ask for a court-appointed lawyer, or for time to retain a lawyer of their own choosing, the hearing may be reset in order to allow time to make the necessary arrangements. After this has been done, the juvenile court judge will ask the youth if he admits to or denies allegations contained in the petition against him.[12] If the juvenile denies the allegations, usually a future date is set at which time the contested petition will be heard. Ordinarily the last consideration at the initial hearing will be a decision concerning the advisability of detaining the youth pending his future hearing.

Contested Hearings   Contested hearings are the most formal proceedings of an otherwise informal process and they constitute a very small proportion of all juvenile court actions. While probation officers perform many prosecutorial functions (and the prosecutorial role is often limited in juvenile court), actual prosecutors are most likely to be present at contested hearings.[13] At such hearings, witnesses may be sworn and cross-examined by the juvenile, usually through his lawyer. These hearings can be rather short — twenty to thirty minutes — or they can take several hours, depending on the number of witnesses, the complexity of the case, and the seriousness of the offense. Because of the inability of prosecutors and defense attorneys to reach a mutually satisfactory resolution of the matter prior to the formal hearing, these hearings are also the most *adversarial* aspect of what is otherwise a largely nonadversarial process.

Lawyers representing juveniles often perceive their role as being distinctly different from what it would be in a criminal court. Most lawyers in juvenile courts believe it is their duty to assist the court in helping the child rather than to aggressively seek an acquittal for the child, especially when they believe the child is guilty and in need of some kind of treatment.[14] These lawyers have cooperative relationships with juvenile court professionals and appear to subscribe to the ideals of the court. Consequently they plead the great majority of juveniles guilty, contest few cases, and frequently negotiate settlements. While a minority of lawyers representing juveniles will conduct themselves as they would in a contested criminal court case, the prevailing mode of operation is nonadversarial and inquisitorial; the parties usually act in the interest of getting to the truth of the case rather than engaging in a winner-take-all courtroom battle.

If the youth is found to be delinquent after a contested hearing or if he admits to the allegation of delinquency, a *disposition hearing* will follow either immediately or at a later date. At this hearing the judge is concerned with attempting to find out why the youth committed the delinquent act or acts, and tries to discover measures that will correct his behavior. The court is usually aided by a report written by the probation officer which deals with the child's social background and his psychological profile. This report includes recommended dispositions and is known as the *social history report*. Probation officers, social workers, psychologists, and welfare case workers may contribute professional opinions concerning the most appropriate disposition in a given case. Often the child's parents, relatives, and even the child himself will present their respective views as to the best resolution of the matter, and all of these opinions and suggestions are taken into consideration by the judge.

Like many decision-makers in the juvenile justice system, the judge has a wide variety of alternatives from which to choose; however, the range of alternatives is either constricted or expanded by the extent of the social services or institutional facilities available in the area. If the judge deems the act to be of limited seriousness and does not consider the youth a serious threat to society, he will normally give him a stern warning and place him on either unsupervised probation or assign him to a probation officer who, because of a large case load, will give the youth limited supervision. An alternative would be to give the youth a sentence but then suspend it for a period of time (e.g., six months); if the youth has committed no new crimes at the end of this period, the court may then remove the finding of delinquency from the records and close the matter. When the law so allows, a fine might be levied or the youth might be ordered, as a condition of probation, to perform certain compensatory tasks such as repainting or repairing structures which have been vandalized or to perform public service tasks such as removing trash from parks and playgrounds.

If the judge believes the act is more serious and that the youth is a threat to himself or others, but not sufficiently dangerous to require actual confinement, he may place him under closely supervised probation. Often the terms of probation include a specific plan of action designed to improve the youth's behavior and may include a referral to a social service agency, public mental health clinic or to a private psychologist. Like the previous alternative, the disposition may include a fine, compensatory labor, or public service.

The most serious cases result in more structured and confined placements. If a halfway house or private institution suitable for the particular youth is available, the judge may arrange for such a commitment; otherwise, he will commit the child either to the custody of a state youth correctional authority or to a particular training or reform school. The frequency with which a juvenile court judge will commit youths to a state institution depends on the judge's faith in such alternatives. Most courts place the great majority of youths on probation and only a very small number are ever committed to a state institution.

In many states, youths committed to juvenile institutions are first sent to a state diagnostic and testing center. After testing and diagnosis, the youth will be assigned to the most appropriate institution or the best placement within a given institution. Except for the least populous states, which may have only one or two juvenile institutions, a state may have a number of juvenile institutions, including reform schools, ranches, forestry camps, halfway houses, and group homes. They also range from maximum security institutions to minimum security facilities with few restraints and with individual rooms. With the exception of some innovative programs, juvenile institutions are often characterized by an aura of brutality and hostility (usually at the hands of other inmates),[15] staff coercion, and harrassment, all of which tends to produce youths who are more delinquent when they come out than when they entered. This is, of course, aggravated by the process of secondary deviance in which many of these youths are essentially rejected by the communities to which they ultimately return. Incarceration in a juvenile facility frequently paves the way for subsequent stays in other juvenile institutions and adult prisons. Charles Manson, the cult leader convicted in the brutal slayings of actress Sharon Tate and several others, was a "graduate" of the Indiana Boys School at Plainfield. Like many features of the juvenile movement, the promise of juvenile corrections is still to be realized.

Current Trends in Juvenile Justice

Since the early 1960's, policy makers, professionals in the field, and the general public have become increasingly concerned with a juvenile justice system that cannot diagnose or cure; with juvenile court judges who are tyrannical rather than solicitous and caring; and with reform schools that do not reform. As a consequence of the tremendous disparity between the *promise* and *performance* of the juvenile justice system, several movements or trends have gradually developed in the hope of strengthening, reforming, or changing the juvenile justice system. These moves are summarized as the "Four D's" — Due process; Decriminalization, Diversion, and De-institutionalization.

Due Process

The juvenile court's original goal of individual diagnosis and treatment, which basically follows the medical model, has come under sharp attack. The optimistic belief of the early reformers that social scientists could cure delinquents is now being seriously questioned. The psychological basis for the medical model has been attacked on the grounds that it fails to consider the deterministic pressures of the social environment which influence and perhaps even *encourage* juveniles to violate legal norms and which seek to adjust juvenile behavior to the existing social environment.[16] The system has also been bitterly attacked on the basis that it deals harshly, unfairly, and disproportionately with the poor and that it ultimately delivers them into the *criminal* justice system.[17] Significant attacks are not being levied upon the basic *precepts* of the criminal justice system, but rather on its *outcomes.*

As was previously mentioned, the juvenile justice movement discouraged lawyers from practicing in juvenile court. Adversarial proceedings were seen as an impediment to the court's central task of diagnosing the delinquent and prescribing appropriate cures, or of protecting dependent or neglected children. As a result, the great majority of juveniles have not been represented by lawyers, and lawyers have seldom appeared in juvenile court. As a consequence of the absence of lawyers, the judge assumed a virtually onmipotent role, performing the normal functions of both judge and attorney.* One result was that the juvenile justice process gradually became more inquisitorial than adversarial. Many observers believed that this lack of checks upon juvenile court judges resulted in arbitrary and capricious treatment being meted out to large numbers of juveniles. Instead of "loving concern and care" many judges have tyrannically attempted to impose their own personal brands of morality on recalcitrant youths.[18]

Perhaps the most notorious example of this was the landmark United States Supreme Court case of *In re Gault.*[19] A petition alleging delinquency was filed in the Gila County (Arizona) Juvenile Court against Gerald Gault, then a fifteen year old, alleging that he made obscene telephone calls to one Mrs. Cook. The petition was not served upon, given to, or even shown to Gerald Gault or his parents at any time. Notice of hearing was cursory, nor were Gerald or his parents told that they were entitled to be represented by counsel. The complaining witness, Mrs. Cook, was not present at the hearing and consequently was not subject to cross-examination. Prior to the hearing she had spoken to the probation officer over the telephone stating that Gerald Gault had made obscene telephone calls to her. Gerald Gault and his parents were not told that

---

*Since juvenile court proceedings have not been considered to be *criminal* cases, and since the hearings were not considered to be *trials*, their results have not been generally subject to review by appellate courts — an open invitation to abuse.

they had a right to confront and cross-examine her or any other witnesses. In addition, they were not told that Gerald did not have to testify or make a statement at the hearing, nor were they warned of the possible consequences of his making a statement. At the conclusion of the last hearing, Gerald Gault was found to be a delinquent and was committed to a state industrial school for an undetermined term, not to exceed six years. While reviewing the essential role of due process of law in the American legal system and the failure of the juvenile justice system to provide such procedural due process, the U.S. Supreme Court stated:

> Accordingly, the highest motives and most enlightened impulses led to a peculiar system for juveniles, unknown to our law in any comparable context. The Constitutional and theoretical basis for this peculiar system is — to say the least — debatable. And in practice, as we remarked in the *Kent* case, the results have not been entirely satisfactory. Juvenile court history has again demonstrated that unbridled discretion, however benevolently motivated, is frequently a poor substitute for principle and procedure. In 1937, Dean Pound wrote: 'The powers of the Star Chamber were a trifle in comparison with those of our juvenile courts...' The absence of substantive standards has not necessarily meant that children have received careful, compassionate, individualized treatment. The absence of procedural rules based upon constitutional principle has not always produced fair, efficient, and effective procedures. Departures from established principles of due process have frequently resulted not in enlightened procedure, but in arbitrariness. The Chairman of the Pennsylvania Council of Juvenile Court Judges has recently observed: 'Unfortunately, loose procedures, high-handed methods and crowded court calendars, either singly or in combination, all too often, have resulted in depriving some juveniles of fundamental rights that have resulted in a denial of due process.'[20]

Failure to observe the fundamental requirements of due process has resulted in instances, which might have been avoided, of unfairness to individuals and inadequate or inaccurate findings of fact along with unfortunate prescriptions of remedy. Due process of law is the primary and indispensable foundation of individual freedom. It is the basic and essential term in the social contract which defines the rights of the individual and delimits the powers the State may exercise over the individual. As Mr. Justice Frankfurter has said, "The history of American Freedom is, in no small measure, the history of procedure." The procedural rules which have been fashioned from the generality of due process are the most effective instruments for distilling and evaluating the conflicts presented by life and our adversary methods. It is these instruments of due process which enhance the possibility that truth will emerge from the confrontation of opposing versions and conflicting data. The Supreme Court concluded its decision in the Gault case by holding that due process requires that juveniles alleged to be delinquents are entitled to the following rights:

Notice: "Process of law requires notice of the sort we have described — that is, notice which would be deemed constitutionally adequate in a civil or criminal proceeding. It does not allow a hearing to be held in which a youth's freedom and his parent's right to his custody are at stake without giving them timely notice, in advance of the hearing, of the specific issues that they must meet."[21] In other words, the youth and his parents must be told what is happening and why.

Right to Counsel: "We conclude that the due process clause of the Fourteenth Amendment requires that in respect of proceedings to determine delinquency which may result in commitment to an institution in which the juvenile's freedom is curtailed, the child and his parent must be notified of the child's right to be represented by counsel retained by them, or if they are unable to afford counsel, that counsel will be appointed to represent the child."[22] This right reintroduces an adversarial element into the proceedings and limits the arbitrary authority of the judge; at a minimum it gives the youth a "say" through an appropriate legal representative.

Self-Incrimination: "We conclude that the constitutional privilege against self-incrimination is applicable in the case of juveniles as it is with respect to adults."[23] The articulation of this right was very important, because until the Gault case, actions against juveniles were not considered criminal actions, and therefore the safeguards built into the criminal justice system could be ignored. This finding meant that the same basic rights an adult offender had against self-incrimination also applied to children.

Confrontation and Cross-Examination: "We now hold that, absent a valid confession, a determination of delinquency and an order of commitment to a state institution cannot be sustained in the absence of sworn testimony subjected to the opportunity for cross-examination in accordance with our law and consitutional requirements."[24] This means that a child cannot be adjudged delinquent solely on the unsworn testimony of witnesses, and that evidence presented by witnesses must be subject to cross-examination. It would not be possible to adjudge Gault a delinquent on the basis of what Mrs. Cook told the probation officer over the telephone. She would have to appear in court and offer her testimony under oath and be subject to cross-examination.

In re Gault sent reverberations throughout the entire juvenile justice system, for in essence, it re-wrote the rules. Predictions of disaster were echoed throughout the land, and some local authorities were convinced the Supreme Court had surely gone too far. Empirical studies of compliance with *Gault* have shown that some juvenile court judges have refused to comply with its requirements or that they comply with only some of them.[25] Other judges have complied with *Gault* in a manner designed to minimize its impact. Where there has been substantial compliance, a major effect has been an increase in legal representation of juveniles. The presence of these lawyers, however, has brought about modest rather than revolutionary change. Rather than transforming juvenile courts into adversarially-oriented tribunals, attorneys appear to have been co-opted and have accepted the values of the juvenile justice system. The system has emerged from the challenge of *Gault* with its basic values intact, but modified to incorporate due process rights.

Diversion

Diversion from the juvenile justice system is an additional development stemming from the recognition that the system often labels and institutionalizes young people. Consequently, alternative methods of handling juvenile cases have been developed. Youths engaging in delinquent activities, especially those of a less serious nature, are routinely sent to a diversion service which refers them to some kind of appropriate treatment agency. This is a voluntary process, although refusal to take part in such a treatment program might result in a reconsideration of the decision not to proceed officially in juvenile court.

Diversion programs, often called Youth Service Bureaus, have been established in many parts of the country. The 1973 National Advisory Commission on Criminal Justice Standards and Goals recommended that youth service bureaus should be established to divert juveniles from the justice system.[26] It is rather ironic that systems have now been established to divert youths from the juvenile justice system, which was itself established to divert them from the criminal justice system!

The use of diversion recognizes the sad fact that the juvenile justice system doles out far more punishment than help, and that often the best interests of the child and of society are better served if the matter is taken out of the court's hands altogether. If the child can be placed in a program where his real problems can be diagnosed and treated, then quite obviously he will be better off. It is also worth remembering that, in spite of the "soft" language of the juvenile courts, juvenile proceedings are still essentially *legal* proceedings and like adult courts, the most that these courts have to offer is variation in punishment. If the child's problem requires something other than punishment (even though the state does not like to refer to its juvenile treatment programs by that name), it will not usually be forthcoming unless it is provided by some agency outside the courts. The following chart provides a comparison between adult and juvenile legal procedural terminology:

COMPARATIVE TERMINOLOGY

Criminal Justice System	Juvenile Justice System
Arrest	Taken into custody
Warrant	Summons
Indictment of Information	Petition
Arraignment	Initial Hearing
Trial	Hearing
Conviction	Adjudication of delinquency
Sentence	Disposition
Jail	Detention Center
Prison	Training school, Industrial school

Many of the diversion projects throughout the country have been quite successful. The problem faced by diversion programs, though, is in the screening of juveniles so that only those who are likely to benefit from treatment will be admitted. Juveniles with a history of serious crimes, especially crimes of violence, are not usually welcome in these programs and there are relatively few diversion or treatment programs which can provide the kind of intensive psychological or psychiatric treatment needed by such juveniles. Of course, many of the juveniles who are accused of those kinds of crimes, especially if they are on the legal borderline with respect to age, are simply dumped on the criminal justice system and tried as adults.

Decriminalization

Status offenses have recently become the subject of considerable concern and criticism. Status offenses, as previously discussed, are grounds for delinquency that are peculiar to children alone. These same acts, if committed by an adult, would not normally be a crime. Examples include truancy, runaway, curfew violations, and some sexual misconduct. Either included under the general category of incorrigibility or spelled out as separate grounds for delinquency are some of the more purely moralistic offenses, such as smoking, swearing, or drinking alcoholic beverages.

It is obvious that contemporary values are no longer in accord with some of these more blantantly moralistic grounds for juvenile delinquency. Also, the realization that the juvenile justice system has not been able to diagnose and correct delinquency has caused many professionals in the area to re-examine the validity and value of using these kinds of behavior as the basis for assigning the label "delinquent." As a result there has been a major trend away from using status offenses against young people. A national commission has recommended the deleting of truancy as a ground for delinquency.[27] Both another national commission and the Board of Directors of the National Council on Crime and Delinquency have advocated the removal of *all* status offenses from the juvenile codes.[28] As a result of this trend toward decriminalization, many states have revised their juvenile codes and some of these states have limited their codes to such basic grounds as the commission of a crime, habitual truancy, or incorrigibility. More liberal attitudes towards the consumption of alcohol and the use of recreational drugs have also shortened the reach of the juvenile court.

De-Institutionalization

De-institutionalization, another contemporary trend, stems from the belief that many youths emerge from the juvenile correction institutions more delinquent than when they entered. Such incarceration frequently paves the way for subsequent stays in other juvenile institutions and adult prisons by producing youths who become both dependent and "institutionalized." Indeed, many adult felons are "graduates" of these "boys schools." Like much of the juvenile justice movement, the promise of juvenile correctional institutions is still to be realized. Consequently, strong criticism has been raised against the practice of committing youths to juvenile correctional institutions. The 1973 National Advisory Commission on Criminal Justice Standards and Goals recommended that no more training schools be built and that existing schools be phased out.[29]

In some states de-institutionalization has resulted from legislative acts which permit the sending of fewer youths (or fewer categories of youths, such as dependent or neglected children) to such institutions. In other states, juvenile corrections administrators have closed institutions or limited their use. In virtually all states some juvenile court judges have lost their faith in these institutions and have made very few commitments to them. This trend, however, is not universal and some states are making greater use of such facilities than others.

Allied with and complementary to the foregoing trends (particularly de-institutionalization), is the movement toward community-based facilities.[30] This trend resulted from the lack of success of correctional institutions and the often remote location of these facilities. Community-based facilities are typically small in size, specialized in nature, and are operated by private organizations or local government. They may include non-residential treatment centers, residential facilities, foster homes, or local juvenile detention centers.

Disillusionment with the lack of accomplishments of the juvenile justice system — in addition to leading to the trends toward diversion, decriminalization, de-institutionalization, and community-based facilities — has also encouraged the development of an attitude or approach known as the *least disruptive alternative*.[31] Those who adhere to this approach believe that the juvenile justice system has counter-productive results, and they also believe that many youths will cease to commit delinquent acts *without* intervention by the juvenile justice system; many of these disruptive children will mature into responsible adults. As a result, they favor as little disruption of the lives of juveniles as is consistent with the need to protect society and the child, and they accordingly recommend the absolute minimum amount of intervention into the life of the child. It can be argued that these trends are reform measures in their orientation and are designed to enable the juvenile justice system to achieve its objectives, and to do so without running counter to the juvenile court's stated values of protection, compassion, and individualized treatment. These trends make such values attainable. Due process, for example, and its concomitant fairness may produce a child more amenable to treatment. Diversion, decriminalization, de-institutionalization, and community-based alternatives are all attempts to bring the system into accord with contemporary values and to enable it to adapt to the challenges which confront it.

There are citizens and professionals, both within and outside the juvenile justice system, whose major concern is with controlling crime. They point to the often appalling crimes of violence committed by juveniles, the massive vandalism of both private and public property, the terrorizing of elderly people by juveniles, and increased gang violence.[32] Adherents of this approach (known as the crime control model) view the rehabilitative attempts of juvenile courts as a failure and argue that the juvenile justice system shelters, permits, and even encourages youths to commit criminal acts which they know to be wrong.[33] Rather than "coddling" young criminals and strengthening their deviant behavior, those who subscribe to the crime control model feel that juvenile offenders should be quickly punished and isolated from the law-abiding community. The crime control model has great faith in the philosophy that punishment will change juvenile behavior. Adherents of this philosophy favor the isolation of juvenile offenders in county jails, detention centers, training schools, and local correctional facilities. Because of demands for control of juvenile crime, money bail is now set in some courts, grounds for waiver to criminal court have been broadened, and mandatory sentencing laws have been instituted. Unlike due process, diversion, decriminalization, and community-based facilities, such practices are directly counter to juvenile court values. Rather than helping to realize the juvenile justice movement's ideal of individualized and compassionate treatment, crime control model practices will strengthen already existing tendencies toward stereotyped and bureaucratic processing similar to the processes of the criminal justice system. If the adherents of the crime control model, both within and outside the juvenile justice system, gain strength, and corresponding practices are instituted throughout the system, then the juvenile justice system will loose its distinctiveness and become more like the criminal justice system. Factors such as the extent and increase of juvenile crime, future effectiveness of the system, and the success of the efforts to reform it may determine whether or not the juvenile justice system will become "criminalized" and thus indistinguishable from the criminal justice system. Should that happen, America'a eighty-year old experiment in "child saving" will come to an end.

Juvenile Justice : The Common View

There are many views of juvenile justice. The preceding paragraphs were largely concerned with the legal dimension of juvenile justice and pointed out the major legal/philosophical problems involved in dealing with youth crime. There is a less legalistic and more common view which reflects the opinions of large segments of the American public. This view sees uncontrolled young people intent on destroying both themselves and their society. This view is based on highly publicized cases, which appear in the news and entertainment media, and also arises from citizens' fear of crime. This view defines juvenile delinquents as violent offenders who seem to remain outside control of the courts — either criminal or juvenile. There are, of course, such people — yet they represent a very small proportion of the juvenile court's case load. By the time these people mature in their misconduct or criminal craft, they "age out" of the juvenile justice system and are dealt with by criminal courts. Moreover, when juveniles *do* commit serious crimes of violence they are usually *not* dealt with leniently.

ITEM: One Christmas Eve a seventeen year-old boy left a party with his date, a girl with whom he was casually acquainted. After leaving the party, he raped her, beat her to death with a tire-iron, and set her body on fire with gasoline. He was found the next day, wandering in the nude in near zero degree weather, still obviously under the influence of drugs. He was sentenced to life in prison.

ITEM: A sixteen year-old Texas youth who had been in an argument with another youth cut his spinal column with a linoleum knife, permanently paralyzing the victim. He said he did it on purpose, that he wanted to hurt the victim "bad." He was held in a juvenile detention facility until he was seventeen and then tried on the felony charge of maiming. He was convicted and sentenced to 20 years in the state penitentiary.

As is often the case in the criminal justice system, the question of class and status plays an important role in outcomes. For example, one case involved the son of a college professor. The boy was described as a terror; anything he could not steal he would break, and if he could not break it, he would spray it with paint. He set fire to houses, smashed windows, shot out the car windows, and committed seemingly endless acts of vandalism, much of it wanton and apparently senseless. His parents consistently denied their son's guilt, and when confronted with evidence which removed any doubt, they became sullen and hostile. The parents went to great trouble and expense defending the boy. The juvenile court was consistently sympathetic with these "concerned" parents and granted their pleas for yet another chance. Shortly before the boy's seventeenth birthday he was caught committing a burglary and subsequently prosecuted as an adult. Juvenile offenders with less spectacular records who appear in court alone or with indifferent parents are typically dealt with less leniently and with considerably less patience.

It is very difficult to say just what is "fair" and what is not; however, it is clear that *many* factors influence how a juvenile will be treated in any given case. What *is* clear is that many juveniles are involved in serious misconduct and it is difficult to always match the right problem with the right remedy. It seems that the problems of juveniles are a lot like the problems of the elderly: time takes care of everything, but time offers very little advice for dealing with new problems as they emerge on the horizon.

Juvenile Justice: An Alternative View

It is easy to be swayed by the newsworthy crimes committed by delinquents. Very seldom do we have the chance to look behind delinquent acts to examine what has really happened. We often find

379

young criminals who have gone through absolutely incredible hardships. One such case involved Noel W., an unwanted illegitimate child who was removed from his mother after authorities found him to be both abused and neglected. He was subsequently adopted by a middle-class couple who had been unable to have children of their own. Shortly after adopting Noel, the woman discovered that she was pregnant and quickly shifted the focus of her attention from Noel to the new child. After the baby was born, his foster parents became largely indifferent toward Noel, and then hostile. Noel was moved to the garage, isolated from the rest of the family, and largely ignored. In school he failed to adjust and experienced considerable difficulty in mastering the tasks assigned to him, further inciting his foster parents' wrath. Finally, when he was twelve, his foster father called the police and simply told them to take Noel away: he and his wife no longer wanted him around. The police took Noel to the county hospital, and he was confined in the psychiatric ward for several months until he could be placed with a social welfare agency. He finally wound up in a group home, from which he frequently ran away only to be returned by the police.

Noel became increasingly withdrawn and uncommunicative. Interestingly, he related to animals and found an injured hawk which he nursed to health. The hawk remained with him wherever he would go. A kind-hearted man in the community heard about Noel's case and volunteered to take him into his home. He bought Noel a car and taught him the basics of auto mechanics, and although his patience was sorely tested, the man persisted in his efforts to "reach" the boy. Unfortunately, one day Noel threatened one of the man's daughters and made an obscene suggestion to her, and the man asked Noel to leave the house. A couple of months later the man learned that Noel had been electrocuted while trying to rescue his hawk from some wires. The boy was buried at county expense in an unmarked grave, never having tasted the joys of life, not yet seventeen years of age. The juvenile courts which had dealt with him had nothing to offer.

Although Noel's case was especially tragic, the juvenile courts constantly see tragedy which most people would find incomprehensible: children who are abused, neglected, frightened, emotionally disturbed — many of whom are simply not wanted by anybody at all. Schools and social service agencies often express concern about the *problem* of such children while showing remarkable indifference to the children themselves. The sad fact is that there are too many problems and too few solutions. Most of these problems are dumped on the *legal* system which has merely been sugar-coated by calling it a *juvenile justice system.*

Consider the following cases, cited by James:

> —Chicago: A 14-year old girl breaks into violent sobs and hugs a social worker when her mother and stepfather tell the judge they do not want her any more. She was drunk when police found her. The social worker indicated the girl turned to alcohol to blur dreadful home conditions and to dull her craving for parental love and understanding.

> —Denver: A little fellow about eight tells the judge that he has no father, has trouble with his mother but likes her, and sometimes feels like leaving home. On Sunday night he 'stayed out late' and then was 'scared to come home,' so he slept on street corners and walked around. The mother wants the boy committed. As the child hangs his head and cries, the judge sentences the youth 'to the home for 30 days.'[34]

It is little wonder that some of these children lash back violently, and there is good reason to fear some of them. They are the products of an inadequate (or in some cases, non-existent) private control system and a public control system which is not yet ready to receive them — until they break forth on society in violence and fury. For example, the police in east Texas were called to the scene of a brutal double murder. The victims, a young husband and wife, had been abducted from a doughnut shop after being robbed and were driven to a remote area where they were taken into a barn. They had their hands wired behind them and were then shot in the head. The police found defecation on the woman's face. The crime was ultimately solved and the criminals brought to trial. One of the defendants, aged 22, was an illiterate drifter. He was the unwanted child of a Los Angeles prostitute and was born with a cleft palate, which was poorly corrected by surgery when the child was nine. His mother did not formally name him, and simply called him the "hare-lipped bastard." For the most part, he raised himself in alleys and streets. He left school in the elementary grades and was constantly in trouble with the authorities. He was dealt with repeatedly by the juvenile courts and social agencies, to no avail. His total disregard for human life — his own included — led to the deaths of his victims, and his hatred of all women was clear in his defecating on the face of his victim. He was sentenced to death.

The human organism is very complex and capable of adapting to considerable stress; however, failures in early maternal-infant bonding accompanied by a dearth of love, warmth, affection, and positive human contact can and do turn people into savages. The first inkling we have of this is when these children bring their problems to school; unfortunately, most schools are unable or unwilling to either recognize or deal with the problems. These problems ultimately come before the juvenile courts which are all too often just a way-station to adult courts. Fortunately, the juvenile courts are able to effectively deal with some of the less serious cases, although even in this respect they are not consistent.

Juvenile Justice And Community Relations

The problems built into our juvenile system present a seemingly endless series of dilemmas. Criminal acts committed by juveniles are usually not prosecuted as such so that hopefully the juvenile can be redeemed; yet the juvenile justice system has proven unable to provide the kinds of remediation needed. It would seem that more often than not, nothing is done: the child remains at liberty to either mature on his own or to "age out" into the criminal justice system. If the state does intervene, it often does so for offenses (status offenses) that are either not criminal in their own right or which are peculiar to children. How does all of this affect community attitudes? In the absence of empirical data, the answer to such a question must remain speculative; however, there is good reason to believe that many citizens are unhappy with the ineffectiveness of the juvenile justice system and public displeasure is likely to focus on the whole criminal justice system.

The police are well aware of the restrictions which are imposed on them in dealing with juvenile cases, and juvenile courts themselves realize that there is little that can be done. Perhaps an effective approach would be to seek greater community involvement in the juvenile justice system. If the misconduct of many juveniles represents hostility based on underlying unhappiness or frustration, then dealing with the underlying problem should eliminate the misconduct. There are two problems with this approach, however. The first is *diagnosis* and the second is *patience*. In considering diagnosis, it may be difficult and time-consuming to find out exactly why a given juvenile behaves in a disruptive fashion — and that is apt to take time and cost money which is not available. As for patience, many people and groups simply do not have much. Those who work with an offender need their efforts reinforced by appropriate responses on the part of the offender; when such reinforcement is not forthcoming (as in the case of Noel), frustration emerges and gives rise to aggression — and the helping relationship is likely to end. This is only human, but it means that those children who need the most help are also the ones least likely to get it.

In the final analysis, people want "closure" for their problems. They want a solution. In many cases, they would rather have a bad solution than none at all. When community members see problems with juveniles — especially when the juveniles differ from them significantly on the basis of such variables as race and class — they are apt to be especially open to "solutions" which they would not find appropriate in cases closer to home. It is easier to see juveniles from "the other side of town" waived to the criminal courts or sent to juvenile detention facilities. Perhaps this is the legacy of our once widely held view that crime is the domain of the "dangerous class," or perhaps it simply represents indifference to those who differ from us.

Perhaps much of the problem with juveniles is that the youth culture, which is constantly changing, tends to be so different from that of adults, and many adults measure the behavior of young people against an inappropriate or outdated set of standards. If this is compounded by cultural differences, the resulting perceptions can be even more at variance. Perhaps adults expect too much from juveniles and too little from themselves, almost as if it is the responsibility of the child to prove he is worthy of being considered a legitimate member of society as opposed to the view that it is society which must shape the child into an adult. It might also be the case that the community has placed too many expectations on schools and too few on the family, and when failure results, both the child and the criminal justice system get blamed.

Summary

Juvenile justice in America grew out of the earlier English practices in which children above the age of seven were usually treated as adults if they were formally accused of a crime. This produced a brutalizing system which ultimately led social reformers to seek better alternatives to dealing with youthful offenders. At first confined children were segregated from adult offenders, but by the end of the nineteenth century an alternative juvenile justice system began to emerge. This alternative system parallels the criminal justice system, but is based on a non-punitive, non-adversarial approach to juvenile offenders in which the court seeks to act as an interested parent on behalf of the child. The goal is not to punish, but rather to set the child on the right track. The juvenile justice system was designed to be informal, supportive, and dedicated to salvaging youths who had gotten into trouble. This alternative system, however, has fallen short of its lofty goals.

In terms of its processes, the juvenile offender (or the dependent or neglected child) comes to the attention of the juvenile court through an intake process which can be initiated by the police, school authorities, or even by parents. The merits of a child's case are examined and efforts are made to dispose of the case with the least possible amount of intervention into the child's life which is consistent with his needs and those of the community. If the matter is serious, the juvenile court must consider whether or not to waive the case directly to the criminal courts. If it retains jurisdiction, then a formal hearing may be held. The youth is not "convicted" in the conventional case, but may be adjudged "delinquent." If that proves the case, then the court must determine what should be done with him. In most cases the child is released back into the community under some kind of supervision; however, in especially serious cases the youth may be placed in state custody in some kind of residential facility.

The juvenile justice system has come under considerable criticism because in many instances the juvenile receives neither the due process afforded adult offenders nor the solicitous care intended by the founders of the system. As a result of the *Gault* case, procedural safeguards have been introduced into the juvenile justice system, although their application has been erratic. These safeguards have also had the effect of converting juvenile court cases into more adversarial hearings, although most lawyers who represent youths tend to be less aggressive on behalf of their clients than they are in adult cases.

The primary thrust in juvenile justice in the past decade has been away from charging juveniles with status offenses. The movement has been characterized by "the four D's": due-process, diversion, decriminalization, and de-institutionalization. Yet the basic problem in juvenile justice is the same as that of the criminal justice system: the conflict between the due-process and the crime control models. In the former, the rights of the accused are paramount, whereas in the latter the safety of society is. Juvenile justice is a complex and difficult area, because attempting to design remedies around age offers little positive guidance, and many of the problems are actually social and psychological problems for which legal remedies are wholly inappropriate anyway.

Discussion Questions

1. Do you think it is still necessary to have special juvenile courts, or could juveniles be more appropriately dealt with by criminal courts?

2. Does diversion in juvenile cases reflect a failure of the juvenile justice system or should diversion be viewed as a "maturing" of the system in the treatments which it offers?

3. What are the chief problems the police are likely to encounter in dealing with juvenile offenders?

4. How can advocates of the crime control model reconcile their perspective with the traditional philosophy of the juvenile court — or can they?

5. How do class, status, and race have the potential for influencing the quality of juvenile justice as it is actually administered?

6. Are community expectations, especially on the part of adults, realistic in so far as they concern juveniles?

7. In what ways can a community assist the juvenile justice system in dealing with youth problems?

8. Why are youths who are in the greatest need of help the least likely to get it?

9. How does the way in which the juvenile justice system works influence public sentiment toward the criminal justice system?

10. Should the police have the authority to make informal "station adjustments" in juvenile cases?

Glossary

INTAKE   The screening process used by a juvenile court.

SECONDARY DEVIANCE   An individual's reaction to his treatment by others which arises from an initial act of misconduct.

SOCIAL HISTORY REPORT   In juvenile courts, the document used by the court in deciding upon a course of action for a given delinquent. It is typically a combination background investigation and psychological evaluation.

WAIVER   In juvenile proceedings, the decision that a juvenile should be bound over to the criminal courts rather than be handled by the juvenile justice system.

Notes

[1] Wayne R. LaFave and Austin W. Scott, Jr., *Handbook on Criminal Law* (St. Paul, Minnesota: West Publishing Co., 1972), pp. 351-352.

[2] Anthony Platt, *The Child Savers* (Chicago: University of Chicago Press, 1969), p. 202.

[3] Some scholars assert that the juvenile justice movement was an attempt by the middle class to impose middle class values upon immigrants and the poor. See Anthony Platt, "The Rise of the Child Saving Movement: A Study in Social Policy and Correctional Reform," *The Annals of the American Academy of Political and Social Science*, 381 (January 1969): 21-38.

[4] The President's Commission on Law Enforcement and Administration of Justice, *Task Force Report: Juvenile Delinquency and Youth Crime* (Washington, D.C.: U.S. Government Printing Office, 1967), p. 3.

[5] For two accounts of early juvenile court procedure, see Julian W. Mack, "The Juvenile Court," *Harvard Law Review*, 23:104; Harvey H. Baker, "Procedure of the Boston Juvenile Court," *The Survey*, 23:643 as reprinted in Frederic L. Faust and Paul J. Brantingham, eds., *Juvenile Justice Philosophy* (St. Paul, Minnesota: West Publishing Co., 1974), pp. 150-196.

[6] LeFave and Scott, *Handbook on Criminal Law*, p. 354.

[7] For a treatment of the police - juvenile relationship see Robert W. Kobetz and Betty W. Bosorge, *Juvenile Justice Administration* (Gaithersburg, Maryland: International Association of Chiefs of Police, 1973).

[8] The quasi-judicial role of the intake officer is considered in Eugene H. Czajhoski, "Exposing the Quasi-Judicial Role of the Probation Officer," *Federal Probation*, pp. 11-12.

[9] For the right to a bail bond in the federal system see *Durst* v *U.S.*, 98 S. Ct. 849 (1978).

[10] *Kent* v *U.S.*, 383 U.S. 541, 86 S. Ct. 1045, 16 L. Ed. 2nd 84 (1966).

[11] *In re Gault*, 387 U.S. 1, 31 18 L. Ed. 3d 527, 87 S. Ct. 1428 (1967).

[12] For an excellent treatment on judging in a juvenile court see Robert M. Emersion, *Judging Delinquents: Context and Pretext in Juvenile Court* (Chicago: Oldine Publishing Co., 1969).

[13] M. Marvin Finkelstem et al., *Prosecution in the Juvenile Courts: Guideline for the Future* (Washington, D.C.: U.S. Government Printing Office, 1973), p. 17.

[14] Anthony Platt, Howard Schecther, and Phyllis Tiffany, *Indiana Law Journal*, 43, No. 3: 637.

[15] Clemens Bartollas, Stuart J. Miller, and Simon Dinitz, *Juvenile Victimization; The Institutional Paradox* (New York: Halsted Press, A Sage Publication, 1976).

[16] Robert W. Balch, "The Medical Model of Delinquency," *Crime and Delinquency* (April 1975): 116-117; Michael H. Longley, "The Juvenile Court and Individualized Treatment," *Crime and Delinquency* (January 1972): 81-82; Martin T. Silver, "The New York City Family Court; A Law Guardian's Overview," *Crime and Delinquency* (January 1972): 96.

[17] Lisa Aversa Richette, *The Throw Away Children* (New York: Dell Publishing Co., 1970).

[18] Silver, "The New York City Family Court," p. 95.

[19] *In re Gault*. For a strong argument that procedural due process rights should apply to dependent-neglect proceedings see Diane M. Faber, "Dependent — Neglect Proceedings: A Case for Procedure Due Process," *Duquesne Law Review* (1971): 651-664.

[20] *In re Gault*, 17-21.

[21] *In re Gault*, 33-34.

[22] *In re Gault*, 41.

[23] *In re Gault*, 55.

[24] *In re Gault*, 57.

[25] Norman G. Kittel, "Juvenile Justice — Twelve Years After Gault," paper presented at the Academy of Criminal Justice Science Convention, Cincinnati, Ohio, 14-16 March, 1979.

[26] Donald R. Cressey and Robert A. McDermott, *Diversion From the Juvenile Justice System* (Washington, D.C.: U.S. Government Printing Office, 1974).

[27] National Advisory Commission, *Community Crime Prevention* (Washington, D.C.: U.S. Government Printing Office, 1973), pp. 70-81.

[28] Board of Directors, *National Council on Crime and Delinquency*, "Jurisdictiotatus Offense Should Be Removed from the Juvenile Court," *Crime and Delinquency* (April 1975): 97-99; President's Commission on Law Enforcement and Administration of Justice, *The Challenge of Crime in a Free Society* (Washington, D.C.: U.S. Government Printing Office, 1973), p. 360.

[29] National Advisory Commission on Criminal Justice Standards and Goals, *Corrections* (Washington, D.C.: U.S. Government Printing Office, 1973), p. 360.

[30] Andrew Rutherford and Osman Bengur, *National Evaluation Program Community-Based Alternatives to Juvenile Incarceration* (Washington, D.C.: U.S. Government Printing Office, 1976).

[31] Edwin M. Schur, *Radical Non-Intervention: Rethinking the Delinquency Problem* (Englewood Cliffs, New Jersey: Prentice-Hall, 1973).

[32] Walter B. Miller, *Violence by Youth Gangs and Youth Groups as a Crime Problem in Major American Cities* (Washington, D.C.: U.S. Government Printing Office, 1975).

[33] The basic crime control model is set forth by Herbert Packer, *The Limits of Criminal Sanctions* (Stanford: Stanford University Press, and London: Oxford University Press, 1968), pp. 149-173.

[34] Howard James, *Crisis in the Courts* (New York: David McKay Co., Inc., 1971), pp. 58-78.

CORRECTIONS: JAILS AND PRISONS

13

"Corrections" is an umbrella term which covers a wide range of concepts and activities. It includes both community supervision of criminal offenders and the actual incarceration of persons accused or convicted of crimes. All in all, corrections is a major component of the criminal justice system, although it has relatively low visibility. Its importance is highlighted by the existence of approximately 4,500 state and local adult correctional agencies in the United States, including about 3,600 probation and parole agencies.[1] This system is responsible for controlling over a quarter of a million people — not including approximately 158,000 others who are confined in local jails on any given day, those who are at liberty within their communities on suspended or probated sentences, or individuals who are on parole from prison. The cost of this effort is staggering: corrections in the United States costs almost six billion dollars a year.[2]

Jails

Jails and prisons are not the same thing. Convicted felons who are incarcerated for more than a year are sent to *prison*. Those who are in *jail* are either awaiting trial or they are serving time (less than a year) for a less serious offense, usually a misdemeanor. In the case of those awaiting trial, many are in jail because they cannot afford bail or because it has been denied. On any given day a substantial number of people are in jail for brief periods of time for some minor offense such as driving under the influence, disorderly conduct, or shoplifting. Most of these people are released within a few hours, either after sobering up or posting a bond. There are many kinds of people in local jails; confined in one facility are "such diverse groups as those persons awaiting trial, inmates serving misdemeanor sentences, suspected mental patients, alleged parole violators, felony prisoners in transit, and chronic drunkenness offenders in the process of 'drying out.' And some jails continue to serve as a place of pretrial detention for juveniles."[3]

The role of jails has expanded over the years; their original purpose (as conceived by Henry II when he provided for the building of the first official jail at the Assize of Clarendon in 1166) was simply to provide a place where suspected offenders could be detained until they were brought to trial.[4] The task of operating the jail, or "gaol" as it was spelled in England and colonial America, fell to the sheriff, a custom which was carried over to the American colonies. In general, jails were *not* places of punishment. Punishment for most crimes was either capital or corporal. Capital punishment meant the death of the offender and corporal punishment involved physical and psychological abuse and included such punishments as branding, maiming, the use of stocks and the dunking stool, and public humiliation.[5]

In the 1600's two major developments changed the nature of corrections. In 1682, under the leadership of William Penn, the Great Law was enacted, one result of which was the establishment of the prison system in which confinement per se was to be used as a form of punishment, thus reducing the number of crimes which were punished by death or maiming.[6] The idea of using incarceration as a punishment filtered down to the local jails, and "punishments for less serious offenses were gradually written into law providing short-term detention in local jails."[7] The second major development, which came in the latter part of the 1600's, was the emergence of the "workhouse." These facilities were originally designed for the unemployed and grew out of the "poor laws" which defined vagrancy and made idleness a crime; however, before long they were also used to house not just vagrants, but petty thieves, prostitutes, and drunks as well. Before long the county jails took on many of the functions of the workhouse, and ultimately county jails emerged as places of confinement for persons awaiting trial, of people who were public nuisances (such as drunks, the mentally ill and others), and for persons being punished for minor crimes.

There are two important points concerning local jails, and taken in combination they explain many of the problems which surround these facilities. The first is that jails are *local* institutions, usually run as a part of the police department or the sheriff's office (See Table 13.1). Jails run by police departments are normally used to hold people whom they arrest pending immediate disposition of their cases. Those who are held in jail for longer periods are usually transferred to the county jail. The second point is that jails are usually considered to be places of short-term confinement.

Table 13.1

STATE AND LOCAL LAW ENFORCEMENT AGENCIES BY TYPE, WITH AND WITHOUT JAILS*

Type of Agency	With Jails	With- out Jails
Sheriff's Department	2,579	438
County Police	6	68
Municipal Police	713	12,562
TOTAL	3,298	13,068

*Source: U.S. Department of Justice, *Criminal Justice Sourcebook, 1978.* Washington, D.C.: U.S. Government Printing Office, 1979. Adapted from Table 1.3, p. 44.

Jails as Local Agencies Jails are a part of *local* government, and for this reason there have been no uniform or national standards regulating their construction, use, or administration. Thus alcoholics, the mentally ill, petty offenders, and hardened criminals have been indiscriminately mixed in most jails. Since jails are part of city or county government, they have had to depend on city councils or county commissions for funding, and local governments have not been generous in funding jails. Moreover, since the jail is a part of the police department or the sheriff's department, it must compete with other parts of their parent agency at budget time. Jails are foced into an *allocational conflict* with the remainder of the agency of which they are a part, and more often than not jails are not a high-priority item among police chiefs and sheriffs. In fact, law enforcement executives tend to view jails "as a sideline to their crime-fighting activities ..."[8] Because of this, and because many law enforcement officials are not especially sympathetic towards those whom they lock up, local jails are usually operated as inexpensively as possible. This means keeping the number of jailers to a minimum and cutting costs wherever possible. Most of the people who work in local jails are not trained for their jobs, but learn as they go. Many of the police officers or deputy sheriffs who work in jails are there as a result of having fallen from favor within the department; being assigned to the jail is not a prestigious job within most departments. Civilian jailers are usually individuals with minimal education and generally make lower salaries which match their limited abilities.

Jails as Temporary Holding Facilities . Unlike prisons, which deal with long-term inmates, jails confine their inmates for relatively short periods of time, in many instances only for a matter of hours. Because of this, the primary emphasis in most jails is on *security* and *custodial convenience*. Security measures are employed to keep inmates from hurting or killing themselves or others, to maintain order within the jail, and to keep the inmates from escaping. When prisoners are first admitted they must surrender any objects which could be used to hurt themselves or others, and they must also give up any valuables they might have for which other inmates might hurt them. The first step is usually that of taking the prisoner's belongings away from him. In many jails prisoners are clothed in special uniforms so they can be easily distinguished from non-prisoners and also for reasons of sanitation.

Security is obviously facilitated by locking prisoners in cells; this keeps them away from one another most of the time and prevents their escape. It also allows a small number of jailers to keep an eye on a large number of prisoners. "Prisoner-proof" toilets and lights provide the functions for which they were intended while also preventing inmates from misusing them. Showers and other cleanup facilities are usually restricted to a common bathing area. This means that vomit and excrement deposited on cell floors often remain there until routine cleanup periods arrive, adding to the foul odor characteristic of many jails. Visitors are restricted and gifts brought to prisoners are closely inspected for contraband items such as drugs, weapons, or tools — if inmates are even allowed to receive gifts. Lights are left on at all hours, and jails are noisy, smelly places where people come and go at all hours of the day.

Although security measures are necessary, they are ultimately degrading and dehumanizing. Prisoners are forced to give up not only their freedom and possessions, but they lose their privacy as well. Because of the custodial restrictions imposed in most jails, there is seldom anything to do, and the atmosphere in most jails is oppressive and depressing. Because jails are short-term places of confinement, few jail administrators feel it is necessary to provide libraries, recreational facilities or health care services for other than emergencies. Although some jails have good food, most do not and in many jails, prisoners are fed only twice a day. Apparently the general sentiment is that prisoners can tolerate prevailing jail conditions because they will not be there all that long anyway.

The result is that jails are thoroughly distasteful places. Richard Velde, former head of the Law Enforcement Assistance Administration, has referred to them as "festering sores in the criminal justice system," and has said that they are, "...without question, brutal, filthy cesspools of crime — institutions which serve to brutalize and embitter men, to prevent them from returning to a useful role in society."[9] All of these and other related problems are the product of circumstances beyond any one person's control. Police chiefs and sheriffs have higher priorities; antiquated facilities cost too much to replace or renovate, especially in times of high inflation and taxpayer revolts. Prisoners themselves often damage or destroy anything they can, and jail administrators are loathe to replace non-essentials destroyed by inmates. Those who work in jails actually have very few options regarding what they can do. If the problem were simply one of dishonesty or incompetence, it would be reasonably easy to solve; unfortunately, all of the participants of the "jail game" are locked into their roles and are guided by their own particular institutional imperatives.

Although informed citizens may be appalled by the conditions in jails, it is probable that the average person on the street knows nothing about them — and could care less! If letters to the editors of local newspapers across the country are any indication of popular sentiment, a great many people feel that those who are in jail are being treated exactly as they ought to be treated. After all, it seems obvious that one does not go to jail for being good, and that people *ought* to be punished for their misbehavior. When prisoners are afforded decent treatment and are given some small modicum of consideration, cries of "coddling criminals" and allegations of turning jails into "country clubs" quickly emerge. Of course, most people never see the inside of a jail and have no idea of what they so quickly and glibly expect others to tolerate. Because of the need for security and institutional convenience, jails are an invisible component of the criminal justice system, and because they are hidden from view, the public is not able to make accurate judgments about them.

Prisons

A person convicted of a serious crime is subjected to major changes in his status. He loses a variety of rights and privileges, some of which may never be restored (such as the right to vote or to enter certain businesses or professions). The most important privilege he stands to lose is his freedom. A substantial proportion of those persons convicted of felonies are sent to prison. There are many kinds of prisons, but the major means by which institutions are classified is by their level of security.

Maximum Security Prisons[10]   From 1830 to 1900 most prisons built in the United States reflected the basic principle of security. These prisons were characterized by high walls, rigid internal security, cage-like cells, sweat shops, a bare minimum of recreation space, and practically nothing else. They kept the prisoners in and the public out, and that was all that was either expected or attempted. Many of these prisons were constructed so well that they have lasted up to the present time; in fact, 56 of them are still in use, although some have been remodeled and expanded.

Any attempt to describe the "typical" maximum security prison is hazardous. One was constructed almost two centuries ago; another was opened in 1972. The largest confines more than 4,000 inmates; another, less than 60. Some contain massive undifferentiated cell blocks, each caging as many as 500 men or more. Others are built in small modules housing less than 16. The industries in some are archaic sweat shops, whereas others have large and modern factories. Many provide absolutely no inside recreation space and only a minimum outside, while others have excellent gyms, recreation yards, and auditoriums. Some are dark, dingy, depressing dungeons, while others are well-lit and sunny. In one, the early warning system consists of cow bells strung along chicken wire atop a masonry wall, while in others closed circuit television and sensitive electronic sensors monitor the corridors and fences.

Maximum security institutions are geared to the fullest possible supervision, control, and surveillance of inmates. Design and program choices optimize security. Buildings and policies restrict the inmate's movement and minimize his control over his environment. Other considerations, such as the inmate's individual or social needs, are responded to only in conformity with security requirements. Trustworthiness on the inmate's part is not anticipated; in fact, the opposite is taken for granted.

Technology has brought much to the design and construction of these institutions, and the development of custodial tools has far outpaced skill in reaching inmates and in using rapport with them to maintain security or control. A modern maximum security institution represents the victory of external control over internal reform.

This kind of prison is invariably surrounded by a masonry wall or double fence with manned gun towers. Electronic sensing devices and lights impose continuous surveillance and control. Inside the institution, the need for security has dictated that men live in cells, not rooms. Doors, which might afford privacy, are replaced by grilles of tool-resistant steel. Toilets are open to view and showers are taken under supervision.

Control, so diligently sought in these facilities, is not limited to structural considerations. All activity is weighed in terms of its relationship to security, and eating meals is no exception. Prisoners often sit on fixed backless stools and eat without knives and forks at tables which do not provide salt, pepper, or other condiments. Visits by outsiders are rigidly controlled; relatives must communicate with inmates by telephone and can see them only through double layers of glass. All contacts take place under the watchful eye of guards, and searches precede and follow visits.

Internal movement is limited by strategic placement of bars and grilles which specifically define where inmates can go. Areas of inmate concentration or possible illegal activity are monitored by correctional officers or by closed circuit television. "Blind spots" — areas which cannot be supervised — are avoided in the design of maximum security prisons. Places for privacy or small group activity are structurally (if not operationally) precluded. As a result, maximum security institutions are characterized by high perimeter security and operational regulations which attempt to curtail movement and maximize control over the inmates.

Medium Security Prisons   Since the early 20th century, means of housing the offender in other than maximum security prisons have been explored. Developments in the behavioral sciences, the increasing importance of education, dominance of the work ethic, and changes in technology have led to modified treatment methods. At the same time, the field services (probation and parole) have increased. Institutions have been established to handle special inmate populations. Prisons began to utilize psychological and sociological knowledge and skills to classify prisoners. Pre-trial holding centers were separated from those holding felons who had already been convicted. Finally, different levels of security (maximum, medium, and minimum) were developed. Much of the major correctional construction in the past 50 years has been of medium security institutions.

Today medium security institutions probably embody most of the ideals and goals of the early correctional reformers. It is in these facilities that the most intensive correctional or rehabilitative efforts are attempted. Inmates are exposed to a variety of programs intended to help them become useful members of society; however, the predominant consideration is still that of security.

Internal security is usually maintained by locks, bars, and concrete walls; by a clear separation of activities; by highly defined movement paths both indoors and outdoors; by schedules and "head counts"; and by sightline supervision and the use of electronic devices. Housing areas, medical and dental treatment rooms, school rooms, recreational and entertainment facilities, counseling offices, vocational training and industrial shops, administrative offices and maintenance facilities are usually clearly separated; occasionally they are located in individual compounds which have their own fences. A complex series of barred gates and guard posts controls the flow of traffic from one area to another. Central control stations keep track of movement at all times. Circulation is restricted to specified corridors or outdoor walks, with certain spaces and movement paths being out of bounds. Closed circuit television and alarm networks are widely used. Locked steel doors predominate, and bars or concrete substitutes line corridors, surround control points, and cross all external windows and even some internal windows as well.

Housing units in medium security prisons vary from crowded dormitories to private rooms with furniture. Dormitories may house as many as 80 persons or as few as 16. Some individual cells have grilled fronts and doors. The variations found in the maximum security prisons are also seen in medium security prisons, but they are not so extreme, possibly because medium security prisons are such a recent development.

Several heartening developments have occurred recently in the construction of medium security prisons. Campus-type facilities have been designed that largely eliminate the cramped oppressiveness of most confinement. Widely separated buildings are connected by meandering pathways, and modulated ground surfaces are designed to reduce monotony. Attractive residences house small groups of inmates in single rooms. Schools, vocational education buildings, gymnasiums, and athletic fields compare favorably with those of the best community colleges, yet external security provided by double cyclone fences and internal security enforced by excellent staff and unobtrusive building design protect the public from the inmates and the inmates from one another.

Minimum Security Prisons   The facilities in this category are diverse but generally have one feature in common. They are relatively open, and consequently custody is a function of *classification* rather than prison hardware. The principal exceptions are the huge prison plantations on which entire penal populations serve time. Minimum security institutions range from large drug rehabiliation centers to small farm, road, and forestry camps located throughout America.

Most but not all minimum security facilities have been created to serve the economic needs of society and only incidentally the correctional needs of the offenders. Cotton is picked, lumber is cut, livestock is raised, roads are built, forest fires are fought, and parks and government buildings are maintained. These are all legitimate tasks for prisoners, especially while our prison system still receives large numbers of offenders who are a minimal threat to themselves or others. Moreover, open prisons probably do serve therapeutic purposes by removing men for the stifling prison environment, separating the young and unsophisticated from the predators, and by substituting controls based on trust rather than on bars. However, these remote facilities have important deficiencies. They seldom provide educational or service resources other than work. Moreover, the predominantly rural labor bears no relationship to the work skills required for the urban life to which most of the inmates will eventually return. Separation of the prisoner from his real world can become almost as complete as it would have been had he been sent to a maximum security prison.

The Institutional Imperative:
The Historical Legacy

Like most other institutions, prisons started out as *instruments*. They were an alternative to the horrible punishments of mutilation or death which were previously inflicted on people convicted of felonies. The death penalty is as old as man himself and has been practiced in nearly all parts of the world. There are several reasons why the death penalty has been so widely used. First, it is quick and easy, or at least it has been so until modern times. Second, the death penalty *did* seem to solve the problem: offenders who received capital punishment certainly did not repeat their crimes! Finally, until recently, life has always seemed cheap. Death has always been man's constant companion and perhaps because in the past it was never very far away, death was not as feared as it is today. High infant mortality rates claimed a large proportion of all newborn babies; diseases which are easily cured or arrested today took a heavy toll before the era of modern medicine and hygiene; and public health disasters like the plague claimed millions of lives and were so catastrophic that when they swept through Europe, many thought the world had come to an end![11] The average person's lifespan was about half of what it is today and the world was seen as a fearful place in which any number of uncontrollable events could take the lives of rich and poor alike. In this context, the death penalty did not seem such a terrible thing; in a sense, it was almost an extension of normality.[12]

Perhaps it was not the death penalty per se that came to disturb people so much as it was the number of crimes for which it could be applied. In eighteenth century England there were over two hundred crimes for which a person could be executed! During the eighteenth century western society went through a period of intellectual change referred to as the Age of Enlightment. New ideas in science and the humanities and new political institutions emerged, and man's perception of himself began to change as the fetters of the medieval period began to fall away. Montesquieu stated that harsh punishments served to undermine morality while Bentham argued his utilitarian position and applied it to the administration of justice. Cesare Beccaria electrified society with his classic *Essay on Crimes and Punishment* which was published in 1764. In this tract Beccaria set forth the radical notions that the prevention of crime was more important than its punishment and that the certainty of punishment was a better deterrent to crime than the severity of punishment. He also urged the use of imprisonment as a punishment for crimes as opposed to the brutal death sentences which were common in his day. He was so concerned about the backlash he expected from his work that he published it anonymously! Instead, his reasoned and compassionate ideas fell on fertile ground and were echoed throughout Europe, marking the turning point in man's perspective on how to deal with offenders.

One of the leading figures in the New World was William Penn, the Quaker leader who founded Pennsylvania. In 1682 Penn's "Great Law" was enacted; it was a humane code which was well ahead of its time. It provided for a house of corrections where punishment took the place of executions. Prisoners were sentenced to hard labor, and the only capital crime was premeditated murder. Although the Great Law was repealed in 1718 after Penn's death, the seeds had been sown. In the latter part of the eighteenth century the United States found itself in the position of trying to figure out how to deal with persons convicted of crimes, and the founding fathers were were well acquainted with the new ideas produced by the Enlightenment. In 1776 the first American Penitentiary Act was passed, although its implementation was delayed by the American Revolution.[13] After the war, the Philadelphia Quakers managed to secure legislation making a wing of Philadelphia's Walnut Street Jail a penitentiary for the housing of felons not under sentence of death. It was to be used exclusively for the *correction* of convicted felons.[14]

After the turn of the century, prisons sprang up in many states: in Kentucky and Virginia in 1800; in Massachusetts in 1805; in Vermont in 1809; in Maryland and New Hampshire in 1812; in Ohio in 1816; and in Georgia in 1817. In the beginning there was conflict over how prisons should manage their inmates. In the "Pennsylvania System" inmates at the Eastern State Penitentiary were kept in solitary confinement and were completely isolated from one another. The prisoners engaged in solitary labor under the supervision of prison officials. The Pennsylvania reformers were certain that if the prisoners were first subjected to enforced idleness and then given work, they would be grateful and the work would instill good habits and discipline in them. From time to time outside visitors would come to the prison and visit with inmates, providing them with instruction in religion and morality. The advocates of the Pennsylvania System believed that inmates would have time to dwell on their misdeeds, become penitent, and ultimately become morally reformed, useful members of society.

A competing model, the "Auburn System," was based on the way prisoners were managed in the New York Penitentiary at Auburn. In this prison inmates were confined in solitary cells, but unlike the Pennsylvania System, they ate and worked together. Although they ate and worked in "congregate" areas, prisoners were not allowed to communicate with one another. Discipline was extremely harsh at Auburn, and if a prisoner committed an infraction, he was quickly subjected to harsh punishment. Eland Lynds, the notorious warden of Auburn (and later of Sing-Sing) believed that all prisoners were cowards and that they could not be reformed until their spirits were broken. He particularly enjoyed administering punishment with a cat-o-nine tails, a whip with barbs of metal in leather strips which gouged flesh out of those being beaten.

Although the Pennsylvania System was popular, it was expensive to build and operate whereas the Auburn System, by using congregate labor, was able to produce more goods. Ultimately the Auburn System prevailed, and throughout the nineteenth century prisons which opened in the United States were based on the Auburn model. During the nineteenth century men who went to prison faced a whole new world: they were subjected to grinding humiliation, beatings, enforced idleness and pointless labor, and a daily regimen which is almost incomprehensible by today's standards.

What we have today essentially represents the results of a modification of the Auburn System, with some advancement in technology. It is a system which was created almost two hundred years ago and which has simply been adapted to contemporary requirements to whatever extent possible. Although the draconian discipline is pretty much gone and enforced silence is no longer maintained, prisons continue to warehouse men under dehumanizing and abnormal conditions. Much of the reform effort is not designed to change the basic nature of prisons per se, but rather to keep people out of them in the first place through community-based correctional schemes, or to get them out early through graduated release programs or parole. Although most states do try to separate inmates through classification techniques, and although the intentional brutality of the nineteenth century is no longer a part of everyday routine, prisons remain what they have always been: dumping grounds for some of society's villains and nuisances.

Part of the problem is the enormous cost most states have invested in their prison systems. This means that it is difficult to stop doing what they have been doing for a long time and start doing something different. The prisons are very much a part of state government and most of them are perpetuated by an inexorable bureaucratic inertia.

A state prison system represents a great deal more than just the warehousing of inmates. It involves the employment of many people whose livelihood is dependent on the continued operation of prisons, and in some states where the prisons run large farms and factories, they represent an economic *asset* to the state, and money-conscious state legislators are reluctant to tinker with this asset. Finally, significant changes in the prison system would require large cash outlays — something that neither politicians nor the public is willing to tolerate, especially in light of the fact that there are no clear acceptable alternatives to the imprisonment of at least some kinds of offenders, and since so much controversy surrounds the purposes of prisons.

Corrections As A Collective Good

For corrections to be a collective good, it must provide some indivisible benefit; it must achieve a positive end which benefits society as a whole. What then are the benefits of corrections? There are several, and they have been individually and collectively used as the justification for maintaining the American system of corrections.

Deterrence   One social benefit of corrections is that the entire process, in all of its many forms, is believed to act as a deterrent to crime. Corrections does this at two levels. The first level involves *general deterrence* and assumes that the punishment of at least some offenders is effective in preventing others from following in their footsteps. *Specific deterrence*, on the other hand, works on the individual offender and assumes that if a person is punished enough for his misbehavior he will not repeat it. Taken together, general and specific deterrence use the punishment meted out by "corrections" to make the pains of crime outweigh its pleasures. This whole concept is based on the idea of "free

402

will" which argues that man can make his own choices for good or ill. This position was taken by Jeremey Bentham (1748-1832), a contemporary of Beccaria.[15] Bentham assumed that man is rational and will consciously choose pleasure over pain. He therefore suggested that a criminal act should carry with it enough pain via punishment to offset its pleasure.

The issue of deterrence, however, is very complex and to a certain extent is poorly understood. It is obvious that punishment does deter some kind of behavior; however, in linking the concept of crime to behavior and in designing penal measures to punish that behavior, the relationship becomes almost unwieldy. For one thing, some deviant "criminal" behavior is irrational and the threat of punishment has little effect. In other words, the use of punishment as a deterrent supposes rationality on the part of the actor — and this is not always the case. When Jack Ruby shot Lee Harvey Oswald, President Kennedy's assassin, he did it in the police station in Dallas, Texas, as Oswald was being escorted by a large group of officers (not only was escape out of the question, but it was also likely that Ruby himself might be shot). In some cases misbehavior is virtually forced on people through the process of secondary deviance, and there are many whose value structure has taught them that their behavior is normatively correct; indeed, this is one of the major problems in a pluralistic society. Schafer recognized this when he noted that the "law is the formal expression of the value system of the prevailing social power." He went on to say that "The law is coercive and negative, but it is also positive in that it affirms the values of the ruling social power. As such it is not always concerned with reality: not what is but what should be is its central concern."[16] If people behave in ways in which *they* believe to be proper, given their circumstances, it is unlikely that they will be deterred by the existence of punishment for that behavior — they are more likely to be deterred by the *probability* of being punished. A good case in point is the national sport of speeding on the highways. Virtually all drivers know that there is a nation-wide speed limit of 55 miles per hour, but how many people abide by that speed limit? Countless drivers have installed radar detectors and citizen-band radios to circumvent the speed limit! The desire to avoid punishment can be dealt with quite effectively by avoiding the people who can punish you! Even in the case of serious crimes, the probability of punishment is relatively low. Many crimes are never reported to the police, and each level of the criminal justice system screens out many offenders.[17] Thus although punishment can and does deter crime, it is important to ask such questions as what *kind* of punishment is the *best* deterrent for *which* crimes? Under what circumstances and by what means is it best applied? What is the relative probability that a given form of punishment will actually be imposed on the person who commits the crime for which it would be the most appropriate form of punishment?

Incapacitation   The collective good of *public safety* is achieved when a person who would harm others is incapacitated. Quite obviously, if a would-be offender is physically restrained from committing crimes, then the crimes he might otherwise commit do not take place.* Putting people in prison is one way of incapacitating them, but it is not clear just how effective imprisonment is. If it makes the offender worse, has anything been accomplished by taking him out of circulation for a few years? Is imprisonment the *best* way to incapacitate? Other techniques can be and have been used. They include such things as deportation, castration, amputation, and psychosurgery — but some of these techniques (even though they might be very effective) are neither ethically nor legally acceptable.

Rehabilitation   The goal of rehabilitation serves the collective good of *social harmony*; it not only restores the equilibrium disturbed by the criminal's acts, but it also renders the offender socially productive. Rehabilitation is, in principle, an ideal solution to the problem of crime and it is a goal which has long been sought by the criminal justice system. The concept of rehabilitation rests on a foundation suggested by the medical model: criminals are "sick" and can be cured. There are, in fact, some mental or physical illnesses which manifest themselves in what we choose to interpret as criminal acts: some forms of temporal lobe epilepsy, organic brain dysfunction, psychoneurotic and character disorders all produce behaviors which can get an individual in trouble with the law. Disturbances in the body's blood chemistry and toxicity resulting from the presence of certain substances can likewise result in dangerous or disruptive behavior. If this is the case, the offender should be considered a medical or psychiatric problem rather than a legal problem — although such neat distinctions are often difficult to make. What becomes even more difficult is to diagnose someone as being "socially" sick — which underlies much of the philosophy of correctional rehabilitation. This problem has been dealt with through vocational training, education, small-group counseling, tattoo removal and a variety

---

*Criminals who are "incapacitated" by being put in prison are not necessarily prevented from committing crimes against other inmates or prison guards!

of other techniques designed to get offenders to give up their misconduct. In spite of the fact that nothing seems to work, we continue to try, and we also continue to try to rehabilitate people by punishing them. As Silberman notes, "As instruments of punishment, prisons have been a resounding success; they never have achieved their goal of rehabilitation."[18] Again, the questions of *who* is to be rehabilitated, *why* it should be done, and *how* it is to be accomplished are important issues. Just what are the relationships between the various forms of punishment and the various kinds of rehabilitation? Do prisons have the wherewithal on the one hand to rehabilitate, and they negate it through the simultaneous experience of imprisonment?

Retribution   Retribution is vengeance, pure and simple. As Packer has said, the "morally derelict" deserve to be punished.[19] Retribution is an ancient concept and one of our most enduring. It goes back to the Roman law, *Lex talionis,* and is an inescapable component of our correctional philosophy. Retribution represents the "setting right" of a wrong and must be considered a collective good, for without retribution, what would be the utility of good behavior? The state imposes retribution for a very good reason: if it were left to the injured party to do so, then some crimes would go unpunished because of the inability of the victim to act against those who harmed him. In other cases, the retribution wrought by the victim would transcend the crime for which it was being administred. It is very difficult for a person to view acts against him in an objective light. Thus the *lex talionis* not only cries out for "an eye for an eye" but it also says, "and nothing more!" The state therefore regulates retribution through the laws which define crimes and set punishments. Through the vehicle of retribution, it secures the consensus of society and the general assent to government by law rather than through personal vengeance.

Through the use of a wide range of correctional efforts, society attempts to achieve a set of transcendant collective goods. They include social harmony, justice (equality under the law), stability, and the ability of citizens to be secure in their homes, persons, and possessions. These collective goods are objectives which the system seeks to achieve through a variety of means, each of which is an instrument that has become an institution. These institutions are highly fragmented and poorly coordinated, and most rest on assumptions that are to some degree questionable.

The Fragmentation Of Corrections

Corrections is not centrally administered within a given jurisdiction, nor do all of its practices fall within the purview of the same agency. In a nutshell, corrections refers to what is done with persons convicted of crimes. Sending them to prison or some other residential facility is only one possibility. In some cases the courts see fit to allow some offenders to remain at large within the community — although with certain restrictions placed on them.

Probation Probation amounts to *constructive custody*; that is, although the person is at large in his community, he is still under the direct control and supervision of the state. This departure from incarceration upon conviction has its roots in a number of earlier practices, such as "benefit of clergy" which began in the 12th century and was based on the claim that clerics should be exempt from the civil courts and should answer to ecclesiastical courts alone where they would receive much lighter treatment. The test of being a "cleric" consisted of being able to read the opening words of verse of the 51st Psalm ("Have mercy upon me, O God, according to thy loving kindness: according unto the multitude of thy tender mercies blot out my transgression"). This was known as the "neck-verse" because a person who could claim benefit of clergy could avoid being hanged for his crime. The practice was later extended to laymen as well as clerics, and it was a major device to modify the severity of the criminal law. The practice was abolished by statute in 1827. The first probation measure in the United States, however, came through the efforts of John Augustus, a Boston shoemaker. In 1841 Augustus, a spectator in the Boston Police Court, was moved to intercede on behalf of a man who had been brought before the court as a common drunkard. Augustus asked the judge to release the drunkard to his custody, which the judge agreed to do. When the man returned to court three weeks later, the judge was impressed with his improvement and he fined him one cent. For the next 18 years Augustus took almost 2,000 defendants from the court and worked with them. In 1878 Massachusetts passed the first probation law, formally creating a practice which rapidly spread throughout the country.

Probation consists of four basic elements:
- The suspension of a sentence;
- The creation of a status;
- The imposition of conditions; and
- Supervision.[20]

Probation is indicated when the safety of the community is not jeopardized and when it is clear that incarceration is not in the offender's best interests. In probation the person who is convicted is given a prison sentence, but the actual execution of the sentence is suspended provided he meets certain conditions under the supervision of a probation officer who is an officer of the court. If the offender satisfies the terms of his probation, he is discharged from his sentence. In order for probation to be effective, its conditions should be carefully tailored to meet the needs of both society and the offender. No conditions should be imposed on the probationer unless they can be met. Obviously, if probation is to be successful, the courts which administer it should have adequate staff and resources to monitor the probationer's progress and to make certain the conditions of the probated sentence are being met. Some of the conditions which the courts may impose include the requirement of steady employment; the avoidance of associates who are ex-convicts; payment of restitution to victims; not changing one's address or marrying without the consent of the court; support of one's spouse and children; and regular meetings with the probation officer. Some states also require probationers to pay the court a fee to offset the administrative cost of the court's services to the probationer. Probation saves the state a considerable sum of money and gives the offender a chance to mend his ways without being deprived of his liberty.

The biggest problems with probation are (1) that it is not given as it should be, and (2) that probationers receive inadequate supervision while on probation. With respect to the former, many individuals receive probation as the result of a negotiated plea in which the offender agrees to plead guilty in return for a probated sentence. Although this may be a proper trade-off in some cases, in others it amounts to a free ride. As to the second issue, that of adequacy of supervision, some probation officers have such large case loads that it is impossible for them to give each probationer the attention he deserves. Some officers simply instruct their probationers to come by and see them at regular intervals at which time they question them on how they are doing — but never follow up to see if the probationer is telling the truth. Properly administered, probation can be one of the most cost-effective and beneficial components of the correctional system.

Confinement   In cases where probation is not indicated, the offender is sentenced to an "active" term. Of course, not all offenders are equal, and it is necessary to segregate prisoners according to their unique requirements. Although prison systems vary a great deal from one state to another, most of them maintain different facilities for different classes of offenders, and in many prisons the first step in the confinement process is the screening of prisoners to see just where within the system they should be placed.

The reception process starts when the inmate is delivered to the prison's admitting unit, which receives inmates from sentencing courts. The inmate is delivered, along with a true copy of the court's commitment, signed by the sentencing judge and impressed with the court's official seal. At the time of admission, the prisoner is provided with a thorough physical examination and is photographed and fingerprinted.

After being admitted, the offender is processed by *classification* personnel who must place the inmate within the system. Where the inmate will be housed is normally based on his age, sex, type of offense, length of sentence, degree of custody risk, and the requirements of the correctional institution itself. Part of this classification process includes the administering of a wide variety of psychological tests which ultimately become a part of the inmate's "jacket" or correctional case summary.

While this screening and classification is in progress, the inmate will also be indoctrinated into the requirements of the world into which he is entering. This entire process is used to develop and coordinate the custody level, work assignment, housing needs, and rehabilitation requirements of the offender so that his placement in the institution will result in both the greatest benefit and the least harm to all parties concerned.

The classification procedure can be divided into four steps and is actually an on-going process. The first step is the referral, a formal report-making recommendation which provides the rationale for the offender's institutional status. The second step is the classification authority's decision (subject to appropriate review) which considers relevant background information, the referral, departmental needs, and the offender's opinions and interests. The classification committees make decisions concerning the offender's assignment and prepare reports providing the necessary instructions and reasons for his assignment. The third step in the classification process is the implementation of the classification decision with respect to custody, work, housing, and program activities. The fourth step is the evaluation of the offender's performance and progress. This evaluation information is collected and utilized in future referrals, classification committee decisions, and assignment implementations.

There are essentially two types of classifications: initial and periodic review. The initial classification usually occurs within two or three weeks after an offender is admitted to an institution. This is the process which includes the utilization of professional examinations, such as psychometric tests, behavioral observation, the collection of background information, receipt of reports of community resources, estimation of the offender's degree of dangerousness, his escape potential, and the development of correctional recommendations. The results of this detailed intake screening are transmitted to the correctional unit to which the inmate is assigned.

The second major type of classification — periodic review (reclassification) — consists of any action which occurs *after* initial classification and which reviews or changes the inmate's status. It may occur for any number of reasons, such as custody review, program review, reassignment, or work release. A periodic reclassification review of all inmates (except death row residents) is required on a regular basis in most prison systems in the United States.

Parole The overwhelming majority of persons who do leave prisons leave them early; they are released on *parole* before they have served their maximum term in prison. Parole is the "release of an offender from a penal or correctional institution, after he has served a portion of his sentence, under continued custody of the state and under conditions which permit his reincarceration in the event of misbehavior."[21] It is similar to probation except that in parole the offender has actually gone to prison before being granted his freedom. In both probation and parole, the offender is technically under state control and must abide by certain conditions. If he violates those conditions, the offender may be placed in confinement. Probation is always granted by the sentencing court, whereas parole is granted by administrative decision either by the correctional institution itself or by a state board of parole.

Another distinction needs to be made, and that is the difference between *conditional release* and parole. Conditional release amounts to an automatic early release from prison based on good behavior or some other criteria. The inmate released from prison on a conditional release remains technically under state supervision until the expiration of the time called for in his maximum sentence. Prisoners released on parole are let out of prison prior to the expiration of their sentence under terms authorized by a parole board, and they also serve the balance of their term under state control. Prisoners released on parole must abide by a set of conditions specified by the parole authority and must report periodically to their parole officer. The decision to grant parole rests with the parole authority, and even though an offender may be eligible for parole, that is no guarantee that it will be granted. Some states and the United States

Prison Bureau release individuals on *mandatory paroles*, which removes the discretionary power of the parole commission and makes parole a "right" after the prisoner has served a specified amount of time. Mandatory paroles are commonly applied during the later months of a prison sentence, even if the inmate has been previously denied parole.

The use of parole was pioneered at the Elmira, New York Reformatory, which confined its inmates under indeterminate sentences. If the individual's behavior was satisfactory, he could be released for a parole term during which he was required to report to a sponsor who kept abreast of his conduct. The system proved satisfactory and was soon adopted in all major prison systems in the United States.

Parole is not, however, a simple matter. Parole authorities must concern themselves with the degree of risk to the public posed by the release of an offender. They must also be sensitive to public sentiment for or against certain individuals who are eligible for parole. They must also consider their own purely subjective impressions of whether or not the offender has "done enough time," as well as the determination of whether or not additional confinement would be more harmful than beneficial. None of these questions have easy answers.

The Power Setting Of Corrections

As Jacobs has pointed out, "prisons do not exist in a vacuum: they are part of a political, social, economic and moral order."[22] Correctional facilities, like all other social institutions, must function within the context of the larger society of which they are a part, and that larger society sets the outer limits which define the role and scope of all public agencies. As one writer has observed, "correctional programs must pass the test of compatibility with public sentiment. That test is administered by the representatives of the people in their legislative role."[23] He goes on to say that politicians are sensitive to public opinion, and if "an unenlightened public calls for an unenlightened correctional measure, the politicians will be strongly influenced by the sentiment of the public."[24]

As an agency of government, corrections operates in a power setting which is different from that of the other elements of the criminal justice system. Like the courts, corrections is largely invisible.* What little most people know of corrections comes from what they see on the news and entertainment media and what they learn through conventional wisdom. Since they do not have access to corrections, people must base their

*The invisibility of the courts stems from public apathy. The public may certainly go to the courts and watch them work. The same cannot be said of correctional facilities.

sentiments on what is available, and for the most part that consists of press reports of notorious criminal cases. And notorious cases, by their nature, deal with offenders whose crimes are particularly repugnant, individuals such as Charles Manson or Richard Speck, two notorious multiple-murderers. The crimes of these types of people are not likely to generate sympathy for either the more conventional prison inmates or the people who must work with them.

Low visibility is compounded by the fact that prisons are *state* agencies, although they serve the needs of local communities. Local communities tend to see prisons problems as *state* problems, problems which *someone else* must solve. In the final analysis, public opinion concerning corrections seems to fall somewhere between indifference and hostility. This means that the improvement of corrections — which costs money — is likely to be a very low priority in most states, even where prison problems are clearly identified and their solutions urgently needed. This was apparently the case in New Mexico prior to the bloody riot which took 33 lives:

> When 11 inmates escaped last December from the Penitentiary of New Mexico in Santa Fe, the state called in Raymond K. Procunier, former director of the California prison system, to look at the prison's security system. On Jan. 14, Procunier issued a scathing indictment of the penitentiary, saying that the prison was overcrowded, understaffed, and, worst of all, that the guards, most of whom were recent high school graduates, had absolutely no training. By failing to staff the prison properly and train the guards, he wrote, New Mexico state officials were 'playing Russian roulette with the lives of inmates, staff and the public.'
> On Feb. 2, New Mexico lost the game of Russian roulette. The penitentiary exploded in the most violent and destructive riot since 43 inmates and hostages were killed at the Attica Correctional Facility in New York in 1971.[25]

A year before the riot at the New Mexico Penitentiary, the State contracted with the American Justice Institute to study its prison industries program; their report concluded that "the Penitentiary of New Mexico was one of the most poorly administered...." prisons the researchers had ever encountered.[26] The situation at the penitentiary was well known — and yet nothing was done.

The "sovereign" of the corrections system is the warden of the particular institution, even though he may report to a state director of corrections. In some states wardens are appointed by governors and in others they are selected on a merit basis; thus some wardens are well-trained and experienced professionals, while in other states they are not. In either event, prisons are dependent on state legislatures for funding, and as is typical with budgeting in government, most prison systems must operate next year pretty much like they did last year, because budgets do not generally encourage or allow a great deal of innovation. Most budgets simply perpetuate what has already been done, with minor modifications. Prison officials can exercise control over some of the productivity within the institution, but usually not enough to make a big difference.

Corrections has no *rivals*; they alone perform their function. Thus there is no basis for comparison in examining "correctional output," unless one wishes to compare units within a prison system or prisons from different states. Even though corrections does not have any *functional* rivals, they do have many *allocational* rivals, for money allocated to prisons is money which is not allocated to some other state agency. This is where the influence of the public through their legislators becomes important. If public lobby groups can exert pressure on legislators to support other interests, then prisons must surely lose — as indeed they do.

It is hard to say who the direct beneficiaries of corrections are. Inmates would definitely argue that they do not directly benefit from corrections, nor does the public see itself as a direct beneficiary of corrections. In fact, it does not even see itself as an *indirect* beneficiary: most citizens probably view prisons as liabilities to the taxpayer. Probably the most important class of direct beneficiaries of the corrections system is composed of those who earn their livelihood from it. This absence of a large and clearly identified body of external direct beneficiaries is one of the major reasons why corrections has such difficulty in getting the funding which it needs to improve its resources and programs.

On the other hand, there are many *sufferers*. The prisoners see themselves as sufferers, as do guards and other correctional workers who must contend with low pay, long hours, and public indifference — not to mention danger and distasteful working conditions. The public sees itself as an indirect sufferer as a result of having to pay for the upkeep of prisons and prisoners, and commercial interests see themselves as sufferers as a result of the productivity of prison industries. In fact, free-world commercial interests have been instrumental in securing restrictive legislation *against* prison labor. Prison industries which might otherwise keep inmates employed in the production of goods have been harshly attacked by private business; two Federal laws were passed which sealed the fate of state prison industries. The first was the Hawes-Cooper Act (1929) which made prison products subject to the laws of the states into which they were shipped; many states followed by passing laws prohibiting the open sale of prison-manufactured goods. The second Federal law was the Ashurst-Sumners Act of 1935 which stopped the interstate shipment of prison products. Thus prison industries, which might have been highly beneficial to both inmates and the states, have been restricted by commercial interests which saw (and still see) themselves as being direct sufferers of corrections.

Corrections has few allies, unless one includes the large number of citizens who wish to reinstate the death penalty and/or make prisons more draconian. Even those who work in other components of the criminal justice system do not identify strongly with corrections. Corrections, unfortunately, stands very much alone and isolated as a public agency.

Dilemmas In Ideology:
Punish, Control, Or Treat?

It has already been mentioned that one of the principal concerns of correctional facilities is that of security; security needs dominate most correctional facilities. But once inmates are secure within their walls, what is to be done with them? Ideally, they should be rehabilitated — made useful for society. They should also be used for institutional purposes; that is, many of the internal housekeeping functions of institutions should be performed by inmates. In addition, those who require medical, dental, and psychiatric services should receive them. Finally, if prisons are places of punishment, then inmates should be punished. Prisons also have what some have called "latent functions," which include the following:

—Slave labor for prison industries.
—Psychic satisfaction for authoritarian employees.
—Reduction of unemployment.
—Subjects for laboratory testing.
—A safety valve for racial tensions in the community by virtue
   of the incarceration of the minority and the poor.
—Birth control.[27]

Just what prisons *ought* to do has become a controversial issue sparked by reports that rehabilitation does not work and a corresponding demand for a more punishment-oriented direction in corrections. Robert Martinson, in a widely-quoted statement, evaluated some 231 rehabilitation programs and concluded that, "With few and isolated exceptions, the rehabilitative efforts that have been reported so far have

413

had no appreciable effect on recidivism."[28] This negative assertion was echoed by respected Harvard scholar James Q. Wilson who stated "Studies done since 1967 do not provide grounds for altering (Martinson's conclusions) significantly."[29] Ernst Van den Haag, one of the principal architects of the emerging Punishment Model of corrections tersely noted that, "Laws threaten, or promise, punishment for crimes. Society has obligated itself by threatening. It owes the carrying out of its threats. Society pays its debts by punishing the offender, however unwilling he is to accept payment."[30] This trend seems to have found receptive listeners; indeed, there are many who fully agree with Wilson when he says that "Wicked people exist. Nothing avails except to set them apart from innocent people."[31] If they are to be set aside, and if corrections *cannot* rehabilitate, then the main focus must be on *control.*

There are, however, a number of scholars on the other side of the fence who argue that rehabilitation is *not* dead.[32] They point out that the criteria for measuring rehabilitation have been flawed and that the assertion that rehabilitation is dead is based in part on citizen unhappiness with crime in general rather than on the individual outcomes of specific rehabilitation programs. Part of the problem is that although the public would like to have prisons rehabilitate their inmates, it has been unwilling to provide the kinds of treatment facilities and personnel needed to accomplish that objective. Prisons are staffed for the most part by correctional officers whose job it is to maintain custody and security. Social workers, psychiatrists, psychologists and educators make up a very small proportion of staff manpower and even they must work within the requirements of institutional security (which is often counterproductive to their rehabilitative efforts). Thus, as Silberman has noted,

> Except in a handful of minimum-security prisons, maintaining custody and order — preventing riots and escapes — overshadows every other consideration. This leads to constant supervision and regimentation and to an incredibly elaborate system of rules and regulations that seem all the more onerous because of the social condemnation and stigmatization that underly them. Even in the most humane institution, life is a constant put-down — a daily challenge to inmates' dignity and sense of self.[33]

Because of their heritage from the days of Eland Lynds and his brutal prisons at Auburn and Sing-Sing, custodial institutions have been tense, harsh, crippling places. The rhetoric of reform and rehabilitation is in reality little more than a recent justification for continuing an old practice; it is no longer acceptable to simply say, "lock them up and throw the key away!" Society needs a theoretical justification for the continued existence of prisons, and as long as we can talk about rehabilitation without having to seriously worry whether or not it takes place, nothing need change. It is clear that we cannot maximize multiple variables simultaneously: we cannot punish, control, cure, and rehabilitate at the same time because each of these goals tends to cancel the other out. It seems we have a tiger by the tail and just can't let go.

Confinement in a custodial institution is punishment. Not only do inmates lose their freedom, but they are also forced to adapt to an abnormal, unpleasant environment. Many of those sent to prison are violent and dangerous people, and once in prison they continue to prey on one another. Thus control *is* important, but the rigorous controls which must be established simply to run prisons also produce an environment which does not allow serious rehabilitation to take place. Simply by learning a vocation or by participating in a program like the Jaycees or Alcoholics Anonymous, one does not become rehabilitated. In fact, many inmates do these things because they know they *have to* if they are to be granted parole at the earliest opportunity.

In conclusion, prisons are a contradiction of ideologies. They attempt to do a number of things at the same time, and they do them with minimal public support, inadequate manpower, antiquated physical plant, and without a clear sense of purpose — other than to see to it that inmates do not get out until the state officially releases them. Few, if any, of the actors involved have any realistic ability to change what they have inherited, and the entire matter is becoming even more complex and difficult as a result of increasing litigation on behalf of prisoner's rights.

The bottom line is that corrections continues to *treat* and *rehabilitate* by *punishing*, and this is done with widespread public approval — in spite of the fact that the public is unhappy with high rates of recidivism! This is characteristic of the relationship between the public and the criminal justice system: all too often it gets what it asks for, but that is not really what it wants or needs. The system is then blamed for the defective product which it gives! Perhaps corrections would be able to eliminate or reduce this conflict of ideology if it would work backwards from the *outcomes* it wants rather than by starting with established *means* and then asking for specific outcomes. If the criminal justice system really wants to rehabilitate offenders, it needs to find out first of all whether rehabilitation is possible and practical. After answering these questions, the correctional system should determine just what kind of setting or design is most likely to produce a rehabilitated offender and then build such facilities. If the system wants to isolate the high-risk offender, that should be reasonably possible to do. The problem is in identifying the high-risk offenders, or in establishing criteria for managing such people. If punishment is desired, then what the criminal justice system needs to do is to conduct research into what kinds of punishments produce what sorts of results — and then to apply them in the most appropriate manner. In fact, perhaps what each state needs is a Department of Corrections *and* a Department of Punishments, each to perform its own function in the most cost-effective and sensible manner possible!

As a minimum, the correctional system requires a great deal more systematic research into such areas as the consequences of sentencing practices and the impact of correctional practices on both the keepers and the kept. Intelligent policies for corrections require good basic information, and although great strides have been made, a great deal of research still needs to be conducted.

Summary

Corrections deals with the supervision and control of persons convicted of crimes. Included within the broad definition of corrections are two primary kinds of custodial institutions: jails and prisons. Although both are custodial institutions, each serves different needs and each is faced with a different set of issues.

Jails are local, short-term places of confinement which are usually administered by a law enforcement agency — either a police department or a county sheriff's office. People accused of crimes are held in jail until they secure a pretrial release either on bail or through a release on their own recognizance. Besides people who cannot secure bail or for whom bail is denied, most accused persons do not spend a great deal of time in *pretrial* confinement. Jails are also used as places of punishment for those who are convicted of minor crimes (misdemeanors). These people usually spend a limited amount of time in jail — normally less than a year. Those who are sentenced to jail are normally sent to the *county* jail for their term; the jails run by police departments are generally only used to temporarily house individuals whom the police arrest pending release on bail.

Prisons are places of confinement for offenders who have been convicted of serious crimes (felonies) and are normally operated by the state. Prisons are usually classified according to their security grade — Maximum, Medium, or Minimum; inmates are assigned to them on the basis of a classification process they undergo when they are first sent to prison. The federal government also maintains a prison system which is administered by the Bureau of Prisons, a part of the Justice Department. Individuals who violate federal laws and who are convicted in federal courts are sent to federal prisons.

The use of prisons as a form of punishment was part of a reform movement which started in the eighteenth century and which became especially popular in the early nineteenth century. This reform sought to find more humane ways of dealing with felons than execution or maiming, and the idea of confining inmates to prisons seemed an ideal solution. At first prisoners were subjected to enforced silence or isolation from other prisoners plus forced labor. The early prisons were fortress-like institutions in which the lives of inmates was carefully and rigorously controlled. Beginning in the late nineteenth century and the early years of the twentieth century, the ideology of imprisonment began to shift, with more emphasis placed on *rehabilitation*. However, the conflicting ideologies of *deterrence, incapacitation, rehabilitation,* and *retribution* all compete with one another in custodial institutions. In spite of this conflict of ideologies, the principal emphasis in most prisons is still on *security*.

Corrections is a highly fragmented aspect of the criminal justice system. For one thing, it is carried out by numerous agencies at a variety of levels. The courts, for example, administer *probation*, which is community supervision of individuals convicted of crimes who have had their sentences suspended with the provision that the offender meet certain conditions. Confinement may take place in city or county jails, state or federal prisons, and may utilize a broad array of institutions which range from massive industrial prisons to rural work camps. Most offenders who actually go to prison are released early on *parole*, which again places them under community supervision at the local level.

Correctional agencies are elements of government and their administration is influenced by this status; they are dependent upon legislators for funding at least some correctional officials are politically appointed. The power setting of corrections is further influenced by the fact that few citizens see themselves as direct beneficiaries of prisons, even though such institutions do produce a collective good. The low visibility of corrections, coupled with public apathy or hostility, has left corrections isolated and underfunded. The conflict of ideologies has added to the confusion and misinformation which surrounds the whole area.

Within prisons, a unique and typically hostile environment exists which pits the kept against their keepers and even inmates against themselves. This is perpetuated by the existence of a strong but informal "inmate code" which at least nominally allows prisoners to adapt to the rigors of confinement. It is, however, counterproductive to the goal of rehabilitation and fosters a corresponding animosity of correctional staff against prisoners.

Discussion Questions

1.   Has the operation of jails by law enforcement agencies helped or hindered them in their relationship with the community — or has it made any difference at all?

2.   Why does the public seem to object to improving the conditions of confinement in local jails? Do you think that the public's harsh attitudes are justified?

3.   How has the historical legacy of prisons locked them into the problems they currently face?

4.   In what ways do contemporary conditions of confinement *harm* the criminal justice system and leave it open to legitimate public criticism?

5.   How much of the public's unhappiness with prisons do you think can be blamed on its own indifference to them?

6.   Many prisons are located in rural areas. Has this had any consequences with respect to how the urban communities feel about them?

7.   Do you think the goal of rehabilitation is consistent with the reality of incarceration?

8.   Why do you think so many citizens are either hostile or indifferent to people in jails and prisons? Could (and should) anything be done to change this?

9.   What impact do you think prison riots have had on public opinion toward corrections?

10.   Does "free world" industry ultimately harm the community through its strong opposition to prison industries?

Glossary

CORRECTIONAL INSTITUTIONS   For the most part, jails (city and county) and prisons (state and federal).

FLAT SENTENCE   A fixed term of imprisonment for a person convicted of a crime.

INCAPACITATION   A correctional doctrine which holds that dangerous offenders are incarcerated to prevent (i.e., incapacitate) them from doing further harm to the public.

INDETERMINATE SENTENCE   A prison sentence which includes a maximum and a minimum amount of time for which the offender may be confined (e.g., 10 - 20 years).

JAIL   A short-term confinement facility normally used for incarcerating persons who are either awaiting trial or who have been convicted of a minor crime for which a jail sentence has been imposed.

LEX TALIONIS   The principle of retaliation; the notion that the punishment should fit the crime — "an eye for an eye; a tooth for a tooth."

PAROLE   A form of early release from prison in which the offender remains under the control of the state, usually subject to a set of conditions mutually agreed to by both the offender and the state.

PRISONS   Places of long-term confinement for those who have been convicted of serious crime.

PROBATION   The delay of imposition of a sentence imposed by a court providing the probationer meet certain conditions imposed upon his liberty.

Notes

[1] Timothy J. Flanagan, David J. van Alstyne, and Michael R. Gottfredson, eds., *Sourcebook of Criminal Justice Statistics - 1981*, U.S. Department of Justice, Bureau of Justice Statistics (Washington, D.C.: U.S. Government Printing Office, 1982), see especially Table 1.2, "State and Local Criminal and Civil Justice Agencies, by Type of Agency or Facility and State," p. 3.

[2] *Sourcebook of Criminal Justice Statistics - 1981*, Table 1.3, "Criminal Justice Expenditures of Federal, State, and Local Governments, by Type of Activity and Expenditure, United States Fiscal Years 1971-1978," p. 4.

[3] Neal Shover, *A Sociology of American Corrections* (Homewood, Illinois: The Dorsey Press, 1979), p. 141.

[4] Harry E. Allen and Clifford E. Simonsen, *Corrections in America: An Introduction*, 2d ed. (Encino, California: Glencoe Publishing Co., Inc. 1978), p. 441.

[5] See Alice Morse Earle, *Curious Punishments of Bygone Days* (Montclair, New Jersey: Patterson Smith, 1969).

[6] Hassim M. Solomon, *Community Corrections* (Boston: Holbrook Press, Inc., 1976), p. 226.

[7] Hassim M. Solomon, *Community Corrections*, p. 226.

[8] Gerald D. Robin, *Introduction to the Criminal Justice System: Principles, Procedures, Practices* (New York: Harper and Row, 1980), p. 327.

[9] Cited in Allen and Simonsen, *Corrections in America*, p. 441.

[10] The description of types of prisons which follows is adapted from the National Advisory Commission on Criminal Justice Standards and Goals report, *Corrections* (Washington, D.C.: U.S. Government Printing Office, 1973), pp. 343-345.

[11] See Barbara W. Tuchman, *A Distant Mirror: The Calamitous 14th Century* (New York: Alfred A. Knopf, 1978), pp. 96-131.

[12] See Albrecht Keller, ed., *A Hangman's Diary, Being the Journal of Master Franz Schmidt, Public Executioner of Nuremberg, 1573-1617*, translated by C.V. Calvert and A.W. Gruner (Montclair, New Jersey: Patterson Smith, 1973).

[13] Allen and Simonsen, *Corrections in America*, p. 29.

[14] Allen and Simonsen, *Corrections in America*, p. 29.

[15] Coleman Phillipson, *Three Criminal Law Reformers: Beccaria, Bentham, and Romily* (Montclair, New Jersey: Patterson Smith, 1970). See also Hermann Mannheim, ed., *Pioneers in Criminology* (Chicago: Quadrangle Books, 1960).

[16] Stephen Shafer, *Theories in Criminology* (New York: Random House, 1969), p. 17.

[17] See Philip H. Ennis, "Crimes, Victims, and the Police," *Transaction* 4 (June 1967): 36-44.

[18] Charles E. Silberman, *Criminal Violence, Criminal Justice* (New York: Vintage Books, 1978), p. 504. See also Douglas Lipton, Robert Martinson, and Judith Wilks, *The Effectiveness of Correctional Treatment: A Survey of Treatment Evaluation Studies* (New York: Praeger Publishers, 1975).

[19] Herbert L. Packer, "The Justification of Punishment," in Rudolph J. Gerber and Patrick D. McAnany, *Contemporary Punishment: Views, Explanations, and Justification* (Notre Dame: University of Notre Dame Press, 1972), p. 183.

[20] Louis P. Carney, *Probation and Parole: Legal and Social Dimensions* (New York: McGraw Hill Book Company, 1977), p. 84.

[21] *Attorney General's Survey of Release Procedures* (Washington, D.C.: U.S. Government Printing Office, 1939), Vol. IV, p. 4.

[22] James B. Jacobs, "Macrosociology and Imprisonment," in David F. Greenburg, ed., *Corrections and Punishment* (Beverly Hills, California: Sage Publishing Company, 1977), pp. 89-107.

[23] Louis P. Carney, *Corrections: Treatment and Philosophy* (Englewood Cliffs, New Jersey: Prentice-Hall, Inc., 1980), p. 102.

[24] Carney, *Corrections*, p. 102.

[25] Michael S. Serrill and Peter Katel, "The Anatomy of a Riot: The Facts Behind New Mexico's Bloody Ordeal," *Corrections Magazine*, April 1980, p. 7.

[26] Serrill and Katel, "The Anatomy of a Riot," p. 24.

[27] C.E. Reasons and R.L. Kaplan, "Tear Down the Walls? Some Functions of Prisons," *Crime and Delinquency* (October 1975): 367. For an especially interesting treatment of the issue of subjects for laboratory testing, see Stephen Gettinger and Kevin Krajick, "The Demise of Prison Medical Research," *Corrections Magazine*, December 1979, pp. 5-14.

[28] Robert Martinson, "What Works? — Questions and Answers About Prison Reforms," *The Public Interest* (Spring 1974): 25.

[29] James Q. Wilson, *Thinking About Crime* (New York: Basic Books, 1975), p. 169.

[30] Ernst Van den Haag, *Punishing Criminals* (New York: Basic Books, 1975), p. 15.

[31] Wilson, *Thinking About Crime*, p. 209.

[32] See Michael Serrill, "Is Rehabilitation Dead?" *Corrections Magazine*, May-June 1975, pp. 3-13, 21-36; Seymour L. Halleck and Ann D. White, "Is Rehabilitation Dead?" *Crime and Delinquency* (October 1977): 372-382.

[33] Silberman, *Criminal Violence, Criminal Justice*, pp. 512-513.

CORRECTIONS: PROBLEMS AND PROSPECTS

14

Corrections has always faced a wide range of both external and internal problems. Recent interest in corrections has led to changes which suggest considerable promise for the criminal justice system as a whole, although other areas continue to be resistant to change. In fact, it seems the whole area of corrections is undergoing change, and much of that change will have a direct impact on local communities.

Corrections In The Criminal Justice System[1]

A substantial obstacle to the development of effective corrections lies in its relationship to the police and courts. Corrections inherits whatever mistakes were made in any earlier step of the criminal justice process. The contemporary view regards society's institutionalized response to crime as the criminal justice *system* and its activities as the criminal justice *process*. This model envisions interdependent and interrelated agencies and programs that will provide a coordinated and consistent response to crime. The model, however, remains a model — it does not exist in reality. Although cooperation between the various components has improved noticeably, it cannot be said that a criminal justice "system" really exists.

Although each element of the system has its own specialized function to perform, none of the elements can perform its tasks without directly affecting the efforts of the others. As a result, while each component must continue to concentrate on improving the performance of its specialized function, it also must be aware of its interrelationships with the other components. When functions overlap, each component must be willing to appreciate and utilize the expertise of the others.

The interrelationships of the various elements must be understood in the context of the purposes for which the entire system is designed. It is generally agreed that the major goal of criminal law administration is to reduce crime through the use of procedures consistent with protection of individual liberty. There is disagreement over how to achieve that goal and what elements are most important. Long sentences of confinement in maximum security penitentiaries were once thought to deter other individuals from committing criminal offenses. It now seems obvious that long periods of imprisonment not only breed hostility and resentment, but also make it more difficult for the offender to avoid further law violations. Long sentences also contribute to the tension within prisons and make constructive programs more difficult. The deterrent effects of a long prison sentence are outweighed by the suffering and alienation of committed offenders which often places them beyond any hope of rehabilitation or reintegration.

Corrections and the Police   The police and corrections are the two elements of the criminal justice system that are farthest apart, both in the sequence of their operations and in their attitudes toward crime and criminal offenders. Cooperation between police and correctional personnel is essential if the criminal justice system is to operate effectively.

The police view the community at large as their responsibility, and removal of known offenders from the community shifts the problem from their area of responsibility to someone else's. Police are more intimately involved than corrections with a specific criminal *offense*. They often spend more time with the victim than with the offender and are influenced by the emotional reactions of the community. As a result, the police may be more receptive to concepts of retribution and incapacitation rather than rehabilitation and reintegration which are the important objectives of corrections.

Correctional personnel seldom see the victims and the strong emotions which surround them. While the police can aim for and achieve a short-range objective (the arrest of the criminal), the correctional staff can only hope for success in the long run. Corrections seeks to assure that an offender will not commit crimes in the future; the response of corrections is less in the direction of what the offender *has done* than in the direction of what he is *likely to do*. This perspective alone places corrections in a unique position within the total criminal justice system.

Corrections, with its long-range perspective, is required to take short-run risks. The release of an offender into the community always contains some degree of risk. All too frequently, the released offenders whom police encounter are those who have turned out to be bad risks. As a result, the police may acquire an imprecise and inaccurate view of corrections. Correctional failures, such as the parole or probation violator, or the individual who fails to return from a furlough, add a burden to already overtaxed police resources and cause increased misunderstanding between police and corrections professionals.

The impact of police practices on corrections is important and often critical to the correctional system's ability to perform its functions properly. The policeman is the first point of contact with the law for most offenders. He is the initiator of the relationship between the offender and the criminal justice system, and he is likewise the ambassador and representative of the society that the system serves. Because contact with the police helps to shape the offender's attitude, the police can potentially influence the individual's future behavior.

The police make a number of policy decisions. They exercise broad discretion in the decision to arrest, and this determines to a large extent the clientele of the correctional system. In fact, police arrest decisions may have a greater impact on the nature of the correctional clientele than the legislative decisions delineating what kinds of conduct are criminal! Police decisions to concentrate on particular types of offenses will directly affect correctional programming. Police and corrections should cooperate closely so that scarce correctional resources may be utilized as effectively as possible.

Carefully used and consistent police discretion could help relieve the present uncertainties and misunderstandings between police and correctional personnel. For instance, community-based correctional programs cannot hope to be successful without police understanding and cooperation. Offenders in these programs are likely to come in contact with the police and the nature of the contact and the police response may directly affect an offender's adjustment. The police should recognize that the nature of their contact with ex-offenders, as with citizens in general, is critically important in developing respect for law and legal institutions. To conduct contacts with the least possible notoriety and embarassment is good police practice and contributes to the correctional process as well.

The police can make affirmative contributions to the success of community-based programs. The police officer knows his community; he knows where resources useful for the offender are available and he knows the pitfalls that may tempt the offender. The police officer is himself a valuable community resource and should be available to correctional programs. This, of course, requires the police to take a view of their role as one which includes the function of preventing crime as well as enforcing the law and maintaining public order.

A better working relationship between the police and corrections is possible only if both recognize that they are performing mutually supportive functions, not conflicting functions. Corrections has indeed been lax in explaining the purposes of its programs to the police and is beginning to realize that much of its isolation in the criminal justice system has been self-imposed. Closer working relationships are developed through mutual understanding and both police and corrections should continue to increase their efforts in this regard. Recruit and inservice training programs for each group should contain discussions of the other's programs. Police should designate certain officers to maintain liaison between correctional agencies and law enforcement and thus help to assure better police-corrections coordination.

Corrections and the Courts   The court has a dual role in the criminal justice system: it is both a participant in the criminal justice process and the supervisor of its practices. As participant, the court and its officers determine guilt or innocence and impose sanctions. In many jurisdictions, the court also serves as a correctional agency by administering the probation system. In addition to being a participant, the court plays another important role. When practices of the criminal justice system conflict with other values in society, the courts must determine which is to take precedence over the other.

In recent years the courts have increasingly found that values reflected in the Constitution take precedence over efficient administration of correctional programs. Some difficulties presently encountered in the relationship between corrections and the courts result primarily from the dual role that courts must play.

There is growing recognition that disparity in sentencing limits corrections' ability to develop sound attitudes in offenders. The man who is serving a 10-year sentence for the same act for which a fellow prisoner is serving 3 years is not likely to be very receptive to correctional programs and is unlikely to respect any of society's institutions. Some courts have attempted to solve the problem of disparity in sentencing through the use of sentencing councils and other similar devices. Appellate review of sentencing would further diminish the possibility of disparity.

The appropriateness of the sentence imposed by the court often determines the effectiveness of the correctional program, because prison confinement is an inappropriate sanction for the vast majority of criminal offenses. As a result, the use of probation and other community-based programs will probably continue to grow. The essential ingredient in the integration of courts and corrections into a compatible system of criminal justice is the free flow of information regarding sentencing and its effect on individual offenders.

The traditional attitude of the sentencing judge has been that his responsibility ended with the imposition of sentence. Many criminal court judges sentence offenders to confinement without fully recognizing what occurs after the sentence is imposed. In recent years, primarily because of the growing number of lawsuits by prisoners, courts have become increasingly aware of the conditions of prison confinement. Continuing judicial supervision of correctional practices to assure that the program applied is consistent with the court's sentence and basic human rights should result in increased interaction between courts and corrections.

Correctional personnel must recognize that they are to some extent officers of the court. They are carrying out a court order and, like other court officers, are subject to the court's continuing supervision. Corrections has little to lose by this development and may gain a powerful new force for correctional reform in the process.

Legal Rights, the Courts, and Corrections   The United States has a strong and abiding attachment to the rule of law, with a rich inheritance of a government of law rather than men. This high regard for the rule of law has been applied extensively in the criminal justice system up to the point of conviction. After that, an offender's fate was quite often determined arbitrarily. This was true of sentencing, for which criteria were absent and from which appeals were both rare and difficult. It was true of the discretion exercised by the institutional administrator concerning prison conditions and disciplinary sanctions. It applied to the exercise by the parole board of discretion to release and revoke.

Within the last two decades, however, the movement to bring the law, judges, and lawyers into relationships with the correctional system has grown rapidly. The American Law Institute took legal initiative in the criminal justice field in drafting the Model Penal Code, which has stimulated widespread recodifications of substantive criminal law at the federal and state levels. Extension of legal aid to the indigent accused was achieved by a series of Supreme Court decisions and by the Criminal Justice Act of 1964 and similar legislative enactments at the state level. This move brought more lawyers of skill and sensitivity into contact with the criminal justice system. The remarkable project on Minimum Standards for Criminal Justice, pursued over many years to completion by the American Bar Association, has also had widespread influence.

The most dramatic impact regarding the correctional system has been the courts' abandonment of their hands-off doctrine in relation to the exercise of discretion by correctional administrators and parole boards. It was inevitable that the correctional immunity from constitutional requirements would come to an end because the Constitution does not exempt prisoners from its protection. Once the courts agreed to review correctional decisions, it was predictable that an increasing number of offenders would ask the court for relief. The courts' willingness to become involved in prison administration resulted from intolerable conditions within many of the prisons.

Over the past two decades in particular, a new and politically important professional group (lawyers) has in effect been added to corrections, and they are not likely to go away. The Supreme Court of the United States has expressed concern that correctional process must avoid the infliction of needless suffering and achieve standards of decency and efficiency of which the community need not be ashamed and by which it will be better protected. Stimulated by the initiative of Chief Justice Burger, the American Bar Association has embarked on an ambitious series of programs to involve lawyers in correctional processes, both in institutions and in the community.

Federal and state legislatures have concerned themselves increasingly with correctional codes and other correctional legislation. The National Council on Crime and Delinquency in 1972 drafted its Model Act for the Protection of Rights of Prisoners. But more important than all these, lawyers and prisoners are bringing (and the courts are hearing) constitutional and civil rights actions alleging unequal protection of the law, imposition of cruel and unusual punishments, and abuse of administrative discretion.

A series of cases has begun to hold correctional administrators accountable for their decision-making, especially where such decisions affect first amendment rights (religion, speech, communication), the means of enforcing other rights (access to counsel or legal advice, access to legal materials), cruel and unusual punishments, denial of civil rights, and equal protection under the law. The emerging view, steadily gaining support since it was first enunciated in 1944 in *Coffin v. Reichard*, is that the convicted offender retains all rights that citizens in general have, except those that must be limited or forfeited in order to make it possible to administer a correctional institution or agency — and no generous sweep will be given to pleas of administrative inconvenience.[2]

Correctional administrators have resisted many of the courts' specific decisions. It is understandably difficult to give up years of unquestioned authority. The courts' intervention has provided corrections with public attention and concern. In the long run, these cases bring new and influential allies to correctional reform.

The law schools have begun to provide training in correctional law. The American Bar Association provides energetic leadership. The Federal Judicial Center develops creative judicial training programs, and judicial administration has finally been acknowledged as an important organizational problem. Federal and state judges in increasing numbers attend sentencing institutes. Bridges are being built between the lawyers and corrections, and this relationship promises to bring about a great many important changes in the future.

Convicted offenders remain within the constitutional and legislative protection of the legal system. The absurdity of attempting to train lawbreakers to obey the law in a system that it itself unresponsive to law should have been recognized long ago. Forcing an offender to live in a situation in which all decisions are made for him is no training for life in a free society. Thus the two sets of alternatives before the judiciary in most cases involving correctional practices are the choice between constitutional principle and correctional expediency, and the choice between an institution that runs smoothly and one that really helps the offender. In exercising their proper function as supervisors of the criminal justice system, the courts have upset practices that have stifled any real correctional progress.

The courts will and should continue to monitor correctional decisions and practices. The Constitution requires it. The nature of the judicial process dictates that this supervision will be done case by case. Some court rulings have, indeed, made the adminsitration of correctional programs much more difficult. Correctional administrators could ease the transition by adopting on their own initiative new comprehensive procedures and practices that reflect constitutional requirements and progressive correctional policy.

The Need for Cooperation in the System   It is unrealistic to believe that the tensions and misunderstandings among the components of the criminal justice system will disappear in the near future. There are unavoidable conflicts of view. The police officer who must subdue an offender by force will probably never see him in the same light as the correctional officer who must win him over with reason. The courts, which must retain their independence in order to oversee the practices of both police and corrections, are unlikely to be seen by either as a totally sympathetic partner.

The governmental institutions designed to control and prevent crime are closely and irrevocably interrelated, whether they function cooperatively or at cross-purposes. The success of each component in its specific function depends on the actions of the other two. The extent to which the institutions can work together will determine in large measure the future course of society's efforts against crime.

Real progress will be made only in the context of a criminal justice system operating as an integrated and coordinated response to crime. Thus corrections must cooperate fully with the other components in developing a system that uses its resources more effectively. If there are persons who have committed legally proscribed acts, but who can be better served outside the criminal justice system at lower cost and little or no increased risk, then police, courts, corrections, legislators, and the public must work together to establish effective diversion programs for such people. If sentencing practices are counterproductive to their intended purposes, a comprehensive restructuring of sentencing must be undertaken.

Problem Areas

People who leave free society and enter the world of corrections — especially those who enter custodial institutions — find themselves in a setting quite unlike anything they have encountered before. The person's status changes and he is confronted with a new and frightening environment. It is out of this context that a number of problems have arisen.

Prisoner Rights   Traditionally, when a person was convicted of a crime and sent to prison he was deemed to have lost his rights: he became a ward of the state and had only those rights which correctional authorities granted to him, and the granting or withholding of rights was believed to be a perfectly proper part of the correctional process. In short, he suffered "civil death" upon conviction.

The courts traditionally maintained a hands-off policy because they believed the complaints raised by offenders actually dealt with privileges, not rights. They also believed that correctional administrators knew what they were doing and that the techniques employed in prisons were not only routine but proper, considering the nature of the clientele with whom prisons dealt. Few judges ever actually visited a prison, and like so many others, assumed that corrections was a world of its own and that there was no need for the courts to intervene.

As it became increasingly clear that corrections was failing and that many of its methods were both harsh and extreme, the courts began to examine correctional practices in the light of Constitutional law. The courts have increasingly accepted the position that offenders are sent to prison *as* punishment, not *for* punishment. Nevertheless, the realities of having to keep a large number of people in forced confinement presents many difficulties. Prisons have attempted to control inmates by placing severe restrictions on them and by gradually releasing those restrictions as the inmate demonstrates that he deserves better consideration.

In the 1944 case of *Coffin* v. *Reichard*, the courts began to shift their policy on the basis of the belief that a "prisoner retains all the rights of an ordinary citizen except those expressly or by necessary implication taken from him by law." Administrative convenience was no longer accepted as a valid basis for denying a prisoner his constitutional rights, and correctional administrators became "subjected to due process standards which require that agencies and programs be administered with clearly enunciated policies and established, fair procedures for the resolution of grievances."[3]

The courts have rendered several decisions which more precisely define the rights of prisoners:

—The right to have reasonable access to the courts.[4]

—The limited right to have access to legal services.[5]

—The right of access to legal materials.[6]

—The right of prisoners to be protected against unreasonable, personal abuse.[7]

—The right of prisoners to have reasonable medical care.[8]

—The limited right of free expression and association.[9]

—The right of prisoners to their religious beliefs, and the limited right to practice their religion.[10]

There are two basic problems with respect to prisoners rights: (1) Correctional administrators and custodians must relinquish the almost unlimited power which they have traditionally had. (2) It is also difficult to define where individual rights of prisoners come into real and legitimate conflict with the administration and operation of a prison unit. It has fallen largely to the courts to find the answers to these complex problems — and the courts have not always been fully realistic in their understanding or interpretation of the issues.

Custodial institutions with large inmate populations depend on an economy of scale for efficiency of operation. This means, to cite but one example, that food service is undertaken for the institution as a whole and involves fixed menus which, although nutritious, allow little choice and limited variety. Black Muslims, however, have argued that their religious beliefs impose certain dietary restrictions on them (no pork) and that by failing to take their dietary restrictions into consideration, prisons deny them their freedom of religion.[11] They sought to have menus altered to accommodate their requirements. Although this can be done (and the courts have required that it *be* done), it imposes an additional burden on the institutions and has generated hostility among other inmates — creating yet another problem for administrators.

Some administrators have been less than enthusiastic over lawsuits which they see as interfering with established procedures and in some cases have refused to comply with the court orders. For example, in 1973 an inmate suit was brought against the Georgia State Prison at Reidsville. A subsequent report found that the prison violated 22 standards for the civil rights and well-being of prisoners, including poor living conditions in the solitary confinement and administrative segregation cells, improper use of force by guards, and racial discrimination in cell and job assignments. The warden refused to comply with the court's orders and had to be replaced.[12]

In some cases the very nature of penal institutions has been considered cruel and unusual punishment. In *Holt v Sarver*, poor personal safety, physical, and rehabilitative conditions were deemed to render the whole Arkansas State prison system an unconstitutional imposition of cruel and unusual punishment.[13] Likewise, in *Jackson* v *Hendrick*, the court ruled that total living, health, overcrowding, and program deficiencies rendered Philadelphia's 3-facility penal system cruel, inhumane, and unconstitutional.[14] Such decisions have placed an enormous burden on both the facilities involved and the entire state government.

Although these cases present the states involved with massive administrative, financial, and operational burdens, in the long run they promise to alleviate much of the unnecessary suffering which has been so common in custodial prisons. They will also help corrections administrators to carefully examine how their institutions are run and to engage in more systematic long-range planning. The whole prisoners' rights movement has also brought prisons — for the first time — under rigorous *outside* scrutiny; a process which has shed light on some appalling practices and which is a significant achievement on behalf of corrections.

Riots When the public *does* focus its attention on prisons, it is usually because of a riot or other major disturbance. Prison riots are essentially a 20th century phenomenon. There were sporadic riots in prisons in the 19th century. As Allen and Simonsen point out, "presumably inmates were either too tired to riot or control was too strict."[15] There was a wave of riots between 1929 and 1932, and from 1950 to 1966 over 100 riots or other major disturbances struck American prisons.[16] The riots appear to have been based on a fairly consistent set of causes including (a) inadequate financial support and official as well as public indifference; (b) substandard personnel; (c) enforced idleness; (d) lack of professional leadership and professional programs; (e) excessive size and overcrowding of institutions; (f) political domination and motivation of management; and (g) unwise sentencing and parole practices.[17]

Hartung and Floch, based on a study of prison riots in 1952, concluded that there are essentially two types of prison riots. The first, which they labeled "brutal riots," arise from the traditional causes of prison riots:

1. Poor, insufficient, or contaminated food.
2. Inadequate, insanitary, or dirty housing.
3. Sadistic brutality by prison officials.
4. Some combination of the first three.[18]

They attribute the overwhelming majority of past prison riots to these causes. The second kind of prison riot they call the "collective riot" and attribute its causes to "mainly ... a combination of certain penal advances and the nature of the maximum custody prison...."[19] The collective riot

> ...stems directly from the specific nature of the prisoner community, and is a good illustration of what can happen when the collective social forces of a community are not integrated into collective goals for the community. This type of riot appears to have been the result primarily of the following combination of sociological and social psychological components:
> 1. The nature of the maximum custody prison.
> 2. The aggregation of different types of inmates within one prison.
> 3. The destruction of semi-official, informal inmate self-government by new administration.[20]

Hartung and Floch presented their views as a hypothesis over thirty years ago and it has proven to be uncannily prophetic. Garson, writing in 1972, did not address the Hartung/Floch hypothesis, but rather examined the use of force vs restraint in prison riots.[21] He confirmed many of the points raised by Hartung and Floch. Garson noted "The 1952 series of prison riots was preceded by a revival of prison reform ...," a condition required by Hartung-Floch for a collective riot.[22]

> ITEM: Last September, James Howard Cobb, 31, of North Little Rock, a prisoner in California, brought a damage suit because, he charged, he was subject to 'willful and malicious

> beatings' while in the Arkansas State Penitentiary. 'On two different occasions plaintiff was harnessed to a plow along with seven other inmates and made to pull a plow from 5 A.M. until 5:30 P.M.,' Cobb's petition charged. It alleged that he and others were then whipped and made to pull harder.[23]

These kinds of conditions had been chronic in the Arkansas system; in a letter smuggled out of the Cummins unit, the writer said,

> We are worked from sunup until sundown at times in rain, cold, snow, until we are soaking wet or half frozen. Like human machines we are talked about, humiliated, beaten, half fed, and when we complain we are told we were sentenced to hard labor and there is nothing illegal in what they are doing.[24]

Trouble broke out at Cummins when 144 inmates went on strike over these conditions. The strike was broken up with state police and tear gas; the men were denied application for parole and the leaders were taken out and whipped.[25]

"Brutal riots" have come about at least in part as a result of traditional inmate grievances. For example, the Oklahoma State Penitentiary at McAlester was severely damaged in July of 1973 after angry inmates took it over and set it on fire. They took hostages and sought as a condition of their release the formation of an inmate council to represent inmates in dealing with the administration. They also sought immediate access to U.S. Justice Department attorneys (and attorneys from the American Civil Liberties Union) and the suspension of a long-time prison employee whom the inmates claimed hated prisoners.[26]

One of the most widely reported prison riots in recent years took place at Attica Prison in New York, September 9-13, 1971. In that riot 11 guards and 32 inmates were killed. The inmates had prepared a lengthy list of traditional grievances, most of which the administration subsequently agreed to accept. The Attica riot, however, was only the bloodiest of a series of riots that took place within a three year period. During the 1960's and 1970's, riots occurred in prisons all around the country, from Florida to Oregon, from California to North Carolina. These prison riots resulted in substantial destruction and death.[27]

The most significant — and horrifying — brutal riot in recent years was the one which took place at the Penitentiary of New Mexico at Santa Fe on February 2, 1980. During that riot 33 inmates were murdered and about 200 others were beaten and raped — all by other inmates. Some victims were first tortured and mutilated. Some were killed when others threw gasoline into their locked cells and burned them alive; one prisoner (who had been convicted for raping and murdering two little girls and their mother) received especially harsh treatment: "inmates reportedly dragged him out of his protective custody cell and turned a blow torch on him. As he screamed with pain, they first burned off his genitals and then moved the torch up his body to his face and burned his eyes out."[28]

In addition to the usual complaints of overcrowding, desire for better food, educational and recreational programs, and inmate complaints about a lack of work, inadequate grievance procedures, and so on, a new and volatile problem is emerging. Many of the young urban Blacks who enter prisons increasingly see themselves as "political prisoners" rather than criminals. The identification along racial or ethnic lines is certainly not limited to Blacks; it is also common among Hispanics and whites. Thus many of the racial tensions which exist in the cities have been magnified by the conditions of confinement in prisons. Racial tensions produce conflict not just between inmates and staff, but among inmates as well. Police crackdowns on violent gangs in major cities have sent many gang members to prison; this has not necessarily broken up gangs, but only moved them to the prisons, where they continue their violent activities.[29]

Control The two preceding problem areas have created a third: control. One of the most basic questions in prison is, "Who runs this place?" Problems which stem from the control of prisons are closely related to the issue of prisoners' rights and inmate violence. Control is *easiest* when it is at its *harshest*. The more rigorously the prison controls its inmates, then the more total the control the staff will have over their charges. Clearly, such draconian control is neither desirable on ethical grounds nor defensible on legal grounds. The question is how much control can the state relinquish (for the sake of prisoners' rights, humane treatment, etc.) before the state *loses* control? The inmate may not choose to exercise his rights in a responsible manner. It is a continuation of a dilemma in the entire criminal justice system; altogether too often middle-class standards of normative behavior are applied to groups who either will not or cannot accept them.

The *collective riot*, described by Hartung and Floch, is a product of this dilemma in control and also illustrates the rapidly changing nature of maximum security institutions. One of the major factors mentioned by Hartung and Floch was "destruction of semi-official, informal inmate self-government by new administration." They go on to note that the prison population is classified into two broad categories of inmates: overtly aggressive individuals and covertly passive individuals.[30]

The first category presents the most problems; if given an opportunity, these prisoners will seize leadership of the inmate community. This leadership has been tacitly recognized in many prisons in the past, and these "leaders" have been given jobs as inmate-assistants, inmate-clerks to either important staff officials or over important functions, thus adding to their power. Administrators have been willing to informally share power with such leaders in return for a "quiet" prison. This process has allowed the creation of an informal inmate government. As Hartung and Floch point out,

> In return for being allowed to operate the prison semi-officially, the inmate leaders relieved the warden of the burden of discipline. If there was an individual prisoner who grumbled too much and too openly, he was 'taken care of' by his leaders. If news of group discontent reached the warden, he suggested that the inmate leaders 'knew what to do,' and they did it. They wanted no trouble that would endanger their positions. Thus the prison floated on an even keel for years, with no serious disturbance.[31]

Reform efforts since the 1940's shattered the sociology of the prisons and deprived the more aggressive and ambitious inmates of their leadership

Many riots seem to occur *after* the displacement of inmate leaders. This has been coupled with an increase in prisoners' rights and the granting of new liberties to inmates. Sanford Bates, former Federal Commissioner of Prisons recognized this problem:

> ...disturbances were in many cases accompanied by the capture of hostages or prison employees by the rioters, and on reflection it can thus be understood that they were literally made possible by the greater liberties accorded to our inmates. If we were willing to return to the rigid program of separate confinement without liberties, we could prevent them![32]

Prison inmates are continuing to divide into racial, ethnic, or gang units and are presenting correctional administrators with some of the most difficult problems in the history of American corrections. Some of these inmates espoused revolutionary or extremist ideologies before coming into prison, and have found fertile grounds for fanning existing hatreds within the prison. The Attica rioters, for example, demanded asylum and safe passage "to some nonimperalist country," and were granted meetings with figures identified with the "new left."[33] The fragmenting of inmates into political cliques, especially those which are antagonistic to conventional ideologies, makes attempts at rehabilitation nearly impossible since that requires acceptance of conventional culture values.[34]

Citizen Expectations Of Corrections

Those involved in criminal justice often make assumptions concerning the will of the public, but in fact what the public wants is really not clear at all. It might be more accurate to speak of *publics*, for the general public is composed of a number of subgroups which can and do vary on nearly any issue. The National Advisory Commission on Criminal Justice Standards and Goals pointed out, "In a democratic nation, responsibility for provision of necessary public services is shared broadly by the citizenry. Decisions are made directly by public interest and demand for services, or indirectly by public neglect." It seems that correctional policy has developed in an environment of "public neglect." The public had no way of knowing what was going on in prisons, and it is highly unlikely that many ordinary citizens consulted the professional literature. Movies and television shows about corrections have likewise been an inadequate source of information because the people and situations they depicted have been either sterile or unrealistic.

This is not to say that members of the public have not had their opinions; the two letters cited below are very clear reflections of opinion:*

Abolish LSP

The suit filed by the Legal Services Project against county officials regarding all present and future inmates of the County Jail is an insult to the taxpayers' intelligence.

As a longtime and overburdened taxpayer whose tax dollars are supporting LSP, jail inmates, lazy welfare clients, illegitimate children of adulterers, etc., I cannot afford the tasty meals, dental care, eye care and glasses, physical examinations and what have you the LSP is demanding for the prisoners.

I am not in favor of furnishing a country club for robbers, murderers, rapists and the no-good elements of our society, most of whom contribute absolutely nothing to the betterment of our environment.

Therefore, if they break the legal rules and laws of our society, preying on innocent victims and business establishments, they do not have any so-called constitutional rights and should thank the taxpayer for a cold meal and a dirty mattress.

As for the Legal Services Project, I cannot think of one nice word to call it and I think it should be abolished immediately.

---

*The author has gone through hundreds of newspapers looking for letters to the editor which reflect opinion on corrections. Many such letters have been located, and nearly all are highly negative. These two are merely an illustration.

Prison Reform

Every week I read about some vote-hungry politician demanding prison reform in the name of humanitarianism. Its bad enough that our country has practically abolished capital punishment (an act which has reaped a tremendous increase in the crime rate), but now many liberals want to reform prisons, which were intended as a means of punishment, into comfortable rehabilitation centers.

If any kind of reform is needed, it is in the opposite direction. Prisons should get back to feeding prisoners a steady diet of bread and beans and making prisoners work 14 hours a day splitting rocks. I'm sure that that kind of reform would result in a reduction of crime.

Many citizens feel quite strongly about criminals and their punishment. Public reaction against penal and correction reform does have a logic to it. It is a way for citizens to symbolically strike out against a whole host of things about which they are unhappy. There are, however, signs that a more compassionate public also exists. For instance, the results of a telephone interview conducted by Smith and Lipsey revealed that the majority of those interviewed supported conjugal visits.[35]

Although there are a number of penal and correctional reform groups, a large proportion of them are adjuncts of radical political entities, ethnic organizations, and counter-culture youth movements. Although in recent years there has been more interest in corrections, especially in first-offender and court volunteer programs, broad-based public support for penal or correctional reform does not yet seem to have been achieved.

Corrections At The Community Level

Incarceration within institutions tends to isolate offenders from society, both physically and psychologically, and cuts them off from schools, jobs, families, and other supportive influences. Incarceration seems to increase the probability that individuals will be indelibly labelled as criminals.[36] Obviously, criminals who are clearly dangerous should be closely confined; however, there are a great many others who do not need such a high degree of custody.

A person who has spent a number of years in confinement may find it rather traumatic to return to free society, and the stresses which he encounters may influence him to return to crime. Community corrections can accomplish two important objectives: (1) it can divert appropriate offenders from custodial institutions, using community-based resources to deal with them, and (2) it can serve as a means for re-introducing an offender who has been in a custodial institution so that his entry back into the community will have a reasonable prospect for success.

Community Corrections in Lieu of Custodial Confinement   Perhaps the best known effort at the use of community corrections in lieu of sending a person to prison is that of probation. In an effective system, probation officers are well aware of their client's overall needs and help them to not only abide by the terms of their probation, but to become productive and useful citizens as well. It is a *treatment program* designed to give the offender an opportunity to correct his ways and conform to society's expectations. If the offender does not seem a suitable candidate for community supervision, his probation may be revoked and he may be returned to prison.

Interested citizens can work with offenders through volunteer programs. Despite the widespread use of volunteers in courts, probation, and parole, there is surprisingly little hard evidence that indicates volunteers are effective.[37] However a study of over 250 reports, monographs, and memoranda found them to be at least as effective in accomplishing their objectives of reducing recidivism and improving the offender's self concept as were the formal methods of rehabilitating offenders.[38]

It would seem that the use of community corrections as an alternative to sending offenders to prison is not only viable, but also desirable. The important consideration is in the screening of candidates for such supervision which they need. There are a variety of community alternatives to confinement, each of which offers certain benefits.

Nonresidential Programs   Nonresidential programs are structured correctional programs which supervise a substantial part of an offender's day but do not include "live-in" requirements. These programs service those people who need more intensive services than probation alone usually offers, yet who are not in need of institutionalization. School and counseling programs, day treatment centers with vocational training, and guided group interaction programs are among the treatment models used, many of which also supply related services to the families of offenders. There have been a number of such programs attempted on an experimental basis, and many have shown promising results. These programs have been used for the most part with juveniles, but they also show promise for adult offenders.

The Community Correctional Center   The popularity of the "community correctional center" concept in recent years has led to a bandwagon effect with rapid growth of a wide variety of programs. The term is often used to mean a relatively open institution located in the neighborhood which uses community resources to provide most of the services required by offenders. The degree of openness varies with offender types, and the use of services varies with availability and offender needs. Such institutions are used for multiple purposes — detention, service delivery, holding, and pre-release.[39]

The lines between community-based and institutional programs are blurring substantially. Many types of community correctional centers exist today, and use such facilities as jails, motels, YMCA's, and surplus army barracks. Some are used as alternatives to penal service, others as adjuncts to institutionalization.

A variant of this approach is the use of work release. Work-release programs began in the 1950's. The practice permits selected inmates to work for pay outside the institution, returning each night after work. Prisoner employment is not new; the work gang for hire is well known in penal history. The work-release concept differs markedly, however, in allowing regular civilian employment, under specified circumstances, for selected low-risk inmates. Initially used mainly with misdemeanants, work-release is now used widely with felons and youthful offenders. Other versions provide for weekend sentences, furloughs, and release for vocational training or educational programs. All such programs help to re-establish links to the community for offenders, and are especially valuable for the offender who is to be released in the near future.

Return To The Community

Most offenders who go to prison are eventually released and they must return to their community or some other place to resume their lives. Many have been changed by their experiences.

The offender released on parole is faced with the formidable task of re-integrating: getting a job, establishing credit, and finding a place to live. Pre-release programs operated by departments of correction attempt to deal with these problems, yet the actual amount and quality of services is limited. One of the biggest problems facing the ex-convict is that of getting a job. One study found that corporations and businesses did not deliberately obstruct ex-offenders in their employment efforts, but that businessmen *were* unhappy with the quality and scope of training inmates receive in prisons.[40] Another study found that small businessmen who had never been victimized reported a significantly greater willingness to hire a criminal offender than did businessmen who had been victims of a crime; however, there was a tendency among businessmen who *had* hired ex-offenders not to hire more of them. The study noted that the offenders who had the best chance of getting hired were car thieves, burglars, drug addicts, and embezzlers; those who had the least chances of being hired were murderers, rapists, and muggers.[41]

Another problem of ex-offenders is that of "civil disabilities," — the legal barring of ex-offenders from certain jobs or professions. These civil disabilities may plague an ex-offender long after he leaves prison. As Reed has noted, laws that create social distance between the public and the ex-offender, like much of the criminal law, are based on a religious morality that equates crime with sin and eternal damnation.[42] In some states ex-offenders may not work as teachers, barbers, funeral directors, insurance agents, accountants or enter medical or law enforcement professions.[43] Many of these arbitrary barriers are starting to fall. In some states there must be a reasonable relationship between the barred occupation and the offenses committed by would-be applicants.

One of the major obstacles faced by many ex-offenders, however, is not that of being barred by law from employment so much as it is a lack of adequate job skills. Many prisons do not have facilities or equipment to teach convicts job skills that would place them in demand in the outside economy; a great many of the jobs performed by inmates are menial or service jobs which require relatively little skill. Of course, one of the major benefits of most pre-release programs is that they assist the offender in locating some kind of employment. Such programs teach the offender how to act in an interview and even send him on job referrals. Although the job the offender gets may not be the best in the world, it *is* a start — often a better start than the offender could have obtained on his own.

Summary

The field of corrections is one of the most troubled components of the entire criminal justice system. Corrections, for example, inherits the flaws of the other elements of the system, for it is the last level of a multi-tiered screening funnel, and inequities and inefficiencies of the other components tends to be deposited on corrections. In spite of the fact that each of the elements of the criminal justice system *ought* to work in an integrated fashion toward a set of common goals, the reality of the system is quite different. The police and corrections are far apart in their work; the police see a criminal as an offender who ought to be punished, and corrections (theoretically) views offenders as people who must be reintegrated into society. The courts have an especially peculiar function: they administer correctional programs (through probation), send prisoners to custodial correctional institutions, and sit in judgment of correctional practices. This latter role has bred some hard feelings between the courts and correctional administrators — especially since the courts, in their role as sentencing agencies, have themselves created some of the problems!

Perhaps the most important step in correction reform in generations has been the abandonment of the "hands-off" policy of the courts towards corrections. The affirmation of the constitutional rights of prisoners has in turn led to a major shift in the advocacy of legal rights for prisoners. Thus prisoners have begun to bring a substantial number of issues before the courts, and for the first time in American correctional history, the custodial institutions are being subjected to outside evaluation — and the results have been dramatic. Brutal and repressive techniques of control and arbitrary procedures (designed around the convenience of administrators) have given way to a more systematic and democratic style of correctional administration. Although correctional officials have resisted this movement, it has persisted none the less and promises to continue into the future. The emerging relationship between corrections and the courts simply highlights the need for careful and cooperative planning among the several elements of the criminal justice system.

There have been a number of problem areas within corrections that have generated both internal and external attention. One has been the area of prisoners' rights. The courts have increasingly come to take the position that offenders are sent to prison *as* punishment, not *for* punishment and have accordingly imposed standards on prisons which safeguard the basic rights of inmates while still allowing the state to exercise necessary confinement and security measures. This movement in the direction of prisoners' rights has itself produced problems. For one thing, many correctional administrators have resisted surrendering some of their enormous power. In addition, it has been very difficult to tell just where prisoners' rights come into direct conflict with legitimate institutional needs.

Another problem in corrections has been that of riots and serious inmate disturbances. These events seem to be largely a product of the 20th century prison, and it would appear that riots fall into two categories: *brutal riots* and *collective riots*. Brutal riots seem to emerge from the traditional negative aspects of confinement — substandard personnel, enforced idleness, etc., whereas the collective riots appear to be a byproduct of both correctional reform and the politicalization of prisoners. The latter problem has been especially severe in prisons and involves the identification of prisoners along racial or ethnic lines. The whole issue of control within prisons has been complicated by these developments, and the objective of rehabilitation has been made all the more difficult to achieve.

It is difficult to guage citizen expectations of corrections; perhaps this is because so much of corrections takes place "out of sight." However, even though a substantial proportion of the public is extrapunitive in its orientation, many do believe in reformation and rehabilitation and would support penal and correctional reform. There is some evidence of this in the large number of volunteers who give time and effort to court programs and other community-based correctional efforts. However, the best description of public attitudes towards corrections probably remains that of neglect.

There has been a growing effort to move corrections into the community. This has the effect of cutting cost and at the same time allowing for programs which can more effectively reintegrate offenders into the communities of which they are a part. These efforts include probation and parole, community treatment centers, halfway houses, and other similar measures.

One of the "final" problems in corrections is the actual reintegration of the offender into society after he has served his term and been released on parole. Few convicts receive worth-while vocational training in prison, and many civil disabilities limit the jobs which ex-offenders may hold. Although progress is being made in this area, many convicts return to hostile communities.

Discussion Questions

1. How does the lack of coordination among the elements of the criminal justice system contribute to public dissatisfaction with how the system works?

2. How do the differing perspectives of police and correctional officials work to the detriment of the community?

3. What has been the impact of recent court decision that values protected by the Constitution must take precedence over administrative convenience in the running of a prison?

4. Do you think it was wise or proper for the courts to abandon its traditional "hands off" doctrine toward prisons?

5. Is there an inconsistency in the notion that people are "sent to prison *as* punishment, not *for* punishment"?

6. How have prison reforms contributed to the problem of prison riots?

7. What are some of the consequences of having prisons run by civil servants rather than by the inmates themselves?

8. Do you think citizens' fear of crime has anything to do with their attitudes towards prisons and prisoners?

9. What role must members of the community play in order to make community-based corrections work?

10. Is the "radicalization" of prison inmates likely to have an impact on community attitudes toward prisons and their inmates? If so, what kind of impact?

Glossary

CIVIL DISABILITIES   In the case of prison inmates, civil disabilities are bars to certain activities or kinds of employment because the individual has been convicted of a crime.

COMMUNITY-BASED CORRECTIONS   An alternative to traditional custodial prisons which seeks to keep convicted offenders in their community, but under proper supervision and guidance (often in conjunction with programs designed to facilitate their rehabilitation).

CONJUGAL VISITS   Family visitation programs which allow the wives and families of inmates to participate in short-term, private visits within the prison.

PRE-RELEASE PROGRAMS   Correctional programs designed to facilitate the re-entry of prisoners into the community prior to their actual release from prison. These programs typically offer counseling, job assistance, financial assistance, etc. They often use a half-way house so the inmate can actually live within the community.

WORK RELEASE   A correctional innovation which allows inmates to hold regular jobs while spending their non-working hours in confinement.

FOOTNOTES

Notes

[1] The material in this section has been adapted from the National Advisory Commission on Criminal Justice Standards and Goals report, *Corrections* (Washington, D.C.: U.S. Government Printing Office, 1973), pp. 5-10.

[2] *Coffin* v *Reichard*, 143 F. 2d 443 (6th Cir. 1944). Cert. denied 325 U.S. 887 (1945).

[3] National Advisory Commission, *Corrections*, p. 19.

[4] *Ex Parte Hull*, 312 U.S. 546 (1941).

[5] *Johnson* v *Avery*, 309 U.S. 483 (1969).

[6] *Younger* v *Gilmore*, 404 U.S. 15 (1971).

[7] *Holt* v *Sarver*, 309 F. Supp. 362 (E.D. Ark. 1970), Affirmed, 442 F. 2d 304 (8th Cir. 1970); *Jackson* v *Bishop*, 404 F. 2d 571 (8th Cir., 1968); *Jordan* v *Fitzharris*, 257 F. Supp. 674 (N.D. Cal. 1966); *Tolbert* v *Bragan*, 451 F. 2d 1020 (5th Cir., 1971); *Weems* v *U.S.*, 217 U.S. 349 (1910); *Wright* v *McMann*, 460 F. 2d 126 (2nd Cir., 1972).

[8] *McCollum* v *Mayfield*, 130 F. Supp. 112 (N.D. Cal., 1955); *Talley* v *Stephens*, 247 F. Supp. 683 (E.D. Ark., 1965).

[9] *Nolan* v *Fitzpatrick*, 451 F. 2d 545 (1st Cir., 1971); *Sobell* v *Reed*, 327 F. Supp. 1294 (S.D. N.Y., 1971); *Sostre* v *McGinnis*, 442 F. 2d 178 (2d Cir., 1971), Cert. denied, 404 U.S. 1049 (1972); *U.S. ex rel Skakur* v *McGrath*, 303 F. Supp. 303 (S.D. N.Y., 1969).

[10] *Barnett* v *Rogers*, 410 F. 2d 995, 1001 (D.C. Cir., 1969); *Long* v *Parker*, 390 2d 816 (3d Cir., 1968); *Gittlemaker* v *Prasse*, 428 F. 2d 1 (3rd Cir., 1970).

[11] *Barnett* v *Rogers*, 410 F. 2d 995, 1001 (D.C. Cir., 1969).

[12] "Georgia Is Struggling to Comply with Reidsville Court Order," *Corrections Magazine*, June 1980, p. 4.

[13] *Holt* v *Sarver*, supra.

[14] *Jackson* v *Hendrick*, 40 Law Week 2710 (Ct. Common Pleas, Pa., 1972).

[15] Harry E. Allen and Clifford E. Simonsen, *Corrections in America: An Introduction*, 2d edition (Encino, California: Glencoe Publishing Co., 1978), p. 59.

[16] Allen and Simonsen, *Corrections in America*, p. 59.

[17] Allen and Simonsen, *Corrections in America*, p. 59.

[18] Frank E. Hartung and Maurice Floch, "A Social-Psychological Analysis of Prison Riots: An Hypothesis," *Journal of Criminal Law, Criminology and Police Science* 47 (May-June 1956): 51.

[19] Hartung and Floch, "A Social-Psychological Analysis of Prison Riots," p. 52.

[20] Hartung and Floch, "A Social-Psychological Analysis of Prison Riots," p. 52.

[21] G. David Garson, "Force Versus Restraint in Prison Riots," *Crime and Delinquency* 4 (October 1972): 411-421.

[22] Garson, "Force versus Restraint in Prison Riots," p. 414.

[23] Robert Pearman, "The Whip Pays Off," *The Nation*, 26 December 1966, p. 701.

[24] Pearman, "The Whip Pays Off," p. 702.

[25] Pearman, "The Whip Pays Off," p. 702.

[26] "Rioters Seek Amnesty, New Inmate Panel," *Oklahoma City Times*, 28 July 1973, p. 1.

[27] "A Mounting Wave of Violence," *U.S. News and World Report*, 27 September 1971, p. 20.

[28] Michael S. Serrill and Peter Katel, "The Anatomy of A Riot," *Corrections Magazine*, June 1980, pp. 12-13.

[29] Kevin Krajick   "At Stateville, the Calm Is Tense," *Corrections Magazine*, June 1980, p. 10; see also "The Menace of the Gangs," pp. 11-14.

[30] Hartung and Floch, "A Social-Psychological Analysis of Prison Riots," p. 53.

[31] Hartung and Floch, "A Social-Psychological Analysis of Prison Riots," p. 54.

[32] Sanford Bates, "Penal Institutions," *National Probation and Parole Journal* (October 1957): 370.

[33] Jack Waugh, "Prisons Fuel Radical Politics," *Christian Science Monitor*, 14 September 1971, p. 1.

[34] See also Erika S. Fairchild, "Politicalization of the Criminal Offender: Prisoner Perceptions of Crime and Politics," *Criminology* 15 (1977): 287-318; see also Ronald Berkman, *Opening the Gates: The Rise of the Prisoners' Movement* (Lexington, Massachusetts: Lexington Books, 1979).

[35] David L. Smith and C. McCurdy Lipsey, "Public Opinion and Penal Policy," *Criminology* 14 (May 1976): 113-124.

[36] Hassim M. Solomon, *Community Corrections* (Boston: Holbrook Press, Inc., 1976), p. 103.

[37] David A. Dowell, "Volunteers in Probation: A Research Note on Evaluation," *Journal of Criminal Justice* 6 (1978): 357-361.

[38] Frank P. Scioli and Thomas J. Cook, "How Effective Are Volunteers?" *Crime and Delinquency* 22 (1976): 192-200.

[39] Adapted from National Advisory Commission, *Corrections*, p. 232.

[40] Walter Jensen and William C. Geigold, "Finding Jobs for Ex-Offenders: A Study of Employers' Attitudes," *American Business Law Journal* 4 (1976): 195-225.

[41] Donald Atkinson, C. Abraham Fenster and Abraham S. Blumberg, "Employer Attitudes Toward Work-Release Programs and the Hiring of Offenders," *Criminal Justice and Behavior* 3 (1976): 335-344.

[42] J.P. Reed, "Civil Disabilities, Attitudes, and Re-Entry: Or, How Can the Offender Reacquire A Conventional Status," *Offender Rehabilitation* 3 (1979): 219-228.

[43] Andrew D. Gilman, "Legal Barriers to Jobs Are Slowly Disappearing," *Corrections Magazine*, December 1979, pp. 68-72.

CRIMINAL JUSTICE AND COMMUNITY RELATIONS: THE FUTURE

15

Many people see the future as nothing more than an extension of the present with some modifications based on changes in technology. To these people, the future is simply a point on a time-line.[1] This linear view of the future is not without some justification, because daily, weekly, or even monthly changes tend to be subtle and logical. Yet at the same time, major changes are occurring even though they may not be immediately apparent. Some of these changes could completely alter the course of the future. These significant changes can take place in two complementary ways: through revolutions in concepts and through technological advances.

To understand the first, it is important to remember that we are guided by certain social realities; society has developed various acceptable ways of interpreting reality — ways which seem to provide answers to important questions and which are consistent with contemporary knowledge. These theories or paradigms may be social, mathematical, or theological, and they may encompass a wide range of human understanding. With the passage of time, however, new information accumulates which is at variance with the existing model or which cannot be explained by it. These bits and pieces become "anomalies" and tend to be treated as curios or artifacts by the theorists. This is why a new finding which is not for the most part congruent with existing knowledge is usually dismissed by the experts. A sudden advance in knowledge through a new discovery or the development of a more comprehensive theory results in a new model emerging which not only provides answers to the old questions, but also takes care of the anomalies as well. These new theories normally render the old ones obsolete and may even be bitterly resisted by the old experts (just as Bertillion resisted fingerprinting in favor of his use of body measurements in identifying criminals). A major example of a revolutionary leap in knowledge based on a theory that altered man's perception of his universe was the shift from Ptolemaic to Copernican cosmology.

Ptolemy, the Greek mathematician/astronomer, proposed the thesis that the earth was the center of the universe and that it remained fixed in position while the heavens rotated about it on a daily basis. This thesis "explained" the arrangement of the heavens for almost 1,200 years. It became an article of faith and was made an integral part of religion, and its influence on life was profound. However, in the 16th century Nicolaus Copernicus found far too many inconsistencies and errors in the Ptolemaic system and ultimately suggested an alternative hypothesis: that the sun was the center of the universe, and that the planets, including earth, rotated around the sun. This concept was revolutionary in every sense of the word, for it completely changed man's perception of the universe and even his role within the scheme of things. Kuhn has developed a theory of the structure of scientific revolutions in which he relates the advancement of man to these kinds of major changes in theories or paradigms; these changes have dramatically altered the nature and quality of life.[2]

The second way in which man significantly alters his perception of himself and his world is through the discovery of processes or technologies which ultimately alter basic relationships. As Toffler points out, the discovery of agriculture revolutionized social history. Agriculture led to the domestication of animals, the establishment of permanent settlements, the division of labor, and the creation of new social arrangements. Another example is the Industrial Revolution (Toffler's "Second Wave") which produced the factory system, industrialism, the mechanization of labor, the development of the modern nation-state, and modern mercantile economics.

Since the 1950's, advances in electronics technology, communications, data processing, fiber optics and other technology fields have led us into a "Third Wave" which has likewise radically altered both physical and social realities. The full impact of this revolution is only now beginning to be seriously felt by large numbers of people.[3] The future promises change — the next one hundred years will perhaps witness more change than all recorded history has noted.

Although we know the future will be different from the present, it is hard to tell just what it will hold. There are many prophets of doom — and they might even be right![4] Heilbronner, for example, gloomily notes that, "The outlook for man, I believe, is painful, difficult, perhaps desperate, and the hope that can be held out for his future prospect seems to be very slim indeed. ...the answer to whether we can conceive of the future other than as a continuation of darkness, cruelty, and disorder of the past seems to me to be no; and to whether worse impends, yes."[5] On the other hand, advances in nearly every field of human endeavor seem to hold a tantalizing prospect for solving many of man's most serious problems. Farming the oceans, for example, seems to offer an alternative to starvation — a threat which is being converted to reality for millions in parts of Africa and Southwest Asia. The discovery and employment of alternative energy sources which do not consume already dwindling supplies of non-renewable fossil fuels is another development which may be forthcoming in the near future. Discoveries in space technology, fiber optics, and cell biology likewise have vast potential for reshaping our future for the better. As Toffler notes:

> Just as the second wave combined coal, steel, electricity, and rail transport to produce automobiles and a thousand other life-transforming products, the real impact of the new changes will not be felt until we reach the stage of combining the new technologies — linking computers, electronics, new materials from outer space and the oceans, with genetics, and all of these in turn, with the new energy base. Bringing these elements together will release a flood of innovation unlike any seen before in human history.[6]

Of course, man is also rapidly developing the means for his own annihilation through this same technology, either as a result of its military application or through his own folly and a lack of respect for the fragile biosphere upon which he is so dependent. Although it is impossible to forecast just how man will use his new technologies, it is obvious that he will have new super-technologies which may be used for good or evil.

The Future Of Justice

Just as technology will change in the future, we can expect the nature of social relationships to change as well. Conflict will continue to be a part of human interaction just as there will continue to be a need to order and regulate the affairs of people. Even though technology and political institutions may change, it is unlikely that human nature will. Therefore we can expect to see changes in society as a whole which will affect both definitions of justice and the means by which it is to be administered.

Morality

Plato, in his Republic, saw justice as consisting of a harmonious relationship among the various components of the social organism; that is, he saw justice as being integrative. As Bodenheimer notes, "Justice is concerned with the fitness of a group order or social system for the task of accomplishing its essential objectives. The aim of justice is to coordinate the diversified efforts and activities of the members of the community and to allocate rights, powers, and duties among them in a manner which will satisfy the reasonable needs and aspirations of the individuals and at the same time promote maximum productive effort and social cohesion."[7] Justice, however, must be more than integrative; it must also ultimately deal with ethical and moral issues — especially when those issues involve conflict and when they operate within a political context. This latter point is important because the public regulation of private morality is always at least slightly behind the times and it is invariably hypocritical. It is behind the times because moral values are always in a state of flux and by the time public policy has come to terms with shifts in moral or ethical values, those values have usually shifted yet again. Justice, at least as it is publicly administered, is always hypocritical because it is based on ideals rather than on realities, and the actual administration of government policy (including justice) often falls considerably short of the ideal, giving rise to criticism of both government and its agents when they do not practice what they preach. The administration of justice will nearly always be somewhat of a contradiction of terms.

The issue of moral values and crime will not fade away in the future. Predicting moral trends is much more difficult than predicting technological trends.[8] Although we can be certain that morality will change, and that its changes will have an influence on the criminal justice system, we cannot be sure of how, when, or even why these shifts will take place. Even as morals change, approaches to their shifts will produce conflict among those who hold differing perspectives. Some individuals will seek to use the legitimacy of the law and the machinery of the political system to support their position; thus, morality will continue to be expressed in terms of power (especially political power) and will remain a source of community conflict.

The real problem with moral conflicts is not that they involve issues upon which reasonable people may disagree, but that they may become issues which polarize groups within the community. When this happens the focus of attention shifts from the moral issue under debate to the nature of the groups in conflict, often pitting them against one another — Blacks against Whites, Catholic against Protestant, and city-dweller against suburbanite. The "troubles" in Northern Ireland and the endless conflict in the Middle East over the Palestinian issue clearly illustrate this phenomenon. The possibility of this kind of conflict arising in this country is slim, but cannot be entirely disregarded.

The Law

The ability of the criminal justice system to act at all is firmly grounded in the laws which define crimes and establish criminal procedures. Any changes in the law will therefore produce a corresponding change within the criminal justice system, and the law is not static. This change can be seen in current movements to eliminate many of the so-called status offenses from the criminal statutes. Such traditional "crimes" as drunkenness, vagrancy, and homosexuality have already been redefined and decriminalized; other offenses are sure to follow. In all probability, the state will move away from defining the practice of morality except in cases where it is necessary to protect the well-being of minors or in which it can be shown that an actual harm will befall the victim. Sexual practices among consenting adults, some forms of gambling, and perhaps even the recreational use of some drugs may be decriminalized. In other words, the concepts of harm and wrong will probably undergo some redefinition — perhaps even to the extent of altering the current relationships between criminal and civil law.

There also appears to be a trend toward the development of stronger consumer protection laws, including those which deal with product liability (the responsibility of a producer for the effects of his product). Although at present this is essentially the domain of the civil law, it is probable that these matters will ultimately come to be regulated at least in part by criminal law as well. As a result, a company which pollutes the environment by dumping toxic substances into rivers or the air may one day find its policy makers facing criminal sanctions. The reason for this shift lies in the nature of the corporation itself. Corporations are legal entities which have the status of a person. They were specifically designed to reduce the liability of their owners. Unfortunately, many corporations have gone beyond any reasonable accountability, especially since the rise of the large, amorphous trans-national corporation. Civil fines against corporations have been recovered in cost hikes, thus fining consumers for the misconduct of the producers while at the same time harming those same consumers. Ultimately criminal responsibility will be placed on those who are responsible for corporate misconduct.

Technology

The future of the criminal justice system cannot be considered apart from the future of technology because the criminal justice system must not only respond to changes in technology, it will actively employ them. The significance of this becomes clear when we note that the number of scientists has been doubling every fifteen years, and most of the scientists who have ever lived are alive today! Rapid advances in technology will require a more sophisticated and highly educated public. This will in turn place increasing demands on the criminal justice system — a process which itself should drive up the level of technical competence of those within the system. These increased competencies will result in improved delivery of even more sophisticated services.

Improved technologies, particularly in communications and in the information and decision sciences, should increase both the efficiency and the effectiveness of the system while reducing manpower requirements, enhancing the quality of outputs while decreasing their total cost, and permitting a greater range of services. In other words, technological advances should enable the criminal justice system to do more, to do it quicker and better, and to do it with fewer people. These same technologies should provide dramatic improvements in such areas as criminal surveillance, crime-scene processing, and crime prediction.[9] Of course, these changes in technology will force the various elements of the criminal justice system to integrate their efforts more effectively, ultimately revitalizing not just the police, the courts, and corrections — but the entire system.

Demography

How and where people distribute themselves in the future will be quite different from that to which we have been accustomed. The large industrial city is a thing of the past, and major population shifts away from the cities will continue. Results of the 1980 census indicate that this trend is already in full swing. The data indicate that even if liberal allowances are made for undercounts, the older cities have suffered a major erosion of their populations since 1970.[10] An especially important trend in the demography of the cities is the "doughnut complex," in which the "hole" is the decaying central city and the "doughnut" is the growing and prosperous suburban and exurban ring.[11]

Three things are happening. First, the central cities are shrinking. Those who can leave them are doing so. Second, non-metropolitan areas are showing rapid growth. Third, there is a demographic shift in the direction of the Sun Belt — the movement of large numbers of people from the northeast and northcentral states to the southwest and western states. The long term impact of these trends will be staggering. For one thing, the role of the central cities is changing dramatically and will continue to do so. When the cities were centers of commerce and industry, they attracted many workers, especially those in blue-collar and service occupations. They have become centers of dependency: places where the unemployed, the unemployable, the sick, the elderly, and the poor go so their private needs can be met through public support. The results are serious: "the greater reality is the city of the poor, with from a fourth (Boston) to a seventh (New York) of the population on welfare, with staggering crime rates and truancy levels (vastly understated by the official reports) that make a mockery of the traditional role of public education as an influence for homegeneity and a route upward for the urban young."[12]

The loss of industry, the flight of the affluent and middle-class to the suburbs, the concentration of the poor in unsafe and unhealthy environments, and increased demands for public services have created major financial and administrative problems for these cities. The long term consequences of this situation are hard to assess; however, one should not overlook the prospect of urban terrorism as inner city youths become increasingly isolated, alienated, and hostile. Unless the cycle of poverty and dependency can be broken, it seems likely that, although the inner cities will become smaller in size, they will become more volatile in nature. The inner cities will almost certainly become breeding grounds for serious violence — violence which itself may take advantage of the advances in technology.

Part of the changing demography includes the alteration of family arrangements. The virtues of the traditional "nuclear family" have long been extolled — the family composed of the breadwinning father, the housekeeping mother, and two children. This kind of family is already a distinct minority of family arrangements and must now compete with a wide range of alternative family styles. The alternates include the single (never married) parent; dyads composed of one parent and one or more children in which the other parent has left through death, divorce or abandonment; homosexual marriages (sometimes with adopted children); solo adult "relationships" and so on. These and many other kinds of alternative family arrangements are already common, but it remains to be seen how they will create, modify, or assign meaning to social values. Like it or not, the future promises to provide enormous variety in living arrangements and this will affect not only basic family law, but an even broader scope of social arrangements. The criminal justice system will have to adapt to these arrangements and the problems they will surely bring.

Community Expectations

Whatever the future may bring, the community will continue to expect certain services from the criminal justice system. Those expectations will arise from the nature of the community itself and will be tempered by the factors discussed below; however, the important thing to remember is that what the community expects will always be subject to change, sometimes subtle and sometimes dramatic.

The Distribution of Scarce Resources

Local governments must operate within the confines of their budgets, and the revenues of any community are limited. Sometimes this means that hard choices must be made. Since much of what is done within criminal justice is labor-intensive, and since salaries are the major source of expenditures, the number of people available to do the work of the system will be limited by the money available to pay them. The bottom line is that scarce resources mean that not all interests within the community will be served (or served as well as they would/could be). This invariably leads to dissatisfaction, and often to complaints of discrimination.

The trend of diminished federal funding for state and local governments will have a major impact on the quantity and quality of services local government can provide. This will very probably be complicated by industrial dislocation, unemployment, and increased demands for local governments to fund large social services programs. Perhaps one of the most important issues for the remainder of the century will be the allocation of scarce resources. Virtually all criminal justice agencies will have to compete for their money, and none of them will be funded at a level which will allow them to provide optimal services.

Competing Demands

The distribution of scarce resources will almost surely result in various segments of the community demanding that their interests be given priority consideration. Not all of these interests are compatible, even though each may be valid in its own right. For example, the goal of increasing minority and female representation in the criminal justice work force (including ranking positions) may properly speak to the issue of equality of opportunity, but it has also proven to be a divisive and bitter issue when the correction of past wrongs involves the creation of new ones. Because of the polarization of this issue, an amicable resolution of the problem in the near future is probably not possible.

The competing demands of crime-control vs due process will also continue to fan passions. An increasingly large segment of the public is simply tired of what it believes to be an arbitrary, capricious, and ineffective criminal justice system which seems to favor criminals over victims. This group is countered by another segment of the population which believes that individual liberties can only be secured through rigid compliance with procedural safeguards that limit what the criminal justice system can do. Thus, the enormous gap between "factual" and "legal" guilt will continue to pit liberal and conservative against one another. Each group will almost certainly attempt to use the political process to impose its wishes on the other.

Changing Patterns in Crime

Community expectations will also be influenced by changing patterns in crime. There can be little doubt that technological advances will also produce new criminal opportunities. This has already proven to be the case with the computer. "Computer crime" is a new and sophisticated area of criminal enterprise which the criminal justice system is only now beginning to recognize.

It is also possible that mass violence, including terrorism and extortion, will become more common during the closing years of the century. This will pose a dilemma for law enforcement, which has traditionally been reactive. If the law enforcement community is to become proactive against this kind of threat, then much more intrusive measures will have to be employed (including widespread use of electronic surveillance) without the kind of probable cause traditionally called for by the courts.

Community Relations: Emerging Tasks

The future will not be easy. If the criminal justice system is to be effective, and if the community is to be a safe and productive place for all of its members, a number of tasks must be accomplished. There must be a reconciliation of the diverse needs within the community. Ours is not a zero-sum society in which anyone's gain is everyone else's loss: to the contrary, as one segment of society improves its position, all segments of society benefit. There must be a clear recognition of the fact that diversity can produce strength and that the criminal justice system is a link which binds all parts of the community together.

Closely related to the reconciliation of diverse needs is the task of establishing mutual support among the community's key functions. Criminal justice requires a community in which social justice is more than rhetoric. To achieve this, all major community processes must work together in harmony and toward the same broad objectives. Schools, churches, and social welfare institutions must become more cohesive in their objectives and must be more willing to support one another and to work with the criminal justice system.

The Need for Dynamic Communication

Perhaps one of the most frustrating problems of the past has been that the diverse elements of the community have shown relatively little inclination to communicate with one another. In general, they have simply used the political processes of the community in a continuing game of one-upmanship. The criminal justice system has been used as a pawn in the process, to the detriment of both the community and the criminal justice system. It is essential that all elements of the community seek an open and honest forum so their respective needs and wishes can be communicated and so that a common understanding can be achieved.

Conclusion

In the closing years of the twentieth century we can look back on nearly one hundred years of history during which the fabric of American society has been dramatically altered. We have gone from a relatively simple, rural, agricultural society to an enormously complex, urbanized, industrial society.

The quality of justice in our communities has likewise been altered dramatically. The law itself has shifted in favor of all members of the community and is no longer simply an instrument of the wealthy. However, some old problems remain and new ones can be expected. Perhaps the test of the twenty-first century will be the extent to which the American community is capable of defining its needs and using its resources to meet them. One thing remains clear: central to the entire issue of the quality of life is the quality of the criminal justice system.

Discussion Questions

1. What kinds of technologies are most likely to have a significant impact on the criminal justice system in the year 2000?

2. Why is it unreasonable to assume that the future will only be a linear extension of the present?

3. What kinds of problems are changes in technology *least likely* to solve?

4. Which is apt to change quicker — the community or the criminal justice system? What will the consequences of this uneven change be?

5. What kind of risks might be involved if technology changes too quickly?

6. Do you think that social and technological changes will make the criminal justice system more of an *institution* or an *instrument*?

7. How will the kinds of changes described in this chapter alter the power setting of criminal justice? Is that good or bad?

8. Why do you think the courts will be the most resistant to change (or will they)?

9. Do you think changing concepts of justice will bring about corresponding changes in how the community thinks justice ought to be administered?

10. Do you think there is really any risk that the criminal justice system could be turned *against* society? What would it take to do that?

Notes

[1] Alvin Toffler, *The Third Wave* (New York: William Morrow and Company, Inc., 1980); see especially Chapter 11, "The New Synthesis."

[2] Thomas S. Kuhn, *Structure of Scientific Revolutions*, 2d ed. Foundation of the Unity of Science Series, Vol. 2, No. 2 (Chicago: University of Chicago Press, 1970).

[3] Toffler, *The Third Wave*, passim.

[4] See L.S. Stavrianos, *The Promise of the Coming Dark Age* (San Francisco: W.H. Freeman and Company, 1976); Robert L. Heilbronner, *An Inquiry into The Human Prospect* (New York: W.W. Norton and Co., 1975).

[5] Heilbronner, *The Human Prospect*, p. 22.

[6] Toffler, *The Third Wave*, p. 164.

[7] Edgar Bodenheimer, *Jurisprudence: The Philosophy and Method of the Law* (Cambridge: Harvard University Press, 1962), p. 177.

[8] Leslie T. Wilkins, "Crime and Criminal Justice at the Turn of the Century," *Annals of the American Academy of Political and Social Science* 480 (July 1973): 13-29.

[9] See Project STAR, *The Impact of Social Trends on Crime and Criminal Justice* (Cincinnati/Santa Cruz: Anderson Davis, 1976).

[10] U.S. Bureau of the Census, *Statistical Abstract of the United States: 1980*, 101st edition (Washington, D.C.: U.S. Government Printing Office, 1980), passim.

[11] George Sternlieb and James W. Hughes, "The Changing Demography of the Central City," *Scientific American* 243 (August 1980): 48-53.

[12] Sternlieb and Hughes, "The Changing Demography of the Central City," p. 53.

Index